Human Behavior Theory

A Diversity Framework

Roberta R. Greene and Nancy Kropf

Second Revised Edition

ALDINETRANSACTION
A Division of Transaction Publishers
New Brunswick (U.S.A.) and London (U.K.)

Library of Congress Catalog Number: 2008055047
ISBN: 978-0-202-36315-8 (cloth); 978-0-202-36316-5 (paper)
Printed in the United States of America

Library of Congress Cataloging-in-Publication Data

Greene, Roberta R. (Roberta Rubin), 1940-
  Human behavior theory : a diversity framework / Roberta R. Greene and Nancy Kropf. -- 2nd rev. ed.
        p. cm.
  Includes bibliographical references and index.
  ISBN 978-0-202-36315-8 (acid-free paper)
    1. Social work with minorities--United States. 2. Cultural pluralism--United States. I. Kropf, Nancy P. II. Title.

HV3176.G77 2009
362.8400973—dc22   2008055047

Contents

1

Defining Social Work Practice within a Diversity Framework

Roberta R. Greene and Nancy P. Kropf

Social work theories, concepts, and practices are often rooted in and reflect the dominant values of the larger society. As a result, forms of treatment may represent cultural oppression and may reflect primarily a Eurocentric worldview. (Sue, 2006, p. xvii)

Culturally competent social work practice has expanded "to promote the full humanity of all voices which have been marginalized in our society." (Hooyman, 1996, p. 20)

This text discusses various approaches to the study of human diversity and of populations at risk for discrimination (Fellin, 2000). It also examines the extent to which these issues receive attention in the human behavior literature. The first chapter provides the historical background and content relevant to cross-cultural social work practice and defines major terms and assumptions. The following chapters explore how the particular assumptions of human behavior theories—psychoanalytic theory, psychodynamic/ego psychology theory, systems theory, symbolic interaction theory, feminist theory, constructionist theory, small group theory, an ecological perspective, and risk and resilience theory—have been used to guide cross-cultural social work practice. Micro-, mezzo-, and macrolevels of diversity issues are discussed.

Introduction

During the twentieth century, various diverse constituencies became more active in political processes, advocating civil rights for minorities, women, and gays and lesbians, and becoming more informed consumers of mental health and social services. In the new millennium, American society will continue to become increasingly diverse, with a marked increase in the proportion of the population who belong to various ethnic and or cultural groups. From an identity perspective, people are becoming increasingly aware of or are rediscovering their ethnic and cultural roots. It is not unusual for people to find themselves working closely in industry, commerce, or services with people from diverse cultural backgrounds. In addition to the demographic changes that are taking place within the United States, the world is becoming more interdependent and connected as a result of technological advances and trade.

These societal forces will clearly have profound implications for social work education and practice. More than ever before, educators will have to help students appreciate the need to learn social work within a diversity framework, as well as how best to deliver cross-cultural social work services. In addition, existing human behavior theory and practice interventions will need to be examined in light of their possible gender, racial, cultural, and class biases (Lecca, Quervalu, Nunes, & Gonzalez, 1998). Thus, the formulation of social work curricula, education of students for a multicultural society, and development of culturally competent practitioners will be a significant issue well into this century.

Historical Advocacy

Readers [of Group Work With the Poor and Oppressed*] will yield increased knowledge of empowerment theory and practice (knowing) that can be generalized to work with all groups, and increased understanding of the ... contemporary social work commitment (feeling).* (Germain, 1985, p. 30)

Over the past three or four decades, historical and social events in the United States have resulted in an increase in the number of groups that either define themselves as minorities or seek redress from the general society. Beginning in the 1960s, tumultuous changes in the body politic, including urban upheavals and the demand for community control, presented social work with "formidable challenges" (Tidwell, 1971, p. 59). During this time, students demonstrated for social and/or political change on college campuses. There were racially motivated riots in major urban areas such as Los Angeles and Detroit. Acts of violence against African Americans were taking place in southern states, where the Civil Rights movement was expanding. The Civil Rights and women's liberation movements, with the accompanied acceleration in social change, required that the social work profession reassess its direction and priorities.

These social and political forces gave impetus to an advocacy approach to social work and its curriculum. Student and faculty activists asserted that cultural group patterns that had historically been less visible in the curriculum should be given more attention (Arnold, 1970; Glasgow, 1971). The strain and struggle to incorporate the study of ethnic and minority group life into the social work curriculum was reflected in professional journals, conferences, and task forces appointed by the Council on Social Work Education (CSWE; Francis, 1973; Mackey, 1973; Miranda, 1973; Murase, 1973; Ruiz, 1973). Moreover, faculty groups within CSWE urged that information about the lifestyles of diverse client groups become an integral part of the educational process.

Reassessment of curricula eventually led to a heightened commitment to understanding diverse groups and "activities related to ethnic minority concerns" (Pins, 1970, p. 30A). As a result, CSWE established accreditation standards that required schools to make a special effort to ensure cultural diversity in their student bodies, faculty, and staff and to provide a curriculum that would include a body of knowledge on women's and minority issues (CSWE, 1970, 1971; Dumpson, 1979).

In 2001–2002, the National Association of Social Workers (NASW) developed standards for culturally competent social work that included the "sociocultural experiences of people of different genders, social classes, religious and spiritual beliefs, sexual orientations, ages, and physical and mental abilities" (NASW, 2001, p. 1; see Table 1.1). The standards were to be used in conjunction with the NASW *Code of Ethics* to help social workers fulfill their moral obligation to provide culturally competent interventions to clients. According to the NASW standards, this requires, among other things, the ability to

- assist people of color;
- address the interrelationship among class, race, ethnicity, and gender;
- assist low-income families;
- work with older adults;
- address the importance of religion and spirituality in the lives of clients;
- explore the development of gender identity and sexual orientation;
- understand the dynamics of immigration, acculturation, assimilation stress, and biculturalism; and
- help people with disabilities.

Fulfilling these obligations necessitates empowerment and community-building skills, outreach to new populations, and training in culturally competent models of practice.

In a similar vein, in 2001–2002, CSWE issued the revised *Educational Policy and Accreditation Standards* (CSWE, 2001). This document "[set] forth the basic requirements for curricular content and educational context that were thought necessary to prepare students for professional social work practice" (p. 3). Specifically, the standards defined the foundation content—knowledge, values, and skills—that would lead to "competent social work practice" (p. 6). Furthermore, the standards mandated that "students gain the knowledge and skills necessary to serve diverse constituencies, addressing clients' age, class, color, culture, disability, ethnicity, family structure, gender, marital status, national origin, race, religion, sex, and sexual orientation" (p. 6). CSWE (2008) has now updated its policy statement to continue the tradition of curriculum mandates that respect differences among people.

Despite the profession's value commitment and increased attention to diversity, content related to diversity in the curricula of schools of social work remains fragmented, reflecting conflicting principles about best practices (Dean, 2001;

Table 1.1
National Association of Social Workers Standards for
Cultural Competence in Social Work Practice

Standard 1. Ethics and Values—Social workers shall function in accordance with the values, ethics, and standards of the profession, recognizing how personal and professional values may conflict with or accommodate the needs of diverse clients.

Standard 2. Self-Awareness—Social workers shall seek to develop an understanding of their own personal, cultural values and beliefs as one way of appreciating the importance of multicultural identities in the lives of people.

Standard 3. Cross-Cultural Knowledge—Social workers shall have and continue to develop specialized knowledge and understanding about the history, traditions, values, family systems, and artistic expressions of major client groups that they serve.

Standard 4. Cross-Cultural Skills—Social workers shall use appropriate methodological approaches, skills, and techniques that reflect the workers' understanding of the role of culture in the helping process.

Standard 5. Service Delivery—Social workers shall be knowledgeable about and skillful in the use of services available in the community and broader society and be able to make appropriate referrals for their diverse clients.

Standard 6. Empowerment and Advocacy—Social workers shall be aware of the effect of social policies and programs on diverse client populations, advocating for and with clients whenever appropriate.

Standard 7. Diverse Workforce—Social workers shall support and advocate for recruitment, admissions and hiring, and retention efforts in social work programs and agencies that ensure diversity within the profession.

Standard 8. Professional Education—Social workers shall advocate for and participate in educational and training programs that help advance cultural competence within the profession.

Standard 9. Language Diversity—Social workers shall seek to provide or advocate for the provision of information, referrals, and services in the language appropriate to the client, which may include use of interpreters.

Standard 10. Cross-Cultural Leadership—Social workers shall be able to communicate information about diverse client groups to other professionals.

Source. National Association for Social Workers. (2001). *Standards for cultural competence in social work practice*. Washington, DC: Author.

Goldberg, 2000; Granger & Portner, 1985; Lister, 1987). The literature on cultural content in social work practice remains diffuse, and there is no consensus on a theoretical framework to address a multicultural constituency (Fong & Furuto, 2001; Yan & Wong, 2005). Nonetheless, the growth of diversity as a social force has become so powerful that the profession must remain committed to preparing social work professionals for effective practice with diverse groups.

Terms

Several terms fall under the rubric of diversity content, each lending itself to a different emphasis in practice. A distinction must be made between terms such as *cultural diversity*, *cultural competence*, and *multiculturalism*. Fong (2001) defined *cultural diversity* as embracing "the multiple dimensions of human identity, biculturalism, and culturally defined social behaviors" (p. 1). Learning about cultural diversity often involves reading about cultures other than one's own. By embracing or accepting the idea of human difference, social work students can become aware of and appreciate the need to work differentially (i.e., expecting to obtain knowledge and modify techniques with each client).

Cultural competence refers to attempting to achieve the ability to "provide services, conduct assessments, and implement interventions that are reflective of the clients' cultural values and norms, congruent with their natural help-seeking behaviors, and inclusive of existing indigenous solutions" (Fong, 2001, p. 1). Such service provision requires that student practitioners learn the knowledge, attitudes, and skills necessary to engage diverse clients. Practitioners also have to be self-aware, especially about their own cultural background and personal history (Leigh, 1998; Lum, 2003, 2007; Lynch & Hanson, 1998).

Multicultural content is another concept used to discuss diversity. It addresses "pluralism, and inclusivity through analyses of power, privilege, oppression, and resistance" (Hyde & Ruth, 2002, p. 241). Multiculturalism also draws attention to relationships in which some people dominate others. Learning about overcoming such inequities can be accomplished by engaging in student classroom- and community-based intergroup dialogue (Nagda et al., 1999). Face-to-face meetings of student groups can provide future practitioners with first-hand understanding of the issues of social injustice and what it means to come from "disenfranchised backgrounds" (Nagda et al., 1999, p. 433). When extended to the clinical encounter, such dialogues may create a sensitive cross-cultural helping environment (see Chapter 2).

The general term *cross-cultural social work* is used throughout this text to define a helping relationship in which the practitioner and those being helped may differ in cultural background, values, and lifestyle (Yan & Wong, 2005). In effective cross-cultural practice, social workers recognize the fact that when they and their client are from different cultures, culturally specific information must be infused into the helping process (Greene, Watkins, Evans, David, & Clark,

2003; see Table 1.2). As discussed in this text, when a practitioner works across cultures, he or she focuses on human behavior in context, including "thoughts, communications, actions, customs, beliefs, values, and institutions of a racial, ethnic, religious, or social group" (NASW, 1999). In general terms, this requires making the professional helping culture more congruent with the client culture.

Diverse Constituencies

There are many perspectives on how ethnic group membership, social class, minority group status, and culture affect individual and group life.... Those who have been assigned official responsibility to help have a particular obligation to be aware of inequality. (Devore & Schlesinger, 1998)

Although there is growing attention to curriculum content relevant to a diverse client constituency, it is important to understand that there is often as much diversity within a particular group as there is between groups. Each client must therefore be seen as an individual who may or may not subscribe to general group norms and beliefs and who should be asked to differentiate his or her own experiences from those of the reference group.

This section presents a general introduction to several diverse groups that are often seen as affected by oppression in the form of social, economic, and legal bias. The list should not be considered exhaustive. In addition, the designations attached to various racial and/or ethnic groups have changed over time and may not now reflect unanimous agreement. Therefore, terms used here and in the following chapters reflect those in general use at the time the particular piece of literature referred to was written.

Social workers need to be aware that language about group membership changes over time and that subpopulations are not homogenous groups. For example, the term *Native American* was used in journal articles in the 1970s, but the term *Indian* has currently come to be preferred. Similarly, the term *elderly* is now rarely used to describe individuals in later adulthood; instead other terms such as *seniors* or *older adults* are used. Social workers should therefore be alert to how individuals or groups of individuals describe or define themselves.

In addition to the language that describes diverse groups, social workers must appreciate intragroup variability. For example, many people who are deaf argue that they are a subculture. That is, instead of perceiving deafness as a disability or a medical condition, many people who are deaf consider themselves members of a cultural group characterized by language: American Sign Language (Dolnick, 1993; *http://www.gallaudet.edu/*). An example of this definition at work was the rejection of Jane K. Fernandes as president of Gallaudet University, a college for the deaf in Washington, DC. As a result of protests by students, faculty, and alumni, Fernandes was ousted from her position shortly after her inauguration. The issue was not whether Fernandes was deaf, but that she was raised in a

Table 1.2
Diversity Principles

- Diversity practice requires a model.
- Diversity practice requires the ability to think critically.
- Diversity practice requires social workers to be learners.
- Diversity content encompasses practice methods, social policy, human behavior in the social environment, research, and field education.
- Diversity content encompasses the selective and differential use of knowledge, skills, and attitudes pertaining to all areas of social work practice.
- Theory building for social work practice with diverse constituencies should reevaluate concepts such as normalcy and deviance.
- Diversity practice involves the use of knowledge or research conducted in a culturally congruent manner to people involved in the study.
- Diversity practice requires an understanding of multiple theories such as systems theory or the ecological perspective.
- Diversity practice requires an understanding of concepts such as privacy and space.
- Using a diversity framework, one views culture as a source of cohesion, identity, and strength as well as strain and discordance.
- A diversity framework needs to provide an understanding of a culture's adaptive strategies.
- Diversity practice requires an understanding of bicultural status.
- The scope of diversity practice encompasses all populations at risk affected by social, economic, and legal biases, distribution of rights and resources, and oppression.
- Diversity practice requires an understanding of a person's behavior as a member of his or her family, various groups and organizations, and community.
- Diversity practice requires that social workers understand the process of inclusion and exclusion.
- Diversity practice requires social workers to understand that individuals and groups may have limited access to resources, live in unsafe environments damaging to self-esteem, and experience their environments as hostile.
- Diversity practice requires an understanding of the effects of institutional racism, ageism, homophobia, and sexism.
- Diversity practice recognizes that social work practice cannot be neutral, value free, or objective.
- Diversity practice requires an appreciation for attitudinal differences between clients and social workers regarding autonomy or self-determination.
- Social workers who are culturally sensitive appreciate differences.
- Diversity practice requires that social workers understand that their decisions may be culture bound or ethnocentric.
- Diversity practice requires social workers to be self-aware, open to cultural differences, and aware of their own preconceived assumptions of diverse groups' values and biases.
- Diversity practice requires social workers to understand their own and the client's belief systems, customs, norms, ideologies, rituals, traditions, and so forth.
- Diversity practice requires social workers to uphold the profession's commitment to social justice.

Table 1.2 (cont.)

- Diversity practice involves the integration of skills and theory grounded in the client's reality.
- Diversity practice recognizes differences in help-seeking patterns, definition of the problem, selection of solutions, and interventions.
- Diversity practice promotes a client's sense of self-efficacy and mastery of his or her environment.
- The most effective social workers in diversity practice differentially use assessment and intervention strategies.
- The most effective workers in diversity practice use a blend of formal and informal resources.

Source. Adapted from Greene, R. R., Watkins, M., Evans, M., David, V., & Clark, E. J. (2003). Defining diversity: A practitioner survey. *Arête*, 27(1), 51–71.

"hearing world" and had only learned American Sign Language when she was twenty-three years old (Farrell, 2006).

> Cultural identity has a profound impact on our sense of well-being within our society and on our mental and physical health. Our cultural background refers to our ethnicity, but is also profoundly influenced by social class, religion, migration, geography, gender oppression, racism, and sexual orientation, as well as family dynamics. All of these factors influence people's social location in our society—their access to resources, their inclusion in dominant definitions of "belonging," and the extent to which they will be privileged or oppressed within the larger society (McGoldrick, Giordano, & Garcia-Preto, 2005, p. 1).

In order to consider more closely concepts of membership and diversity, several groups will be examined. They include the following:

1. minority groups (people of color; race), defined by limited political power;
2. ethnic groups, characterized by a shared peoplehood;
3. women, distinguished by gender roles and power issues;
4. older adults, affected by devalued status;
5. members of certain social classes, affected by economic and educational (dis)advantage, especially those living in poverty;
6. people with developmental disabilities, perceived as being limited by handicap;
7. people of varying sexual and gender orientations, affected by misconceptions of lifestyle and affectional ties;
8. religious groups, defined by their spiritual needs, religious beliefs, and practices;
9. oppressed populations, faced by discrimination and limited political power; and
10. new Americans, characterized by their choice to make a new life in the United States.

Case studies that illustrate social work practice with these diverse groups appear in subsequent chapters.

Minority Groups

Social work practice with minority clients addresses individuals, families, and members of communities who historically have been oppressed or have had limited power in U.S. society (J. W. Green, 1999; Lum, 2007). Devore and Schlesinger (1998) suggested that the term *minority group* be used to mean the underprivileged in a system of ethnic stratification. However, Hopps (1987) proposed *people of color* as the best term to define those individuals "most affected by racism and poverty" (p. 161). Because minority group members are in a relatively less powerful position in society, they may be denied access and opportunities available to others, such as adequate housing, employment, and health care (Institute of Medicine, 1994, 2003; Min, 2005).

The term *minority* has been extended over the years to include more groups, including people affected by racism, poverty, or discrimination. However, the term has no scientific criteria and often is defined differently by government policies and regulations and by group members themselves (Hopps, 1987). Among the groups that have been included by law in the term *minority* are American Indians, Alaska Natives, African Americans, Asian Americans, Americans from the Pacific Islands, and Hispanics of various national ancestry. Developmentally disabled persons also are protected by law (Public Law No. 95-602). Women (despite their numbers), gay men, lesbian women, older adults, and people with Spanish surnames sometimes are referred to as minorities.

There is no scientific agreement about the meaning of the term *race* (J. W. Green, 1999; Johnson, 1987). Race is currently considered by most social scientists to be a social concept with no standing as a scientific or analytic category (J. W. Green, 1999). The disuse of the term *race* as a scientific category relates to the understanding that there are only superficial physical differences between people, such as skin color, and that people differ more within a race than between races.

Because people of color have experienced oppression, stereotyping, and denial of opportunity, the term *race* is often associated with the stratification of power (J. W. Green, 1999). Therefore, there is concern among members of the social work profession about how color differences are portrayed and "the uses to which (group classification) might be put. [At the same time,] social workers must be alert to the possible misuse of 'color blindness' as a way to avoid remediation of the effects of past discrimination" (Hopps, 1987, p. 162).

Ethnic Groups

Members of an ethnic group think of themselves as being a "people" or as having a common culture, history, and origin. An ethnic group maintains a distinction between its members and perceived outsiders; nevertheless, it is "a dynamic system constantly changing, adjusting, and adapting to the wider environment of which it is a part" (Holzberg, 1982, p. 254). Ethnic groups consist of subgroups with diverse lifestyles, languages, histories, and cultural strengths and supports. In addition, there is considerable variation in cultural and life situations among subgroups of people identified as members of a particular minority or ethnic group.

In addition to the way that people identify themselves, there is also a cultural perception about various ethnic groups. After the tragedies of September 11, 2001, for example, negative cultural bias was focused upon people with physical characteristics of Middle Eastern heritage. Soon after the events of 9/11, Representative John Cooksey from Louisiana (R–Monroe) stated that Middle Eastern men who wear turbans looked like they were wearing diapers on their heads. After apologizing for this statement, he continued to advocate for the racial profiling of people from the Middle East, stating, "we know the faces of the terrorists and where they're from" (as quoted in Firestone, 2001). In this situation, the emotions and experiences of 9/11 created negative bias toward people of Middle Eastern ethnicity.

Women

Every known society has a gender-based definition of economic and social roles. Although every society makes a distinction between gender roles, the way in which gender is symbolized varies across cultures. Stockard and Johnson (1992) pointed out that although women's status in a culture is multidimensional, "there is no evidence, historical or contemporary, of any society in which women as a group have controlled the political and economic lives of men" (p. 91). In addition to possible structural inequities, the concern in social work practice is whether practitioners have differential perceptions of clients by gender that adversely affect the help rendered (Heyman, 2000; Jayaratne & Ivey, 1981).

Gender-sensitive social work practice, although variously defined, usually incorporates a therapeutic model that rejects traditional power arrangements for both men and women (Lather, 1991). Many feminists have suggested that gender-sensitive practice follows a therapeutic model that would produce a non-sexist role model, espouse self-actualization regardless of role stereotyping and social demand, and provide for women with a feminist ego ideal or role model (Van Voorhis, 2008). For example, Tice (1990) proposed that a gender-inclusive curriculum would not collapse the "multiplicity of women's expressions, preoccupations, and experiences into the universal woman" (p. 136). Similarly, Gilligan's (1982) *In a Different Voice* suggested that human development texts need to consider differences among women of color and among women in general in divergent historical circumstances (see Chapter 11).

Older Adults

Every society ascribes certain qualities to its older members. Reviews of the contemporary literature indicate that attitudes toward older adults are mixed at best (Hooyman & Kiyak, 2005). In the youth-oriented society of the United States, the image of the older person as unproductive is common place (Butler, Lewis, & Sunderland, 1998). The view has been so pervasive that the term *ageism* has been coined to describe the prejudice and stereotype applied to older people (Butler, 1969). Ageism is an attitude that can result in actions that subordinate a person or group because of age, bringing about unequal treatment. That ageism exists in the mental health field has been well documented in numerous studies indicating that allied health professionals are reluctant to deal with older adults (Greene, 2008). Throughout the 1960s, gerontologists (Posner, 1961; Soyer 1960; Wasser, 1964) urged social workers to counteract negative societal attitudes and work with older adults and their families.

Despite professionalization and efforts to eliminate stereotypes, many misconceptions and barriers to effective service remain, and shortages in social work personnel continue to be projected (Scharlach, Damron-Rodriguez, Robinson, & Feldman, 2000). It is now projected that by 2030 one out of every five persons in this country will be sixty-five years of age or older (Administration on Aging, 2000). In response to the growth in the older population and in acknowledgment of the need for an increase in social workers trained in gerontology, the John A. Hartford Foundation of New York City made a major commitment of resources to develop a sustained, focused, and centralized effort to strengthen the social work profession's response to the older population (CSWE/SAGE-SW, 2001). The major objective is to expand the depth of gerontological content in schools of social work, ultimately producing graduates who are better prepared to serve older adults and their families.

Members of Varying Socioeconomic Classes

There is no consensus about whether or how to identify, measure, and classify different social strata. Although conceptions about social and economic inequality and stratification are complex, they generally deal with maldistribution of wealth, variation in educational attainment, occupations, and patterns of deference accorded certain groups (Devore & Schlesinger, 1998). One often-used means of classifying social strata, however, is the six-part classification by Hollingshead and Redlich (1958a, 1958b). It categorizes members of the

1. upper-upper class: the most wealthy (often "old wealth");
2. lower-upper class: the newly wealthy;
3. upper-middle class: successful professionals and business people;
4. lower-middle class: white-collar workers;
5. upper-lower class: blue-collar workers; and

6. lower-lower class: unemployed persons and recipients of public assistance.

In a study of the "average" person's conception of social class, Coleman and Rainwater (1978) found that people tend to associate social class with social standing (namely social rank) no matter how achieved. Although respondents used the social class concept to refer to high or low status and acceptance, they wished it was used to refer to "a person's true quality [and] moral goodness" (p. 17).

Issues of culture and poverty have been controversial. Most social workers took exception to the "culture of poverty" argument. This argument attributed the conditions of the ghetto to the personal pathologies of its inhabitants (e.g., people in poverty are not motivated or are lazy) and characterized minority families in negative terms (Lewis, 1966). W. Ryan (1971) coined the term *blaming the victim* to describe how the ills of society, such as unemployment, low wages, and crowded living quarters, are attributed to the people suffering from them. Ryan suggested that conditions in the ghetto would change only when White society decided to accept structural and governmental reform or a change in the balance of power. The effect of rethinking these social concepts led to a shift of focus in curriculum from the pathology of clients to a strengths model (Saleebey, 2004, 2005).

The social work profession traditionally has had a strong interest in social welfare, such as how to redress incongruities between client needs and resources and how to serve low-income clients. However, there is strong evidence that fewer and fewer social workers are interested in serving people in poverty (Perry, 2003; Specht & Courtney, 1995; Weiss, 2006). Not only do social work students and social workers in the field distance themselves from poor people, but the research literature has suggested that clinical assessments and psychotherapeutic interventions may reflect a biased middle-class ideology (Franklin, 1986). This bias may be related to the mainstream emphasis on individualism in which being poor is believed to be a personal failing (Weiss, Gal, Cnaan, & Maglejlic, 2004). Equally important to how social workers perceive clients is the way in which such clients perceive their own economic and political opportunities. This was brought home by witnessing the lack of attention given to survivors of 2005's Hurricane Katrina who happened to live in the Ninth Ward, an area of New Orleans that already had poor resources (Greene, 2008a). A large section of the U.S. population lives at or below the poverty threshold and is at risk for economic insolvency. In 2007, Congress approved the first minimum wage increase since 1997, which will raise the hourly wage by $2.10 by mid-2009. The current federal minimum wage of $5.85 per hour translates into $234 per 40-hr work week or $12,168 per year. The poverty level for a two-person household is $13,690 (U.S. Department of Health and Human Services, 2007). Clearly, a single parent working at a full-time minimum wage job is unable to earn an income that exceeds the poverty level.

Even individuals who earn an adequate salary may be one crisis away from financial stress. With health care costs continuing to increase, a health care diagnosis and treatment may create economic distress for individuals and families. In a study on the relationship between health care costs and bankruptcy, Himmelstein, Warren, Thorne, and Woolhandler (2005) reported that in 2001, between 1.9 and 2.2 million Americans filed bankruptcy related to medical causes. Within this group, the average out-of-pocket expenses were more than $11,000, and the majority (75 percent) of individuals had health insurance at the time of their health diagnosis.

People with Developmental Disabilities

People who have variations in developmental processes that impair cognitive and social functioning are known as being developmentally disabled. The identification of people who have a developmental disability has greatly influenced legislative and regulatory policy. According to the U.S. Department of Health and Human Services (2005), individuals are termed *developmentally disabled* if they experience substantial physical or mental limitations before age twenty-two in three or more of the following major life activities:

- capacity for independent living,
- economic self-sufficiency,
- learning,
- mobility,
- receptive and expressive language,
- self-care, or
- self-direction.

Individuals with developmental disabilities who are seeking social services are most likely to have been diagnosed as having mental retardation, cerebral palsy, autism, orthopedic problems, hearing problems, epilepsy, or specific learning disabilities. These clients are more likely to be poor; to be strained by care demands; and to need counseling, multiple supportive services, and advocacy. Without appropriate services and supports, the choices open to people with developmental disabilities, such as where they live, work, or play, may be minimal. The social work role in assisting developmentally disabled clients is expanding rapidly to meet these needs (Kropf & Malone, 2004).

Black and Weiss (1991) discussed the *social construction of disability*—the idea that people with chronic illness and disability often face discrimination in U.S. society and are viewed by many activists and scholars as being an oppressed minority group (Fine & Asch, 1988; D. M. Fox, 1986). Indeed, decades ago, some human services professionals who sought to implement normalization principles noted that "handicappism" should be added to racism, sexism, and ageism as an example of institutionalized oppression.

This form of social discrimination requires social work interventions to increase societal participation and access to services. Much more needs to be done to ensure that people with disabilities can lead fuller lives (Mackelprang & Valentine, 1996). Simply using a diagnostic–medical explanation of disability can further exacerbate a client's situation. Rather, clients should be assessed and helped from a person–environment perspective that stresses abilities rather than disabilities and uses client strengths to overcome environmental barriers and attain fuller community participation (DePoy & Gilson, 2004; Gilson & DePoy, 2002).

Sexual and Gender Identity

Although *sexual identity* and *gender identity* are different constructs, these terms are frequently combined to define the gay/lesbian/bisexual/transgender community. However, several aspects of gender and sexual identity form a person's concept of self and others (C. Ryan & Futterman, 1998). *Gender identity* is the individual's personal sense of being male or female; *gender role* encompasses the social and cultural expectations that accompany being male or female. *Sexual orientation* refers to sexual attraction and behaviors. Although *gender identity* and *sexual identity* may have related components, these terms are not synonymous and represent different aspects of one's sense of self.

The groundbreaking work of Kinsey indicated that a minority of people are "purely" heterosexual (Kinsey, Pomeroy, & Martin, 1948; Kinsey, Pomeroy, Martin, & Gebbard, 1953); nevertheless, a gay or lesbian orientation was considered deviant and pathological until fairly recently. Prior to 1973, homosexuality was included in the American Psychiatric Association's *Diagnostic and Statistical Manual of Mental Disorders* and was defined as a mental illness requiring treatment. However, because homosexuality had never been shown to meet the definition of mental disorder, this portrayal of gays and lesbians was challenged. On December 15, 1973, the American Psychiatric Association board of directors voted to no longer consider homosexuality a psychiatric disorder, and it is currently viewed as a particular lifestyle (Harrison, Wodarski, & Thyer, 1992).

Nevertheless, many misconceptions about the sexual orientation of gays and lesbians remain. Conflicting and inaccurate definitions of homosexuality and the perpetuation of myths often impede social work services (Donahue & McDonald, 2005; Van Den Bergh, 2004). Research has underscored the fact that homosexual men and women have diverse developmental experiences, family constellations, roles, and personalities (Cohen & Murray, 2006; Crawford, 1988; Woodman, 1987).

Homophobia is a belief system that supports negative myths and stereotypes about gays and lesbians. Such beliefs may lead to the use of offensive language and a devaluation of homosexual lifestyles, and they also may erroneously suggest that discrimination on the basis of lifestyle is justifiable (Parents, Family, and Friends of Lesbians and Gays, 2006). Because practitioners who subscribe to a homophobic belief system are less likely to understand homosexual clients and can seriously undermine their therapeutic work, it is important for practitioners to clarify their belief systems and to obtain accurate information about this client constituency (Hash & Cramer, 2003).

Transgender people have different gender affiliations from the physical characteristics that define them as male or female. Although many sexual identity issues were discussed in the medical and psychiatric literatures much earlier, this phenomenon has only gained attention in recent decades. In 1966, Dr. Harry Benjamin published a text, *Transsexual Phenomenon*, that disputed the dominant theory that transsexuals had mental disorders. His conclusion was that people who were transsexual had endocrine disorders and, because of these medical conditions, were entitled to more compassionate responses than they were receiving from the psychiatric community.

Gender identification is different from sexual identity, and people who are transgender may be either heterosexual or gay/lesbian. As Gainor (2000) argued, however, transgenderism and homosexuality are deeply linked politically because "they are treated as different aspects of a similar deviance by the dominant, patriarchal, heterosexual community" (p. 144). People who are transsexual may physically alter their appearance cosmetically (e.g., men and women may dress in clothes of the opposite gender, men may wear makeup, women may bind their breasts), and some may choose to undergo medical procedures to align their physical appearance with their gender identity (e.g., take hormones, have sexual reassignment surgery). Sadly, people who are transgender are at high risk for being abused, being victims of hate crimes, and being marginalized by family and other social institutions (Gainor, 2000; Witten & Eyler, 1999).

Religious Groups

Although the definition of religion is complex, it usually includes reference to a supernatural power or being, a sense of faith, and how a person perceives his or her ultimate concerns (Canda & Furman, 1999). In addition to a person's spirituality, religion also tends to refer to an institutionally patterned system of beliefs, values, and rituals. Because social workers sometimes perceive religion as a private concern of clients, they may ignore spiritual issues in professional practice (Sanzenbach, 1989). Recent literature has increasingly questioned this assumption and has suggested that understanding a client's religious beliefs and practices is important in assessing individual and collective behavior (Canda & Furman, 1999). It is important for social workers to know about a person's sense of spirituality in order to understand that person's maturational development and coping (Bricker Nelson, Nakashima, & Canda, 2007). In addition, knowledge of religious beliefs, values, and rituals enables practitioners to better comprehend the culture in which the client lives (Pellebon & Anderson, 1999).

Oppressed Populations

Diversity content in social work education involves discussion of groups of people who have experienced or are experiencing the effects of social and economic injustice, including all forms of discrimination at the personal and societal levels (Greene, Taylor, Evans, & Smith, 2002). This type of discrimination may not always be visible, as with the historical and sometimes current discrimination of Jewish, Muslim, and Mormon people, who have been discriminated against for their faiths. Effective cross-cultural social work practice also addresses strategies of intervention to achieve social and economic justice and to combat the causes and effects of institutionalized forms of oppression (CSWE, 1992). Social workers who understand and use advocacy and empowerment techniques can be instrumental in assisting clients to exert their personal, political, and economic power.

New Americans

Social workers will be challenged to serve people who have come to the United States from around the globe, as the United States is becoming increasingly populated by immigrants from Asia, South and Central America, and the Caribbean. To aid in serving this population, Elaine Congress (2004) introduced an assessment tool that includes the following 10 areas:
- reasons for relocation,
- legal status,
- time in the community,
- language spoken at home and in the community,
- health beliefs,
- crisis events,
- holidays and special events,
- contact with cultural and religious institutions,
- values about education and work, and
- values about family—structure, power, myths, and rules. (p. 252)

Acculturation is an important concept used to understand the immigration experience. It is defined as the degree to which a person subscribes to mainstream culture, and it may vary along a continuum from most to least acculturated. The extent of acculturation depends on such factors as the individual's degree of urbanization, the number of generations that have passed since the original family member came to the United States, the extent to which a person may prefer to retain linguistic and cultural differences, or political beliefs about the mainstream culture.

Over the past several decades it has become evident that *assimilation,* or the process of diverse racial and ethnic groups coming together to share a common culture, an ideal of many new Americans, may have a negative side. Many immigrants do not want to become indistinguishable from mainstream culture and "throw off the cultures of their homeland as so much old clothing, that would no longer be needed" (Alba, 1985, p. 5). This realization is apparent, given the numerous discussions in social work journals about how to provide social work services in an increasingly diverse society and among immigrants to the United States who arrived at different times and may have varying beliefs regarding their assimilation path.

Finally, many social workers who espouse a postmodernist approach, as expressed in feminist theory (see Chapter 11) and social constructionism (see Chapter 6), have challenged the accepted or traditional ways of thinking about clients in categories, such as "women" or "African American" (Scott, 1989; Tice, 1990; see Chapter 2 for a discussion of whether human behavior theory can be universal). Rather, they have suggested that social workers be open to multiple meanings, respect clients' multiple perspectives, and "celebrate [client] differences" (Sands & Nuccio, 1992, p. 489).

Evolving Theoretical Approaches to Diversity

The cross-cultural and pluralistic perspective in social work implies a conscious effort to break loose from the tendency to see social work practice exclusively in terms of one culture, class, or nation. (Sanders, 1974, p. 86)

Human diversity content is multidimensional, addressing numerous communities and groups and encompassing multiple sources for effective practice. Diversity content and applications are presented in all domains of social work education. The expanded knowledge base supporting social work practice within a diversity framework encompasses cognitive information, skill-based techniques, and methods for developing self-awareness and an affirming appreciation for cultural variations or differences.

Social work's commitment to a diversity framework originally reflected an appreciation and understanding of the consequences of diversity in ethnic background, gender, race, class, sexual orientation, and culture in a multicultural society. The ability to work with and to understand individual lifestyles and the distinct needs and aspirations of diverse ethnic groups and special populations, to view these differences nonjudgmentally and with respect, and to incorporate this understanding into practice has been seen as fundamental to culturally sensitive social work practice (Greene, 2008a). The goal continues to be effective practice with people of both genders in varying cultural, socioeconomic, and life situations.

The differential use of theory-informed practice with diverse populations is central to cross-cultural client–social worker encounters. The ability to organize the helping process and to work sensitively with diverse populations requires the selective and differential use of knowledge, attitudes, and skills pertaining to social welfare policy, research methods, practice methods, human behavior theory, as well as an evaluation of the effectiveness of interventions in the field

(Greene et al., 2003; see Table 1.2). Although this book emphasizes the application of human behavior theory to social work practice with diverse constituency groups, it initially explores the multiple sources of learning to achieve practice competency.

An Overview of Culturally Competent Practice

A vast body of knowledge identifies how ethnicity and membership in various social class groups shape approaches to the problems of living. (Devore & Schlesinger, 1998, p. 3)

Three of the traditional elements of social work learning are involved in developing culturally competent practice: knowledge, skills, and attitudes.

Knowledge

The knowledge component, or culture-specific information, overlaps with the attitude or value dimension and is broad, cutting across all curriculum areas including field practicum. The knowledge component, in large measure, stems from the idea that false assumptions and prejudice can most readily develop when people lack information or have misinformation about a member of a particular group. Moreover, it is imperative to understand the impact of oppression, as well as a cultural group's history, normative life experiences, and family and community patterns. The practitioner then must be able to individualize or understand how these factors affect a particular client's life experiences (Schlesinger & Devore, 1995).

Detailed information on and facts about diverse populations are necessary to combat myths and stereotypes. For example, Kim (1973) pointed out that "the myth that Asian-Americans comprise a homogeneous model minority ignores the many difficulties these heterogeneous populations face" (p. 44). He suggested that practitioners need to know that communities referred to as Asian American contain groups with great variations in their immigration patterns; size; group cohesion; stability; and educational, professional, political, and economic life. In addition, a particular client must be assessed to ascertain his or her interpretation of cultural and other life experiences.

Skills

Factual information alone may not improve specific practice behaviors (Castex, 1993; Gallegos & Harris, 1979; Ifill, 1989; Proctor & Davis, 1983). Teaching approaches that help students move beyond cognitive learning, including a focus on affective processes and skills development, are increasingly popular. Skills necessary to provide culturally competent social work services include those for interacting interpersonally, gathering information, developing relationships, and constructing helpful interventions. Skill development has routinely included methods for interviewing as well as for giving practice feedback on basic facilitative skills such as attending, responding, reflecting, questioning, and summarizing feelings (Sue, 2006).

To provide cross-cultural social work, practitioners must become competent in the skills necessary for providing services not only to individuals, but to families and groups (see Chapters 9 and 10). Delivering family-centered interventions from a cross-ethnic or cross-cultural perspective involves being open to cultural differences, understanding the relativity of practitioners' own biases, and providing a culturally relevant assessment for families of different cultural backgrounds (Burke, 1982; McGoldrick, Preto, Hines, & Lee, 1991; Stack, 1975; Suzuki, Ponterotto, & Meller, 2000). A critical component of effective practice is to begin with understanding the family system of which one is a member—who are the people with whom one feels kinship? As family forms become more diversified, it is important to acknowledge that everyone "knows family" through the membership of his or her own family system.

Attitudes

Researchers have argued for at least five decades that a social worker's feelings and attitudes toward minority clients, particularly when hidden and negative, potentially interfere with effective interracial practice (Lum, 2003). Briar (1961) and Fischer (1978) assessed the impact of client group membership, such as race and social class, on the clinical judgment process. They found that clinicians tended to assess working-class clients more negatively than middle-class clients. Similarly, practitioners working with older clients were found to be influenced by their emotional response to that population (Genevay & Katz, 1990). A classic study by Hollingshead and Redlich (1958b) established the effects of social class on mental health and diagnosis, and an equally well-known study by Broverman, Broverman, Clarkson, Rosekrantz, and Vogee (1970) pointed out that the effects of therapists' bias on judgments about the mental health of clients were related to client gender.

These interests, sentiments, feelings, attitudes, values, awarenesses, judgments, and so forth compose the affective or value-oriented content of cross-cultural social work (Montalvo, 1983). Affective learning, usually thought of as experiential, requires an exploration and clarification of the practitioner's worldview. Through affective learning, practitioners often focus on an awareness of their own cultural upbringing so that they will develop the ability to distinguish their own worldview from that of others (Chau, 1989, 1990). Practitioners may approach affective learning through modeling behavior in role plays; examining popular-culture movies; reading novels or autobiographies; writing a "coming out" letter; or discussing a person's first encounter with racism, sexism, or classism (Freedman, 1990). This could take the form of candid discussion and labs.

Self-Awareness

Experiential learning opportunities can narrow the gap between a practitioner's personal life and his or her work expectations. Experiential learning is increasingly conceptualized in behavioral terms and includes opportunities, such as participant observation or social simulations, for practitioners to explore how they should act during an interview of a client. Experiential learning in the classroom and the field practicum begins the process that allows social workers to understand and interact with people who are culturally different from themselves.

Ideally, experiential experiences can enable students who wish to become effective in cross-cultural social work to confront and possibly overcome their biases and to better understand how members of a community articulate their own problems and concerns (J. Fox, 1983). Self-awareness, which encompasses the ability to challenge preconceived ideas and attitudes about particular client populations, is the goal of much affective learning. This involves a gradual and ongoing process of becoming more receptive to cultural differences. The process begins with awareness, or increasing one's consciousness of people and events outside one's own experience; moves to openness, a further ability to accept information about and experiences with those who are culturally different; and results in an immediate alertness to others (Montalvo, 1983). Because this self-knowledge enables practitioners to be more culturally responsive and "give unbiased attention to concerns of the larger society and those unique to racial and ethnic groups" (Chau, 1990, p. 131), it is said to heighten the skills component.

Multiculturalism

The traditional perspective on the culturally competent model of social work practice has received major attention in the social work literature. However, theorists are increasingly suggesting a different but complementary view that greater understanding of the client is insufficient for effective practice. Rather, the practitioner's "competence ... is best understood as (developing) greater understanding of herself, of her reactions to client differences, and of cultural limitations and barriers" (R. G. Green et al., 2005, p. 192). Multicultural approaches also attempt to equalize the power between the social worker and client and focus on how a client describes and explains his or her own worldview. Meaning is co-constructed in the conversational process or dialogue. That is, when the social worker and client meet in the relationship, new meanings arise in the interaction through mutual self-reflection (Yan & Wong, 2005).

Diversity and Large-Scale Social Change

A diversity framework must be understood from an ecological perspective, extending multicultural issues from the individual to the family, group, community, societal, and political levels (Bronfenbrenner, 1979; Carter & McGoldrick, 2005). A larger scale perspective draws practitioners' attention to the collective contributions people make to culture, encompassing collective identity; societal histories; patterns of power, privilege, and oppression; and belief systems (McGoldrick & Carter, 2005). Furthermore, the ecological perspective helps practitioners better comprehend how microsystems, especially families, are affected by the macroenvironment, encompassing economic and political climates (Schriver, 2003). Social workers engaged in social change need to understand the patterns of how social and economic resources are allocated as well as the ways in which policy and legislative decisions affect ethnic stratification and political power (Solomon, 1976; see Chapter 11).

Group Work: Promoting Cultural Healing

Ethnic groups have differing degrees of power over material resources and political power (Greene, 2008a). Culturally sensitive social work practice with groups encompasses understanding how a group experience can universalize the needs of minority ethnic group members, affirm groups' cultural traditions and experiences, and equalize power differentials (Davis, 1984; Lee, 1989). Thus, social justice, an attempt to remedy societal inequities, is at the core of cross-cultural social work practice.

Two types of social justice groups are described in this section: (a) those that are part of restorative justice efforts, and (b) intergroup dialogue. Both of these types seek to transform community challenges by beginning the interaction within a small-group setting. With an orientation to creating more functional communities, both types of groups are consistent with the goals of the social work profession.

Restorative Justice

Restorative justice groups may be used to promote healing when a social wrongdoing has occurred. A basic tenet of restorative justice is that crime violates people, their relationships, and the entire community in which it occurs (Holtquist, 1999; Zehr, 2002). Efforts to repair damage that is a result of wrongdoing can begin by bringing together those who have been wounded, including the perpetrator of the action.

Principles of restorative justice have their roots in several cultural traditions. Methods of restorative justice weave together traditions from the Maori of New Zealand and First Nations tribes in Canada, along with the peace-making philosophy of the Mennonites, among others (Braithwaite, 2002). Currently, various components of restorative justice are found in numerous countries, including the United States, Canada, Brazil, Belgium, Bulgaria, Rwanda, China, Thailand, Romania, New Zealand, Australia, South Africa, and others (Van Ness & Strong, 2006).

What constitutes groups that have the purpose to promote healing and justice? First, there is the sense of community and connectedness that implies a relationship (albeit, one that is in need of repair) between those who have been victimized and those who have perpetrated harmful acts. Zehr (2002) stated:

> Many cultures have a word that represents this notion of centrality of relationships: for the Maori, it is communicated by *whakapapa*; for the Navaho, *hozho*; for many Africans, the Bantu word *ubuntu*. Although the specific meanings of these words vary, they communicate a similar message: all things are connected to each other in a web of relationships. (pp. 19–20)

Furthermore, wrongdoing such as criminal acts tear at the fabric of these relationships. Logically, healing comes from repairing these rips instead of extending separation and damage through current practices that are part of the criminal justice system.

Two primary types of groups are involved in the practice of restorative justice. One is *family group conferencing*, which has its roots in the Maori culture of New Zealand in the late 1980s (Johnstone, 2002). In the family group conference, the victim and his or her family and supports are typically joined by the offender and his or her family and supports. In addition, members of criminal justice agencies may participate. The goal is to come to an agreement about dealing with the offense, including restitution. In addition, however, there is attention to the underlying reasons why the wrongdoing took place, and a goal is to prevent further offenses (Masters & Roberts, 2000).

A second kind of group is the *circle*. With origins in the First Nation tribes of Canada, circles can be peacemaking groups, sentencing circles, healing circles, or community dialogues (Zehr, 2002). The facilitators of these groups are often termed the *circle keepers* and lead the process of the circle, provide synthesis of interactions that take place, and offer additional insights. Other participants of the circle may include victims, offenders or perpetrators, justice officials, family members, and community members. Particular topics that might be addressed within the various types of circles include the context and consequences of the offense, the needs and experiences of the victim or the offender, community norms that have been violated, and other related issues. Following is an example of using circles that has been excerpted from Braithwaite (2002, p. 103):

> In the North Minneapolis African American circles, a series of circles is held for each juvenile offender. The first is the interview circle at which the offender and his/her parents meet with the circle volunteers to determine if they want to go through the program. The young offender's crime is not mentioned in this circle. At the meeting, the young person's needs and interests are considered so individual members of the circle can act as mentors. A second circle is held in which a social compact is made (which involves a commitment by the offender). Another circle is held for the victim. A fourth circle, the healing circle, is held for the victim and the offender. Other circles monitor the social compact, culminating in a celebration circle where the group celebrates the young person's completion of the agreement.

Intergroup Dialogue

Intergroup dialogue is another tool that focuses specifically on social justice issues. Like the groups focused on restorative justice, intergroup dialogue is a nontherapeutic model. Intergroup dialogue provides an opportunity for increased contact between diverse members to create an opportunity for greater understanding and reduced prejudice. In this way, it provides a structure for social workers to impact prejudice, mistrust, and oppression that contribute to segregation and inequality within society (Rodenborg & Huynh, 2006).

Various components are essential parts of this group experience. First, an environment must be fostered to provide participants with the opportunity to speak and listen in a safe setting. Part of promoting a safe place is selecting a neutral environment for the group, establishing rules of communication and dialogue to which the members can adhere, and promoting relationship-building among the participants. This last condition implies that "participants are asked to suspend assumptions, confirm their unfamiliarity with each other, be spontaneous, and prepare for unanticipated consequences" (Dessel, Rogge, & Garlington, 2006, p. 304).

Pettigrew's (1998) model for intergroup dialogue includes components to foster positive contact within the group. In the first phase, facilitators work to create a safe place for members to learn about their shared human experiences. Rodenborg and Huynh (2006) described the importance of identifying and increasing "friendship potentials" among members; that is, similarities that transcend cultural differences within the group. During the second phase, differences among members are explored. The tone is to honor and share cultural differences, and the value of various practices and beliefs is stressed. During this phase, content related to privilege and discrimination is woven into the discussion. The ideal is that in the final phase a new identification will be adopted by the members. Differences are overcome and the group members start to have more inclusive identities.

Research on outcomes of intergroup dialogue has identified key processes that are related to more successful experiences. As one might expect, the communication process is critical to developing a more inclusive sense of identity. Two processes are strongly associated with bridging differences between group members within the dialogue (Nagda, 2006). One is being *engaged* with others in the group by sharing about oneself, asking questions of others, and reconsidering ideas. The second is *building alliances* among group members, working out differences, and considering various actions that can be completed to accomplish social justice goals within these processes. The facilitator has an important role in assisting the diverse membership of the group to be actively involved and to participate in creating an agenda for social change (Nagda, Spearman, Holley, & Harding, 1995) and in promoting peace around the world (*http://traubman. igc.org/global.htm*).

References

Administration on Aging. (2000). *Statistics on the aging population.* Retrieved September 5, 2007, from *http://www.aoa.gov/prof/Statistics/statistics.asp.*

Alba, R. D. (1985). *Italian-Americans: Into the twilight of ethnicity.* Englewood Cliffs, NJ: Prentice Hall.

Arnold, H. D. (1970). American racism: Implications for social work. *Journal of Education for Social Work, 6,* 7–12.

Benjamin, H. (1966). *Transsexual phenomenon.* New York: Julian.

Black, R. B., & Weiss, J. O. (1991). Chronic physical illness and disability. In A. Gitterman (Ed.), *Handbook of social work practice with vulnerable populations* (pp. 137–164). New York: Columbia University Press.

Braithwaite, J. (2002). *Restorative justice and responsive regulation.* New York: Oxford Press.

Briar, S. (1961). Use of theory in studying the effects of client social class on students' judgments. *Social Work, 6,* 91–97.

Bricker Nelson, H., Nakashima, M., & Canda, E. R. (2007). Spiritual assessment in aging: A framework for clinicians. *Journal of Gerontological Social Work,* 48(3/4), 331–347.

Bronfenbrenner, U. (1979). *The ecology of human development.* Cambridge, MA: Harvard University Press.

Broverman, I., Broverman, D., Clarkson, I., Rosekrantz, P., & Vogee, S. (1970). Sex role stereotypes and clinical judgments of mental health. *Journal of Consulting and Clinical Psychology,* 34, 1–7.

Burke, J. L. (1982). Suggestions for a sex-fair curriculum in family treatment. *Journal of Education for Social Work,* 18(2), 98–102.

Butler, R. N. (1969). Directions in psychiatric treatment of the elderly: Role of perspectives of the life cycle. *The Gerontologist,* 9, 134–138.

Butler, R. N., Lewis, M., & Sunderland, T. (1998). *Aging and mental health: Positive psychosocial and biomedical approaches* (5th ed.). Austin, TX: PRO-ED.

Canda, E. R., & Furman, L. D. (1999). *Spiritual diversity in social work practice.* New York: Free Press.

Carter, B., & McGoldrick, M. (Eds.). (2005). *The expanded family life cycle: Individual, family, and social perspectives* (3rd ed.). Boston: Allyn & Bacon.

Castex, G. (1993, February). *Using diversity in the classroom to understand diversity: Challenges and techniques.* Paper presented at the 39th Annual Program Meeting of the Council on Social Work Education, New York, NY.

Chau, K. L. (1989). Sociocultural dissonance among ethnic minority populations. *Social Casework,* 70, 224–230.

Chau, K. L. (1990). A model for teaching cross-cultural practice in social work. *Journal of Social Work Education,* 26, 124–133.

Cohen, H. L., & Murray, Y. (2006). Older lesbian and gay caregivers: Caring for families of choice and caring for families of origin. In R. R. Greene (Ed.), *Contemporary issues of care* (pp. 275–298). New York: Haworth Press.

Coleman, R. P., & Rainwater, L. (1978). *Social standing in America: New dimensions of class.* New York: Basic Books.

Congress, E. (2004). Cultural and ethical issues in working with culturally diverse patients and their families: The use of the culturagram to promote culturally competent practice in health care settings. *Social Work in Health Care,* 39(3/4), 249–262.

Council on Social Work Education. (1970). *Manual of accrediting standards revisions.* New York: Author.

Council on Social Work Education. (1971). *Manual of accrediting standards for graduate professional schools of social work.* New York: Author.

Council on Social Work Education. (1992). *Curriculum policy statement for master's degree programs in social work education.* Alexandria, VA: Author.

Council on Social Work Education. (2001, 2008). *Educational policy and accreditation standards.* Alexandria, VA: Author.

Council on Social Work Education/SAGE-SW. (2001). *Strengthening the impact of social work to improve the quality of life for older adults and their families: A blue print for the new millennium.* Alexandria. VA: Authors.

Crawford, S. (1988). Cultural context as a factor in the expansion of therapeutic conversation with lesbian families. *Journal of Strategic and Systemic Therapies,* 7(3), 2–10.

Davis, L. E. (1984). *Ethnicity in social group work practice.* New York: Haworth Press.

Dean, R. G. (2001). The myth of cross-cultural competence. *Families in Society,* 82, 623–630.

DePoy, E., & Gilson, S. F. (2004). *Rethinking disability: Principles for professional and social change.* Monterey, CA: Brooks/Cole.

Dessel, A., Rogge, M. E., & Garlington, S. B. (2006). Using intergroup dialogue to promote social justice and change. *Social Work,* 51, 304–315.

Devore, W., & Schlesinger, E. G. (1998). *Ethnic-sensitive social work practice* (5th ed.). Boston: Allyn & Bacon.

Dolnick, E. (September 1993). Deafness as a culture. *Atlantic Monthly,* 37, 12.

Donahue, P., & McDonald, L. (2005). Gay and lesbian aging: Current perspectives and future directions for social work practice and research. *Families in Society,* 86, 359–366.

Dumpson, J. B. (March 1979). *Education for practice with and for black Americans: An historical perspective.* Paper presented at the 25th Annual Program Meeting of the Council on Social Work Education, Boston, MA.

Farrell, E. (November 10, 2006). A protest topples a president. *Chronicle of Higher Education.* Retrieved February 16, 2007, from *http://chronicle.com/weekly/v53/i12/12a03901.htm.*

Fellin, P. (2000). Revisiting multiculturalism in social work. *Journal of Social Work Education,* 36, 261–278.

Fine, M., & Asch, A. (Eds.). (1988). *Women with disabilities: Essays in psychology, culture, and politics.* Philadelphia: Temple University Press.

Firestone, D. (October 10, 2001). South Louisiana: A call for terrorist profiling. *New York Times.* Retrieved February 16, 2007, from *http://query.nytimes.com/gst/fullpage. html?res=9F00EFDA1F3CF933A25753C1A9679C8B63.*

Fischer, J. (1978). *Effective social work practice: An eclectic approach.* New York: McGraw-Hill.

Fong, R. (2001). Culturally competent social work practice: Past and present. In R. Fong & S. Furuto (Eds.), *Culturally competent practice: Skills, interventions, and evaluations* (pp. 1–9). Boston: Allyn & Bacon.

Fong, R., & Furuto, S. (Eds.). (2001). *Culturally competent practice: Skills, interventions, and evaluations.* Boston: Allyn & Bacon.

Fox, D. M. (1986). AIDS and the American health policy: The history and prospects of a crisis of authority. *Milbank Quarterly,* 64 (Suppl. 1), 7–33.

Fox, J. (1983). Affective learning in racism courses with an experiential component. *Journal of Social Work Education,* 19, 69–76.

Francis, E. A. (Ed.). (1973). *Black task force report.* New York: Council on Social Work Education.

Franklin, D. L. (1986). Does client social class affect clinical judgment? *Social Case-work*, 67, 424–432.

Freedman, E. (1990). Fear of feminism? An interview with Estelle Freedman. *Women's Review of Books*, 7(5), 25–26.

Gainor, K. A. (2000). Including transgender issues in lesbian, gay, and bisexual psychology: Implications for clinical practice and training. In B. Greene & G. L. Croom (Eds.), *Education, research, and practice in lesbian, gay, bisexual, and transgender psychology: A resource manual* (pp. 131–160). Thousand Oaks, CA: Sage.

Gallegos, J. S., & Harris, O. D. (1979). Toward a model for inclusion of ethnic minority content in doctoral social work education. *Journal of Education for Social Work*, 15(1), 29–35.

Genevay, B., & Katz, R. S. (Eds.). (1990). *Countertransference and older clients*. Newbury Park, CA: Sage.

Germain, C. (1985). The place of community work within an ecological approach to social work practice. In S. H. Taylor & R. W. Roberts (Eds.), *Theory and practice of community social work* (pp. 30–55). New York: Columbia University Press.

Gilligan, C. (1982). *In a different voice*. Cambridge, MA: Harvard University Press.

Gilson, S. F., & DePoy, E. (2002). Theoretical approaches to disability content in social work education. *Journal of Social Work Education*, 38, 153–165.

Glasgow, D. (1971). The black thrust for vitality: The impact on social work education. *Journal of Education for Social Work*, 7(2), 9–18.

Goldberg, M. (2000). Conflicting principles in multicultural social work. *Families in Society*, 81, 12–21.

Granger, J. M., & Portner, D. L. (1985). Ethnic- and gender-sensitive social work practice. *Journal of Social Work Education*, 21, 38–47.

Green, J. W. (1999). *Cultural awareness in the human services: A multi-ethnic approach*. Boston: Allyn & Bacon.

Green, R. G., Kiernan-Stern, M., Bailey, K., Chambers, K., Claridge, R., Jones, G., et al. (2005). The Multicultural Counseling Inventory: A measure for evaluating social work student and practitioner self-perceptions of their multicultural competencies. *Journal of Social Work Education*, 41, 191–208.

Greene, R. R. (2008a). *Human behavior theory and social work practice*. New Brunswick, NJ: Aldine Transaction.

Greene, R. R. (2008b). *Social work with the aged and their families* (3rd ed.). New Brunswick, NJ: Aldine Transaction.

Greene, R. R., Taylor, N. J., Evans, M. L., & Smith, L. A. (2002). Raising children in an oppressive environment. In R. R. Greene (Ed.), *Resiliency: An integrated approach to practice, policy and research* (pp. 241–276). Washington, DC: NASW Press.

Greene, R. R., Watkins, M., Evans, M., David, V., & Clark, E. J. (2003). Defining diversity: A practitioner survey. *Arête*, 27(1), 51–71.

Harrison, D. F., Wodarski, J. S., & Thyer, B. A. (Eds.). (1992). *Cultural diversity and social work practice*. Springfield, IL: Charles C Thomas.

Hash, K., & Cramer, E. P. (2003). Empowering gay and lesbian caregivers and uncovering their unique experiences through the use of qualitative methods. *Journal of Gay & Lesbian.Social Services*, 15(1/2), 47–63.

Heyman, J. (2000). *The widening gap*. New York: Basic Books.

Himmelstein, D. U., Warren, E., Thorne, D., & Woolhandler, S. (2005). Illness and injury as contributors to bankruptcy. *Health Affairs*, W563–W573. Retrieved July 8, 2007, from *http://content.healthaffairs.org/cgi/reprint/hlthaff.w5.63v1.pdf*.

Hollingshead, A. B., & Redlich, F. C. (1958a). *Social class and mental illness: A community study*. New York: Wiley.

Hollingshead, A. B., & Redlich, F. C. (1958b). Social stratification and psychiatric disorders. In H. D. Stein & R. A. Cloward (Eds.), *Social perspectives on behavior* (pp. 449–455). New York: Free Press.

Holtquist, S. E. (1999). Nurturing the seeds of restorative justice. *Journal of Community Practice*, 6(2), 63–77.

Holzberg, C. S. (1982). Ethnicity and aging: Anthropological perspectives on more than just minority elderly. *The Gerontologist*, 22, 240–257.

Hooyman, N. (1996). Curriculum and teaching: Today and tomorrow. In *White paper on education—Today and tomorrow* (pp. 11–24). Cleveland, OH: Case Western Reserve University Press.

Hooyman, N., & Kiyak, H. A. (2005). *Social gerontology* (7th ed.). Needham Heights, MA: Allyn & Bacon.

Hopps, J. G. (1987). Minorities of color. In A. Minahan (Ed.-in-Chief), *Encyclopedia of social work* (18th ed., pp. 161–171). Silver Spring, MD: NASW Press.

Hyde, C. A., & Ruth, B. J. (2002). Multicultural content and class participation: Do students self-censor? *Journal of Social Work Education*, 38, 241–256.

Ifill, D. (1989). Teaching minority practice for professional application. *Journal of Social Work Education*, 25, 29–35.

Institute of Medicine. (1994). *Balancing the scales of opportunity: Ensuring racial and ethnic diversity in the health professions*. Washington, DC: National Academy Press.

Institute of Medicine. (2003). *Unequal treatment: Confronting racial and ethnic disparities in health care*. Washington, DC: National Academy Press.

Jayaratne, S., & Ivey, K. V. (1981). Gender differences in the perceptions of social workers. *Social Casework*, 62, 405–412.

Johnson, H. C. (1987). Human development: Biological perspective. In A. Minahan (Ed.-in-Chief), *Encyclopedia of social work* (18th ed., pp. 835–850). Silver Spring, MD: NASW Press.

Johnstone, G. (2002). *Restorative justice: Ideas, values, debates*. Portland, OR: Willan.

Kim, B. (1973). Asian-Americans: No model minority. *Social Work*, 18, 44–53.

Kinsey, A. C., Pomeroy, W. B., & Martin, C. E. (1948). *Sexual behavior in the human male*. Philadelphia: W.B. Saunders.

Kinsey, A. C., Pomeroy, W. B., Martin, C. E., & Gebbard, P. H. (1953). *Sexual behavior in the human female*. Philadelphia: W.B. Saunders.

Kropf, N. P., & Malone, D. M. (2004). Interdisciplinary practice in developmental disabilities. *Journal of Social Work in Disability & Rehabilitation*, 3(1), 21–36.

Lather, P. (1991). Staying dumb? Student resistance to liberatory curriculum. In *Getting smart: Feminist research and pedagogy with/in the postmodern* (pp. 123–152). New York: Routledge.

Lecca, P., Quervalu, I., Nunes, J., & Gonzalez, H. (1998). *Cultural competency in health, social, and human services*. New York: Garland.

Lee, J. A. B. (1989). *Group work with the poor and oppressed*. New York: Haworth Press.

Leigh, J. (1998). *Communication for cultural competence*. Boston: Allyn & Bacon.

Lewis, O. (October 1966). The culture of poverty. *Scientific American*, 215, 19–25.

Lister, L. (1987). Ethnocultural content in social work education. *Journal of Social Work Education*, 20, 31–39.

Lum, D. (2003). *Social work practice and people of color: A process stage approach* (5th ed.). Belmont, CA: Wadsworth.

Lum, D. (2007). *Culturally competent practice: A framework for understanding diverse groups and justice issues* (3rd ed.). Monterey, CA: Brooks/Cole.

Lynch, E., & Hanson, M. (1998). *Developing cross-cultural competence* (2nd ed.). Baltimore: Brookes.

Mackelprang, R., & Valentine, D. (1996). *Sexuality and disability*. New York: Haworth Press.

Mackey, J. E. (Ed.). (1973). *American Indian task force report*. New York: Council on Social Work Education.

Masters, G., & Roberts, A. (2000). Family group conference for victims, offenders and communities. In M. Liebmann (Ed.), *Mediation in context* (pp. 140–154), London: Kingsley.

McDonald-Wikler, L. (1987). Developmental disabilities. In A. Minahan (Ed.-in-Chief), *Encyclopedia of social work* (18th ed., pp. 422–434). Silver Spring, MD: NASW Press.

McGoldrick, M., & Carter, B. (2005). Remarried families. In B. Carter & M. McGoldrick (Eds.), *The expanded family life cycle: Individual, family, and social perspectives* (pp. 417–435). Boston: Allyn & Bacon.

McGoldrick, M., Giordano, J., & Garcia-Preto, N. (Eds.). (2005). *Ethnicity and family therapy* (3rd ed.). New York: Guilford Press.

McGoldrick, M. J., Preto, N. G., Hines, P. M., & Lee, E. (1991). Ethnicity and family therapy. In A. S. Gurman & D. P Kniskern (Eds.), *Handbook of family therapy* (pp. 546–582). New York: Brunner/Mazel.

Min, J. W. (2005). Cultural competency: A key to effective future social work with racially and ethnically diverse elders. *Families in Society*, 86, 347–357.

Miranda, M. (Ed.). (1973). *Puerto Rican task force report*. New York: Council on Social Work Education.

Montalvo, F. (1983). The affective domain in cross-cultural social work education. *Journal of Social Work Education*, 19, 48–53.

Murase, K. (Ed.). (1973). *Asian American task force report: Problems and issues in social work education*. New York: Council on Social Work Education.

Nagda, B. A. (2006). Breaking barriers, crossing borders, building bridges: Communication processes in intergroup dialogues. *Journal of Social Issues*, 62, 553–576.

Nagda, B. A., Spearmon, M. L., Holley, L. C., & Harding, S. (1995). Bridging differences through intergroup dialogues. In S. Hatcher (Ed.), *Peer programs on a college campus: Theory, training and "voice of the peers"* (pp. 378–414). San Jose, CA: Resources.

Nagda, B. A., Spearmon, M. L., Holley, L. C., Harding, S., Moïse-Swanson, D., Balassone, M. L., et al. (1999). Intergroup dialogues: An innovative approach to teaching about diversity and justice in social work education. *Journal of Social Work Education*, 35, 433–449.

National Association of Social Workers. (1999). *Code of ethics of the National Association of Social Workers*. Retrieved September 11, 2007, from *http://www.naswdc. org/pubs/code/code.asp*.

National Association of Social Workers. (2001). *NASW standards for cultural competence in social work practice*. Retrieved August 1, 2007, from *http://www.socialworkers. org/practice/standards/NASWCulturalStandards.pdf*.

Parents, Family, and Friends of Lesbians and Gays. (2006). Retrieved September 3, 2007, from *www.pflag.org/*.

Pellebon, D. A., & Anderson, S. C. (1999). Understanding the life issues of spiritually-based clients. *Families in Society*, 80, 229–238.

Perry, R. (2003). Who wants to work with the poor and homeless? *Journal of Social Work Education*, 39, 321–341.

Pettigrew, T. F. (1998). Intergroup contact theory. *Annual Review of Psychology*, 49, 65–86.

Pins, A. M. (1970). Entering the seventies: Changing priorities for social work education. *Social Work Education Reporter*, 18(1), 30A.

Posner, W. (1961). Basic issues in casework with older people. *Social Casework*, 42, 234–239.

Proctor, E. K., & Davis, L. E. (1983). Minority content in social work education: A question of objectives. *Journal of Education for Social Work*, 19(2), 85–93.

Rodenborg, N., & Huynh, N. (2006). On overcoming segregation: Social work and intergroup dialogue. *Social Work With Groups*, 29(1), 27–44.

Ruiz, J. (Ed.). (1973). *Chicano task force report*. New York: Council on Social Work Education.

Ryan, C., & Futterman, D. (1998). *Lesbian and gay youth: Care and counseling*. New York: Columbia University Press.

Ryan, W. (1971). *Blaming the victim*. New York: Pantheon Books.

Saleebey, D. (2004). "The power of place": Another look at the environment. *Families in Society*, 85, 7–16.

Saleebey, D. (2005). *The strengths perspective in social work practice* (4th ed.). Boston: Allyn & Bacon.

Sanders, D. S. (1974). Educating social workers for the role of effective change agents in a multicultural, pluralistic society. *Journal of Education for Social Work*, 10(2), 86–91.

Sands, R. G., & Nuccio, K. (1992). Post-modernization feminist theory and social work. *Social Work*, 37, 489–502.

Sanzenbach, P. (1989). Religion and social work. *Social Casework*, 70, 571–572.

Scharlach, A. E., Damron-Rodriguez, J., Robinson, B., & Feldman, R. (2000). Educating social workers for an aging society: A vision for the twenty-first century. *Journal of Social Work Education*, 36, 521–538.

Schlesinger, E. G., & Devore, W. (1995). Ethnic-sensitive practice. In R. L. Edwards (Ed.-in Chief), *Encyclopedia of social work* (19th ed., Vol. 1, pp. 902–908). Washington, DC: NASW Press.

Schriver, J. M. (2003). *Human behavior and the social environment: Shifting paradigms in essential knowledge for social work practice* (4th ed.). Boston: Allyn & Bacon.

Scott, D. (1989). Meaning construction and social work practice. *Social Service Review*, 63, 39–51.

Solomon, B. B. (1976). *Black empowerment: Social work in oppressed communities*. New York: Columbia University Press.

Soyer, D. (1960). Reverie on working with the aged. *Social Casework*, 50, 291–294.

Specht, H., & Courtney, M. E. (1995). *Unfaithful angels: How social work has abandoned its mission*. New York: Free Press.

Stack, C. (1975). *All our kin: Strategies for survival in a black community*. New York: Harper & Row.

Stockard, J., & Johnson, M. M. (1992). *Sex and gender in society*. Englewood Cliffs, NJ: Prentice Hall.

Sue, D. W. (2006). *Multicultural social work practice*. New York: Wiley.

Suzuki, L. A., Ponterotto, J. G., & Meller, P. J. (Eds.). (2000). *Handbook of multicultural assessment: Clinical, psychological, and educational applications* (2nd ed.). San Francisco: Jossey-Bass.

Tice, K. (1990). Gender and social work education: Directions for the 1990s. *Journal of Social Work Education*, 26, 134–144.

Tidwell, B. J. (1971). The black community's challenge to social work students to confront their biases. *Journal of Education for Social Work*, 7(3), 59–65.

U.S. Department of Health and Human Services. (2005). *ADD fact sheet*. Retrieved September 21, 2007, from *http://www.acf.hhs.gov/programs/add/Factsheet.html*.

U.S. Department of Health and Human Services. (2007). *2007 federal poverty guidelines.* Retrieved July 8, 2007, from *http://aspe.hhs.gov/poverty/07poverty.shtml.*

Van Den Bergh, N. (2004). Defining culturally competent practice with sexual minorities: Implications for social work practice. *Journal of Social Work Education*, 40, 221–238.

Van Ness, D. W., & Strong, K. H. (2006). Restoring justice. *Journal of Religion & Spirituality in Social Work*, 23(1/2), 93–109.

Van Voorhis, R. M. (in press). Feminist theories and social work practice. In R. R. Greene (Ed.), *Human behavior theory and social work practice.* New Brunswick, NJ: Aldine Transaction.

Wasser, E. (1964). The sense of commitment in serving older persons. *Social Casework*, 45, 443–449.

Weiss, I. (2006). Factors associated with interest in working with the poor. *Families in Society*, 87, 385–394.

Weiss, I., Gal, J., Cnaan, R. A., & Maglejlic, R. (2004). Social work education as professional socialization: A study of the impact of social work education upon students' professional preferences. *Journal of Social Service Research*, 31, 13–31.

Witten, T. M., & Eyler, A. E (1999). Hate crimes against the transgendered: An invisible problem. *Peace Review*, 11, 461–468.

Woodman, N. J. (1987). Homosexuality: Lesbian women. In A. Minahan (Ed.-in-Chief), *Encyclopedia of social work* (18th ed., pp. 805–812). Silver Spring, MD: NASW Press.

Yan, M. C., & Wong, Y. R. (2005). Rethinking self-awareness in cultural competence: Toward a dialogic self in cross-cultural social work. *Families in Society*, 86, 181–188.

Zehr, H. (2002). *The little book of restorative justice.* Intercourse, PA: Good Books.

2

The Social Work Interview:
Legacy of Carl Rogers and Sigmund Freud

Roberta R. Greene

*Self-awareness is the first growth to self-realization.... Social workers can facilitate
the process of self discovery by employing additive empathic responses [that] focus on
deeper feelings. (Hepworth, Rooney, Larsen, Rooney, & Strom-Gottfried, 2005, p. 522)*

The purpose of this chapter is to examine how such assumptions "imported"
from Carl Rogers and Sigmund Freud and "amalgamated" into social work
practice affect cross-cultural social worker–client interactions (Briar & Miller,
1971, p. 59). The chapter first outlines Rogers's and Freud's major premises about
the helping process and explores how concepts about what constitutes effective
therapeutic techniques have shaped the interviewing process. It then examines
how postmodern theorists have shifted social workers' attention to the interview
as a conversation with inherent cultural meaning (Schriver, 2003). Finally, the
chapter examines whether these assumptions about the social work interview,
both implicitly and explicitly stated in the social work literature, are effective
when applied in practice with diverse populations.

Whether conducted with individuals, families, or groups, the social work
interview is the most consistently and frequently used practice intervention
(Compton, Galaway, & Cournoyer, 2004; Kadushin & Kadushin, 1997). Many
of the ideas central to an effective social work interview are derived from the
human behavior theory assumptions of Rogers and Freud. For example, the
widely accepted practice principle—tuning in to client feelings—is based on
Freud's assumption that the therapist's role is to interpret a client's hidden feelings in order to expand the client's self-awareness. And the assumption that
the cardinal feature of an effective interview is establishing rapport is based on
Rogers's conclusion that it is critical for the helping person to express empathetic
understanding in order to promote client self-actualization (Greene, 2008a;
Hepworth et al., 2005; Raskin, 1985).

The Rogerian assumptions discussed in this chapter suggest that in an effective interview, the practitioner: affirms the client's worth and dignity; supports

client self-determination; forges a therapeutic relationship; and communicates with empathy, authenticity, and genuineness. The Freudian or psychoanalytic assumptions explored suggest that the social worker listen to client feelings, interpret latent or hidden meanings, develop client insight or understanding, assess client behaviors and motivation, and maintain professional authority and control in the interview. In contrast, postmodern theorists believe that practitioners and clients share the responsibility for ascribing meaning to life situations.

For several decades, practice methods texts pointed out the necessity of addressing clients' cultural backgrounds in the interviewing process (Mizio, 1972). For example, Perlman (1957) argued that a client's behavior is both shaped and judged by cultural expectations and the various roles they play. Kadushin (1972) cautioned that the social distance between the client and social worker could be a barrier to communication, and that class, color, age, and gender "are some of the subcultural differences which might separate interviewer and interviewee" (p. 89). Northen (1982) suggested that a social worker pay attention to the constellation of a client group and learn to work across ethnic lines.

Practice texts continue to urge practitioners to develop the ability for sincere acceptance of other people, regardless of their similarities or differences so that they will be able to fulfill the functions of professional social work practice (Cournoyer, 2007). For example, Compton and colleagues (2004) discussed how to communicate across cultures. They suggested that engaging people from different cultures necessitates sensitivity, openness to differences, and a willingness to know other cultures and oneself. Sheafor and Horejsi (2005) provided guidelines for working with vulnerable groups, encompassing clients who are poor, have brain injuries, are at risk for suicide, or are battered women. In a revision of a classic text, Kadushin and Kadushin (1997) pointed out that white interviewers need to recognize and be consciously aware that they, too, have a culture. These authors provided a list of characteristics of the culturally sensitive interviewer, summarized in Table 2.1. Although these chapters are useful, most practice books continue to have specialized chapters or sections on diversity issues rather than infusing these distinctions throughout their texts.

The Social Work Interview

Interviewing in social work is generally consider a means of collecting data in five areas: (a) client's accounts; (b) accounts of others; (c) questions and tests, either verbal or written; (d) observations; and (e) records of other professional or institutional systems. Social work interviews are distinguished by their *context*, providing parameters that set the scope, extent, and nature of the interview; *purpose and limits*, establishing specific ends/goals while limiting extraneous materials; and *specialized role relationships*, conforming to expected behaviors for the client and social worker (Compton et al., 2004).

Some theorists believe that a social work interview is a communication process composed of practice skills that should be guided by a theoretical orientation

Table 2.1
Characteristics of the Culturally Sensitive Interviewer

The culturally sensitive interviewer

- Approaches all interviewees with respect, warmth, acceptance, concern, interest, and empathy.
- Avoids client stereotypes and addresses mistrust and suspicion.
- Strives to develop an explicit awareness of client culture.
- Recognizes cultural patterns of help-seeking behaviors and preferences in intervention.
- Accepts the obligation of learning about different client cultures.
- Because of limitations in cultural knowledge, adopts a learning stance.
- Is aware of indigenous culture's strengths.
- Is aware that clients may have been disenfranchised or faced discrimination.

Source. Summarized from Kadushin, A., & Kadushin, G. (1997). *The Social Work Interview: A Guide for Human Service Professionals* (4th ed., pp. 347–348). New York: Columbia University Press.

(Greene, 2007; Shulman, 2005). Theoretical orientations shape what the practitioner tends to see, what he or she makes of it, and what he or she tends to do about it (Greene, 2008c). Theories of human behavior that are useful to social work practitioners "identify, describe, explain, and predict a world of stimuli and observations" in the practice role (Siporin, 1975, p. 101). That is, theories of human behavior must present assumptions suitable both to explore the pertinent and to translate a practitioner's observations into practice principles.

A Practice Skill

Practice skills refer to the "how" of helping (i.e., to purposeful, planned, instrumental activity through which tasks are accomplished and goals are achieved) (Cournoyer, 2007). Of necessity, practice skills must allow social workers to accomplish the best treatment interventions. Social work interviewing skills provide an enabling process with a recognized and agreed-upon purpose to help people resolve or cope more effectively with identified problems undermining their social functioning.

Interviewing skills are professional behaviors or techniques central to gathering information for appropriate assessment and successful intervention outcomes. Interview techniques structure the relationship between and among client(s) and the social worker, and they organize the therapeutic tasks necessary to carry out an interactive helping approach.

In large measure, discussions in the social work literature reflect the view that, irrespective of theoretical orientation, effective interviews conform to a general structure, manifest certain properties, and reflect the use of the same skills by interviewers (Hepworth et al., 2005).

Common properties of the clinical interview discussed in social work practice methods texts tend to include establishing rapport, responding empathetically, relating as a genuine person, starting where the client is, exploring problems and client meaning, structuring social worker responses, seeking concreteness in client problem identification, formulating treatment or intervention goals and negotiating contracts, and instilling client change-oriented skills. Although there is not a fixed order, these interview skills are often presented as a phase-specific process: preparing, beginning, exploring, assessing, contracting, working and evaluating, and ending (Cournoyer, 2007).

Rogerian Influences on the Social Work Interview: Basic Assumptions

Significant personality change does not occur except in a relationship. (Rogers, 1957, p. 98)

Valuing the Individual and the Right to Choose

Carl Rogers, the founder of the person-centered approach to counseling, had a major influence on social work practice, so much so that many of his value assumptions became tenets. Rogers is best known for his humanistic view that suggests that people have intrinsic worth and a natural tendency toward growth that can be facilitated by a warm and caring practitioner–client relationship (Rogers, 1957, 1961). His belief in the intrinsic value of all human beings, fundamental to all democratic societies, underlies the very existence of social work (Briar & Miller, 1971; see Table 2.2).

The right of client self-determination is another value orientation derived from the humanistic school and is an integral part of the matrix of social work ethics and beliefs. The principle of the right to client self-determination suggests that social workers who serve as facilitators and assist clients in making their own choices and decisions provide clients with a positive method of problem-solving experience.

Perlman (1965), an early social work practice theorist, provided a definition of client self-determination that speaks to its powerful force in social work practice:

> Self-determination, then, is the expression of our innate drive to experience the self as cause, as master of one's self. Its practical every day experience builds into people's maturation process because it requires the recognition of the actual, the consideration of the possible.... Self-determination is based upon a realistic view of freedom. Freedom, in essence, is the inner capacity and outer opportunity to make reasoned choice, among possible socially acceptable alternatives. (p. 421)

The right to self-determination has high priority in an effective social work interview (Greene, 2008d; Kadushin & Kadushin, 1997; National Association of Social Workers, 1999; Sheafor & Horejsi, 2005). Nonetheless, client self-determination is usually not seen as unconditional and sometimes is discussed as a right, influenced or even restricted by certain situations and conditions, particularly those conditions considered to be immoral and/or criminal acts.

Table 2.2
The Person-Centered Approach: Basic Assumptions

- People are trustworthy, capable, and have a potential for self-understanding and self-actualization.
- Self-actualization is a lifelong process.
- People develop and grow in a positive manner if a climate of trust and respect is established. Individual growth is promoted through therapeutic and other types of relationships.
- Positive attributes of the helping person, including genuineness, acceptance, and empathetic understanding, are necessary conditions for effective helping relationships.
- Respecting the subjective experiences of the client, fostering freedom and personal responsibility and autonomy, and providing options in therapy facilitate the client's growth.
- The helping person is not an authority. The helping person is someone who, through his or her respect and positive regard, fosters positive growth.
- Clients are capable of self-awareness and possess the ability to discover more appropriate behaviors. Clients, as do all people, have a propensity to move away from maladjustment toward psychological health.
- The practitioner should focus on the here-and-now behavior in the client–social worker relationship. The content of the helping relationship also should emphasize how the client acts in his or her world.
- Getting to know the true self is a major goal of the helping relationship.
- The aim of the helping relationship is to move the client toward greater independence and integration.

Source. Greene, R. R. (2008-a). Carl Rogers and the person-centered approach. In R. R. Greene (Ed.), Human Behavior Theory and Social Work Practice. New Brunswick, NJ: Aldine Transaction.

For example, McDermott (1982) raised thorny questions about the principle of a client's right to self-determination: Does the right to self-determination commit the social worker to support policies or decisions he or she may find unacceptable? Does the principle require the social worker to stand idly by while a client brings disaster upon himself or herself? McDermott went on to answer these questions: A social worker can, without violating the principle of self-determination, attempt to persuade the client of the desirability of adopting or not adopting a particular course of action. However, the real threat in situations that limit the right to self-determination is using the helping relationship as an opportunity to manipulate the client or to coercively exercise illegitimate authority. "The more insidious powers of the 'hidden persuader' ... threaten our liberty" (p. 87).

Under the following four conditions a social worker may consider assuming a paternalistic, or authoritative, role:

1. when the client is a child and lacks the capacity to make an informed decision;
2. when the client is mentally incompetent and is unable to understand the results of his or her decisions;
3. when the consequences of a client's actions are far-reaching or irreversible, such as in suicide; and
4. when the temporary interference with a client's liberty ensures future freedom and autonomy (Abramson, 1985).

The extent to which a social worker affirms a client's right to self-determination rests, in large measure, on the practitioner's perceptions of the helping role and the helping process (Reamer, 2006). For example, does the social worker perceive his or her role as the provider of solutions? Does the social worker erroneously perceive a particular client as a member of a group—such as a member of an oppressed community—lacking in strength and problem-solving capacity (Solomon, 1976)?

In practice situations, the social worker may often face conflict between his or her social responsibility and a client's right to self-determination (e.g., in the controversy concerning a mentally ill person's right to refuse treatment or a homeless person's right to refuse shelter). Some social work functions, such as protective services for children, older adults, and persons who are mentally impaired, also carry legal authority that may limit client self-determination (Murdach, 1996).

Working with particular client populations may present ethical conflict and countertransference issues (see below) for social workers when client behaviors and practices differ from their own (Brandell, 2004). These conflicts may prevent a social worker from making every effort to foster maximum self-determination on the part of the client (National Association of Social Workers, 1999). For example, when the AIDS pandemic began, legal and ethical issues as well as the stigma attached to HIV challenged social workers to reaffirm their profession's traditional values of advocacy (Compton et al., 2004; C. C. Ryan & Rowe, 1988).

The extent to which a client's right to self-determination is affirmed in the client–social worker relationship is also influenced by the helper–client power differential. A power differential between a client and social worker can be brought about by differences in gender, respective cultural identities, or group connections (Pinderhughes, 1995). Pinderhughes cautioned that because power is an important factor in social worker–minority relationships, a client's sense of powerlessness may be reinforced in the cross-cultural encounter more readily and more frequently than expected. Therefore, practitioners must encourage and empower clients and guard against putting them in a one-down position (see Chapter 11). Finally, Pinderhughes suggested that the ideal social worker–client relationship affirms self-determination and fosters growth because the relationship is based on a partnership of mutual respect in which both parties search for common solutions.

Establishing a Client–Social Worker Relationship: Empathy, Genuineness, and Warmth

The Therapeutic Relationship

Rogers (1957) hypothesized that clients will experience significant personality change only within a warm and caring therapeutic relationship. This assumption still dominates the social work profession's helping process: Most social work theorists agree that the client–social worker relationship is central to the clinical social work process and is a positive opportunity for facilitating client change (see Table 2.3).

As early as 1951, Biestek considered the client–social worker relationship a dynamic interaction and psychological connection between people that is "the soul of social casework" (p. 370). Other early theorists such as Hollis (1964) saw the relationship as the keystone of the casework process and basic to all treatment, and Perlman (1957) stated that "all growth-producing relationships, of which the casework relationship is one, contain elements of acceptance and expectation, support and stimulation" that are necessary for client change (p. 57). Most current practice methods texts continue to discuss the therapeutic relationship as a communication based on the emotional interaction between people necessary to client self-development, growth, and problem-solving capacity (Boyle, Hull, Mather, Smith, & Farley, 2006; Kadushin & Kadushin, 1997; Shulman, 2005).

Empathy, Genuineness, and Warmth

Another key idea about the nature of the social work interview derived from the Rogerian perspective is that positive change will occur if the practitioner displays three core attitudes: (a) empathy, or the ability to deal sensitively and

Table 2.3
The Rogerian Helping Relationship

Client	Social Work Therapist
Establishes self-trust	Values the client in a free environment
Is open to experience	Establishes a therapeutic climate
Is open to self-evaluation	Promotes client's self-exploration
Experiences freedom to grow	Provides genuineness, positive regard, and empathy
Moves to a new self-concept	Experiences a renewed sense of caring

Source. Greene, R. R. (2008-a). Carl Rogers and the person-centered approach. In R. R. Greene (Ed.), *Human Behavior Theory and Social Work Practice.* New Brunswick, NJ: Aldine Transaction.

accurately with client feelings; (b) nonpossessive warmth, or acceptance of the client as an individual; and (c) genuineness, or authenticity (Rogers & Dymond, 1957).

These characteristics of effective helping professionals are known as the core conditions or essential facilitating qualities (Cournoyer, 2007). Communicating with empathy and authenticity and with a nonjudgmental attitude have come to be considered the necessary and sufficient conditions for facilitating personality change (Asay & Lambert, 1999; see also Table 2.4). Forty years of research on outcomes continues to delineate the principal elements of therapy that account for client improvement, suggesting that the helping process is a form of healing with Rogers's core ingredients necessary to *any* form of successful intervention (Frank & Frank, 1991; Hubble, Duncan, & Miller, 1999; Norcross & Newman, 1992).

The therapeutic factors necessary for the practitioner to bring about positive change include the following:

1. exploring extratherapeutic factors (i.e., what clients bring to therapy and what influences they have in their lives);
2. building a collaborative client–practitioner relationship involving trust and collaboration;
3. fostering positive expectations, including hope and optimism;
4. using generative techniques that promote growth and transformation (Lambert, 1992).

Table 2.4
Guidelines for the Social Worker Practicing in the Rogerian Tradition

---

- Examine your own belief system. Review your attitudes about the self-worth of each individual's potential to use the helping relationship effectively.
- Deliberate about whether you have the capacity and are able to promote an atmosphere of warmth and trust within the helping relationship.
- Involve the client in a therapeutic relationship in which he or she takes the lead in describing his or her experiences and in expressing feelings.
- Show respect for the subjective experiences of the client by echoing his or her concerns accurately.
- Focus on the here-and-now experiences within the interview. Develop a process in which the client can learn that he or she can trust his or her own experiences.
- Use interviewing techniques that express genuineness, empathy, and congruence.
- Accept and interpret the client's life experiences that may stand in the way of his or her positive self-evaluation.
- View the helping relationship as an opportunity to facilitate growth (for both client and therapist) and promote self-evaluation.

Source. Greene, R. R. (2008-a). Carl Rogers and the person-centered approach. In R. R. Greene (Ed.), *Human Behavior Theory and Social Work Practice.* New Brunswick, NJ: Aldine Transaction.

Relationship-Building and Empathy: Cultural Applications

Social work theorists have increasingly come to question whether there is a universal approach to helping and facilitating client change. Various theorists have presented the view that effective social work service across a diverse population involves identifying cultural factors that may be barriers to establishing rapport and effective communication in the social work interview. For example, such barriers may include a reluctance to reveal problems to others, to reflect on what may be perceived as personal inadequacies, or to acknowledge a history of discrimination and mistrust. Still other barriers to forming an effective therapeutic client–social worker relationship in the social work interview may include the cultural norm of not discussing family business with outsiders, and an inability of the client and social worker to discern the other's intended meanings (Hepworth et al., 2005).

Understanding a client's worldview or cultural frame of reference is an essential dimension of empathy, facilitating interpersonal understanding across cultures (Cain, 2002). Having empathy allows the social worker to share the client's state of mind. The social worker feels *with* rather than *for* the client (Kadushin & Kadushin, 1997). Although social worker empathy is said to be an essential condition for successful practice, putting oneself in the client's shoes is not an easy matter. Achieving empathy in the social work interview is made difficult by the erroneous belief that all people are the same (Gibbs, 1985). This assumption that empathy is grounded in human sameness is often expressed in the social work literature. So, too, is the belief that specific social worker behaviors transmit universal messages with predictable interpretations.

Bachelor (1991) found considerable variation in clients' interpretations of empathy and concluded that empathy is not a universal construct, thus adding doubt to the value of a strict emphasis on skill building as a means to practice effectiveness. From this perspective, the goals of multicultural competence may be better served by learning experiences that focus on the skills of adaptive, reflective responses, by which—as Duncan, Solovey, and Rusk (1992) suggested—the social worker can "accommodate a wide variety of interpersonal styles and meaning systems" (p. 39).

The idea that all practitioners can learn to deliver the same interview skills in the same way, rather than adapt their techniques to different client contexts, may lead to *cultural countertransference*, or unconscious assumptions about human behavior that are based on prevailing cultural beliefs (Bernardez, 1982, p. 8). That is, for the practitioner to assume the client is the same as himself or herself, when attempting to be empathetic, can result in "a decidedly nonempathetic helping response, especially when the client is from a group that has been marginalized or demeaned by the prevailing culture" (Kaplan, 1990, p. 8). Maintaining empathy during the interview process is also difficult when the social worker overidentifies with the client. This form of countertransference is a result of the practitioner placing his or her own expectations for behavior on the client (Compton et al., 2004).

In examining empathy in psychotherapy with women, theorists at the Stone Center at Wellesley College (Jordan, 1997; Miller & Stiver, 1991) proposed that people yearn for connections with others, yet tend to keep a large part of themselves out of connection. These theorists believe that being out of connection, or not relating in a disclosing manner, occurs more frequently among women because women are socialized to appear less (sexually) available and more compliant. Therefore, for psychological growth to occur in the therapeutic relationship, mutual empathy and mutual empowerment must occur. The sense of mutuality in therapy, in their view, is based on a true sense of authenticity that allows for equally true engagement and is seen as part of relational cultural theory in which the client and social worker see beyond themselves (Freedberg, 2007).

From a cross-cultural point of view, the theoretical underpinning of the social work interview must assume knowledge of a client's culture to allow the social worker to develop different skills and strategies in the interview. Perhaps the best known technique for achieving an empathetic connection that does not apply across cultures is maintaining eye contact. For many Indian clients, eye contact may cause uneasiness, and a method of looking elsewhere is recommended (Edwards & Edwards, 1980). Of course, to some extent, the practice of maintaining eye contact varies with the individual, often depending on his or her adoption of mainstream ideas and values (Kadushin & Kadushin, 1997). Therefore, it is always important to individualize the seemingly universal suggestion to maintain positive eye contact.

It is necessary to use culture-specific information to enhance the cross-cultural interviewing process. For example, among several Indian tribes, it is useful to use a term such as *sister*, *brother*, *father*, and so on, rather than the person's name, to discuss someone who has died, because it is a violation of tradition to use a dead person's name. Such cultural sensitivity to clients who follow this tradition enhances the empathetic response of the social worker (Edwards & Edwards, 1980). As forms of address convey status and level of intimacy, social workers must carefully weigh how they address clients by name. Especially in the use of first names, the age of a client and the length of time the social worker has been seeing the client are important factors to consider (Kadushin & Kadushin, 1997).

Relationships and Empathy: Alternative Perspectives

Social Constructionism

How would you know when someone truly accepts you (Cournoyer, 2007)? How can a social worker who shares few of the client's life experiences achieve empathetic responses in the interview? The social worker may have to accept the fact that he or she is likely to have little experience that may lead to empathy, and therefore needs to be more ready to listen and more open to learning from the client (Kadushin, 1972). Scholars and practitioners who espouse the utility of constructionist thought for social work practice have argued that empathy and unconditional positive regard are not practitioner behaviors but can only be realized through client perceptions and interpretations and in experiences between people (Allen, 1993; Dean, 1993; Duncan et al., 1992; Gergen, 2001; see Chapter 6 on constructionist thought). Therefore, the core conditions would be experienced in a highly idiosyncratic manner according to the specific and unique meaning system of the client:

> Empathy is *not* ... a specific therapist behavior or attitude ... a means to gain a relationship.... Rather, empathy is therapist attitudes and behaviors that place the client's perceptions and experiences above theoretical content and personal values. Empathy is attempting to work within the expressed meaning system of the client. (pp. 34–35)

A common theme in the cross-cultural literature is that practitioner empathy can lead to an understanding of difference. Ironically, the assumption that empathy is a transcultural phenomenon, or an attribute shared by all human beings, has not been documented. The assumption also does not recognize that the helping process takes place in a societal context in which racism, classism, sexism, heterosexism, and so forth can occur, negatively influencing an empathetic relationship (Arredono, 1999; Cain, 2002; Ridley, 1995).

Ethnographic Interviews

James Green's (1999) model of cross-cultural social work attempts to address the limitations of the general features of the helping interview. He proposed that careful listening, openness and honesty, and an effort to gain rapport and develop empathy are not enough when interviewing minority or ethnic clients. He suggested that social workers take a learning stance to understand client meanings so as to communicate with competence across cultures. He argued that a practitioner's caring response cannot be contrived, nor may he or she rely solely on empathy and openness to get in touch with a client's feelings. Rather, the practitioner who is culturally competent must use ethnographic interviews to comprehend what the client knows and how that knowledge is used in everyday activities.

The ethnographic approach to the social work interview delineates culture-specific cognitive and behavioral structures to go beyond general statements about helping and caring for others (Clark, 2004; Comas-Diaz, 2000; Comas-Diaz & Jacobsen, 1991). The goal of an ethnographic interview is to reduce practitioner ethnocentrism and to increase bicultural sensitivity (Ho, 1995; Spradley, 1979). To help the social worker appropriately assess client problems and provide effective social work interventions, this perspective on cross-cultural social work focuses the social work interview on "localized group-specific categories of how the world is organized to generate an insider's perspective" (Green, 1999, p. 72).

A Five-Stage Model

Gibbs (1985) authored a five-stage model of interpersonal orientation to treatment in which the client evaluates the social worker while the social worker is attempting to establish a relationship and to assess the client's problems (see Table 2.5). The model, which was intended to overcome problems of misdiagnoses and early termination found among many Black clients, explores and offers practice suggestions for initial interviews that set the tone of the helping relationship and establish the boundaries of treatment. The focus of the model is on the content of verbal and nonverbal interactions between the social worker and client, and the goals they agree need to be accomplished. Furthermore, the model examines practitioner behaviors, which are evaluated in each stage by the client according to his or her treatment priorities. The social worker dimensions of counselor competence are Rogers's warmth, empathy, congruence, and unconditional positive regard for the client.

Table 2.5
Model of Interpersonal Orientation to Treatment

Client Evaluation Stage (Theme of Evaluation)	Counselor Behavior Response (Dimension of Competence)
I. Appraisal ("sizing up")	I. Personal authenticity ("genuineness")
II. Investigation ("checking out")	II. Egalitarianism (status equalization)
III. Involvement (social interactions)	III. Identification (positive identity)
IV. Commitment (personal loyalty)	V. Acceptance (empathy, support)
VI. Engagement (task involvement)	VII. Performance (task performance)

Source. Gibbs, J. T. (1985). Treatment relationships with Black clients. Interpersonal U.S. instrumental strategies. In C. B. Germain (Ed.), *Advances in Clinical Social Work Practice* (p. 188). Silver Spring, MD: NASW Press.

Stage I of the model is the *appraisal stage*, during which the client sizes up the social worker, is generally aloof, and evaluates the personal authenticity of the worker. Stage II is the *investigation stage*, characterized by the client checking out the practitioner, usually by challenging the social worker's qualifications and background. Stage III, *the involvement stage*, begins when the client believes the social worker is able to deal effectively with [his or her] differences and begins a process of client self-disclosure. The relationship during Stage III is based on a sense of perceived mutuality and positive identification. The client may ask the social worker to be involved in his or her community activity.

During Stage IV, the *commitment stage*, the client expresses more personal regard for the social worker and is more active in the treatment process. This is the point at which the client should recognize that the practitioner has demonstrated acceptance through empathetic and supportive behaviors. Stage V, the *engagement stage*, is the final stage of treatment, when the client and social worker engage in mutually defined tasks. The attention to tasks acknowledges the interpersonal competence of the social worker.

Gibbs based her model on research that suggested that Black clients tend to evaluate the interpersonal competence of the social worker in terms of

- personal authenticity, or being perceived as genuine, real, and down to earth;
- egalitarianism, equalizing perceived differences from an ethnic or socioeconomic background;
- identification, resolving problems without pressuring clients to relinquish their sense of ethnic identity and cultural values;
- acceptance, empathizing with clients to the extent that the clients are provided nonjudgmental attitudes and support; and
- performance, cooperating in the treatment process.

Gibbs's model is illustrative of the idea that problems in cross-cultural communication can result from failure to personalize the client–social worker relationship. Rather, effective interviewing with diverse populations requires that the practitioner "treat a universalistic situation in a particularistic way" with interpersonal competence involving mutual trust (Gibbs, 1985, p. 190).

Relationships across Racial/Ethnic Lines

Some theorists have developed another model for thinking about client–social worker relationships across racial/ethnic lines. They suggest that social workers think of themselves and their clients as *bicultural* (i.e., as people who have retained certain aspects of their "original culture" and adopted other features of the dominant or majority culture; D. W. Sue, 2006).

This approach requires that the practitioner understand how ethnic group membership governs behavior, values, and norms, recognizing that people who are bicultural have learned about and adopted aspects of mainstream culture. People's ability to live in two cultures falls along a continuum—from those who are most ethnically traditional to those who have adopted most aspects of mainstream culture (Pedersen, 1997).

Therefore, social workers will want to become self-aware about where they are on the continuum, asking themselves what they know about their own values, expected role behaviors, and historical experiences. Practitioners will need similar knowledge about clients and their belief systems. In order to form a relationship, the social worker and client will have to address the incongruities between values, norms, and worldviews that may not be shared. In this way, barriers to forming a therapeutic alliance and expressing appropriate empathy may be overcome.

Freud's Influence on the Social Work Interview: Basic Assumptions

Mental processes that are conscious are within awareness; preconscious mental processes are capable of becoming conscious "without much ado"; and unconscious mental processes are outside awareness and cannot be studied directly. (Freud, 1956, p. 256)

Listening to Client Feelings, Interpreting Meaning, and Developing Client Insight

Social workers' strong interest in Freudian explanations of human behavior dates back to at least the 1920s and lasted throughout the 1950s, well into the 1960s, and beyond (Baker, 1985; Briar & Miller, 1971; Greene, 2008b). Among the most important assumptions that many social workers adopted from Freud's psychoanalytic thinking is the view that all behavior is determined in a pur-poseful and orderly way and can therefore be explained (Freud, 1956). Other psychoanalytic principles adopted in social casework include a primary focus on clients' intrapsychic mental processes and on their past experiences. Taken together, these assumptions lead to an emphasis on the clinician interpreting client feelings and helping a client develop insight (Briar & Miller, 1971; see Tables 2.6 and 2.7).

Hamilton (1958) contended that "caseworkers must sometimes bring to the attention of the client ideas and feelings, whether acceptable or not, of which [he or she] was previously unaware" (p. 26). Kadushin (1972) proposed that to achieve the purpose of the interview, it is necessary to "move ... from a surface statement of the [client's situation] to a more personal, emotional meaning of the content" (p. 96). In addition, Kadushin believed it important for the social work interviewer to distinguish between *clarification*, mirroring what the client has said and of which he or she is therefore aware, and *interpretation*, making explicit what the client is feeling but of which he or she is not yet aware.

Table 2.6
Assumptions about the Psychoanalytically Oriented Helping Person

- Examining and explaining the symbolic nature of symptoms is the path to reconstruction of past events, particularly childhood traumas.

- Uncovering pertinent repressed material and bringing it to consciousness is a necessary ingredient in the helping process.

- Expressing emotional conflicts helps to free the individual from traumatic memories.

- Reconstructing and understanding difficult early life events will be curative.

- Using the relationship of the helping person and client as a microcosm of crucial experiences is an important part of the helping relationship.

- Developing self-awareness and self-control are the goals of social work intervention.

Source. Greene, R. R. (2008-b). Classical psychoanalytic thought, contemporary developments, and clinical social work. In R. R. Greene (Ed.), *Human Behavior Theory and Social Work Practice*. New Brunswick, NJ: Aldine Transaction.

Table 2.7
Guidelines for Psychodynamically Oriented Practitioners

- Accept that all behavior has meaning and can be explained.

- Engage in active listening to ascribe meaning to the material the client produces in the helping relationship.

- Evaluate the relative outcomes of the psychosexual stages by observing and analyzing present derivative behaviors.

- Assess the relative use and pattern of ego defenses. Weigh the flexibility or fragility as well as level of maturity of ego defenses.

- Pay attention to your own motivations and feelings.

- Allow the client to reflect on his or her feelings, thoughts, and behaviors in a nonobtrusive manner.

- Provide interpretations of fantasies, feelings, and events described. Allow for feedback about the interpretations' efficacy.

Source. Based on Greene, R. R. (2008-b). Classical psychoanalytic thought, contemporary developments, and clinical social work. In R. R. Greene (Ed.), *Human Behavior Theory and Social Work Practice*. New Brunswick, NJ: Aldine Transaction.

Social work texts continue to teach the traditional technique of social workers reflecting client feelings as a means of enhancing client self-awareness (Boyle et al., 2006; Compton et al., 2004; Kadushin & Kadushin, 1997). Interpreting client feelings that are beyond clients' conscious recognition—a technique used by social workers who adopt ego psychology and cognitive therapies—is also recommended as an intervention so that "people can genuinely learn about themselves" (Boyle et al., 2006, p. 35). Various techniques are used to focus a client's attention on feelings at greater depth. Furthermore, social workers are urged to respond in ways that affirm their understanding of client's inner feelings (Hepworth et al., 2005).

Because client self-awareness is generally seen as a key ingredient of mental health, social work practitioners have tended to view interpretation of client meanings as critical to the helping process. Some social work theorists have contended that insight through interpretation focuses on a generic view about a client's need to receive a different viewpoint, and that such insight is most important in therapeutic endeavors (Hepworth et al., 2005).

Achieving *insight* involves the social worker obtaining a client's essential history and discovering historical influences on present difficulties to achieve a curative effect. The social worker's purpose from a psychodynamic point of view is to uncover "discrepancies between statements and actions, gaps, silences, repetitions, and omissions, which are clues to a person's inner experience" (Siporin, 1975, p. 245). Interpreting the client's meaning from information presented in the interview often is viewed as the most important element of the social work helping process. Although under question (Blong Xeong, Tuicomepee, LaBlanc, & Rainey (2006), the goal of the client–social worker relationship from this perspective is to help the client attain self-awareness through self-disclosure and social worker interpretation.

Transference and Countertransference

According to Freud, client self-awareness may be hampered by the intrusion of irrational thoughts into the therapeutic process. Freud offered two concepts for understanding the client–social worker relationship as a here-and-now microcosm of past intrapsychic events: transference and countertransference. *Transference* was defined as the client's special interest or feelings about the practitioner brought into the clinical experience, but based on earlier authority relationships. *Countertransference* was defined as the social worker's reaction to the client based on past events or feelings that could interfere with therapeutic work.

Freud's belief that a client can be helped by re-experiencing past feelings within the therapeutic encounter is frequently expressed in social work practice texts (Shulman, 2005). For example, Northen (1982), in her text on clinical social work practice, stated that although they may or may not be based on accurate perceptions, "feelings, attitudes, and patterns of responses are transferred from earlier relationships" into present situations (p. 42). She also made reference to the social worker being self-aware so he or she does not "transfer attitudes from [his or her] past onto the client" (p. 42).

Because transference and countertransference have been defined as a mixture of conscious and unconscious distortions of reality, social work practitioners have characteristically contended that these phenomena are obstacles to the helping process (Northen, 1982; Perlman, 1957). Over the years, however, the definition of countertransference has broadened and emerged as an experience in the therapeutic relationship that can make a positive contribution (Greene, 2008d; Peabody & Gelso, 1982). The literature increasingly addresses countertransference issues in social work with various populations, including people who are terminally ill, mentally ill, members of countercultures, or homosexual (Buckingham & Rehm, 1987; Buckingham & Van Gorp, 1988; Dunkel & Hatfield, 1986). In addition, theorists have suggested that a key issue in working with older adults is an ability to recognize practitioner misconceptions and biases (Abramson, 1985; Butler & Lewis, 1973; Greene, 2008d; Reamer, 1988; Sprung, 1989).

Dunkel and Hatfield (1986) pointed out that social workers in health care have identified the following eight countertransference issues in working with persons with AIDS that, if understood, may enhance the treatment process:

1. fear of the unknown—the fear that the "true" means of transmission of HIV remain unknown,
2. fear of contagion—the fear that not all precautionary measures have been identified,
3. fear of death and dying—the fear of dealing with one's sense of mortality,
4. denial of helplessness—gaining control through feelings of omnipotence or power,
5. fear of homosexuality—unresolved feelings about gays that ghettoize or marginalize the client,
6. overidentification—overinvesting time and energy in the client to the point of loss of objectivity,
7. anger—unconscious feelings that "blame the victim" for his or her "predicament," and
8. need for professional omnipotence—the social worker as an authority who does not respect the client's right to human dignity and self-determination.

Because social workers believe in an egalitarian society, they may not be aware of transference and countertransference problems (Paviour, 1988). However, when the concepts of countertransference and diversity are considered together, a different dimension is added to the client–social worker encounter. By attending to countertransference, practitioners can deepen their understanding of diverse client groups (Palombo, 1985).

Self-Disclosure

Kadushin (1972) contended that "the core of traditional casework derives from theoretical conceptions which have limited applicability to many lower-class clients. Traditional casework is more applicable to the neurotic, introspective, articulate client whose problems are primarily intrapsychic" (p. 89). The view remains that it may be harmful to not express distressful information. However, the idea that cultural variables influence self-disclosure is better understood. For example, when and how emotions are experienced may vary from one culture to another (Kitayama, Markus, & Kurokawa, 2000).

Because Chinese American clients often stress collective identity formation and emotional interdependence, they "'match' disclosure behavior with the social norms governing the interpersonal standards of the [traditional Chinese] society" (Ow & Katz, 1999, p. 620). That is, Chinese-American clients may focus on maintaining interpersonal harmony and unity rather than engaging in what could be negative self-disclosure (Chung, 2006). In addition, Chinese-American clients often cannot understand free association as a method of understanding, because they tend to believe that verbalization is a discipline and language is to be used with precision (A. S. Ryan, 1985). Chinese-American clients also may think it unacceptable to express inner conflict. Therefore, a social worker who "encourages ... self-expression may seem to a Chinese client to be leading away from peace of mind" (A. S. Ryan, 1985, p. 335).

Insight

Self-understanding and introspection may be viewed differently by various cultures (Edwards & Edwards, 1980). Edwards and Edwards pointed out that many Indian clients believe that people should be able to understand one another; therefore, constant questioning about past or present events may not build a therapeutic alliance. From this perspective, it should not be necessary for the client to explain to the social worker his or her problem in great detail. Rather, the professional should be able to understand.

The therapeutic relationship must take into account "the intrapsychic meanings of ethnic sense of belonging and identification, the meaning and utilization of cultural symbols ... and the various functions of language" (Sotomayor, 1977, p. 203). How accurate the interpretation of client feelings is across culture, class, and gender groups remains a serious concern. Because insight attainment in treatment became the primary goal of treatment under the Freudian-influenced model, social workers had to face the issue of how to treat clients and problems thought to be unsuited to a psychoanalytic approach (Briar & Miller, 1971). The primacy of insight-oriented therapy led to an implied value hierarchy about who is a suitable candidate for therapy that may still linger today (i.e., who is considered a "bonafide" or motivated client for certain forms of treatment interventions).

Assessing Client Behaviors and Motivation

Assessment is said to be fundamental to social work and has been defined in various ways: It refers to a process between the social worker and client in which information is gathered, analyzed, and synthesized to provide a person-in-environment picture of the client's strengths and challenges (Cournoyer, 2007; Hepworth et al., 2005). Members of the diagnostic and psychosocial schools of social work practice have been particularly influenced by Freudian theory and have based their assessments on a format of evaluation/diagnosis, treatment, and cure (Hamilton, 1958; Hollis, 1964; Perlman, 1957). For example, Perlman (1957) stated that the social work diagnostic interview includes an exploration of the balance among ego ("the personality's problem-solving apparatus"; p. 17), superego ("the personality's automatic punishment-or-reward system"; p. 11), and id (the "life force"; p. 10). Perlman and others of the diagnostic and psychodynamic schools believed that the purpose of the social work interview was to assess and bring about a better relative balance among ego, superego, and id.

Kadushin (1972), who also proposed that the interview involved a diagnostic process, later stated that the social work interview is designed to keep the client focused on affective material and to encourage the interviewee to reveal himself or herself. The social worker's role is to interpret affective materials, to help clients become more aware of their feelings, and to seek therapeutic change through the client–social worker relationship.

Many contemporary approaches to direct practice in social work incorporate the concept of study or assessment as the basis of intervention (Brandell, 2004). However, the emphasis on the accumulation of client data to form an assessment continues to come under question. Social workers trained in diagnostic assessment and treatment should be alert to the "potential bias inherent in any one ethnocentric educational approach" (Chandler, 1980, p. 348). Practitioners also need to be aware of biases in differential diagnoses and differential treatment regimens and need to be sure assessment and interventions are appropriate for a member of a particular ethnic population.

Finally, many theorists are concerned that the helping process be based on client–practitioner shared meanings of events. For example, Lowe (1991) cautioned that "numerous cases of ethnic differences in expectations of treatment can be traced to cultural distinctions embedded in belief systems and norms of culturally appropriate behavior" (p. 43). S. Sue and Zane (1987) suggested that culturally sensitive assessment involves three major guidelines:

1. Social workers must define the problem in a manner that is consistent with the client's belief system.
2. Expectations for change must be consistent with the client's cultural values.
3. Treatment goals must be compatible with the client's perceived outcome goals.

Maintaining Professional Authority and Control in the Interview

Many social workers, particularly those identified with the psychodynamic school of thought, have adopted Freud's view that the course of the helping process is determined by the clinician. From this perspective, the social worker guides, structures, or, some might say, takes charge of the interview (Biestek, 1951). *Resistance* to social worker authority is defined as a normal reaction to the idea of being helped. Resistance also has been attributed to client effort to hold on to the familiar, a lack of client motivation or capacity, and client fear of change or of the unknown. For example, Shulman (2005) suggested that practitioners should expect that issues related to authority theme are an expected part of the helping process and can present barriers to change. Likewise, Northen (1982) proposed that the client needs to come to understand the nature and extent of the social worker's legitimate authority, and the social worker needs to come to understand the client's need to control or to submit to the social worker's authority (p. 205).

Client self-disclosure and social worker interpretation as part of the context of the helping relationship have increasingly come under question. For example, helping professionals may face clients who have reasonable grounds for resistance to control (Edelman, 1982). Professionals may need to take care when rationalizing their authority and defining what they consider normal behaviors. Individual verbal therapies, with their roots in Freud, often put clients in a paradoxical situation: Although client self-disclosure is generally considered necessary for successful counseling outcomes, there may be many complex intrapsychic, interpersonal, and sociocultural reasons that affect a client's willingness to self-disclose.

Because most therapy with black clients is conducted by white therapists who are likely to inhibit self-disclosure in their black clients, Ridley (1984) argued that a "shared failure" may result (p. 1237). Some client reluctance to disclose personal information can be attributed to "playing it cool" or to maintaining a "healthy cultural paranoia." Ridley also attributed many such failures in disclosure to the ineffectiveness of the helping person who does not address the client's often negative interracial experiences in the therapy. In a similar vein, Edwards and Edwards (1980) pointed out that many Indian clients are suspicious of Anglo people in authority and approach many social workers with great caution. In addition, Indian people often are taught to deal with problems within their own family and tribal settings. The use of unnecessary reliance on the view that the social worker is an authority in the relationship may "eventuate in raw coercion" and, at the very least, may raise a serious concern about how self-determination coincides with case planning (Briar & Miller, 1971, p. 40).

There has been considerable discussion about the place of self-disclosure and interpretation as primary techniques in the social work interview. Although theorists from the existential, client-centered, and Gestalt schools of thought have argued against interpretation as a therapeutic technique, most other theorists believe interpretation is a key therapeutic intervention. These latter theorists posit that interpretation, although varying in content with the theoretical orientation of the worker, offers the client a different point of view that prepares him or her for change (Claiborn, 1982; Hepworth & Larsen, 1987).

Alternative Perspectives

Finding Meaning: Alternative Perspectives

When examining the effectiveness of a particular therapeutic technique, such as those used in interviewing, theorists usually discuss which clients are "good" or "bad" candidates for that particular method. The discussion tends to encompass information about how social worker or client blind spots inhibit goal attainment. Rarely does the discussion include the limitations of the theory or paradigm itself. However, questions are increasingly being asked about the frameworks used as the theoretical underpinnings for practice skills (Anderson & Goolishian, 1988; Dean & Fenby, 1989; Lax, 1992; Weick, 1983; White & Epston, 1990).

Social work scholars continue to provide suggestions for an eclectic use of theory-informed practice skills necessary for social work practice with diverse populations. Practitioners are moving from traditional intrapsychic therapies to an eclectic, more systemic approach to intervention (DeHoyos, 1989; Ephross & Greene, 1992). Many believe the move to a multitheoretical, multimodal approach to helping will not minimize the role of verbal techniques. Rather, an eclectic, more systemic approach may offer the potential for a variety of interventions, including social environmental changes (DeHoyos, 1989; De-Hoyos & Jensen, 1985; see Chapters 10 and 11 for a discussion of change in macrolevel systems).

Positivist (Objective) and Postpositivist (Subjective) Theory

Two human behavior perspectives about such questions have dominated the social sciences and have been infused into social work thinking about how to proceed with interview practice techniques. *Positivist* or *objectivist theory* assumes that social phenomena have a real existence that is factual and can be studied through natural science research methods, and that underlying universal laws can be discovered (Guba, 1990). That is, psychological knowledge about the client can be discovered with the help of practitioner interpretation.

Postpositivist or *subjectivist theory*, as in Rogers's humanistic approach, takes the stance that social reality exists in or is a creation of human consciousness, and that people are proactive in its creation (Foucault, 1980). The only reality, then, is in the person's consciousness. The client's social reality cannot be studied as such but must be experienced with the client (Burrell & Morgan, 1979; Martin & O'Connor, 1989).

Postmodern thinkers do not subscribe to the view that behavior A causes B; rather, behavior is an outcome of complex personal, social, cultural, and historical contexts and meaning is personal—created through language and social interactions. "Social workers should not expect to know in advance what the outcome of clinical interactions will be" (Pozatek, 1994, p. 397). They should take a "not-knowing" stance, learning from the client during the therapeutic conversation (Gilligan & Price, 1993).

Another shift in emphasis from the social constructionist viewpoint is the importance of intuitive knowing (McNamee & Gergen, 1992; Van Den Bergh & Cooper, 1986; Weick, 1993). Social work theorists are increasingly engaged in debate about whether social work is an applied science based on empirical knowledge or a process or an art understood by analyzing and codifying the performance of master practitioners (Weick, 1993). Postmodern thinkers have proposed that knowledge is created through social discourse within a historical and sociopolitical context. That is, practitioners may create knowledge at the local level or at the front line of practice. Knowledge thus becomes a process of creation in the client–social worker interaction or what Schon (1983) so aptly called "knowing-in-practice" (p. 62). From this perspective, social work may be considered an art: Students learn knowledge and skills from master artists (Weick, 1993).

Interviewing Differentially

Less frequently addressed in the social work literature is the need for social workers to adapt their interviewing techniques to different client contexts to better communicate across gender and culture. There is, however, a small body of literature that specifically addresses diversity and the interviewing process. The ability to conduct a skillful social work interview with diverse populations may require the selective and differential use of both human behavior theory and practice methods, and an evaluation of the effectiveness of person–environment interventions (Compton et al., 2004). It has been argued that the differential use of theory-informed practice with diverse populations is central to cross-cultural client–social worker encounters, and that such differential use of theory for practice allows help to be given and used within age- and gender-appropriate cultures.

In the postmodern approach, the social worker generally does not ask predetermined interview questions but encourages a search for understanding (for an invaluable description of postmodern ideas, see Laird, 1993). That is, the practitioner explores the client's ideas about the nature of what might be considered "individual dysfunction" (McNamee & Gergen, 1992). Social workers who have adopted a postmodern approach focus on the client's definition of the situation, emphasize the client's unique meaning of events, and ask questions that lead to a collaborative view of solutions.

The manner in which the practitioner works with the client to define the situation may be portrayed as circular (see Figure 2.1). Tomm (1994), who

Figure 2.1
A Framework for Distinguishing Four Major Groups of Questions.

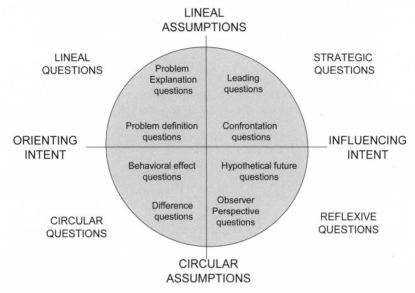

From Tomm, K. (1994). Interventive interviewing: Part III. Intending to ask lineal, circular, strategic, or reflexive questions? In K. Brownlee, P. Gallant, & D. Carpenter (Eds.), Constructionism and Family Therapy (pp. 117-156). Thunder Bay, Canada: Lakehead University Printing.

provided an example framework of circular questioning, distinguished four major groups of questions that practitioners may ask. *Lineal orienting questions* are those that presuppose that normative data can be collected about each client (e.g., "What problems brought you to see me today?"). *Circular questions* are primarily exploratory (e.g., "How is it we find ourselves together today?"). *Strategic questions* are based on an assumption the practitioner holds about the client (e.g., "When are you going to take charge of your life and start looking for a job?"). And *reflexive questions* are intended to place the client in a reflexive position or to trigger the consideration of new options (e.g., "If your depression suddenly disappeared, how would your life be different?"). According to DeJong and Berg (2002), when they put clients in the position of being experts on their own lives, social workers put aside as much of their own frame of reference as possible. They take a *not-knowing position*, relying on the client's perceptions and explanations and being informed by the client (Anderson & Goolishian, 1992). However, this alternative view of the clinical social work encounter has yet to firmly take hold.

References

Abramson, M. (1985). The autonomy–paternalism dilemma in social work practice. *Social Casework*, 66, 387–393.

Allen, J. (1993). The constructivist paradigm: Values and ethics. In J. Laird (Ed.), *Revisioning Social Work Education: A Social Constructionist Approach* (pp. 31–54). New York: Haworth Press.

Anderson, H., & Goolishian, H. (1988). Human systems as linguistic systems. *Family Process*, 27, 371–395.

Anderson, H., & Goolishian, H. (1992). The client is the expert: A not-knowing approach to therapy. In S. McNamee & K. J. Gergen (Eds.), *Therapy as Social Construction* (pp. 25–39). Newbury Park, CA: Sage.

Arredono, P. (1999). Multicultural counseling competencies as tools to address oppression and racism. *Journal of Counseling and Development, 77,* 102–108.

Asay, T. P., & Lambert, M. J. (1999). The empirical case for the common factors in therapy: Quantitative findings. In M. A. Hubble, B. L. Duncan, & D. Miller (Eds.), *The Heart and Soul of Change* (pp. 23–55). Washington, DC: American Psychological Association.

Bachelor, A. (1991). Comparison and relationship to outcome of diverse dimensions of the helping alliance as seen by client and therapist. *Psychotherapy*, 28, 534–549.

Baker, E. (1985). Psychoanalyses and a psychoanalytic psychotherapy. In I. J. Lyn & J. P. Garske (Eds.), *Contemporary Psychotherapies* (pp. 19–68). Columbus, OH: Merrill.

Bernardez, T. (1982, May). *Cultural Countertransference in the Psychotherapy of Women.* Paper presented at the 26th Annual Meeting of the American Academy of Psychoanalysis, Toronto, Ontario, Canada.

Biestek, F. P. (1951). The principles of client-self-determination. *Social Casework*, 32, 369–375.

Blong Xiong, Z., Tuicomepee, A., LaBlanc, L., & Rainey, J. (2006). Hmong immigrants' perceptions of family secrets and recipients of disclosure. *Families in Society*, 87, 231–239.

Boyle, S. W., Hull, G. H., Mather, J. H., Smith, L. L., & Farley, O.W. (2006). *Direct Practice in Social Work.* Boston: Pearson Education.

Brandell, J. (2004). *Psychodynamic Social Work.* New York: Columbia University Press.

Briar, S., & Miller, H. (1971). *Problems and Issues in Social Casework.* New York: Columbia University Press.

Buckingham, S. L., & Rehm, S. J. (1987). AIDS and women at risk. *Health and Social Work*, 12(1), 5–11.

Buckingham, S. L., & Van Gorp, W. G. (1988). Essential knowledge about AIDS dementia. *Social Work*, 31, 112–115.

Burrell, G., & Morgan, G. (1979). *Sociological Paradigms and Organisational Analysis.* London: Heinemann.

Butler, R. N., & Lewis, M. C. (1973). *Aging Mental Health: Positive Psychological Approaches.* St. Louis, MO: Mosby.

Cain, D. (2002). *Classics in the Person-Centered Approach: The Best of the Person-Centered Review.* Ross-on-Wye, England: PCCS Books.

Chandler, S. M. (1980). Self-perceived competency in cross-cultural counseling. *Social Casework*, 61, 347–353.

Chung, I. (2006). A cultural perspective on emotions and behavior: An empathic pathway to examine intergenerational conflicts in Chinese immigrant families. *Families in Society*, 87, 367–376.

Claiborn, C. D. (1982). Interpretation and change in counseling for negative emotions.

Journal of Counseling Psychology, 30, 164–171.

Clark, J. (2004). *Beyond Empathy: An Ethnographic Approach to Cross Cultural Social Work Practice.* Retrieved September 21, 2007, from *http://www.mun.ca/cassw-ar/papers2/clark.pdf.*

Comas-Diaz, L. (2000). An ethnopolitical approach to working with people of color. *American Psychologist, 55,* 1319–1325.

Comas-Diaz, L., & Jacobsen, F. N. (1991). Ethnocultural transference and countertransference in the therapeutic dyad. *American Journal of Orthopsychiatry, 61,* 392–402.

Compton, B. R., Galaway, B., & Cournoyer, B. R. (2004). *Social Work Processes* (7th ed.). Belmont, CA: Wadsworth.

Cournoyer, B. (2000). *The Social Work skills Workbook* (3rd ed.). Monterey, CA: Brooks/Cole.

Cournoyer, B. (2007). *The Social Work Skills Workbook* (5th ed.). Monterey, CA: Brooks/Cole.

Dean, R. (1993). Teaching a constructivist approach to clinical practice. In J. Laird (Ed.), *Revisioning Social Work Education: A Social Constructionist Approach* (pp. 55–75). New York: Haworth Press.

Dean, R. G., & Fenby, B. L. (1989). Exploring epistemologies: Social work action as a reflection of philosophical assumptions. *Journal of Social Work Education, 25,* 46–53.

DeHoyos, G. (1989). Person-in-environment: A tri-level practice model. *Social Casework, 70,* 131–138.

DeHoyos, G., & Jensen, C. (1985). The systems approach in American social work. *Social Casework, 66,* 490–497.

DeJong, P., & Berg, I. (2002). *Interviewing for Solutions* (2nd ed.). Monterey, CA: Brooks/Cole.

Duncan, B. L., Solovey, A. D., & Rusk, G. S. (1992). *Changing the Rules: A Client Directed Approach to Therapy.* New York: Guilford Press.

Dunkel, J., & Hatfield, S. (1986). Countertransference issues in working with persons with AIDS. *Social Work, 31,* 114–118.

Edelman, M. (1982). The political language of the helping professions. In H. Rubenstein & M. H. Block (Eds.), *Things That Matter: Influences on Helping Relationships* (pp. 63–76). New York: Macmillan.

Edwards, E. D., & Edwards, M. E. (1980). American Indians: Working with individuals and groups. *Social Casework, 25,* 498–506.

Ephross, J., & Greene, R. R. (1992). Social workers' perceived knowledge and use of human behavior theory. *Journal of Social Work Education, 29,* 88–98.

Foucault, M. (1980). *Power/Knowledge: Selected Interviews and Other Writings, 1972–1977.* New York: Pantheon Books.

Frank, J. D., & Frank, J. B. (1991). *Persuasion and Healing: A Comparative Study of Psychotherapy* (3rd ed.). Baltimore: Johns Hopkins University Press.

Freedberg, S. (2007). Re-examining empathy: A relational-feminist point of view. *Social Work, 52,* 251–260.

Freud, S. (1956). On psychotherapy. In *Collected Papers* (Vol. 1, pp. 256–268). London: Hogarth.

Gergen, K. (2001). Psychological science in a post-modern context. *American Psychiatry, 56,* 203–213.

Gibbs, J. T. (1985). Treatment relationships with black clients: Interpersonal U.S. instrumental strategies. In C. B. Germain (Ed.), *Advances in Clinical Social Work Practice* (pp. 179–190). Silver Spring, MD: NASW Press.

Gilligan, S., & Price, R. (1993). *Therapeutic Conversations.* New York: Norton.

Green, J. W. (1999). *Cultural Awareness in the Human Services: A Multi-Ethnic Approach*. Boston: Allyn & Bacon.
Greene, R. R. (Ed.). (2007). *Social Work Practice: A Risk and Resilience Perspective*. Monterey, CA: Brooks/Cole.
Greene, R. R. (2008-a). Carl Rogers and the person-centered approach. In R. R. Greene (Ed.), *Human Behavior Theory and Social Work Practice*. New Brunswick, NJ: Aldine Transaction.
Greene, R. R. (2008-b). Classical psychoanalytic thought, contemporary developments, and clinical social work. In R. R. Greene (Ed.), *Human Behavior Theory and Social Work Practice*. New Brunswick, NJ: Aldine Transaction.
Greene, R. R. (Ed.). (2008-c). *Human Behavior Theory and Social Work Practice*. New Brunswick, NJ: Aldine Transaction.
Greene, R. R. (2008-d). *Social Work with the Aged and Their Families* (3rd ed.). New Brunswick, NJ: Aldine Transaction.
Guba, E. G. (Ed.). (1990). *The Paradigm Dialog*. Newbury Park, CA: Sage.
Hamilton, G. (1958). A theory of personality: Freud's contribution to social work. In H. J. Parad (Ed.), *Ego Psychology and Casework Theory* (pp. 11–37). New York: Family Service of America.
Hepworth, D. H., Rooney, R. H., Larsen, J., Rooney, G. D., & Strom-Gottfried, K. (2005). *Direct Social Work Practice: Theory and Skills* (7th ed.). Belmont, CA: Wadsworth.
Hepworth, D. H., & Larsen, J. A. (1987). Interviewing. In A. Minahan (Ed.-in-Chief), *Encyclopedia of Social Work* (18th ed., pp. 996–1008). Silver Spring, MD: NASW Press.
Ho, D. (1995). Internalized culture, culturocentrism, and transcendence. *Counseling Psychologist*, 23(1), 4–24.
Hollis, F. (1964). *Casework: A Psychosocial Therapy*. New York: Random House.
Hubble, M. A., Duncan, B. L., & Miller, S. (Eds.). (1999). *The Heart and Soul of Change*. Washington, DC: American Psychological Association.
Jordan, J. V. (1997). *Women's Growth in Diversity: More Writings from the Stone Center*. New York: Guilford Press.
Kadushin, A. (1972). The racial factor in the interview. *Social Work*, 17(3), 88–98.
Kadushin, A., & Kadushin, G. (1997). *The Social Work Interview: A Guide for Human Service Professionals* (4th ed.). New York: Columbia University Press.
Kaplan, A. (1990). Empathy and its vicissitudes. In J. Surrey, A. Kaplan, & J. Jordan (Eds.), *Work in Progress: Empathy Revisited* (pp. 6–12). Wellesley, MA: Wellesley Centers for Women.
Kitayama, S., Markus, H. R., & Kurokawa, M. (2000). Culture, emotion, and well-being: Good feelings in Japan and the United States. *Cognition and Emotion*, 14, 93–124.
Laird, J. (Ed.). (1993). *Revisioning Social Work Education*. New York: Haworth Press.
Lambert, M. J. (1992). Implications of outcome research for psychotherapy integration. In J. C. Norcross & M. R. Goldfried (Eds.), *Handbook of Psychotherapy Integration* (pp. 3–45). New York: Basic Books.
Lax, W. D. (1992). Postmodern thinking in a clinical practice. In S. McNamee & K. J. Gergen (Eds.), *Therapy as Social Construction* (pp. 69–85). Newbury Park, CA: Sage.
Lowe, R. (1991). Postmodern themes and therapeutic practices: Notes towards the definition. *Dulwick Centre Newsletter*, 3, 41–53.
Martin, P. Y., & O'Connor, G. G. (1989). *The Social Environment: Open Systems Applications*. New York: Longman.
McDermott, F. E. (1982). Against a persuasive definition of self-determination. In H.

Rubenstein & M. H. Block (Eds.), *Things That Matter: Influences on Helping Relationships* (pp. 77–88). New York: Macmillan.

McNamee, S., & Gergen, K. J. (Eds.). (1992). *Therapy as Social Construction*. Newbury Park, CA: Sage.

Miller, J. B., & Stiver, I. P. (1991). *A Relational Reframing of Therapy Work in Progress* (No. 52). Wellesley, MA: Wellesley Centers for Women.

Mizio, E. (1972). White worker–minority client. *Social Work*, 17(3), 82–86.

Murdach, A. D. (1996). Beneficence re-examined: Protective intervention in mental health. *Social Work*, 25, 458–461.

National Association of Social Workers. (1999). *Code of Ethics of the National Association of Social Workers*. Retrieved September 11, 2007, from *http://www.naswdc.org/pubs/code/code.asp*.

Norcross, J. C., & Newman, C. F. (1992). Psychotherapy integration: Setting the context. In J. C. Norcross & M. R. Goldfried (Eds.), *Handbook of Psychotherapy Integration* (pp. 3–45). New York: Basic Books.

Northen, H. (1982). *Clinical Social Work*. New York: Columbia University Press.

Ow, R., & Katz, D. (1999). Family secrets and the disclosure of distressful information in Chinese families. *Families in Society, 80*, 620–628.

Palombo, J. (1985). Self psychology and countertransference in the treatment of children. *Child and Adolescent Social Work Journal*, 2(1), 36–48.

Paviour, R. (1988). The influence of class and race on clinical assessments by MSW students. *Social Service Review*, 62, 684–693.

Peabody, S. A., & Gelso, C. J. (1982). Countertransference and empathy: The complex relationship between two divergent concepts in counseling. *Journal of Counseling Psychology*, 29, 240–245.

Pedersen, P. B. (1997). *Culture-Centered Counseling Interventions: Striving for Accuracy*. Thousand Oaks, CA: Sage.

Perlman, H. H. (1957). *Social Casework: A Problem Solving Process*. Chicago: University of Chicago Press.

Perlman, H. H. (1965). Self-determination: Reality or illusion? *Social Service Review*, 39, 410–421.

Pinderhughes, E. (1995). Direct practice overview. In R. Edwards (Ed.-in-Chief), *Encyclopedia of Social Work* (19th ed., Vol. 1, pp. 740–751). Washington, DC: NASW Press.

Pozatek, E. (1994). The problem of certainty: Clinical social work in the postmodern era. *Social Work*, 39, 396–403.

Raskin, N. (1985). Client-centered therapy. In S. J. Lynn & J. P. Garske (Eds.), *Contemporary Psychotherapies Models and Methods* (pp. 155–190). Columbus, OH: Merrill.

Reamer, F. G. (1988). AIDS and ethics: The agenda for social workers. *Social Work*, 33, 460–464.

Reamer, F. G. (2006). *Social Work Values and Ethics*. New York: Columbia University Press.

Ridley, C. (1984). Clinical treatment of the nondisclosing black client: A therapeutic paradox. *American Psychologist*, 39, 1234–1244.

Ridley, C. R. (1995). *Overcoming Unintentional Racism in Counseling and Therapy*. Thousand Oaks, CA: Sage.

Rogers, C. R. (1957). The necessary and sufficient conditions of therapeutic personality change. *Journal of Consulting Psychology*, 21, 95–103.

Rogers, C. R. (1961). *On Becoming a Person*. Boston: Houghton Mifflin.

Rogers, C. R., & Dymond, R. F. (Eds.). (1957). *Psychotherapy and Personality Change*. Chicago: University of Chicago Press.

Ryan, A. S. (1985). Cultural factors in casework with Chinese-Americans. *Social Casework*, 66, 333–340.

Ryan, C. C., & Rowe, M. J. (1988). AIDS: Legal and ethical issues. *Social Casework*, 69, 324–333.

Schon, D. (1983). *The Reflective Practitioner: How Professionals Think in Action*. New York: Basic Books.

Schriver, J. M. (2003). *Human Behavior and the Social Environment: Shifting Paradigms in Essential Knowledge for Social Work Practice* (4th ed.). Boston: Allyn & Bacon.

Sheafor, B. W., & Horejsi, C. R. (2005). *Techniques and Guidelines for Social Work Practice* (7th ed.). Boston: Allyn & Bacon.

Shulman, L. (2005). *The Skills of Helping Individuals, Families, Groups, and Communities* (5th ed.). New York: Wadsworth.

Siporin, M. (1975). *Introduction to Social Work Practice*. New York: Macmillan.

Solomon, B. B. (1976). *Black Empowerment: Social Work in Oppressed Communities*. New York: Columbia University Press.

Sotomayor, M. (1977). Language, culture and ethnicity in developing self-concept. *Social Casework*, 58, 195–203.

Spradley, J. P. (1979). *The Ethnographic Interview*. New York: Harcourt, Brace & Jovanovich.

Sprung, G. M. (1989). Transferential issues in working with older adults. *Social Caseworker*, 70, 597–602.

Sue, D. W. (2006). *Multicultural Social Work Practice*. New York: Wiley.

Sue, S., & Zane, N. (1987). The role of culture and cultural techniques in psychotherapy: A critique and reformulation. *American Psychologist*, 42, 37–45.

Tomm, K. (1994). Interventive interviewing: Part III. Intending to ask lineal, circular, strategic, or reflexive questions? In K. Brownlee, P. Gallant, & D. Carpenter (Eds.), *Constructivism and Family Therapy* (pp. 117–156). Thunder Bay, Ontario, Canada: Lakehead University.

Van Den Bergh, N., & Cooper, L. B. (Eds.). (1986). *Feminist Visions for Social Work*. Silver Spring, MD: NASW Press.

Weick, A. (1983). Issues in overturning a medical model of social work practice. *Social Work*, 28, 467–471.

Weick, A. (1993). Reconstructing social work education. In J. Laird (Ed.), *Revisioning Social Work Education* (pp. 11–30). New York: Haworth Press.

White, M., & Epston, D. (1990). *Narrative Means to Therapeutic Ends*. New York: Norton.

3

Symbolic Interactionism: Social Work Assessment, Language, and Meaning

Roberta R. Greene, Joan Ephross Saltman,
Harriet Cohen, and Nancy Kropf

The ability of humans to understand and organize their experiences is directly
related to a tendency to construct worldviews or perspectives from which each
life experience is assessed, understood, and then acted upon. These meanings are
used to take action, to plan for the future, and by their very nature are reflective of
peoples' culture and individual life experiences. (Blundo & Greene, 2007, p. 162)

[Assessment is] a differential, individualized, and accurate identification and evalu-
ation of the problems, people, and situations and of their interrelationships, to serve
as a sound basis for differential helping interventions. (Siporin, 1975, p. 224)

The next three chapters of the text focus on theories of human behavior that
may be used to guide social work assessment processes—each with its own set
of principles that suggests how to approach assessment content (Greene, 2008;
Hepworth, Rooney, Larsen, Rooney, & Strom-Gottfried, 2005). This chapter
discusses assumptions derived from symbolic interaction theory. Based on the
study of factors such as the development of the self that bridge sociology and
psychology, the philosophical stance of symbolic interaction theory can be useful
to social workers conducting cross-cultural interviews.

Social workers focus on understanding the person-in-environment, viewing
the client within the context of his or her life situation in order to achieve a
sound assessment (Meyer, 1993). Cross-cultural social work assessment requires
individualizing clients by gathering culturally sound information about them,
establishing shared meanings on issues and events, and getting to know their
own stories (Greene, 2007; Meyer, 1993). Because symbolic interaction theory
is organized around concepts that emphasize the significance of cultural symbols
and explains the development of collective meaning in various cultural groups,
it provides a set of ideas for obtaining culturally sensitive information.

One of the key assumptions of symbolic interaction theory is that people differ largely because they have learned different symbolic vocabularies through

social interaction and use them to interpret life experiences. From this vantage point, social worker–client communication processes, in which language, words, and meaning are at the core, can be a means of understanding and incorporating information on cultural strengths in the assessment process.

The term *symbolic interactionism* was coined by Herbert Blumer in 1937 to describe how people make meaning of life's experiences. Symbolic interaction theory rests on the premise that reality is not a given but is developed through participation in social groups and interaction with their members. Therefore, the tenets of the theory can be applied in client assessment to increase awareness of how cultural expectations may vary between and within cultures. Because symbolic interaction theory strongly emphasizes the use of language as a tool for interaction, it is also useful in analyzing social worker–client encounters (Munson, 1981).

Social Work Assessment and Symbolic Interaction

Emerging conceptual frameworks [for assessment] are more contextual, incorporating a rigorous examination of the complex interactions and interdependence inherent in person-in-environment configurations. Within a contextual framework, available data can be organized in multiple ways, offering alternative potential approaches to effective change. (Mattaini, 1990, p. 237)

Social Diagnosis

All social work interventions begin with an assessment or an understanding of the client situation. Since as early as 1917, when Mary Richmond published her work *Social Diagnosis*, the general approach to social work practice has been to collect the "nature of social evidence" (pp. 38–40) and interpret data that lead to the "social diagnosis" (pp. 342–363). That being said, assessment content and the way in which the social worker and client communicate can vary greatly depending on the underlying assumptions of the theory (or theories) and practices being used.

Assessment traditionally has been defined as a means of identifying and explaining the nature of a problem to appraise it within a framework of specific elements and to use that appraisal as a guide to action (Perlman, 1957). Its purpose, whether the difficulty rests with an individual, family, group, or community, is to bring together the various facets of the client's situation to determine intervention strategies. Assessment of an individual requires that the social worker evaluate the interrelationship among biopsychosocialspiritual variables, getting to know the person—his or her motivations, strengths, weaknesses, capacity to change, and opportunities for growth.

Mutual Meanings

Because of its emphasis on language and symbols as influences that shape the world, symbolic interaction theory can give practitioners a new perspective on what constitutes an assessment. Because assessment may erroneously be under-stood as solely an information-gathering activity, the idea that it also is based on a dynamic, individualized social worker–client relationship cannot be sufficiently underscored. From the symbolic interaction perspective, verbal exchanges of meanings between the client and social worker are at the heart of the assessment process. That is, "language is more than a means of communicating about real-ity: it is a tool for constructing reality" (Spradley, 1979, p. 17). Understanding a client's life meaning is an interactive process of interpreting, evaluating, and defining the situation until the client and social worker arrive at a mutually shared orientation regarding person-in-the-environment interventions.

When thinking about the nature of symbolic interaction, practitioners can create an interactive and dynamic assessment process that fosters the partici-pation of the client in information gathering and analysis of the situation. The interest in client participation, if not creation of the assessment, recognizes that from the symbolic interaction point of view, people are active shapers, if not creators of their life situation. Assessment, then, is the ongoing process of building mutual understanding between the client and social worker that goes on throughout the treatment process, facilitating the achievement of viable, culturally sound solutions.

Culture and Assessment

Symbolic interactionism is especially useful for overcoming culture-bound thinking that can set up barriers to understanding between the client and social worker (Ephross & Greene, 1991). Such barriers may be attributed to dif-ferences between the client and social worker in the meaning of events that can stem from differences in gender, age, sexual orientation, race or ethnic background, social class, or religion. For example, Lum (2003) proposed that an ethnic-oriented assessment should aim for a psychosocial balance between objective, external factors of the community, and subjective, internal reactions. Lum went on to state that ethnic beliefs, family solidarity, community support networks, and other cultural strengths are intervening factors in the assessment process.

Similarly, Dieppa (1983) cautioned that assessment of ethnic minority clients often tends to evaluate internal and external liabilities rather than include an identification of positive cultural strengths. Causative factors tend to be placed with individual and family psyche, and solutions are couched in terms of mental health treatment when they should, in Dieppa's view, include an understanding of oppressed populations and social problems within an ecological framework. Furthermore, Romero (1983) argued that when assessing minority clients, prac-titioners need to understand "the socioeconomic stresses that are compounded by poverty, racism, oppression" and the lack of access to educational, legal, and health care systems (p. 91).

Developing the Self Through Interaction

Each individual, through the construction and expression of his or her own unique meanings, contributes to the collective "dictionary" of meanings shared by the groups to which he or she belongs, while simultaneously incorporating each groups' [sic] meanings into his or her own individual worldview. (Knauff, 2006, p. 21)

The Self and Personal Meaning

Symbolic interaction theory, the "baseline of all constructivist approaches" (Fleck-Henderson, 1993, p. 223) is used to account for the development of the self as well as the formation of group, community, and societal institutions. According to symbolic interaction theory, the self is an outcome of social participation. Blumer (1969) argued that meanings are not imposed on people, nor is behavior simply a response to the environment. Rather, meanings arise out of social interaction as people confront and create the world around them.

Said another way, the formation of the self is based on shared, cultural linguistic labels and meanings. Each time individuals confront the world, they must interpret it—through their unique set of personal meanings—so that they may act. The use of symbols allows people to understand someone else's role and to elicit from others the proper behavior. According to symbolic interactionists, the personality is built through this interaction with others. That is, people learn how to behave and how to predict the responses of others through the process of socialization in primary group experiences (Blumer, 1969). As a result of such ongoing social participation, an individual's personal meanings are derived, modified, and refined.

Mead's Definition of Self

George Herbert Mead (1925) was another theorist who addressed the societal formation of the self. He proposed that the self is "a social structure that engages in reflective activity, and emerges through the transfer of interpreted meanings (to and from others)" (Mead, 1934, p. 5). The largest portion of the self includes internalization of community and societal norms and standards, a sense of who one ought to be, and how one measures up to societal demands. The self comprises definitions of life roles one plays (e.g., spouse, agency administrator, parent) and how well one is playing those roles. The self also includes a picture of oneself as good or bad, attractive or ugly, and so forth (Ephross & Greene, 1991).

In this context, the attitudes of others, or the social "me," is a central force in shaping human behavior. Do I define myself in response to others? How do people experience themselves and others? What do people have in mind when they say *I* or *me*? These series of expectations for behavior become synthesized into what Mead (1925) called the *generalized other*.

Social work theorists have applied the concept of the generalized other to examine the critical issue of character development in a hostile environment

(Chestang, 1972). This issue recognizes that racism and discrimination, particularly in the form of institutional injustices, profoundly affect the lives of ethnic minorities through a socialization process by the majority group that devalues minority individuals. For example, Chestang argued that institutionalized racism gives rise to an individual feeling of distrust, suspicion, and rage that may result in "a diminished sense of self-worth, and low self-esteem" (p. 44). That is, children may accept the negative attributions of self to make it in the majority society, often "sacrificing pride in victory" or "casting off a part of themselves" (pp. 47–49).

Chestang (1972) proposed that, to be successful in a hostile environment, children must adapt to two systems: (a) the dominant or sustaining system that is the source of economic and political power and (b) the nurturing system—the family and community that provide comfort and strength. This notion of the dual perspective (Norton, 1976, 1978) offers a dynamic way of describing and working with minority clients to resolve dissonance between the sustaining and nurturing aspects of self.

Sotomayor (1977) also traced critical aspects of self-development to "majority-minority of color group relationships in this country … [that produce] social stratification and conflict" (pp. 195–198). She suggested that the sense of belonging, critical in the development of the self-concept, becomes "blurred if one's language, cultural patterns, and ethnic experiences are not reflected and supported, but rather given negative connotation in the environment" (p. 196). In contrast, a growing body of literature suggests that resilience is enhanced by an ethnic family's cultural values and provision of mutual psychological support (Genero, 1998; McCubbin, Thompson, Thompson, & Futrell, 1998). In addition, there is increasing evidence that by socializing children to have a positive racial or ethnic as well as personal identity and by providing them with strategies to resist discrimination, families can effectively raise children in an oppressive society (Greene, Taylor, Evans, & Smith, 2002).

Definition of Meaning

Symbolic interactionism sees meanings as social products, as creations that are formed in and through the defining activities of people as they interact. (Blumer, 1969, p. 5)

Background

Symbolic interaction theory has its origins in social psychology and considers behavior to result from the fact that people are social beings. The theory emphasizes people's symbolically organized experiences and meanings negotiated in face-to-face interaction (Fleck-Henderson, 1993). Symbolic interaction theorists examine people's participation in social groups and the way in which societies and their institutions develop. In addition, symbolic interactionists examine how individuals learn to assign meanings to feelings, experiences, social forms, and structures; as well as how families, groups, organizations, and communities develop unique sets of meanings through such social participation (Bruner, 1986; see Table 3.1).

Culture and Meanings

Culture comprises the abstract values, beliefs, and perceptions of the world that lie behind people's behavior. These shared beliefs are not static; rather, they shape behaviors within a range of variation. The evolving interaction between and among people produces the orienting features of a particular culture or group membership. *Collective behavior* is the term used to refer to the social aspects of behavior and the social context that gives behavior meaning. Because people participate in small groups, creating within them social ideals, values, and norms, symbolic interaction theorists suggest that individuals create cultures and the various social structures of which society is composed (Cooley, 1902).

Consideration of client culture is an important issue in social work assessment. Limited understanding of any individual's cultural meanings and thinking about his or her life situation may lead the social worker to culture-bound solutions. *Culture-bound thinking* refers to the formulation of ideas based on assumptions about the world and reality based only on one's own culture (Haviland, 1990). Pedersen (1976) called the therapist lacking in cross-cultural sensitivity "the culturally encapsulated counselor" (p. 24), that is, a therapist who evaluates the client's life circumstances according to criteria more suitable to the personal or professional ideas of the counselor rather than to the day-to-day experiences of the client.

Table 3.1
Basic Assumptions of Symbolic Interaction Theory

- Humans are a self-conscious, reflective, thinking species.
- Personality development is a process of learning to assign meaning to symbols. This learning process occurs through interaction with real and symbolic others.
- Individual and group meanings arise from human interaction.
- Behavior is symbolic and largely rests on linguistic processes.
- The self is a social structure that arises through social interaction.
- The self is derived through taking the attitudes, perceptions, and actions of others toward oneself and one's own and internalizing their meaning.
- Deviance is nonnormative behavior. Conceptions of deviance and norms are constructed by society.
- The differences among people are largely the result of people's having learned different symbolic vocabularies for interpreting life experiences.
- Change results from the development of new systems of meanings.

Source. Ephross, P. H., & Greene, R. R. (1991). Symbolic interactionism. In R. R. Greene & P. H. Ephross (Eds.), *Human Behavior Theory and Social Work Practice* (p. 208). Hawthorne, NY: Aldine de Gruyter.

The client's cultural reality in problem specification can be identified through *cultural mapping*. This involves identifying and linking localized or culture-specific sources of the (minority) client's solutions in the therapy. *Social mapping*, in contrast, involves identifying and locating all ethnic groups in the area; describing the social organization of the community; describing the beliefs and ideological characteristics of the residents of the community; recording the patterns of wealth, its accumulation, and its distribution; describing the patterns of mobility, both geographical and social; and providing information on access and utilization of human services providers (Cochrane, 1979).

Ethnic Membership

Ethnic membership is an example of a social group created through collective social interaction and participation. *Ethnicity* generally refers to the shared social and cultural heritage of a group of people. Members of an ethnic group may also share ideas, perceptions, feelings, and behavior (Ho, 1992). To understand ethnicity, it is necessary to examine the values, signs, and behavioral styles through which individuals signal their identity in cross-cultural encounters (Green, 1999).

Religiosity and Spirituality

Religiosity and spirituality are other dimensions of human culture that significantly affect clients and the collective behavior of social work professionals; they can also be viewed through a symbolic interaction perspective (Canda, 1989). *Religion* has been defined as "the communal expression of faith in institutional forms" (Joseph, 1987, p. 14). That is, the meaning of God and religion evolve in the lifelong development of the self in communal interaction with others. *Spirituality* has been described as a way of recognizing the oneness and interconnectedness of all life, and of connecting with its transcendent dimensions (Tisdell, 2000; Weiss, 1999). Spirituality involves a personal search for meaning in life that is relational, connecting individuals with self and others. An individual explores his or her purpose in life that is meaningful, creative, and responsible (Frankl, 1984).

Historically, social work has attached different meanings to whether the exploration of a client's spirituality or religion is congruent with social workers' professional role. Social work has its roots in the sectarian institutions of the late nineteenth century and the views and meanings attributed to charity and community service (Canda, 1986). Many services for children, older adults, and the seriously mentally ill can be traced to that era. Early "service providers" helped the indigent as part of their religious duty to people who were less fortunate, whereas social work "volunteers" viewed helping others as their religious calling.

In the early twentieth century, as social services became more professionalized, case workers attached a different meaning to religion and its infusion in

spouses, coworkers; abstract objects such as anger, compassion, loyalty; and physical objects such as buildings, open spaces (e.g., parks, roadways). Although these aspects of Blumer's definition have received relatively little attention in the social and behavioral sciences, the fields of architecture and design have incorporated these principles into their professions. The constructed environment, from large spaces such as parks to smaller spaces such as the family home, creates a system of emotional meaning that influences individuals' sense of identity. This can be seen even in young children, who create playhouses and clubhouses to reflect their personalities and sense of self (Marcus, 1995).

The symbols that are created to have meaning beyond a particular picture or logo are part of the manufactured environment. In the blitz of media branding, for example, images and symbols have changed the ways in which society thinks about resources and consumption. In her book about children and brand identification, Juliet Schor (2004) discussed how advertisers are reaching out to very young children to create brand loyalty. She studied 300 fifth- and sixth-grade children to analyze their involvement in the consumer-driven U.S. culture. She reported that the average 10-year-old had memorized about 400 brands, the average kindergartner could identify some 300 logos, and from as early as age 2 kids are "bonded to brands." In other words, cultural meanings that are connected to symbols are recognized by and evoke an emotional response in even very young children.

Beyond messages that are created from objectives, meaning is also derived from the configuration of the environment. Smith and Bugni (2006) suggested that symbolic interaction theory helps explain connections between the built environment and human thoughts, feelings, and emotions. From a social work perspective, understanding of a client's environment provides insight into the meaning that this space has in the client's understanding of self. Within the assessment process, the created or manufactured environment has symbolic meaning in the perception of self (as well as the perception of family and community life) and needs to be noted by the practitioner. For example, a family that lives in a neighborhood that has parks and well-maintained streets is given a message of being valued within the community. Conversely, a family that lives in a neighborhood that is in decay with abandoned buildings and unsafe roads takes in a message of being devalued.

Configuration of the environment creates meanings about how various groups are positioned within the social environment as well. From the perspective of environmental racism, several studies have documented the disproportionate number of toxins and pollutants that are located in proximity to communities of color. For example, research was conducted on Superfund hazardous waste sites located in Florida (Stretesky & Hogan, 1998). The findings indicated that these highly toxic areas were disproportionately located in proximity to Hispanic and African American communities. Likewise, other environmental dangers such as poor air quality, dangers related to mining practices, and toxicity in water sources have been noted within communities and reservations of persons of color (Brook, 1998; Higgins, 1993). These findings have resulted in grassroots efforts to promote principles of environmental justice, which seeks to transform current practices that value production and industry over individuals and communities. As the Environmental Justice Resource Center stated, environmental justice "brings to the surface the ethical and political questions of who gets what, why, and how much" (Bullard, n.d.).

Meaning and the Language of the Social Work Profession

Symbolic interactionism can help practitioners understand culturally different interpretations of similar social experiences, explore meanings such as those of the members of undervalued groups, and attend to the social aspects of intense emotions. (Forte, 2004a, p. 391)

Language

Language is central to the social work process in interviewing, listening, recording, and understanding social worker–client communication. Because people have the capacity for language, they are self-aware and capable of self-reflection in a therapeutic encounter (Efran, Lukens, & Lukens, 1990). Although there are ways of communicating that are nonverbal, verbal communication between the client and social worker is the primary helping tool. Symbolic interactionism offers a framework for examining the language of communication and its development, limitations, distortions, significance, content, and symbolic nature.

Whorf (1956) proposed that the way people think is largely determined by the words they use. From this perspective, if clients perceive verbal communication as abusive or evasive, it can be a serious barrier to a genuine helping relationship. Clichés, ready-made phrases, and technical jargon often can be perceived negatively (Bloom, 1980; Burgest, 1973). Language used in everyday speech as well as social work jargon may be viewed as a potent force in society.

Language can not only express ideas and concepts but may actually shape them. It has been hypothesized that language is not simply an encoding process but rather is a shaping force that predisposes people to act in a certain way. "Language is not separate from action—it is a particular form of action" (Efran et al., 1990, p. 21). For example, a single Navajo verb contains its own subject, objects, and adverbs and can translate into an entire English sentence. Therefore, in the Navajo language, "words paint a picture in your mind" (Watson, 1993, p. 34). This premise suggests that if the social worker can understand the ongoing process of interaction between the client and the groups and social structures of which the client is a part, then the social worker can begin to enter the client's world of meaning, seeing the world as the client sees it (Ephross & Greene, 1991).

From a symbolic interaction perspective, a personal meaning system is constructed via exchanges and interchanges with others. The process of guided autobiography is an example of how language guides the process of self-interpretation (Brown-Shaw, Westood, & deVries, 1999; Randall & Kenyon, 2001). This process involves individuals, often in a collective setting, who look backward through the various experiences and stages of their lives. This process is beneficial to "help us gain access to memories and to organize them in a way that honors the complex threads that shape our lives so that we can present them as a unique and richly woven fabric of life—which indeed they are" (Birren & Cochran, 2001, p. 5).

Language and Societal Structures

Symbolic interactionists explore the functions of language in the socialization process. Most interaction, according to symbolic interactionists, occurs through the use of symbols, primarily language. Therefore, language is a vehicle of communication between members of the group: It establishes relationships and solidarity, is a "declaration of the place and psychological distance" held by the group's various members, and is used in the coordination of the activities of the group (Sotomayor, 1977, p. 198).

Other theorists have argued that labels can become the instruments of social control. For example, Edelman (1982) proposed that the client–social worker encounter, as a social situation, is affected by the political language of the helping professions. He cautioned that, although categorization of problems is necessary to science and indeed to all perceptions, it also is necessary to guard against the use of client labels or the description of treatment techniques as a means of political power and control. For example, to speak of "seclusion" or a "quiet room" rather than solitary confinement may mask the difficulties encountered by patients who are confined against their will. At worst, language may encompass derogatory terms or language habits that are "instruments of control devised to prevent or diminish communication and/or conflict" (Baird, 1970, p. 265).

Social workers can learn valuable interviewing techniques through *sociolinguistics*, or the study of the social context of language. From this perspective, the client–social worker interview is an interactive process that is subject to interpretation. For example, messages between the client and social worker become clarified through the language or conversation (see Table 3.2; see Chapter 6 for a discussion of constructionist theory).

Finally, although social work historically used symbolic interaction as a theoretical foundation for assessment and practice, over the decades the theory has declined in significance in the social work literature. In a thoughtful analysis of symbolic interaction in practice, Forte (2004a) traced the close relationship between pioneers in the social work profession and early symbolic interaction

Table 3.2
Guidelines for Social Workers: A Symbolic Interaction Approach

- Acknowledge that the client has his or her own personal system of meaning derived through interaction with others and the environment.
- Engage in active listening to ascertain the client's meaning of past experiences and present events.
- Communicate an interest in understanding the symbolic meanings of the client.
- Choose your words carefully.
- Let your client be your teacher as to the symbols and meanings in his or her world. Do not assume that your client's experiences are the same or mean the same as yours.
- Reflect the meanings you have ascribed to the client to be sure you have understood correctly.
- Assess with the client whether or not the client's personal meanings or his or her view of events contribute to the presenting problem.
- Determine with the client if and how personal meanings of significant others and reference groups are understood and may contribute to his or her difficulties.
- Share with the client your own meanings and interpretations of events.
- Remember that the agency or the organizational structure in which you work has a system of meanings that contribute to the social worker–client encounter. Be aware that the way in which your client perceives the help available will affect the social worker–client relationship.
- Learn to use nonverbal as well as verbal communication. Participate in the helping process.
- Contract with the client to help him or her interpret events differently and to negotiate new meanings.

Source. Ephross, P. H., & Greene, R. R. (1991). Symbolic interactionism. In R. R. Greene & P. H. Ephross (Eds.), *Human Behavior Theory and Social Work Practice* (p. 223). Hawthorne, NY: Aldine de Gruyter.

theorists. In particular, he described how George Herbert Mead chaired a committee at Hull House and was involved in the early settlement house movement. Forte argued that the relationship between social work practice and symbolic interaction theory was bidirectional: The theory informed practice, and practice influenced the development of the theory.

In a related article, Forte (2004b) advocated that social work should reclaim social interactionism as an important foundation for current assessment and practice. He carefully chronicled aspects of contemporary social work assessment and processes and highlighted their connection to the symbolic interaction theory base. In particular, the connection of professional language and the definition of social problems can best be understood through a symbolic interaction perspective.

References

Baird, K. E. (1970). Semantics and Afro-American liberation. *Social Casework*, 51, 265–269.

Birren, J. E., & Cochran, K. N. (2001). *Telling the Stories of Life through Guided Auto-biographical Groups*. Baltimore: Johns Hopkins University Press.

Bloom, A. A. (1980). Social work and the English language. *Social Casework*, 61, 332–338.

Blumer, H. (1969). *Symbolic Interactionism*. Englewood Cliffs, NJ: Prentice Hall.

Blundo, R., & Greene, R. R. (2007). Survivorship in the face of traumatic events and disasters: Implications for social work. In R. R. Greene (Ed.), *Social Work Practice: A Risk and Resilience Perspective* (pp. 160–176). Monterey, CA: Brooks/Cole.

Brook, D. (1998). Environmental genocide: Native Americans and toxic waste. *American Journal of Economics and Sociology*, 57, 105–113.

Brown-Shaw, M., Westwood, M., & deVries, B. (1999). Integrating personal reflection and group-based enactments. *Journal of Aging Studies*, 13(1), 109–119.

Bruner, J. (1986). *Actual Minds: Possible Worlds*. Cambridge, MA: Harvard University Press.

Bullard, R. D. (n.d.). *Environmental Justice in the 21st Century*. Retrieved September 5, 2007, from *http://www.ejrc.cau.edu/ejinthe21century.htm*.

Burgest, D. R. (1973). Racism in everyday speech and social work jargon. *Social Work*, 18(4), 20–25.

Cain, D. S. (2007). The effects of religiousness on parenting stress and practices in the African American family. *Families in Society*, 88, 263–272.

Canda, E. R. (1986). A conceptualization of spirituality for social work: Its issues and implications. *Dissertation Abstracts International*, 47 (7-A), 2737–2738. (UMI No. 8625190).

Canda, E. R. (1989). Religious content in social work education: A comparative approach. *Journal of Social Work Education*, 25, 36–45.

Chestang, L. (1972). *Character Development in a Hostile Environment* (Occasional Paper No. 3). Chicago: University of Chicago, School of Social Service Administration.

Cochrane, G. (1979). *The Cultural Appraisal of Development Projects*. New York: Praeger.

Cohen, H. L., Thomas, C. T., & Williamson, C. (2008). Religion and spirituality as defined by older adults. *Journal of Gerontological Social Work*, 51(3/4), 284-299.

Cooley, C. H. (1902). *Human Nature and the Social Order*. New York: Scribner.

Council on Social Work Education. (2001). *Handbook of Accreditation Standards and Procedures* (Rev. ed.). Alexandria, VA: Author.

Dieppa, I. (1983). A state of the art analysis. In G. Gibson (Ed.), *Our Kingdom Stands on Brittle Glass* (pp. 115–128). Silver Spring, MD: NASW Press.

Edelman, M. (1982). The political language of the helping professions. In H. Rubenstein & M. H. Block (Eds.), *Things That Matter: Influences on Helping Relationships* (pp. 63–76). New York: Macmillan.

Efran, J. S., Lukens, M. D., & Lukens, R. J. (1990). *Language Structure and Change: Frameworks of Meaning in Psychotherapy*. New York: Norton.

Ellor, J. W., Netting, F. E., & Thibault, J. M. (1999). *Religious and Spiritual aspects of Human Service Practice*. Columbia: University of South Carolina Press.

Ephross, P. H., & Greene, R. R. (1991). Symbolic interactionism. In R. R. Greene & P. H. Ephross (Eds.), *Human Behavior Theory and Social Work Practice* (pp. 203–226). Hawthorne, NY: Aldine de Gruyter.

Fleck-Henderson, A. (1993). A constructivist approach to "Human behavior and the social environment I." In J. Laird (Ed.), *Revisioning Social Work Education: A Social Constructionist Approach* (pp. 219–238). New York: Haworth Press.

Forte, J. A. (2004a). Symbolic interactionism and social work: A forgotten legacy, part 1. *Families in Society*, 85, 391–401.

Forte, J. A. (2004b). Symbolic interactionism and social work: A forgotten legacy, part 2. *Families in Society*, 85, 521–531.

Frankl, V. E. (1984). *Man's Search for Meaning* (3rd ed.). New York: Simon & Schuster.

Furman, L. D., Benson, P. W., Grimwood, C., & Canda, E. (2004). Religion and spirituality in social work education and direct practice at the millennium: A survey of UK social workers. *British Journal of Social Work*, 34, 767–792.

Genero, N. P. (1998). Culture, resiliency, and mutual psychological development. In H. I. McCubbin, E. A. Thompson, A. I. Thompson, & J. A. Futrell (Eds.), *Resiliency in African-American Families* (pp. 31–48). Thousand Oaks, CA: Sage.

Gieryn, T. F. (2002). What buildings do. *Theory and Society*, 31, 35–74.

Green, J. W. (1999). *Cultural Awareness in the Human Services: A Multi-Ethnic Approach.* Boston: Allyn & Bacon.

Greene, R. R. (Ed.). (2008). *Human Behavior Theory and Social Work Practice.* New Brunswick, NJ: Aldine Transaction.

Greene, R. R. (Ed.). (2007). *Social Work Practice: A Risk and Resilience Perspective.* Monterey, CA: Brooks/Cole.

Greene, R. R., Taylor, N., Evans, M. L., & Smith, L. A. (2002). Raising children in an oppressive environment. In R. R. Greene (Ed.), *Resiliency: An Integrated Approach to Practice, Policy, and Research* (pp. 241–276). Washington, DC: NASW Press.

Haviland, W. A. (1990). *Cultural Anthropology.* New York: Holt, Rinehart, & Winston.

Hepworth, D. H., Rooney, R. H., Larsen, J., Rooney, G. D., & Strom-Gottfried, K. (2005). *Direct Social Work Practice: Theory and Skills* (7th ed.). Belmont, CA: Wadsworth.

Higgins, R. R. (1993). Race and environmental equity: An overview of the environmental justice issue in the policy process. *Polity*, 26, 281–300.

Ho, M. K. (1992). *Minority Children and Adolescents in Therapy.* Newbury Park, CA: Sage.

Imre, R. W. (1971). A theological view of social casework. *Social Casework*, 52, 578–583.

Joseph, M. V. (1987). The religious and spiritual aspects of clinical practice: A neglected dimension of social work. *Social Thought*, 6, 12–23.

Karner, T. X., & Bobbitt-Zeher, D. (2006). Losing selves: Dementia care as disruption and transformation. *Symbolic Interaction*, 28, 549–570.

Knauff, W. S. (2006). Herbert Blumer's theory of collective definition in the battle over same-sex marriage: An analysis of the struggle to control the meaning of marriage in America from a symbolic interaction perspective. *Journal of Human Behavior in the Social Environment*, 14(3), 19–43.

Lee, E. O., & Sharpe, T. (2007). Understanding religious/spiritual coping and support resources among African American older adults: A mixed-method approach. *Journal of Religion, Spirituality, & Aging*, 19(3), 55–75.

Lowenberg, F. M. (1988). *Religion and Social Work Practice in Contemporary American Society.* New York: Columbia University Press.

Lum, D. (2003). *Social Work Practice and People of Color: A Process Stage Approach* (5th ed.). Belmont, CA: Wadsworth.

Marcus, C. C. (1995). *House as a Mirror of Self: Exploring the Deeper Meaning of Home.* Berkeley, CA: Conari Press.

Mattaini, M. A. (1990). Contextual behavior analyses in the assessment process. *Families in Society,* 71, 236–245.

McCubbin, H. I., Thompson, E. A., Thompson, A. I., & Futrell, J. A. (Eds.). (1998). *Resiliency in African-American Families.* Thousand Oaks, CA: Sage.

Mead, G. H. (1925). The genesis of the self and social control. *International Journal of Ethics,* 35, 251–277.

Mead, G. H. (1934). *Mind, Self, and Society.* Chicago: University of Chicago Press.

Meyer, C. (1993). *Assessment in Social Work Practice.* New York: Columbia University Press.

Munson, C. E. (1981). Symbolic interaction theory for small group treatment. *Social Casework,* 62, 167–174.

National Association of Social Workers. (2001). *NASW Standards for Cultural Competence in Social Work Practice.* Retrieved August 1, 2007, from *http://www.socialworkers.org/practice/standards/NASWCulturalStandards.pdf.*

Neiderman, R. (1999). *The Conceptualization of a Model of Spirituality.* Unpublished doctoral dissertation, the University of Georgia, Athens.

Norton, D. G. (1976). Working with minority populations: The dual perspective. In B. Ross & K. Khinduka (Eds.), *Social Work in Practice.* New York: NASW Press.

Norton, D. G. (1978). *The Dual Perspective: Inclusion of Minority Content in the Social Work Curriculum.* New York: Council on Social Work Education.

Pedersen, P. (1976). The field of intercultural counseling. In P. Pedersen, W. J. Lonner, & J. G. Draguns (Eds.), *Counseling Across Cultures* (pp. 17–41). Honolulu: University of Hawaii Press.

Perlman, H. H. (1957). *Social Casework: A Problem Solving Process.* Chicago: University of Chicago Press.

Randall, W. L., & Kenyon, G. M. (2001). *Ordinary Wisdom: Biographical Aging and the Journey of Life.* Westport, CT: Praeger.

Richardson, G. E. (2002). The metatheory of resilience and resiliency. *Journal of Clinical Psychology,* 58, 307–321.

Richmond, M. (1917). *Social Diagnosis.* New York: Russell Sage Foundation.

Robbins, S. P., Chatterjee, P., & Canda, E. (1998). *The Nature of Theories in Contemporary Human Behavior Theory.* Boston: Allyn & Bacon.

Romero, J. T. (1983). The therapist as social change agent. In G. Gibson (Ed.), *Our Kingdom Stands on Brittle Glass* (pp. 86–95). Silver Spring, MD: NASW Press.

Sanzenbach, P., Canda, E. E., & Joseph, M. (1989). Religion and social work: It's not that simple. *Social Casework,* 70, 571–575.

Schor, J. (2004). *Born to Buy: The Commercialized Child and the New Consumer Culture.* New York: Simon & Schuster.

Siporin, M. (1975). *Introduction to Social Work Practice.* New York: Macmillan.

Smith, R. W., & Bugni, V. (2006). Symbolic interaction theory and architecture. *Symbolic Interaction,* 29, 123–155.

Sotomayor, M. (1977). Language culture and ethnicity in developing self-concept. *Social Casework,* 58, 195–203.

Spradley, J. P. (1979). *The Ethnographic Interview.* New York: Harcourt, Brace & Jovanovich.

Stretesky, P., & Hogan, M. J. (1998). Environmental justice: An analysis of Superfund sites in Florida. *Social Problems,* 45, 268–287.

Tisdell, E. J. (2000). Spirituality and emancipatory adult education in women adult educators for social change. *Adult Education Quarterly,* 50, 308–335.

Vance, D. E., Struzick, T. C., & Russell, T. V. (2007). Spiritual and religious implications of aging with HIV: A conceptual and methodological review. *Journal of Religion, Spirituality, & Aging*, 19(3), 21–42.

Walton, E. (2007). Evaluating faith-based programs: An introduction from the guest editor. *Research on Social Work Practice*, 17(2), 171–173.

Watson, B. (1993). Navajo code talkers: A few good men. *Smithsonian*, 24(5), 34–35.

Weisman, C. B., & Schwartz, P. (1989). Spirituality: An integral part of aging. *Journal of Aging and Judaism*, 3(3), 110–115.

Weiss, J. (1999). *A Qualitative Investigation of Counseling Students' Attitudes toward Addressing Spiritual Issues in Counseling.* Unpublished doctoral dissertation, the University of Georgia, Athens.

Whorf, B. L. (1956). *Language Thought and Reality.* New York: Wiley.

4

Erikson's Eight Stages of Development: Different Lenses

Nancy P. Kropf and Roberta R. Greene

The phenomenon and the concept of social organization, and its bearing on the individual ego was, thus, for the longest time, shunted off by patronizing tributes to the existence of "social factors." (Erikson, 1959, p. 18)

One of the most important professional judgments social workers are called on to make in assessment is whether a client's behavior is appropriate to his or her stage of development. The many questions to be addressed include ascertaining when and why a certain behavior began, how long it has persisted, whether the behavior is acceptable in a sociocultural group or related to a client's gender or ethnic background, and whether the behavior interferes with one or more of a client's roles (Northen, 1987).

The theorist who has provided one of the most widely used approaches to answering these questions and who made a major contribution to the conceptualization of a developmental approach to ego mastery is Erik Erikson. Erikson was one of the few great personality theorists (Carl Jung was another) to view development as a lifelong process (Hogan, 1976). Erikson proposed that development occurs in eight life stages, starting at birth and ending with old age and death. He viewed each stage of development as a new plateau for the developing self or ego to gain and restore a sense of mastery within the context of social factors (Greene, 2008).

In contrast to Sigmund Freud, Erikson is noted for his attention to social phenomena (Erikson, 1974). To account for social forces, Erikson turned to social anthropology, ecology, and comparative education for social concepts. According to Greene (2008), in keeping with his emphasis on the social world, Erikson reformulated the concept of *ego identity* to encompass mutuality between the individual and his or her society. He hypothesized that there exists a "mutual complementation of ethos and ego, of group identity and ego identity" (Erikson, 1959, p. 23).

An understanding of the natural, historical, and technological environment was among the factors Erikson considered part of ego identity and necessary for a true clinical appraisal of the individual. Central to Erikson's (1964a) philosophy was the idea that a "nourishing exchange of community life" (p. 89) is key to mental health: "All this makes today's so-called biological adaptation a matter of life cycles developing within their communities changing history" (Erikson, 1959, p. 163).

Erikson restated the nature of identity, linking the individual's inner world with his or her unique values and history (Coles, 1970; Hogan, 1976). He proposed that membership identities, including social class, culture, and national affiliation, provide people with the collective power to create their own environment. Society—through its ideological frameworks, roles, tasks, rituals, and initiations—"bestow[s] strength" (Erikson, 1964b, p. 91) and a sense of identification on the developing individual. Social influences, including economic, historical, and ethnic factors, were stressed, as was the view that people are socialized positively to become part of the historical and ethnic "intertwining of generations" (p. 93).

Although Erikson has been credited with adding a much-needed social dimension to the psychoanalytic perspective on clinical intervention, he also has been criticized for what some have called his White, heterosexual, male-defined life cycle of adult development (Berzoff, 1989; Gilligan, 1982; Kravetz, 1982; Schwartz, 1973). For example, social work educators such as Schwartz (1973) and Wesley (1975) have argued that Erikson's theory, widely read in courses in human growth and development, contributed to sexism within the social work curriculum. Wesley noted that in *Childhood and Society* (1950), Erikson devoted seventeen pages to the development of the male adolescent and a single paragraph to that of the female. She contended that such bias contributed to stereotyped concepts of women.

Still other theorists have questioned whether Erikson's theory of development effectively captures the experience of racial and ethnic minorities (Logan, 1981; Poster, 1989). For example, Chestang (1984) proposed that although establishing a sense of identity is a basic human need, understanding the process and its dynamics among African Americans requires further consideration of the special characteristics inherent in realizing racial identity. Theories of personality formation and development are increasingly taking into account differences in life span events and episodes (Boxer & Cohler, 1989; Cornett & Hudson, 1987; Newman & Newman, 2005; Sophie, 1986). In addition, nonstage theories of human development are increasingly discussed as an alternative, for example, Germain's (1992, 1997) ecological approach to development and Thyer's (1992) behavioral perspective, which examines principles of social learning theory as an explanation for behavior. This reexamination of Erikson's approach is marked by an interest in developmental continuations for individuals in diverse populations. Such research is producing a contemporary study of the ecology of the life course (Boxer & Cohler, 1989; Greene, 2008; Haraeven, 1996).

Basic Assumptions of Development: A Critique

Each successive step in development, then, is a potential crisis because of a radical change in perspective.... Thus, different capacities use different opportunities to become full-grown components of the ever-new configuration that is the growing personality. (Erikson, 1959, p. 57)

Defining Life Span Development

Development across the life cycle is the focus of Eriksonian psychosocial theory, a theoretical approach that involves analysis of social and environmental factors that produce changes in thought and behavior. Erikson's life cycle approach was to view the tendency of an individual's life to form a coherent, lifelong experience and to be joined or linked to lives of those in previous and future generations (see Table 4.1).

Table 4.1
Eriksonian Theory: Basic Assumptions

- Development is biopsychological and occurs across the life cycle.

- Development is propelled by a biological plan; however, personal identity cannot exist independently of social organization.

- The ego plays a major role in development as it strives for competence and mastery of the environment. Societal institutions and caretakers provide positive support for the development of personal effectiveness. Individual development enriches society.

- Development is marked by eight major stages at which time a psychosocial crisis occurs.

- Personality is the outcome of the resolution—on a continuum from positive to negative—of each of these crises. Each life stage builds on the success of former stages, presents new social demands, and creates new opportunities.

- Psychosocial crises accompanying life stages are universal or occur in all cultures. Each culture offers unique solutions to life stages.

- The needs and capacities of the generations are intertwined.

- Psychological health is a function of ego strength and social supports.

- Confusions in self-identity arise from negative resolution of developmental crises and alienation from societal institutions.

- Therapy involves the interpretation of developmental and historical distortions and the curative process of insight.

Source. Greene, R. R. (2008b). Eriksonian theory: A developmental approach to ego mastery. In R. R. Greene (Ed.), *Human Behavior Theory and Social Work Practice.* New Brunswick, NJ: Aldine Transaction.

Erikson's perspective on development was derived from the biological principle of *epigenesis*, the idea that each stage depends on resolutions of the experiences of prior stages. Epigenesis suggests that "anything that grows has a ground plan, and out of that plan parts arise, each part having its time of special ascendancy, until all parts have arisen to form a functioning whole" (Erikson, 1959, p. 53). Erikson (1982) defined epigenesis as

> a progression through time of a differentiation of parts. This indicates that each part exists in some form before "its" decisive and critical time normally arrives and remains systematically related to all others so that the whole ensemble depends on the proper development in the proper sequence of each item. Finally, as each part comes to its full ascendance and finds some lasting solution during its stage, it will also be expected to develop further under the dominance of subsequent ascendancies, and most of all, to take its place in the integration of the whole ensemble. (p. 29)

Personality development, then, is said to follow a proper sequence, emerge at critical or decisive times in a person's life, progress over time, and be a lifelong integrative process. However, epigenesis, the assumption that future functioning is determined by history and biology, has met with criticism. Feminist scholars have taken exception to the view that gender determines successful functioning. They contend that although women's development is different than men's, its uniqueness does not make it inferior (Gilligan, 1982; see Chapters 5 and 11 for a further discussion).

As individual life spans have increased, there has also been a critique about how this model of personality development is biased toward the earlier life experiences. In fact, the model suggests that the years sixty and older are fairly undifferentiated for the aging adult. However, Capps (2005) reconceptualized Erikson's stages to include two additional ones for later life. Both of these involve a recapitualization back to earlier life stages, specifically trust versus mistrust and autonomy versus shame. With the onset of very late life, the older adult faces the psychosocial crisis of feeling a sense that he or she will have the adaptive ability and/or resources to continue to function as optimally as possible. Additionally, successful adaptation includes reconceptualizing one's identity in situations in which physical or cognitive functioning is diminished. The inability to make these adaptations will lead to feelings of shame. Similar to critiques based upon gender and race/ethnicity, there are perceptions that Erikson's theory has not extended late enough into older ages.

Personality Development in Eriksonian Theory

From an Eriksonian epigenetic perspective, personality develops through a predetermined readiness "to interact with a widening social radius, beginning with the dim image of a mother and ending with mankind" (Erikson, 1959, p. 54). The healthy personality begins to develop in infancy. Over time, the child, "given a reasonable amount of guidance, can be trusted to obey inner laws of development, laws which create a succession of potentialities for significant interaction with those who tend him" (p. 54).

Erikson argued that identity not only emerges in stages but also involves restructuring or resynthesis. The view that personality development involves new configurations at different life stages is called *hierarchical reorganization*. This is the concept that development over time is linear and refers to changing structures and organization that permit new functions and adaptations over time (Shapiro & Hertzig, 1988). Erikson (1959) believed that, through a series of psychosocial crises and an ever-widening circle of significant relations, the individual develops "a new drive-and-need constellation" and "an expanded radius of potential social interaction" (p. 21).

Although Erikson proposed that individuals have a readiness to interact with a widening circle of other people throughout their lives, he emphasized that psychological individuation is paramount. Feminist scholars and others have taken exception to this view of ideal adult development (Berzoff, 1989; Gilligan, 1982). For example, feminist scholars have contended that women's experience of connectedness (including mothering, nurturing, and caretaking) should be valued as the catalyst for self-development (Bricker-Jenkins, Hooyman, & Gottlieb, 1991; Van Den Bergh & Cooper, 1987; see Chapter 11).

In addition, Ho (1992) suggested a cross-cultural framework for examining development. He cautioned that practitioners can misconstrue closeness between family members, particularly mother and child, among many Latinos or Asian American families. Similarly, among many minority adolescents, autonomy is not determined solely by moving out of the home. Rather, it is expected that family members will continue to live in extended households.

Critique of Life-Stage Models of Development

Erikson's (1959) most important and best known contribution to personality theory is his model of eight stages of ego development. In this life cycle approach, he proposed that development is determined by shifts in instinctual or biological energy, occurs in stages, and centers around a series of eight psychosocial crises. As each stage emerges, a psychosocial crisis fosters change within the person and in his or her expanding interconnections between self and environment. Crises offer the opportunity for new experiences and demand a "radical change in perspective" or a new orientation toward oneself and the world (Erikson, 1963, p. 212). The result is an "ever-new configuration that is the growing personality" (Erikson, 1959, p. 57).

Erikson emphasized that one stage of development builds on the successes of previous stages. Difficulties in resolving earlier psychosocial issues may foreshadow further difficulties in later stages. Each stage of development is distinguished by particular characteristics that differentiate it from preceding and succeeding stages (Newman & Newman, 2005). The notion that development occurs in unique stages, each building on the previous one and having its own emphasis or underlying structural organization, is called *stage theory* (see Figure 4.1). Erikson argued that personality is a function of the outcome of each life stage. The psychological outcome of a crisis is a blend of ego qualities resting between two contradictory extremes or polarities. This means an individual's personality reflects a blend of ego qualities such as trust or mistrust.

Social workers and other human services professionals refer to several theories of personality development that are based upon assumptions of sequential, universal stages. In addition to Erikson, other well-known stage theorists include Sigmund Freud, Heinz Hartmann, Margaret Mahler, Jean Piaget, and Lawrence Kohlberg (Germain, 1991). Although stage theories continue to be used by practitioners, their utility and universality are increasingly being questioned.

As stated in Chapter 3, social work assessment is used to explore needs and resources as a process to select interventions and treatment modalities for a client. From a practice perspective, a person's progression throughout life may be evaluated by the normative (and therefore desirable) standards proposed by Eriksonian theory. As with other stage or phase theories, the perspective of normative patterns of development and transition implies that a different progression is undesirable, involves unresolved conflicts and issues, and is deviant. Interventions by the practitioner become attempts to assist a client with fitting into the stages or resolving previously unresolved internal issues.

Figure 4.1.

Erik Erikson's Psychosocial Crisis

	1	2	3	4	5	6	7	8
Old Age								Integrity vs Despair **WISDOM**
Adult hood							Generativity vs Stagnation **CARE**	
Young Adulthood						Intimacy vs isolation **LOVE**		
Adolesence					Identity vs Identity Confusion **FIDELITY**			
School Age				Industry vs Inferiority **COMPETENCE**				
Play Age			Initiative vs Guilt **PURPOSE**					
Early Childhood		Autonomy vs Shame, Doubt. **WILL**						
Infancy	Basic Trust vs Basic Mistrust **HOPE**							

Erik Erikson's psychosocial crises. From Erikson, E. (1982). *The Life Cycle Completed* (pp. 56–57). New York: Norton. Reprinted with permission.

Unfortunately, the use of a model in which stages are mastered in a linear sequence does not consider cultural variations in lifestyle decisions and behaviors. If practitioners are uninformed about influences of gender, racial or ethnic, religious, sexual orientation, or cohort variations in clients' development, decisions about treatment approaches may prove to be inappropriate or even harmful.

The critique of stage theories, including Eriksonian theory, is related to the assumptions of fixed sequence development. For example, the identity development of gays and lesbians has been found to be different from that of heterosexuals, as well as to have intragroup variations (Boxer & Cohler, 1989; Sophie, 1986). The whole concept of timing of events, both in the individual's personal history as well as his or her sociocultural setting, has an impact on the progression and mastery of developmental tasks (Germain, 1991; Sophie, 1986). As Boxer and Cohler stated, "It is precisely this social definition of the course of life which transforms the study of the life span or life cycle into the study of the life course" (p. 320). The question then becomes whether any fixed, determined sequence of life tasks adequately addresses an understanding of human development during changing cultural, social, and political eras.

Eight Stages of Development: Diversity Perspectives

The ego is learning effective steps toward a tangible collective future, that is developing into a defined ego within a social reality. (Erikson, 1959, p. 22)

Erikson outlined eight stages of development spanning birth through death. This section summarizes each of the stages and discusses the associated developmental tasks. An additional component is a brief critique based on individual and cultural group differences in development for each stage. Cultural influences on issues related to various stages are examined, and the concept of mastery of developmental tasks is explored.

Stage 1: Basic Trust Versus Basic Mistrust   Birth – 18 months

Erikson (1959) believed that "enduring patterns for the balance of basic trust over basic mistrust" are established from birth until about age two (pp. 64–65). He viewed the establishment of trust as the "cornerstone of the healthy personality" and the primary task during this first stage (p. 58). The resolution of each psychosocial crisis, according to Erikson, results in a basic strength or *ego quality*. He indicated that the first psychosocial strength that emerges is *hope*, the enduring belief in the attainability of primal or basic wishes. Hope is related to a sense of confidence and stems primarily from the quality of maternal care a person receives. Although Erikson focused on the development of healthy personalities, he acknowledged that the resolution of each crisis produces both positive and negative ego qualities. He identified a tendency toward *withdrawal* (detachment) from social relationships as the negative outcome of the first life crisis. Erikson proposed that tendencies later in life toward low self-esteem, depression, and social withdrawal are indications that there may have been difficulty during the first developmental stage. In working with clients who have these behaviors, practitioners need to become knowledgeable about the history of their relationships. Clients with difficulties in these areas may internalize their anger or employ strategies to avoid engaging with others.

Chestang (1972) argued that Erikson did not sufficiently address the consequences of injustice, inconsistency, and feelings of impotence on personality development. He suggested that character development of members of groups who are treated differently by virtue of their living in a hostile environment must be examined in the context of institutional disparity. Chestang went on to suggest that a *deficit model*, or one viewing an individual's adjustment as pathological, is not an acceptable assessment when societal structures have impeded development through "excessive shaming" and "repeated environmental assault" (pp. 46–48). Rather, it is necessary to ask how an individual's personality has adapted to or transcended these provocations (Cohen & Greene, 2005; Greene, 2007).

Stage 2: Autonomy Versus Shame   /8- 3 yrs

Autonomy, or a sense of self-control without loss of self-esteem, involves the psychosocial issues of holding on and letting go. In contrast, *shame*, the feeling of being exposed or estranged from parental figures, involves a child's feeling that he or she is a failure and, as a result, his or her lack of self-confidence. A successful resolution of the psychosocial crisis of autonomy versus shame results in the positive ego quality *will*, or the unbroken determination to exercise free choice. Will's antipathic counterpart is *compulsion*, the repetitive behavior used to restrict impulses. Compulsion is the negative result of autonomy versus shame.

In this stage of development, independence or separation is the desired outcome. For Erikson, male identity formation is an antecedent to intimacy in relationships with others. However, more recent research has shown that women's development is more relational and less individualistic than that of men and has seen this as a strength in women (Hartling & Ly, 2000; Walker & Miller, 2001). These theories specifically recognize and value the different patterns of women's development, focusing on the importance of attachments in women's development and the importance of relationships throughout life (Gilligan, 1982; Miller, 1976; Miller & Stiver, 1991).

The emergence of female voices in life span development has challenged assumptions of earlier theorists. In theories that bring an analysis of a strengths perspective to women's development, the ability to maintain attachments to others is seen as positive and functional. Women's ability to be connected has the goal of sustaining and affirming creativity and cooperation in family life (Berzoff, 1989). Miller (1984) suggested that the capacity to adapt to others is central to being empathetic. A reconceptualization of attachments in a feminist framework implies that relatedness, not merely autonomy, is a desirable state.

Stage 3: Initiative Versus Guilt   3 -5

During the stage of initiative versus guilt, as a result of being willing to go after things and to take on roles through play, the child develops a sense of purpose. However, if he or she is overly thwarted, a feeling of *inhibition* or restraint prevents freedom of thought and expression from developing (Erikson, 1977). Erikson echoed Freud when he stated that girls "lack one item: the penis; and with it, important prerogatives in some cultures and classes" (Erikson, 1964a, p. 81). As was typical of Erikson, he identified the source of the inequality he noted not in some form of biological determinism, as did Freud, but rather in the inner workings of certain societies (Hoare, 2002). Erikson (1963) stressed that, at this stage, the child engages in an active investigation of his or her environment, and the family remains the radius of significant human relations.

However, Erikson departed from traditional psychoanalytic thought when he proposed that, during this stage, children are more concerned with play and with the pursuit of activities of their own choosing than they are with their sexuality. Some theorists (Gilligan, 1982) have taken issue with Erikson's concepts relating play activity to biologically based "masculine and feminine imitative" (Erikson, 1959, p. 82). For example, in research at a playground, Lever (1976) noted that boys fought over the rules of a game, whereas girls tended to leave the game when disputes arose. She interpreted this finding as showing that girls quit the game to sustain their friendships. In addition, Ho (1992) pointed out that because play content, feelings, and fantasies vary from group to group and within different societies, practitioners need to be cautious about applying one set of norms when working with young children and their families. Part of the assessment process needs to include investigation of the meanings and outcomes of children's play, and specifically the private meanings held by the client.

Stage 4: Industry Versus Inferiority   6 - 12

This life stage occurs between ages six and twelve. Classically trained psychoanalysts believed that this is a time when the sexual drive lies dormant (or is sublimated) and children enjoy a period of relative rest, known as the *latency period* (Corey, 2005). Erikson (1959) broke with psychoanalytic thinking by suggesting that the central task of this time is to achieve a sense of *industry*. Developing industry is a task involving "an eagerness for building skills and performing meaningful work" (p. 90). The crisis of industry versus inferiority can result in a sense of competence or a blend with its opposite, *inertia* (a paralysis of thought and action that prevents productive work). Success at creating and making things together with one's neighbors and schoolmates is a critical task in the child's expanding physical and social world at this time (Erikson, 1982; Newman & Newman, 2005).

Attitudes toward productivity may vary among and within cultures. For example, Sue and Sue (1990) discussed the importance of tribal allegiances for many American Indians, whose identity and security are entwined with their tribal affiliation. Productivity is valued as a communal good and less as a reflection of individual success. This concept also is different from the cultural values of Native Australians. In their social order, a rite of passage to manhood is the *walkabout*, which is the practice of being alone in the environment, demonstrating one's ability to survive independently in one's world (White & Epston, 1990). In the social work assessment process, the strategies and symbolic rituals that accompany a sense of industry must be examined with the particular client.

Stage 5: Identity Versus Identity Confusion   /2-/8

From ages twelve through twenty-two, the adolescent develops into the young adult. The central task of this stage, according to Erikson (1963), is to form a stable identity, which he defined as "a sense of personal sameness and historical continuity" (p. 153). *Identity*, which involves the establishment of personal identity, autonomy from parents, acceptance of one's sexual preference, and commitment to a career, also depends on social supports that permit the child to formulate successive and tentative identifications. This process culminates in an overt identity crisis in adolescence. During adolescence, an individual struggles with the issues of how "to be oneself" and "to share oneself with another" (Erikson, 1959, p. 179). The peer group becomes the critical focus of interaction.

The person who forms a relatively healthy identity views the world of experience with a minimum of distortion and defensiveness, and a maximum of mutual activity. *Fidelity*, or the ability to sustain loyalties, is the critical ego quality that emerges from this stage. *Identity confusion* is based on a summation of the most undesirable and dangerous aspects of identification at critical stages of development (Newman & Newman, 2005). Severe conflicts during this stage can result in *repudiation*, or a rejection of alien roles and values.

Erikson (1964b) viewed identity as "a new combination of old and new identification fragments" (p. 90). He believed that identity is more than the sum of childhood identifications. The individual's inner drives and his or her endowments and opportunities, as well as the ego values accrued in childhood, come together to form a sense of confidence and continuity about "inner sameness" and "one's meaning for others" (Erikson, 1959, p. 94). Absorption of personality features into a "new configuration" is the essence of development during this stage (Erikson, 1959, p. 57). Erikson proposed that identity formation is a lifelong developmental process. For example, positive involvement with community (e.g., volunteering, participating in service-learning activities) and positive experiences within the family during this time of life provide a foundation to be a healthy and generative adult later in life (Lawford, Pratt, Hunsberger, & Pancer, 2005). In addition, the ability to retain one's belief in oneself as well as one's lifestyle and career (often a focus of therapy) can be enhanced throughout life.

However, the universality of this stage of identity has also been disputed. In cross-cultural and multicultural research on adolescent development in the United States, Canada, India, and Romania, evidence has suggested that the adolescent life period varies significantly across cultures and communities (Chatterjee, Bailey, & Aronoff, 2001; Chatterjee & Curl, 2005). In fact, the period of "extended adolescence" (e.g., ages 18–22) does not appear in many cultures. In places like the United States, where many young adults are still financially dependent upon parents and still in school, this period is closely aligned with early adolescence. In cultures where young adults move into adult roles of work and parenting during this time, the psychosocial issues have greater similarity to those of mature adulthood.

As this life period is one of tremendous social identity formation, adolescence identity crisis is frequently explored in the literature. The task for the practitioner is to evaluate how the adolescent perceives and internalizes the images that confront him or her. In forming an adult identity, adolescents may struggle with images that are negatively portrayed, such as overtly masculine lesbian women or feminine gay men. In addition, Ho (1992) expressed concern that attitudes of young Asian Americans toward themselves often are negatively influenced by a society whose media constantly bombard them with the superiority of Western values. In addition, there has been increasing concern about the role of educators who do not positively reinforce feminine identity, which contributes to a negative identity formation among young women, particularly with regard to self-esteem (American Association of University Women, 1991). There has also been the suggestion in the literature that identity formation for African American adolescents "may be more problematic because of negative messages they receive from the dominant society" (Gibbs & Moskowitz-Sweet, 1991, p. 580).

Stage 6: Intimacy Versus Isolation   /8–35

Erikson's sixth stage involves a mature person's ability to form intimate relationships. This occurs between ages twenty-two and thirty-four. Corresponding to Freud's genital stage, the stage of intimacy versus isolation focuses on the psychosocial modality of "being able to lose and find oneself in another" (Erikson, 1959, p. 179). The radius of significant relations expands to include partnerships in friendship and love and encompasses both cooperative and competitive aspects. *Love*, or a mutual devotion that can overcome "the antagonisms inherent in a divided function," is the emerging ego strength (Erikson, 1968, p. 289). Shutting out others, or *exclusivity*, is a sign that an individual has not been successful in reaching intimacy (Newman & Newman, 2005).

Erikson (1968) subscribed to Freud's view that the criterion for defining a mature person is the ability "to love and work" (p. 289). On the one hand,

Erikson agreed with Freud that intimacy includes mutuality of orgasm with a loved partner of the opposite sex with whom one shares mutual trust and the continuing cycle of work, recreation, and procreation. However, he also perceived intimacy as being more than sexual gratification, but also an interest in another's well-being as well as in intellectually stimulating interactions. On the other hand, Erikson (1959) suggested that the psychoanalytic perspective on mature generativity "carries a strong cultural bias" and that various societies might define the capacity for mutual devotion differently (p. 102).

Erikson's sixth stage relates to the intimate social relationships that develop during early adulthood. However, this assumes that opportunities, structures, and resources are available that promote interaction and intimacy. His stages also suggest that relationship skills develop during certain chronological age ranges. Both of these assumptions do not consider the life course development stages of people with developmental disabilities.

The ability to enter into adult relationships and roles is a result of a person's social skills and the availability of social opportunities (Pridgen, 1991). Therefore, social functioning is not solely an individual process but depends on the opportunities that exist in a particular environment. Communities may be structured in such a way that promotes or inhibits a person's ability to function adequately. As Germain (1991) put it, competent communities are those that are structured to promote the functioning of all members.

One group that has historically lacked social and vocational options is people with cognitive and psychiatric disabilities. Because of the limited opportunities afforded them, their ability to work, love, and hold adult family roles has been compromised. Rather than providing increased opportunities for people with disabilities, many communities restrict individuals from social participation through segregated work and living environments (DeWeaver & Kropf, 1992). A grassroots effort from within the disability movement is changing this oppressive paradigm. Current models of supporting individuals with disabilities involve *person-centered planning*, which is a process to maximum goodness of fit between an individual's preferences and residential/vocational/social opportunities (DePoy & Gilson, 2004; O'Brien, Ford, & Malloy, 2005).

Lack of opportunity also affects the ability to form more intimate relationships. Erikson (1959) defined intimacy as the ability to be lost in another person. However, intimacy issues for people with disabilities have been a source of controversy and concern (Abramson, Parker, & Weisberg, 1988; Howard, Lipsitz, Sheppard, & Steinitz, 1991). Historically, society has not allowed sexual expression among people with disabilities, and the intimate relationships of these individuals have been discouraged and suppressed. Sadly, the 1927 Supreme Court upheld a Virginia law that allowed for forced sterilization of individuals who were deemed "feebleminded," a law that had been enacted to keep people with disabilities from having sexual experiences and bearing children. Over the course of the next four decades, more than 50,000 individuals received this compulsory surgery (Wehmeyer, 2003).

Despite many barriers to intimate relationships, some people with disabilities do become parents. Part of the intimacy versus isolation stage of development is the desire and ability to have children. Most parents with intellectual disabilities function in the less severe ranges of disability (Schilling, Schinke, Blythe, & Barth, 1982). However, even more highly functioning parents with disabilities report having little preparation for assuming a parenting role. In addition to possible inadequate socialization, these mothers and fathers may lack other psychological, social, and environmental resources that can enhance their caregiving ability (Whitman, Graves, & Accardo, 1989). To be successful in their roles, many parents with mental disabilities need ongoing educational and support, which is not provided by many families or service providers.

Stage 7: Generativity Versus Stagnation $35 - 55$

This stage occurs in adulthood between ages thirty-four and sixty and is concerned with "establishing and guiding the next generation" (Erikson, 1968, p. 290). The psychosocial crisis centers around "the ability to take care of others" (Erikson, 1959, p. 179). The radius of significant relations extends to dividing labor and sharing households. Broadly framed, generativity encompasses creativity through producing a family; mentoring a student, colleague, or friend; and engaging in career and in leisure activities.

Generativity versus stagnation involves the ability to take care of others; the inability to care for others sufficiently or to include them significantly in one's concerns results in the negative ego quality *rejectivity*. What is commonly called a "midlife crisis" may actually be an inability to satisfactorily resolve Erikson's stage of generativity versus stagnation.

The concept of generativity is currently being reexamined. Generativity has been expanded to include activities external to the family that are more diffuse (e.g., mentoring and craft development). Within families, adults who score higher on measures of generativity have more positive and caring behaviors toward their older parents (Peterson, 2002). Other researchers have examined multiple caregiving roles of women, especially those who are sandwiched between the needs of their elderly parents and their teenage or young-adult children (Sands & Richardson, 1986). Therefore, practitioners often work with middle-aged caregivers who are frequently involved in the demands of caretaking even as they are reassessing their interpersonal relationships, their physical well-being, and their work and achievements.

Likewise, the concept of *stagnation*, or the absence of involvement and inclusivity, is being studied more fully. Furthermore, this concept involves both low levels of involvement with others and a lack of interest in oneself (Bradley & Marcia, 1998).

Another example of the reexamination of Erikson's concept of middle adulthood is Cornett and Hudson's (1987) examination of middle-aged gay men. Their discussion of generativity explored whether gays are able to successfully achieve a state of generativity, because most gays have no offspring. They proposed that generativity can be attained through alternative avenues, such as careers, hobbies, volunteer activities, and relationships with cohorts of younger gays. Cornett and Hudson argued that gay men can be involved in promoting and guiding younger generations through means other than actual parenthood. They cited contributions by brilliant, productive, and creative middle-aged gay men through the ages, such as Socrates, Walt Whitman, and Tennessee Williams. The histories of these great men point to the need of the practitioner to explore alternative options with clients. A feeling of generativity is achieved not simply through caregiving for blood-related family members.

Stage 8: Integrity Versus Despair 55-60 (death)

The final stage, which is concerned with late-life events, begins at about age sixty and lasts until death. The issue of this psychosocial crisis is how a person is able to grow older with integrity in the face of impending mortality. Integrity is achieved by individuals who have few regrets, who have lived productive lives, and who cope as well with their failures as they do with their successes. The person who has successfully achieved a sense of integrity appreciates the continuity of past, present, and future experiences. He or she also comes to accept the life cycle, to cooperate with the inevitabilities of life, and to experience a sense of being complete. *Wisdom*, or the active concern with life in the face of death, characterizes those who are relatively successful in resolving this stage (Erikson, Erikson, & Kivnick, 1986).

The "self story" or "autobiography" is part of this integrative process (Randall & Kenyon, 2001). A life review process

> according to Erikson, can help create an acceptance of one's one and only life cycle with few or no regrets. It does this by helping individuals integrate memories into a meaningful whole, and [providing] a harmonious view of past, present, and future. (Haber, 2006, p. 157)

The process of retelling one's life stories is an important dimension in integrating events across the life span for many individuals.

Erikson's notion that one stage of life is intimately related to all of the others comes full circle at the end of life. His view that the needs and capacities of the generations intertwine is reflected in his statement that the development of trust in children depends on the integrity of previous generations: "Healthy children will not fear life if their elders have integrity enough not to fear death" (Erikson, 1950, p. 269).

Despair, in contrast, predominates in those who fear death and who wish life would give them another chance. The older person who has a strong sense of despair feels that life has been too short and finds little meaning in human existence, having lost faith in himself or herself and others. The person in whom despair predominates has little sense of world order or spiritual wholeness (Butler, 1969). *Disdain*, or a scorn for weakness and frailty, characterizes those who are relatively unsuccessful in resolving integrity versus despair.

Antonovsky and Sagy (1990) "rejected the Eriksonian notion of stages that are epigenetically determined, universal, and clearly demarcated age-wise" (p. 367). They also proposed that Erikson did not give ample attention to the tasks of the later years of life. They questioned why there is no further development during almost forty years of the life cycle—from the time an individual emerges from the stage of generativity versus stagnation until he or she enters the stage of integrity versus despair. They then suggested that Erikson's formulations be used to examine how a life cycle transition is characterized by a number of major life tasks. Furthermore, they differentiated between tasks and outcomes of a given stage; for example, the successful outcome of the crisis of integrity versus despair is integrity. However, it is possible to conceptualize a process of personal needs and social demands that may arise during this stage, such as retirement transition and a concern for maintaining one's health. Finally, Antonovsky and Sagy proposed that the exploration of psychosocial developmental tasks within a historical context, as suggested, allows for an enriched cultural-specific understanding of adult human development.

Differential Assessment as a Foundation for Intervention

Although norms are necessary, rapid changes in life-styles and the conditions of life make it difficult for workers and clients to assess the adequacy of functioning, as do the varied cultural backgrounds of clients. (Northen, 1987, p. 179)

In social work practice, the assessment phase includes collecting information on a client's functional status (see Tables 4.2 and 4.3). This process also involves making sense of this information by understanding it within the framework of a theoretical perspective. Although Eriksonian theory provides a life-stage perspective on development, what would be considered successful mastery of the life stages may be different among various cultural groups and among different people. As discussed in the previous section, gender and disability status—and often cultural characteristics—have an impact on progression through the eight stages proposed by Erikson.

In social work, the value placed on individualism and autonomy has had a major effect on the profession's knowledge base. The effect of this individualistic paradigm can be seen in various aspects of assessment and treatment (see Table 4.4). Even the terminology used in professional practice reflects a desired state of autonomy (e.g., in the term *codependency* for women with addicted partners, or *welfare dependents* for women who use public assistance programs). Practice interventions often have a goal of helping people separate from others. This

Table 4.2
Questions for Life Histories

Make a self-evaluation of good, neutral, or bad:

1. Trust/autonomy: To what extent do you think you were well cared for and well guided through your first years? How easily do you interact with others without feeling shy or ashamed?
2. Initiative: To what extent do you enjoy starting new activities? Were you easily kept back by feelings of guilt in your pre-school years?
3. Industry: Were you a hard working pupil in the early school years? Did your teachers indicate that you were good enough?
4. Identity: Did you belong to a group of friends in your teens? Did you feel like you knew yourself? Did you know how to behave towards other people?
5. Intimacy: Do you remember your first love? Did you establish a close relationship with anyone? How do you remember that person?
6. Early generativity: In the first half of your working life, did you do things that were meaningful for other individuals? For the next generation?
7. Late generativity: In the second half of your working period, did you do things for other people? The next generation?

Source. Rennemark, M., & Hagberg, B. (1997). Social network patterns among the elderly in relation to their perceived life history in an Eriksonian perspective. *Aging & Mental Health, 1,* 323.

could encompass helping a family secure a group home residence for a relative with a disability, assisting a couple through divorce mediation, helping older workers with retirement planning, or helping a mother on public assistance find job training.

The way social work has been taught is not immune from the effects of paradigms built on values of individualism. Back in the early 1970s, schools of social work were admonished for teaching sexist content in the curriculum (Schwartz, 1973). In more recent years, issues related to assessment of members of various groups (e.g., elderly people, people with disabilities, gays and lesbians) have continued to surface in the professional literature (e.g., DePoy & Gilson, 2004; DeWeaver & Kropf, 1992; Hunter & Hickerson, 2002; Mellor & Ivry, 2002).

As a result, progress appears to have been made in representing the experiences of diverse groups of people because content on race, ethnicity, sexual orientation, and gender is now a mandated part of the social work curriculum. However, others proclaim that an additive model is insufficient to address the fundamental problems of "doing social work" based on an individualistic model. Some in the profession advocate a paradigmatic shift that includes a focus on relatedness and interdependence rather than on autonomy and individualism (Falck, 1988; Kravetz, 1982; Tice, 1990).

As suggested by feminist scholars, practice needs to move beyond a separation model (Watkins & Iverson, 1998). The assessment process must include a focus

Table 4.3
Assessment Questions

Stage	Questions to Explore
Trust versus Mistrust	How hopeful is the client?
	How socially attached is the client?
	How well does the client appear to trust the social worker?
Autonomy versus Shame	Does the client appear to move ahead with a sense of will or determination?
	Does the client seem to have a strong or relatively weak sense of self-control?
	Does he or she appear lacking in self-confidence?
Initiative versus Guilt	To what degree does the client have a sense of purpose?
	Does he or she move into opportunities?
	Does he or she face new events with trepidation?
Industry versus Inferiority	How competent does the client seem in handling his or her affairs?
	Does the client seem relatively productive?
Identity versus Identity Confusion	How comfortable is the client with bonding with others?
	Does the client have a relatively "good" sense of self?
Intimacy versus Isolation	How comfortable is the client in loving and sharing with others?
Generativity versus Stagnation	How willing is the client to care for others and be cared for him- or herself?
Integrity versus Despair	Does the client pass along his or her ideas to the next generation?
	Has the client come to terms with his or her life and with others close to him or her?
	Does he or she have a relative comfort with his or her mortality?

Source. Greene, R. R. (2008). *Eriksonian Psychosocial Theory.* New York: Wiley.

on helping clients in various life situations with the transitions they face. Instead of "letting go," however, assessment and treatment may have the goal of helping clients "loosen" relationships, as in the case of a family investigating residential placements. When relationships must be terminated, as in the case of retirement from a job, social work assessment must also be prepared to tell clients who have lost relationships to "grab on" to new ones, such as through joining a senior citizen's group in the community. Berzoff (1989) suggested that a more relational model of practice would move into a modality of working in group settings instead of emphasizing individual models of treatment, as the current one does.

Postmodern theorists have argued that Erikson's theory is becoming less relevant (Schachter, 2005). Viewing the psychosocial theory from a postmodern perspective, Schachter made the case that although Erikson's theory was intended to be a universal theory that would transcend time-bound and local contexts, it is increasingly less applicable to current social conditions that are far more complex than those discussed by Erikson. In a similar vein, Ermann (2004) argued that Erikson's developmental model, in which an individual goes through the normative identity crisis in adolescence, leading to a long-lasting identity, is no longer viable. Ermann contended that because society is in such a state of flux, "today's individual is in a continuous developmental crisis" (p. 209). In an article on the changing nature of the patriarchal family, Sjodin (2004) agreed that because of the dynamic nature of social change, "our entire social contract is being rewritten" (p. 264).

Therefore, assessing the functional status of a client involves more than understanding that individual's behavior (see Tables 4.3 and 4.4). Considerations of environmental influences need to be included in the assessment process, such as opportunities and resources that do not exist for certain groups of clients. For example, throughout their lives, people with intellectual disabilities have limited social support networks (Malone, 1990). Furthermore, adults with these disability conditions often express a desire to make more friends and meet new people (Flynn & Saleem, 1986; Mest, 1988; see Chapter 10 for a discussion of social support networks). In the assessment process for clients with mental retardation, community-level factors can have an important influence on an intervention plan. The focus of the intervention may move from an individual- to a system-change direction that is more inclusive of all people regardless of personal characteristics such as age, race and ethnicity, gender, disability status, sexual orientation, or religious affiliation.

Erikson's Recent Critique

In 1970, at 68 years of age, having completed a full career of writing and clinical work, Erikson retired from his professorship at Harvard, examining his own work and that of others in the field. Additional information about Erikson and his life works was made available in 2002 in a book by Carol Hoare (2002), *Erikson on Development in Adulthood: New Insights From the Unpublished Papers*. She reviewed unpublished papers from the Erikson collection at the Houghton Library at Harvard University and a transcript of the 1971 Conference on the Adult sponsored by the American Academy of Arts and Sciences. Hoare concluded that a content analysis of Erikson's works enabled her to reveal "new images" of his developmental concepts (p. vi). She learned that Erikson believed that his linear depiction of development was limiting and did not capture the complexity of people's lives. Furthermore, he argued that viewing life's milestones, such as marriage and retirement, as the essential elements of development did an injustice to describing the meaning of *adult*.

Table 4.4
Guidelines for the Eriksonian-Style Practitioner

- Understand that your client is engaged in a lifelong process of personality development in which the practitioner can be instrumental in promoting growth.

- Engage the client in a self-analysis, which results in a developmental history.

- Distinguish with the client his or her relative successes and difficulties in resolving psychosocial crises.

- Determine areas of development that have led to a distortion of reality and a diminution in ego functioning.

- Interpret the client's developmental and historical distortions. Ask for client confirmation of your interpretations.

- Develop the client's insight and understanding about unresolved normative crises and their historical implications.

- Identify ways in which the client can use his or her ego strengths to cope more effectively with his or her environment. Explore how these coping strategies can be put into action.

- Clarify how and in what ways various social institutions support or fail to support the client's psychosocial well-being.

- Seek means of enhancing the client's societal supports.

- Promote the client's developing a new orientation to his or her place in the social environment.

Source. Greene, R. R. (2008). Eriksonian theory: A developmental approach to ego mastery. In R. R. Greene (Ed.), *Human Behavior Theory and Social Work Practice.* New Brunswick, NJ: Aldine Transaction.

Erikson initiated a conference on adult development that addressed six difficulties he perceived in the field:

1. Freud's idea that adulthood was not a time of growth and further development had been too influential.
2. Because of this influence, adults were viewed as physically developed children.
3. Theorists appeared to be unable to separate early childhood development from its origins in childhood.
4. When adult development was studied, development was addressed as a chronological phenomenon composed of marker events rather than a time of qualitative difference.
5. Concepts of adulthood and the views of adult normalcy were limited.
6. Developmentalists tended to view behavior from a mainstream perspective limited by class and ethnocentric biases (Hoare, 2002).

In short, Erikson critiqued his own work as overly concerned with normative events. He asked for a fresh inquiry about normal adult development that
would reveal the ideal and images of the generative caring person (Greene,
2008). Erikson's lifelong exploration of what it means to be an adult led him
to question why so many adults led "restricted versions of what they might yet
become, whereas others always [seemed] to create resilient, fresh renditions of
themselves throughout the adult years" (Hoare, 2002, p. vii).

References

Abramson, P. R., Parker, T., & Weisberg, S. R. (1988). Sexual expression of mentally
retarded people: Educational and legal implications. *American Journal of Mental
Retardation*, 93, 328–334.
American Association of University Women. (1991). *Shortchanging Girls, Shortchanging
America.* Washington, DC: Author.
Antonovsky, A., & Sagy, S. (1990). Confronting developmental tasks in the retirement
transition. *The Gerontologist*, 30, 362–368.
Berzoff, J. (1989). From separation to connection: Shifts in understanding women's
development. *Affilia*, 4, 45–58.
Boxer, A. M., & Cohler, B. J. (1989). The life course of gay and lesbian youth: An im-
modest proposal for the study of lives. *Journal of Homosexuality*, 17, 315–355.
Bradley, C. L., & Marcia, J. E. (1998). Generativity-stagnation: A five-category model.
Journal of Personality, 66, 39–64.
Bricker-Jenkins, M., Hooyman, N. R., & Gottlieb, N. (Eds.). (1991). *Feminist Social
Work Practice in Clinical Settings.* Newbury Park, CA: Sage.
Butler, R. N. (1969). Directions in psychiatric treatment of the elderly: Role of perspec-
tives of the life cycle. *The Gerontologist*, 9, 134–138.
Capps, D. (2005). The decades of life: Relocating Erikson's stages. *Pastoral Psychol-
ogy*, 53(1), 3–32.
Chatterjee, P., Bailey, D., & Aronoff, N. (2001). Adolescence and old age in twelve com-
munities. *Journal of Sociology and Social Welfare*, 28(4), 121–159.
Chatterjee, P., & Curl, A. (2005). Community and adolescence in four societies. *Social
Development Issues*, 27(1), 35–54.
Chestang, L. (1972). *Character Development in a Hostile Environment* (Occasional Paper
No. 3). Chicago: University of Chicago, School of Social Service Administration.
Chestang, L. (1984). Racial and personal identity in the black experience. In B. W. White
(Ed.), *Color in a White Society* (pp. 83–94). Silver Spring, MD: NASW Press.
Cohen, H., & Greene, R. R. (2005). Older adults who overcame oppression. *Families
in Society*, 87, 1–8.
Coles, R. (1970). *Erik H. Erikson: The Growth of His Work.* Boston: Little, Brown.
Corey, G. (2005). *Theory and Practice of Counseling and Psychotherapy.* Belmont, CA:
Wadsworth.
Cornett, C., & Hudson, R. A. (1987). Middle adulthood and the theories of Erikson,
Gould, and Vaillant: Where does the gay man fit? *Journal of Gerontological Social
Work*, 10(3/4), 61–73.
DePoy, E., & Gilson, S. F. (2004). *Rethinking Disability: Principles for Professional and
Social Change.* Monterey, CA: Brooks/Cole.
DeWeaver, K. L., & Kropf, N. P. (1992). Person with mental retardation: A forgotten
minority in social work education. *Journal of Social Work Education*, 28, 36–46.
Erikson, E. H. (1950). *Childhood and Society* (1st ed.). New York: Norton.

Erikson, E. H. (1959). *Identity and the Life Cycle*. New York: Norton.

Erikson, E. H. (1963). *Childhood and Society* (2nd ed.). New York: Norton.

Erikson, E. H. (1964a). Inner and outer space: Reflections on womanhood. *Daedalus*, 93, 1–25.

Erikson, E. H. (1964b). *Insight and Responsibility*. Toronto, Ontario, Canada: McLeod.

Erikson, E. H. (1968). *Identity, Youth, and Crisis*. New York: Norton.

Erikson, E. H. (1974). *Dimensions of a New Identity*. New York: Norton.

Erikson, E. H. (1977). *Toys and Reason*. New York: Norton.

Erikson, E. H. (1982). *The Life Cycle Completed*. New York: Norton.

Erikson, E. H., Erikson, J. M., & Kivnick, H. Q. (1986). *Vital Involvement in Old Age*. New York: Norton.

Ermann, M. (2004). Guest editorial. *International Forum of Psychoanalysis*, 13, 209–210.

Falck, H. S. (1988). *Social Work: The Membership Perspective*. New York: Springer.

Flynn, M. C., & Saleem, J. K. (1986). Adults who are mentally handicapped and living with their parents: Satisfaction and perception of their lives and circumstances. *Journal of Mental Deficiency Research*, 30, 379–387.

Germain, C. B. (1991). *Human Behavior and the Social Environment: An Ecological View*. New York: Columbia University Press.

Germain, C. B. (1992). A conversation with Carel Germain on human development in the ecological context. In M. Bloom (Ed.), *Changing Lives: Studies in Human Development and Professional Helping* (pp. 406–409). Columbia: University of South Carolina Press.

Germain, C. B. (1997). Should HBSE be taught from a stage perspective? In M. Bloom & W. C. Klein (Eds.), *Controversial Issues in Human Behavior in the Social Environment* (pp. 33–48). Boston: Allyn & Bacon.

Gibbs, J. T., & Moskowitz-Sweet, G. (1991). Clinical and cultural issues in the treatment of biracial and bicultural adolescents. *Families in Society*, 72, 579–592.

Gilligan, C. (1982). *In a Different Voice*. Cambridge, MA: Harvard University Press.

Greene, R. R. (Ed.). (2007). *Social Work Practice: A Risk and Resilience Perspective*. Monterey, CA: Brooks/Cole.

Greene, R.R. (2008). Psychosocial theory. In B. Thyer (Ed.-in-Chief) *Comprehensive Handbook of Social Work and Social Welfare: Human Behavior in the Social Environment* (pp. 229-255). Hoboken, NJ: John Wiley & Sons.

Greene, R. R. (2008). Eriksonian theory: A developmental approach to ego mastery. In R. R. Greene (Ed.), *Human Behavior Theory and Social Work Practice*. New Brunswick, NJ: Aldine Transaction.

Greene, R. R. (Ed.). (2008). *Human Behavior Theory and Social Work Practice*. New Brunswick, NJ: Aldine Transaction.

Haber, D. (2006). Life review: Implementation, theory, research, and therapy. *International Journal of Aging & Human Development*, 63(2), 153–171.

Haraeven, T. K. (1996). *Aging and Generational Relations over the Life Course: A Historical and Cross-Cultural Perspective*. Hawthorne, NY: Aldine de Gruyter.

Hartling, L. M., & Ly, J. (2000). *Relational References: A Selected Bibliography of Theory, Research, and Applications* (Project Report No. 7). Wellesley, MA: Wellesley Centers for Women.

Ho, M. K. (1992). *Minority Children and Adolescents in Therapy*. Newbury Park, CA: Sage.

Hoare, C. H. (2002). *Erikson on Development in Adulthood: New Insights from the Unpublished Papers*. New York: Oxford University Press.

Hogan, R. (1976). *Personality Theory: The Personological Tradition*. Englewood Cliffs, NJ: Prentice Hall.

Howard, R., Lipsitz, G., Sheppard, F., & Steinitz, L. Y. (1991). Sexual behavior in group residences: An ethics dilemma. *Journal of Contemporary Human Services*, 72, 360–365.

Hunter, S., & Hickerson, J. C. (2002). *Affirmative Practice: Understanding and Working with Lesbian, Gay, Bisexual, and Transgender persons*. Washington, DC: NASW Press.

Kravetz, D. (1982). An overview of content on women for the social work curriculum. *Journal of Education for Social Work*, 18(2), 42–49.

Lawford, H., Pratt, M. W., Hunsberger, V., & Pancer, S. M. (2005). Adolescent generativity: A longitudinal study of two possible contexts for learning concern for future generations. *Journal of Research on Adolescence*, 15, 261–273.

Lever, J. (1976). Sex differences in games children play. *Social Problems*, 23, 478–487.

Logan, S. M. L. (1981). Race, identity, and black children: A developmental perspective. *Social Casework*, 62, 47–56.

Malone, D. M. (1990). Aging persons with mental retardation: Identification of the needs of a special population. *Gerontology Review*, 3(1), 1–14.

Mellor, M. J., & Ivry, J. (Eds.). (2002). *Advancing Gerontological Social Work Education*. New York: Haworth Press.

Mest, G. M. (1988). With a little help from their friends: Use of social support systems by persons with retardation. *Journal of Social Issues*, 44, 117–125.

Miller, J. B. (1976). *Toward a New Psychology of Women*. Boston: Beacon Press.

Miller, J. B. (1984). *The Development of Women's Sense of Self*. Unpublished manuscript, Wellesley College, Wellesley, MA.

Miller, J. B., & Stiver, I. P. (1991). *A Relational Reframing of Therapy*. Wellesley, MA: Wellesley Centers for Women.

Newman, B. M., & Newman, P. R. (2005). *Development through Life: A Psychosocial Approach* (8th ed.). Monterey, CA: Brooks/Cole. (To be read in conjunction with Erikson.)

Northen, H. (1987). Assessment in direct practice. In A. Minahan (Ed.-in-Chief), *Encyclopedia of Social Work* (18th ed., pp. 171–183). Silver Spring, MD: NASW Press.

O'Brien, D., Ford, L., & Malloy, J. M. (2005). Person centered funding: Using vouchers and personal budgets to support recovery and *employment* for people with psychiatric disabilities. *Journal of Vocational Rehabilitation*, 23(2), 71–79.

Peterson, B. E. (2002). Longitudinal analysis of midlife generativity, intergenerational roles, and care giving. *Psychology and Aging*, 17, 161–168.

Poster, M. (1989). *Critical Theory and Poststructuralism: In Search of a Context*. Ithaca, NY: Cornell University Press.

Pridgen, N. H. (1991). Community-based counseling services for deaf and hard-of-hearing individuals. *Families in Society*, 72, 174–176.

Randall, W. L., & Kenyon, G. M. (2001). *Ordinary Wisdom: Biographical Aging and the Journey of Life*. Westport, CT: Praeger.

Rennemark, M., & Hagberg, B. (1997). Social network patterns among the elderly in relation to their perceived life history in an Eriksonian perspective. *Aging & Mental Health*, 1, 321–331.

Sands, R. G., & Richardson, V. (1986). Clinical practice with women in their middle years. *Social Work*, 31, 36–43.

Schachter, E. P. (2005). Erikson meets the postmodern: Can classic identity theory rise to the challenge? *Identity*, 5, 137–160.

Schilling, R. F., Schinke, S. P., Blythe, B. J., & Barth, R. P. (1982). Child maltreatment and mentally retarded parents: Is there a relationship? *Mental Retardation*, 20, 201–209.

Schwartz, M. C. (1973). Sexism in the social work curriculum. *Journal of Social Work Education*, 9(3), 65–70.

Shapiro, T., & Hertzig, M. E. (Eds.). (1988). Normal growth and development. In *American Psychiatric Press Textbook of Psychiatry* (pp. 91–121). Washington, DC: American Psychiatric Press.

Sjodin, C. (2004). The power of identity and the end of patriarchy: Reflections on Manuel Castells' book on the network society. *International Forum of Psychoanalysis*, 13, 264–274.

Sophie, J. (1986). A critical examination of stage theories of lesbian identity development. *Journal of Homosexuality*, 12(2), 39–51.

Sue, D. W., & Sue, D. (1990). *Counseling the Culturally Different: Theory and Practice* (2nd ed.). New York: Wiley.

Thyer, B. A. (1992). A behavioral perspective on human development. In M. Bloom (Ed.), *Changing Lives: Studies in Human Development and Professional Helping* (pp. 410–418). Columbia: University of South Carolina Press.

Tice, K. (1990). Gender and social work education: Directions for the 1990s. *Journal of Social Work Education,* 26, 134–144.

Van Den Bergh, N., & Cooper, L. B. (1987). Feminist social work. In A. Minahan (Ed.-in-Chief), *Encyclopedia of Social Work* (18th ed., pp. 610–618). Silver Spring, MD: NASW Press.

Walker, M., & Miller, J. B. (2001). *Racial Images and Relational Possibilities* (Talking Paper No. 2). Wellesley, MA: Wellesley Centers for Women.

Watkins, M., & Iverson, E. (1998). Youth development principles and field practicum opportunities. In R. R. Greene & M. Watkins (Eds.), *Serving Diverse Constituencies: Applying the Ecological Perspective* (pp. 167–198). New York: Aldine de Gruyter.

Wehmeyer, M. L. (2003). Eugenics and sterilization in the heartland. *Mental Retardation*, 41(1), 57–60.

Wesley, C. (1975). The women's movement and psychotherapy. *Social Work*, 20(2), 120–124.

White, M., & Epston, D. (1990). *Narrative Means to Therapeutic Ends*. New York: Norton.

Whitman, B. Y., Graves, B., & Accardo, P. J. (1989). The mentally retarded parent in the community: Identification and method and needs assessment survey. *American Journal of Mental Deficiency*, 91, 636–638.

5

Role Theory and Social Work Practice

Kathryn H. Thompson and Roberta R. Greene

Humans are never just individuals trying to meet their own needs. They are social in nature and live out their lives in the context of social systems and their constituent roles. The meeting of individual needs is intimately caught up in the dynamics of the system as a whole. (Longres, 2000, p. 45)

Historical Background

Theories that attempt to explain how group norms and values are established, how groups achieve a division of labor, and what contributes to systems maintenance are of great interest to social workers (Longres, 2000; Strean, 1974). Therefore, it is not surprising that the concept of social roles is viewed as making an important contribution to the understanding of human behavior and the social environment, and the theory is infused into several social work practice models (Greene, 2008; Hollis, 1964, 1977; Perlman, 1968).

Role theory came to the fore in social work practice during the 1960s and early 1970s, when there was renewed interest in environmental factors that influence personality (Davis, 1986; Ephross-Saltman & Greene, 1993; Stein & Cloward, 1958). According to Hamilton (1958), social workers' increased attention to the concept of social roles represented a "revolution" in the social sciences and a return to a stronger focus on the social perspective on behavior (p. xi). Writing at the zenith of the social work profession's interest in intrapsychic processes as the explanation for human behavior, Hamilton believed role theory would offer social and cultural insights that would no longer "restrict the social worker to a consideration of how the client feels about his [or her] situation" but would allow the professional to "be equally attuned to the effects on the client of ethnic, class, and other significant group determinants of behavior" (p. xi).

Since the 1970s, however, researchers have reexamined role theory, particularly the underlying assumptions about gender roles, family definitions, and hierarchical structures within families that are based on role relationships (Carter & McGoldrick, 2005). Feminist scholars particularly have been concerned that role theory has not appropriately addressed questions about gender roles and family structure and that role theory has been used uncritically to maintain systems within which devalued and inferior roles are ascribed to women. In a similar vein, scholars are reviewing the changing role of fathers.

Another area in which role theory has gained prominence is research and practice in later life caregiving issues. As the older population grows, greater numbers of families will have some responsibility to provide care and support to older family members. Role theory, used to understand earlier life stages within families, has utility for understanding issues of later life care provision as well (e.g., Kang, 2006; Reid & Hardy, 1999).

This chapter explores the perspectives of social role theory for culturally sensitive and gender-sensitive social work practice. It applies social role concepts to the assessment process and client–social worker interaction. Applications of social role constructs to human behavior and the implications of these for devalued social roles and groups in society are discussed (see Table 5.1).

Table 5.1
Role Theory: Basic Assumptions

- Certain behaviors are prescribed (by us and by other elements of our social system) relative to our position within that system.
- Every role involves both our own expectations and abilities and with one or more others.
- The notion of role expectation implies that there are certain social norms that set the outside limits for congruent, nonconflicted interactions, and transactions between positions within the system and between systems.
- There are emotionally charged value judgments to how people carry out their roles both on the part of the person occupying the role position and others.
- Social functioning may be seen as the sum of the roles performed by a human system.
- The concept of role, role functioning, role expectations, and role transactions may be used to increase the knowledge base used for the assessment of the problem situation. Role failure and/or role conflict will tend to follow:
  a. The loss or absence of resources necessary to a system's ability to perform a role well.
  b. When systems are thrust into new roles without knowing the role expectations.
  c. When there is a new role expectation on the part of interacting systems.
  d. When there is a conflict of role expectations within the cluster of roles carried by one system.
  e. When there is ambiguity on the part of the system as to role expectations.
  f. When the individual, a member of social system, is [disabled or challenged] in physical, intellectual, or social capacities demanded of the role.
  g. When high feelings or crisis situations suddenly and without warning disrupt previous effective role patterns (Perlman, 1962).

Source. Compton, B., & Galaway, B. (1989). *Social Work Processes* (4th ed., pp. 131–132). Chicago: Dorsey. Copyright 1984 by the Dorsey Press. Reprinted with permission.

Attention to Culture

The construct of role was proposed as a way of "studying and describing the interaction of two members of a social group as they adjust to each other within a social system," thereby permitting an analysis of diverse interpersonal systems (Turner, 1974, p. 319). Social workers were urged to use role analysis to better understand and treat marital difficulties, child-rearing issues, and workplace concerns. Because role theory explores the changing societal context in which behavior is defined and explains how novel or context-specific individual behavior is influenced by the social environment, it was argued that it contributes to an understanding of the personal and social dimensions of behavior across culture and gender.

Cultural relativity is inherent in role theory, directing attention to the way in which values govern a particular family and its country of origin when conceptualizing role behaviors. For example, traditional Asian/Pacific families are heavily influenced by Confucian philosophy and ethics, which strongly emphasize specific roles and the proper relationships among people in those roles (M. K. Ho, Rasheed, & Rasheed, 2003). Practitioners need to be aware that in families influenced by Confucian philosophy, the wife may be assigned a different status in the family structure and role expectations of the parent–child relationship are well defined; these Confucian values may conflict with those of mainstream American society. Practitioners should therefore, as a general principle, explore where family members were born as well as their level of education and income. This information can provide a rough gauge of the degree of the client's acculturation and assimilation and, consequently, of possible cross-cultural role conflict within the family, between the family and its current American environment, and between the social worker (and agency) and the family or its individual members.

Role Theory: A Person-in-Environment Paradigm

Individuals are connected to social systems through the roles they occupy in them. Roles are at the same time an element of the individual and an element of a social system. They represent the joint boundary between the two, the point at which person meets environment. (Longres, 2000, p. 41)

Role theory provides a set of constructs for understanding human behavior that arises out of group life. It perceives human behavior as a pattern of reciprocal relationships in which there is a set of culture-specific attitudes, beliefs, values, and expectations about how people should conduct themselves in particular situations. The concept of role addresses how people learn what behaviors are expected, permitted, or prohibited within their families and social groups; it explains human behavior as flowing from internalized social prescriptions, motivated by the nature of group identification on the one hand and bounded by status assignments on the other (Biddle, 1979). Role theory constructs can be understood by examining the role of student: *How does my culture view women getting an education? Does my family give me encouragement? Do I perceive myself as a college-bound "A" student?*

An individual's role must be viewed in reference to other roles, usually those that are paired, such as parent–child or client–social worker. Because roles are interrelated, what constitutes a claim for one party is an obligation for another. If a child is expected to go to college, families do their best to support this effort. In a similar vein, Longres and Bailey (1979) contended that female liberation must consider male liberation. Role expectations, therefore, are influenced by the interactive contexts in which people find themselves.

Although role theory examines the attitudes and behaviors expected of people in a particular position, it holds that others' expectations always influence the expectations of the self. That is "it is the relation of the individual's perception of his [or her] own role to its perception by others that largely determines the nature of his [or her] social functioning" (Linton, 1936, p. 171): *Because I am shy, I wonder how I will behave when I enter a room of strangers? What will they think of me?* The concept of social role then serves as a link for understanding an individual's emotional life, behavior, and place in society. Because roles are simultaneously "an element of the individual and an element of a social system," the concept of role exemplifies the person-in-environment paradigm (Longres, 2000, p. 41).

Binary Role Performance

Role performance should not be described in a binary (either/or) fashion (Thorne & Yalom, 1982). Categories such as gender, race, and class may be too simplistic to be useful in social work practice (Van Voorhis, 2008). For example, what is considered "masculine" behavior is a generalization that often ignores the existence of a continuum of acceptable behavior for either gender. In addition, role performance may require a certain type of behavior in one role set and a totally different behavior in another. Often it is this experience of moving back and forth across roles that creates tension within relationships. For example, a police officer must have the ability to make powerful, instantaneous decisions within this work role. At home, however, the officer must be able to negotiate a relationship with a spouse, be loving, and suspend judgment with his or her children. These role sets (police officer, spouse, and parent) require different types of role performance that might be difficult to navigate. The officer may work with a social work practitioner around the issues of enacting different types of roles within the home and on the job.

Although prescriptions of society are powerful factors contributing to human behavior, they do not subsume the multiple, diverse contributions of simultaneous roles that people enact. These broad categories blur the distinctions between role prescriptions that arise from the individual's particular locale and simultaneous gender, race, and class roles. "Since most people in pluralistic societies participate simultaneously in more than one reference group [a group whose values guide one's actions], the picture becomes more complicated" (Shibutani, 1961, p. 275). In addition, cohort changes in role expectations also blur definition around roles. Acculturation patterns in immigrants will change role expectations from one generation to another; for example, the concept of filial piety has changed across generations of Asians who have moved to the United States. The older generation may define role performance of a caregiver (who culturally is either the daughter or daughter-in-law) differently than that of the younger generation. This discrepancy can create tension within the family and can create potential risk situations such as family discord or emotional abuse (C. J. Ho, Weitzman, Cui, & Levkoff, 2000; Kim, 2001).

Tice (1990) argued that the very use of dichotomous (role) categories is in itself oppressive. For example, feminists have suggested that gender role descriptions convey "the sense of roles being fixed and dichotomous as well as separate but equal" (Hare-Mustin, 1989, p. 72). This approach also implies a harmonious balance of roles and hence may obscure conflict and power differentials (Atwood, 2001; Gottlieb, 1987; Valentich & Gripton, 1984). For example, this power differential may play out in parents treating daughters differently than sons, devaluing and limiting girls' choices (Atwood, 2001). Instead of creating false dichotomies, Hare-Mustin suggested constructing a client–practitioner reality within the therapy that considers the social, economic, and political context and the inequalities of power that accompany class, race, gender, and age. Sands and Nuccio (1992) specifically urged feminists to speak of a particular woman, rather than the universal woman.

Multiple Roles

Role theory holds that all organized groups have a division of labor; the delineation of these labor roles establishes the status structure, for which reciprocal roles, in turn, are defined. All individuals are simultaneously engaged in a multiplicity of roles (e.g., career woman, wife, mother, group spokesperson, daughter, friend, sister, activist, student, and teacher). Individuals enact multiple roles both within as well as across several categories; moreover, they show idiosyncratic variations in their commitments to each role, and these commitments also vary across time for the same individuals.

Multiple role engagement creates opportunity for role conflict and for role strain, but it also creates opportunity for stress-buffering effects of one role to offset stress-creating effects of another role. Until recently, most of the research on caregiving focused on the caregiver's burden, shedding little light on the psychological well-being, benefit, or resiliency conferred by the caregiving experience (Chappell & Reid, 2002; Farran, Keane-Hagerty, Salloway, Kupferer, & Wilken, 1991; Tebes & Irish, 2000). In the caregiver burden approach, the emphasis is on how a person who provides care can alleviate stress and more effectively cope with care expectations, leading to the development of meaningful practice interventions such as respite care and support groups. However, the idea that caregiving is only a burden does not give credence to how people benefit from adversity, thus skewing perceptions of the caregiving experience and limiting the selection of strengths-based interventions (McMillen, 1999; Riley, 2007).

Systems Levels

One way to clarify types of roles is by the levels of group organization to which they apply. Some roles are specific to (a) the microlevel of family and a circle of close friends, (b) the mesolevel of community and other nonfamily small groups or organizations, or (c) the macrolevel of national (or global) organization. Still other roles may be thought of as "cross-cutting" the micro-, meso-, and macrolevels. These tend to be triggered by biological characteristics of the person (e.g., gender, race, and age) and by group dynamics such as scapegoat, caretaker, or leader (see Figure 5.1).

Figure 5.1
Types of roles: levels and categories.

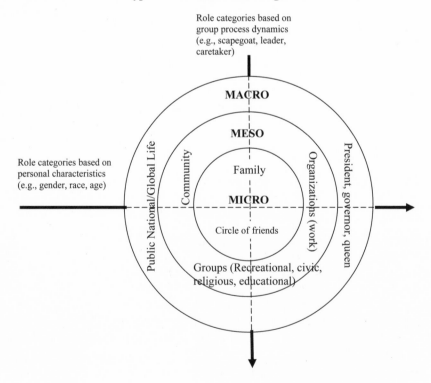

Much of the attractiveness of role theory to social scientists is its applicability to macrolevel (organizational) as well as microlevel (individual) phenomena. For example, a given social structure may be viewed as a system of role behaviors. To the extent to which individuals in a society enact normative role behaviors (i.e., fulfill their socially obligated behaviors), social structure is maintained (Merton, 1957, 1958; Parsons, 1942). An application of this assumption of role theory was provided by Max Weber (1958a, 1958b) and others to explain the organizational model known as bureaucracy. Key to their concept of bureaucracy was rational role assignment based solely on technical qualifications (Merton, 1957); disciplined engagement in prescribed roles by occupants; and a resulting status structure that avoided role confusion, ambiguity, and conflict (Reissman, 1958).

Role theory has primarily focused on the "downward" impact of societal influences on individuals, families, and subgroups; yet individuals impact society through their daily role performance as both carriers and harbingers of societal change (Kluckhohn & Strodtbeck, 1961, p. 38). That is, behavior is shaped by societal expectations, but people also influence societal values for these behaviors. For example, the implications of changing gender roles on family structure cannot be understood without considering socioeconomic and political factors that shape society (Bem, 1979). At the same time, the individual and his or her "changing sex roles are a sound barometer of a more pervasive change within a society" (Lipman-Blumen, 1976, p. 67). An example of this mutual influence between roles and society's shifting attitudes was seen as women entered the workforce in increasing numbers.

Role Variations and Changing Role Expectations

Early contributors to role theory observed that although "roles are culturally determined patterns of behavior, [and the] culture sets the limits of variation of roles, … alternative roles may be available in a given culture" (Sutherland & Woodward, 1940, pp. 250–253). Theorists have suggested that social position, role, authority, and prestige are derived from how people behave toward one another and are *not* predetermined (Blumer, 1969; Mead, 1934). That is, behavior cannot be understood simply by examining status positions, cultural prescriptions, norms, values, sanctions, role demands, and social system requirements. Rather, behavior must be understood by examining social interaction (social role performance) and the meaning that people attribute to it (perception and values attached to social role performance).

Gender Role Expectations

Normative expectations, or common understandings for role behavior, depend, among other things, on gender, age, and class (Davis, 1986). Sex-typing, a process through which a culture socializes male and female children into masculine and feminine adults, is a key example of how culture prescribes behavioral norms for what is appropriate behavior. Bem (1974, 1981, 1987) argued that because each person's culture implicitly and explicitly communicates that gender is one of the most important categories in social life, children develop a "spontaneous readiness to impose a gender-based classification system on social reality, a spontaneous readiness to see reality as carved naturally into gender categories" (1987, pp. 264–265).

Standards for what constitute appropriate emotional behaviors, for example, need to be reevaluated and constructed socially and closely tied to gender role expectations (Shields, 1987). In a study to explore the social meaning of emotional behavior, Shields found a double standard for how people viewed emotionality. For example, in the case of anger, different criteria were applied in evaluating anger displays in men than in women. Such examples illustrate the power of gender role stereotypes in U.S. society. Each gender is evaluated differently on the basis of social norms or beliefs about what is appropriate behavior.

Fatherhood

Expectations about the role of fathers have been changing: Recent studies on paternal roles suggest that the old prototypical division of male and female roles now exemplifies fewer and fewer U.S. families and that society is expanding the ways fathers are perceived (Shears, Summers, Boller, & Barclay-McLaughlin, 2006). The responsibilities of fatherhood now tend to include assuming legal paternity, giving emotional support, and caregiving, as well as providing economic support (Peart, Pungello, Campbell, & Richey, 2006; Strug & Wilmore-Schaeffer, 2003). A father's involvement can encompass a range of behaviors that include the child, such as engaging in face-to-face activities, phoning, or writing, as well as in direct caregiving (Leite & McKenry, 2006).

According to Ihinger-Tallman, Pasley, and Buehler (1995), four conditions must be present in order for a man to develop and maintain the identity of a father:

1. The paternal role must have meaning;
2. The man must have a commitment to the socially prescribed duties of the paternal role;
3. The expectations of the community must foster a father's ability to respond and maintain contact with his children; and
4. A man's peers within the community must reinforce and support paternal behavior (p. 69).

Same-Sex Families

One of the major social and political changes of the past decade has been the advent of a greater array of formalized commitments for same-sex couples. At this point, Massachusetts is the only U.S. state that has legalized same-sex marriage, but several other countries (e.g., Canada, Spain, The Netherlands, and Belgium) have enacted legalized marriage for same-sex couples. Within the United States, several states and localities are establishing civil unions or domestic partnerships that provide some level of social recognition to same-sex couples.

As same-sex couples have greater opportunity to form legitimized partnerships, roles within the context of the committed relationships also begin to change. Issues related to parenting, for example, become less polarized around "mommies" and "daddies." Within same-sex couples, role division is not around gender lines but is more determined by the skills and qualities that each individual brings to the family. Although there continues to be political backlash against same-sex families, empirical evidence indicates that children who are raised in same-sex households do well socially, psychologically, and educationally (Patterson, 2006).

Caregiving Grandparents

Although grandparents have always played a role in taking care of grandchildren, demographers began to note a startling role change around 1990, with increasing numbers of grandparent-headed households. More recent data suggest that this trend has continued (Casper & Bryson, 1998). Based on a national survey of 3,477 grandparents in 1997, Fuller-Thomson and Minkler (2001) found that 10 percent of U.S. grandparents had taken on primary responsibility for raising one or more grandchildren for a period of at least 6 months at some point in the grandparent's lifetime.

Role expectations and the way in which family members anticipate their lives unfolding provide temporal markers for family events (Burnette, 2000; Burton, 1996; Force, Botsford, Pisano, & Holbert, 2000; Waldrop & Weber, 2001). Because there is a general timing to family transitions and events, role transitions that occur according to societal expectation are called *on time*; those that seem to violate the expected timetable are termed *off time*. Grandparent-headed households are generally off time, may cause caregiver stress, and may adversely affect child and grandparent health (Greene, 2005). However, this role can also provide unexpected rewards (Bullock, 2004).

Grandparent-headed households are more likely to be families of color living in the South (Bullock, 2004). Because grandparent caregiving has disproportionate effects on low-income women, it therefore may be seen as a women's issue (Minkler, 1999). The disproportionate representation of African Americans and Latinos, as well as higher poverty rates in kinship care families, raises questions about access to proper health care services and rates of underemployment (Greene, 2008).

Stigmatized Roles

Stigmatized roles are an outcome of social interaction and consist of "discredited," "tainted," or "discounted" attributes (Goffman, 1963, p. 3). Placing an individual in a stigmatized role is understood as a means of creating social distance and justifying social control. Stigmatized individuals (e.g., those who may have a mental or physical disorder, be imprisoned, be unemployed, or be a member of a particular race or religion) are characterized as possessing "an undesired differentness from what the group anticipated" (Goffman, 1963, p. 5). This stigmatization could be used to oppress or usurp power from those individuals. For example, older adults living with HIV may be doubly stigmatized as they are negatively perceived as being old and as having HIV-positive status (Emlet, 2006).

Other stigmatized roles impact the experience of the entire family unit. For example, grandparents who are raising grandchildren because of HIV may experience stigma (Poindexter, 2002). Another example is parents who have sons or daughters with a mental illness, which is a condition that carries a stigma within U.S. culture (Kelly & Kropf, 1995). In both of these family situations, the care providers experience stigma in their role because of a situation that has affected their family system.

Applications of Role Theory to Social Work Practice

The utilization of role theory in the study phase would inevitably induce the worker to investigate what demands for social performance are being made on the client, by whom, and in what social context. (Strean, 1974, p. 329)

Assessment and Intervention

Role theory has been used in social work assessment and intervention to better understand clients' many roles; their prescribed patterns of behavior; and the valuation of associated gratification and stress that may affect social functioning of individuals, families, groups, communities, organizations, and the client–social worker relationship.

Social workers may use a role theory orientation in client assessment to help understand the client's perception of his or her various roles and to discern the impacts of role expectations arising from the client's original and current ethnic group, religion, social class norms, and community norms that in turn affect the client's ideas, feelings, and behavior (Strean, 1974). Role analysis requires that social workers obtain a full picture of the client's person–environment context, allowing them to better understand the complexities and ramifications of the client's presenting problem.

In other situations, social workers may be working with a client who is in a role situation in which he or she has limited understanding of or expectation for effective role performance. For example, Kropf and Robinson (2004) described various pathways into caregiving for custodial grandparents. One, the immediate pathway, involves a rapid and unexpected ascent into the role—as in the case of a violent or sudden death of a parent, abandonment, or incarceration. When a grandparent becomes the immediate care provider for a grandchild, there is a rapid transition from the role of grandparent to parent. These transitions can create a number of challenging issues that can be brought to the attention of the social worker.

A role analysis includes all of the demands that contribute to the client's social functioning. For example, it may include the fact that a woman is a wife, a mother, a daughter, and a worker and that she is expected to fulfill these roles in highly particular ways shaped by the past as well as current context and reference groups. These multiple roles interact with one another, with other ascribed roles (such as race, gender, class, age), with the client's cultural and temporal contexts, and with roles prescribed to others with whom the client is in reciprocal role relationships. A comprehensive role assessment must also include refined knowledge of the normative role expectations specific to the client's geographic locale, which in turn gives further context to each role performance. Hence, role analysis requires the inclusion of socioeconomic, cultural, and biopsychological data (Greene, 2008).

An analysis of family roles may sometimes be accompanied by an examination of family rules. Jackson (1977a, 1977b) first identified family rules as the implicit or explicit norms that organize family interaction and function to maintain a stable system, sometimes limiting expression of a family member's behavior. However, rules are not necessarily stereotypes, cultural preconceptions, or a priori categories about proper role behavior. They are observable patterns of the interactional and collaborative aspects of family relationships, something as simple as "No one interferes with Uncle George's Sunday nap." Although this example is fairly innocuous, problems in functioning often stem from these types of family role patterns. Examples of more problematic relationships that exist within families are the child who becomes the care provider for an alcoholic parent, or the teenager who enacts the violence witnessed between his parents in his relationship with his girlfriend.

A comprehensive social work assessment from the perspectives advanced by role theory includes six dimensions:

1.   *Assessment of role competency as the basis for determining social functioning.* Adapted from work by John O'Brien and Ron Gerhard (1978), Table 5.2 provides guidelines for assessing client role performance. These guidelines offer an approach to client assessment that examines competency in various social roles as the centerpiece of evaluation in a mental health system. Assessing role performance emphasizes the client's current behaviors and opportunities to interact. Such goal-directed behaviors are related to fundamental social needs and expectancies. Most adults have (or need opportunities to have) primary connections in a number of the following role areas:

   • in the immediate household and with extended family,
   • with their spouse or life partner,
   • with child(ren),

- with friends,
- with neighbors and community groups,
- with associates on the job,
- with other teaching and helping persons or agencies (p.16).

2. *Assessment of the impacts of multiple roles and expectations on social functioning.* Because roles prescribe the daily interactions between persons, social workers can also use role analysis to better understand how a client is meeting his or her needs in a complex of roles (Anderson, Carter, & Lowe, 1999). For most people, engagement in multiple and varied roles (assuming that enough of these roles are valued by their social group and society as a whole) characterizes the "good life." Barriers to accepting

Table 5.2
Role Theory: Practitioner's Guide to Assessment

Various role behaviors may be identified as associated with competent social functioning by adults within the context of the sociocultural milieu in which the client lives and the reference groups with which the client is identified. These include:

Household/family member
Performing such tasks as household upkeep and cleaning, shopping for, planning, and preparing meals; laundry, ironing. Sharing and nurturing others.

Self-health care
Self-monitoring one's health status and practicing self care habits including grooming, exercising, and stress reduction. Negotiating the arrangements for medical assistance.

Worker/wage earner
Developing the knowledge and skill for doing selected work and carry these out in a work setting.

Friend
Obtaining satisfactory and nurturing interactions with males and females.

Spouse/life partner
Engaging in interpersonal and intimate communication and shared activities. Giving and receiving mutual support.

Parent
Carrying out responsibilities to provide safety, nurturing/caring, and teaching role responsibilities.

Neighbor/community member
Participating in the life of the social group and immediate environment. Engaging in civic responsibility.

Source. Adapted and expanded from O'Brien, J., & Gerhard, R. (1978). [Original materials prepared for mental health workers in the Georgia Mental Health Institute Consortium, Atlanta].

roles or fulfilling them competently may be evaluated to understand the discontinuities in person–environment fit.

3. *Assessment of the stressors arising from role conflict as an approach to evaluating social functioning.* Contradictory sets of prescriptions for an individual's role performance that require the person to respond simultaneously to incompatible expectations inevitably (a) cause the person to violate someone's expectations and (b) create considerable tension. Parsons (1951) was one of the first to propose that conflicting sets of legitimized role expectations are an obvious source of strain and frustration, causing difficulty for the individual and within the system. Feminists maintain that the expectation that women will simultaneously "be feminine" and "act just like a man" in the workplace holds great potential for role conflict (Freeman, 1984; Hooyman & Cunningham, 1986).

4. *Assessment of the impact on role performance arising from role overload on social functioning. Role overload* refers to occasions when a person must perform a series of roles (tasks) that are not necessarily in conflict but are more demanding than he or she can handle. For example, single mothers in the United States increasingly live with their children in conditions of poverty and are especially vulnerable to role overload. Similarly, single fathers, a small but growing client population, experience similar difficulty with role overload as they juggle child care and home management with wage-earning responsibilities (Kost, 2001; Peart et al., 2006; Shears et al., 2006). Ironically, people may experience role loss, particularly as they age and retire. Because role performance and social participation are important to self-esteem, role loss may have a negative influence on life satisfaction.

5. *Assessment of consequences for individuals and families generated by discomplementarity in family roles.* Social workers are interested in how family members carry out numerous roles on a daily basis, all of which are played out with other family members. By studying the process of the rights and duties associated with family membership and by learning what is desirable in a particular family (e.g., a caregiving family), the social worker can help a family achieve its goals. Understanding mutually dependent and reciprocal roles and how and whether there is a harmonious fit is the key to understanding the family unit (McGoldrick, 1990; Parsons, 1964; Parsons & Bales, 1955). Concerted or joint action is facilitated when people play conventional or well-established roles and share the way in which roles are defined. As long as people agree about the claims and obligations that constitute their respective parts, role reciprocity or cooperation is maintained (Shibutani, 1961). However, this does not mean that all role occupants prosper or benefit equally (McGoldrick, 1989).

6. *Assessment of roles in light of increased cross-cultural sensitivity.* Cross-cultural research has suggested that there may be great differences in how families enact roles (M. K. Ho et al., 2003; Tseng & Hsu, 1991). Among the differences that lead to differential assessment and intervention are those that concern family value systems, sociopolitical histories, role definitions and structures, communication patterns, and relative acculturation to U.S. culture. These differences also affect who a family turns to for help, how a family defines its problem, and the family's specific help-seeking behaviors and expectations.

Difficulties in Role Performance

Assessment eventuates in a mutual understanding of how a client is experiencing challenges in role performance. These challenges stem from the fact that people occupy multiple roles such as parent, child, social worker, wife, mother, or rabbi. Negative outcomes may include the following:

*   *role ambiguity*, arising when a person is uncertain about the behaviors associated with a particular role;
*   *role conflict*, arising when a person has contrary or incompatible demands in several roles, such as providing care to an older parent and getting to work on time;
*   *role incapacity*, existing when an individual cannot perform a role, such as with an injured volleyball team member;
*   *role incongruity*, occurring when two or more people disagree about the expectations for a specific role, such as what makes a "good" spouse;
*   *role overload*, occurring when a person may occupy more roles than he or she can perform adequately, such as when a student who must work and be a parent and wife becomes sick; and
*   *role strain*, arising when an individual experiences too many demands in one role, such as a student having multiple assignments due on one day (Compton, Galaway, & Cournoyer, 2004; Sheafor & Horejsi, 2005).

Family Therapy: Redefining Family Roles

Openness to Role Change

Social workers need to be open to the idea that role expectations vary not only in culturally relative and culturally distinctive ways but, within a given culture, with regard to their clarity and rigidity. When societies (or communities) are relatively stable, a person's status is relatively clear, with limited tolerance for variation. In a rapidly changing society, there is less consensus over rights and duties, and the avenues of advancement or variation are not so clearly marked. When rigidly held role prescriptions are challenged by large numbers of people—as occurs in periods of rapid social change—reactions are stimulated to reaffirm the "old order," and considerable social conflict surrounds role prescription.

Practitioners will undoubtedly come across these conflicts in their social work practice. One example concerns the debate about whether gay couples should be allowed to adopt children, thus fulfilling their desire for parenthood. Role theory suggests that "there is nothing intrinsically negative about changing roles" (Lipman-Blumen, 1976, p. 67). For example, the increase in female-headed households and the greater labor force participation of women signal changing roles for men and women in U.S. society. Although the valuation of these changes may differ widely among different members of the society, the changes themselves are inherently neither good nor bad.

Nonetheless, the impact of rapid social change in the United States on the emergence of social conflict over role prescriptions confronts people daily. During recent decades, demographic, socioeconomic, and political circumstances have changed society dramatically. These changes, coupled with political events such as the Civil Rights movement, the war on poverty, and the women's movement, have brought about a serious reexamination of fundamental beliefs, values, and standards for social behavior. As a result, many of the ground rules for how people behave and express their needs have become ambiguous, if not challenged outright. According to Martin and O'Connor (1989), the phenomenon of ambiguous roles is so common that the "hegemony of a few values, norms, and mores that formerly constrained the actions of family, neighbor, friend, and stranger has given way to a variety of competing standards" (pp. 5–6).

Practice Implications

In the 1950s, when family therapy began, the family was different from how it would become in subsequent years—people married younger and had larger families, and fewer women worked outside the home. These societal conditions became equated with gender role stereotypes that account for much of the polarity and inequality between the two genders and that often underpin the theory base that may continue to intrude in clinical social work practice (McGoldrick, 2002).

Parsons (1954) developed a framework for family role functioning that greatly affected social work practice. His theory focused on how the family functioned and maintained itself as a unit based on the role assignment of its members. His portrayal of the family from the 1940s to the 1960s emphasized a married couple and their children, or the nuclear family. Family was defined as having two major functions: (a) socializing children, or imparting societal values and beliefs; and (b) maintaining the emotional health of family members. Parsons also viewed age and gender as critical organizing features of the family. This translated into two dichotomous roles: (a) the male *instrumental* role, which focused on getting things done by earning a living outside the family; and (b) the female *expressive* role, which emphasized nurturance and caretaking inside the family. The conceptualization of the stay-at-home mother and a breadwinning father became known as "the normal family" (Boss & Thorne, 1989, p. 79).

This view of role definition was challenged because it presented an idyllic view of a family unencumbered by multiple demands or issues of power. This view ignored the conflicting pressures in the body politic and economy of the day, as well as how families were changing with regard to socially expected behavior (Sherman, 1976). Theorists concerned with women's issues called for a reexamination of the changing gender/sex, racial/ethnic, generational, and occupational roles and the effect these contexts have on social work practice (Boyd-Franklin, 2003; Carter & McGoldrick, 2005; Laird & Green, 1999; Slater, 1999).

Theorists and practitioners have worked to change what many believed to be an outdated and romanticized view of the family. This view of the family did not recognize or legitimate a range of family structures, including situations of single women and men, single-parent families, extended families, lesbian and gay households, childless heterosexual couples, elderly unmarried couples, and elderly communities.

The Client–Social Worker Relationship: Clarifying Respective Role Expectations

An understanding of role conflict, in the client, in the worker-client relationship, often in the practitioner's own roles, is especially important because of the strains such conflict can create. (Hamilton, 1958, p. xiii)

One of the most important tasks specific to the assessment phase is clarification of a client's role expectations. By examining the client–social worker relationship as a social system comprising complementary roles, the social worker can better understand the helping process. Does the client expect the social worker to provide advice? A needed resource? The role of the social worker will be prescribed by client expectations, how the social worker perceives the role, and how he or she enacts the role. Therefore, the practitioner must not only consider the role expectations of clients, but must become aware of his or her perceptions, behaviors, feelings, and special vulnerabilities arising from role expectations he or she brings to the therapeutic encounter (Greene, 2008).

Define the Situation

Social theorists have suggested that when an individual enters the presence of another person, he or she attempts to acquire as much information about the other as possible. Such information helps a person *define the situation*; that is, the person's behavior is not a direct response to environment but constitutes a succession of adjustments to interpretations of what is going on (Goffman, 1963; Shibutani, 1961, p. 41). Clients enter into the helping process wondering what is expected of them and what they may expect of the social worker. For example, as clients approach the reception desk of a social agency for the first time, they bring with them a particular notion of how to behave in their role. They even react to the furnishings and the practitioner's office.

Connecting with Clients

Client dissatisfaction can arise when he or she and the social worker have substantially different perceptions of the social worker's activities. Barriers between the client and the social worker can result when client expectations are not clear to social workers and when the client is not aware of the social worker's expectations. Theorists have proposed that, to assist in overcoming these difficulties, the social worker develop a process of educating clients to appropriate role behaviors and clarify the roles of both the client and practitioner. This mutual client–social worker discussion of role expectations and goals—*role induction*—is achieved by determining client expectations, explaining the nature of the helping process, and defining the client–social worker relationship as one of partners seeking a common solution (Hepworth, Rooney, Larsen, Rooney, & Strom-Gottfried, 2005).

How an applicant undertakes the role of client does not clarify how the social worker utilizes knowledge of the client's role-embedded context in cross-cultural social work. By becoming more aware of the client's reference groups, the social worker may more readily understand the client's social standards (expectations of how a role should be played), likely reference group sanctions, and preference for some values and behaviors. Social workers must simultaneously be alert to clues from a client regarding individual differences from the norms of the reference group, the degree of identification with the norms and the group, and potential conflicts arising from the client's efforts to manage an array of role expectations that may be in conflict with his or her current status or family and culture of origin. Practitioners must also examine these issues for themselves.

Greene (2008) contended that understanding the client–social worker encounter as a pattern of reciprocal roles allows social workers to communicate more effectively and to address distortions in the communication process. Such an interactional view recognizes the potential for certain client groups to evoke countertherapeutic responses. That is, certain client groups, such as individuals with mental or physical challenges or older adults, may be more likely to elicit problematic responses from a particular social worker. These responses may be understood as a divergence in role expectations or role enactment between the therapist and client. The social worker's responsibility in cross-cultural practice is to strive to attain this clarity.

References

Anderson, R. E., Carter, L., & Lowe, G. (1999). *Human Behavior in the Social Environment: A Social Systems Approach* (5th ed.). Hawthorne, NY: Aldine de Gruyter.

Atwood, N. C. (2001). Gender bias in families and its clinical implications for women. *Social Work, 46*, 223–236.

Bem, S. (1974). The measurement of psychological androgyny. *Journal of Consulting and Clinical Psychology, 42*, 155–162.

Bem, S. (1979). Theory and measurement of androgyny: A reply to the Pedhazur-Tetebaum and Locksley-Cohen critiques. *Journal of Personality and Social Psychology*, 37, 1047–1054.

Bem, S. (1981). *Bem Sex-Role Inventory Professional Manual*. Palo Alto, CA: Consulting Psychologists Press.

Bem, S. (1987). Gender schema theory and the romantic tradition. In P. Shaver & C. Hendrick (Eds.), *Sex and Gender* (pp. 251–271). Newbury Park, CA: Sage.

Biddle, B. J. (1979). *Role Theory: Expectations, Identities and Behaviors*. New York: Academic Press.

Blumer, H. (1969). *Symbolic Interactionism*. Englewood Cliffs, NJ: Prentice Hall.

Boss, P. G., & Thorne, B. (1989). Family sociology and family therapy: A feminist linkage. In M. McGoldrick, C. Anderson, & F. Walsh (Eds.), *Women in Families: A Framework for Family Therapy* (pp. 78–96). New York: Norton.

Boyd-Franklin, N. (2003). *Black Family Therapy: Understanding the African-American Experience* (2nd ed.). New York: Guilford Press.

Bullock, K. (2004). The changing role of grandparents in rural families: The results of an exploratory study in southeastern North Carolina. *Families in Society*, 85, 45–54.

Burnette, D. (2000). Latino grandparents rearing grandchildren with special needs: Effects on depressive symptomatology. *Journal of Gerontological Social Work*, 33(3), 1–16.

Burton, L. M. (1996). Age norms, the timing of family role transitions, and intergenerational caregiving among aging African American women. *The Gerontologist*, 36, 199–208.

Carter, B., & McGoldrick, M. (Eds.). (2005). *The Expanded Family Life Cycle: Individual, Family, and Social Perspectives* (3rd ed.). Boston: Allyn & Bacon.

Casper, L. M., & Bryson, K. R. (1998). *Co-Resident Grandparents and Their Grandchildren: Grandparent Maintained Families*. Washington, DC: U.S. Census Bureau, Population Division.

Chappell, N. L., & Reid, R. C. (2002). Burden and well-being among caregivers: Examining the distinction. *The Gerontologist*, 42, 772–780.

Compton, B., & Galaway, B. (1989). *Social Work Processes* (4th ed.). Chicago: Dorsey.

Compton, B. R., Galaway, B., & Cournoyer, B. R. (2004). *Social Work Processes* (7th ed.). Belmont, CA: Wadsworth.

Davis, L. V. (1986). Role theory. In F. J. Turner (Ed.), *Social Work Treatment* (pp. 541–563). New York: Free Press.

Deutsch, M., & Krauss, R. M. (1965). *Social Psychology*. New York: Basic Books.

Emlet, C. (2006). "You're awfully old to have this disease": Experiences of stigma and ageism in adults 50 years and older living with HIV/AIDS. *The Gerontologist*, 6, 781–790.

Ephross-Saltman, J., & Greene, R. R. (1993). Social workers' perceived knowledge and use of human behavior theory. *Journal of Social Work Education*, 2, 88–98.

Farran, C., Keane-Hagerty, E., Salloway, S., Kupferer, S., & Wilken, C. (1991). Finding meaning: An alternative paradigm for Alzheimer's disease family caregivers. *The Gerontologist*, 31, 483–489.

Force, L. T., Botsford, A., Pisano, P. A., & Holbert, A. (2000). Grandparents raising grandchildren with and without a developmental disability: Preliminary comparisons. *Journal of Gerontological Social Work*, 33(4), 5–21.

Freeman, J. (Ed.). (1984). *Women: A Feminist Perspective*. Palo Alto, CA: Mayfield.

Fuller-Thomson, E., & Minkler, M. (2001). American grandparents providing extensive child care to their grandchildren: Prevalence and profile. *The Gerontologist*, 41, 201–209.

Goffman, E. (1963). *Stigma: Notes on the Management of Spoiled Identity*. Englewood Cliffs, NJ: Prentice Hall.

Gottlieb, N. (1987). Sex discrimination and inequality. In A. Minahan (Ed.-in-Chief), *Encyclopedia of Social Work* (18th ed., pp. 561–569). Silver Spring, MD: NASW Press.

Greene, R. R. (2005). Students living in the care of grandparents. In C. Franklin, M. Harris, & P. Allen-Meares (Eds.), *The School Services Source Book* (pp. 737–744). New York: Oxford Press.

Greene, R. R. (2008). *Social Work with the Aged and Their Families* (3rd ed.). New Brunswick, NJ: Aldine Transaction.

Hamilton, G. (1958). Foreword. In H. D. Stein & R. A. Cloward (Eds.), *Social Perspectives on Behavior* (pp. xi–xiv). New York: Free Press.

Hare-Mustin, R. T. (1989). The problem of gender in family therapy theory. In M. McGoldrick, C. M. Anderson, & F. Walsh (Eds.), *Women in Families: A Framework for Family Therapy* (pp. 61–77). New York: Norton.

Hepworth, D. H., Rooney, R. H., Larsen, J., Rooney, G. D., & Strom-Gottfried, K. (2005). *Direct Social Work Practice: Theory and Skills* (7th ed.). Belmont, CA: Wadsworth.

Ho, C. J., Weitzman, P. F., Cui, X., & Levkoff, S. E. (2000). Stress and service use among minority caregivers to elders with dementia. *Journal of Gerontological Social Work*, 33(1), 67–88.

Ho, M. K., Rasheed, J. M., & Rasheed, M. N. (2003). *Family Therapy with Ethnic Minorities* (2nd ed.). Thousand Oaks, CA: Sage.

Hollis, F. (1964). *Casework: A Psychosocial Therapy*. New York: Random House.

Hollis, F. (1977). Social casework: The psychosocial approach. In J. B. Turner (Ed.-in-Chief), *Encyclopedia of Social Work* (17th ed., pp. 1300–1308). Washington, DC: NASW Press.

Hooyman, N. R., & Cunningham, R. (1986). An alternative administrative style. In N. Van Den Bergh & L. B. Cooper (Eds.), *Feminist Visions for Social Work* (pp. 163–168). Silver Spring, MD: NASW Press.

Ihinger-Tallman, M., Pasley, K., & Buehler, C. (1995). Developing a middle range theory of father involvement postdivorce. In W. Marsiglio (Ed.), *Fatherhood Contemporary Theories, Research, and Social Policy* (pp. 57–77). Thousand Oaks, CA: Sage.

Jackson, D. D. (1977a). Family rules: Marital quid pro quo. In P. Watzlawick & J. Weakland (Eds.), *The International View* (pp. 21–30). New York: Norton.

Jackson, D. D. (1977b). The study on the family. In P. Watzlawick & J. Weakland (Eds.), *The International View* (pp. 2–20). New York: Norton.

Kang, S. Y. (2006). Predictors of emotional strain among spouses and adult child caregivers. *Journal of Gerontological Social Work*, 47(1/2), 107–131.

Kelly, T. B., & Kropf, N. P. (1995). Stigmatized and perpetual parents: Older parents caring for adult children with life-long disabilities. *Journal of Gerontological Social Work*, 24(1/2), 3–16.

Kim, J.-S. (2001). Daughters-in-law in Korean caregiving families. *Journal of Advanced Nursing*, 36, 399–408.

Kluckhohn, F., & Strodtbeck, F. L. (1961). *Variation in Value Orientations*. Westport, CT: Greenwood Press.

Kost, K. (2001). The function of fathers: What poor men say about fatherhood. *Families in Society*, 82, 499–508.

Kropf, N. P., & Robinson, M. M. (2004). Pathways into caregiving for rural custodial grandparents. *Journal of Intergenerational Relationships*, 2(1), 63–77.

Laird, J., & Green, R. J. (1999). *Lesbian and Gay couples, and Families: A Handbook for Therapists*. San Francisco: Jossey-Bass.

Leite, R., & McKenry, P. (2006). A role theory perspective on patterns of separated and divorced African-American nonresidential father involvement with children. *Fathering*, 4(1), 1–21.

Linton, R. (1936). *The Study of Man*. New York: Appleton-Century-Croft.

Lipman-Blumen, J. (1976). The implications for family structure of changing sex roles. *Social Casework*, 57, 67–79.

Longres, J. F. (2000). *Human Behavior in the Social Environment* (3rd ed.). Belmont, CA: Wadsworth.

Longres, J. F., & Bailey, R. H. (1979). Men's issues and sexism: A journal review. *Social Work*, 24, 26–32.

Martin, P. Y., & O'Connor, G. G. (1989). *The Social Environment: Open Systems Applications*. New York: Longman.

McGoldrick, M. (2002). *Re-Visioning Family Therapy: Race, Culture, and Gender in Clinical Practice*. New York: Guilford Press.

McGoldrick, M. J. (1989). Women through the family life cycle. In M. J. McGoldrick, C. M. Anderson, & F. Walsh (Eds.), *Women in Families: A Framework for Family Therapy* (pp. 200–226). New York: Norton.

McGoldrick, M. J. (1990, October). Presentation at the Georgia State University Professional Continuing Education Series, Atlanta, GA.

McMillen, J. (1999). Better for it: How people benefit from adversity. *Social Work*, 44, 455–468.

Mead, G. H. (1934). *Mind, Self, and Society*. Chicago: University of Chicago Press.

Merton, R. K. (1957). *Social Theory and Social Structure*. Glencoe, IL: Free Press.

Merton, R. K. (1958). Bureaucratic structure and personality. In H. D. Stein & R. A. Cloward (Eds.), *Social Perspectives on Behavior* (pp. 577–584). New York: Free Press.

Minkler, M. (1999). Intergenerational households headed by grandparents: Contexts, realities, and implications for policy. *Journal of Aging Studies*, 13, 199–219.

O'Brien, J., & Gerhard, R. (1978). [Original materials prepared for mental health workers in the Georgia Mental Health Institute Consortium, Atlanta].

Parsons, T. (1942). Age and sex in the social structure of the United States. *American Sociological Review*, 7, 604–616.

Parsons, T. (1951). *The Social System*. New York: Free Press.

Parsons, T. (1954). *Essays in Sociological Theory*. New York: Free Press.

Parsons, T. (1964). Age and sex in the social structure. In R. L. Coser (Ed.), *The Family: Its Structure and Functions* (pp. 251–266). New York: St. Martin's Press.

Parsons, T., & Bales, R. F. (1955). *Family Socialization and Interaction Process*. Glencoe, IL: Free Press.

Patterson, C. (2006). Children of gay and lesbian parents. *Current Directions in Psychological Science*, 15(5), 241–244.

Peart, N., Pungello, E. P., Campbell, F., & Richey, T. G. (2006). Faces of fatherhood: African American young adults view the paternal role. *Families in Society*, 87, 71–83.

Perlman, H. H. (1962). The role concept and social casework: Some explanations. *Social Service Review*, 36, 17–31.

Perlman, H. H. (1968). *Persona: Social Role and Responsibility*. Chicago: University of Chicago Press.

Poindexter, C. P. (2002). "It don't matter what people say as long as I love you": Experiencing stigma when raising an HIV-infected grandchild. *Journal of Mental Health and Aging*, 8, 331–348.

Reid, J., & Hardy, M. (1999). Multiple roles and well-being among midlife women: Testing role strain and role enhancement theories. *Journal of Gerontology: Social Sciences, 54B,* S239–S338.

Reissman, L. (1958). A study of role conceptions in bureaucracy. In H. D. Stein & R. A. Cloward (Eds.), *Social Perspectives on Behavior* (pp. 221–227). New York: Free Press.

Riley, J. (2007). Caregiving: A risk and resilience perspective. In R. R. Greene (Ed.), *Social Work Practice: A Risk and Resilience Perspective* (pp. 239–262). Monterey, CA: Brooks/Cole.

Sands, R. G., & Nuccio, K. (1992). Post-modernization feminist theory and social work. *Social Work*, 37, 489–502.

Sheafor, B. W., & Horejsi, C. R. (2005). *Techniques and Guidelines for Social Work Practice* (7th ed.). Boston: Allyn & Bacon.

Shears, J., Summers, J. A., Boller, K., & Barclay-McLaughlin, G. (2006). Exploring fathering roles in low-income families: The influence of intergenerational transmission. *Families in Society*, 87, 259–268.

Sherman, S. N. (1976). The therapist and changing sex roles. *Social Casework*, 57(2), 93–96.

Shibutani, T. (1961). *Society and Personality*. Englewood Cliffs, NJ: Prentice Hall.

Shields, S. A. (1987). Women, men and the dilemma of emotion. In P. Shaver & C. Hendrick (Eds.), *Sex and Gender* (pp. 229–250). Newbury Park, CA: Sage.

Slater, S. (1999). *The Lesbian Family Life Cycle*. Urbana: University of Illinois Press.

Stein, H. D., & Cloward, R. A. (Eds.). (1958). *Social Perspectives on Behavior.* New York: Free Press.

Strean, H. S. (1974). Role theory. In F. J. Turner (Ed.), *Social Work Treatment* (pp. 314–342). New York: Free Press.

Strug, D., & Wilmore-Schaeffer, R. (2003). Fathers in the social work literature: Policy and practice implications. *Families in Society*, 84, 503–511.

Sutherland, R., & Woodward, J. L. (1940). *Introduction to Sociology*. New York: Lippincott.

Tebes, J. K., & Irish, J. T. (2000). Promoting resilience among children of sandwiched generation caregiving women through caregiver mutual help. *Journal of Prevention & Intervention in the Community*, 20(1/2), 139–158.

Thorne, B., & Yalom, M. (1982). *Rethinking the Family: Some Feminine Questions*. New York: Longman.

Tice, K. (1990). Gender and social work education: Directions for the 1990s. *Journal of Social Work Education*, 26, 134–144.

Tseng, W. S., & Hsu, J. (1991). *Culture and Family Problems and Therapy*. New York: Haworth Press.

Turner, F. J. (1974). *Social Work Treatment*. New York: Free Press.

Valentich, M., & Gripton, J. (1984). Ideological perspectives on the sexual assault of women. *Social Service Review*, 58, 448–461.

Van Voorhis, R. M. (in press). Feminist theories and social work practice. In R. R. Greene (Ed.), *Human Behavior Theory and Social Work Practice*. New Brunswick, NJ: Aldine Transaction.

Waldrop, D. P., & Weber, J. A. (2001). From grandparent to caregiver: The stress and satisfaction of raising grandchildren. *Families in Society*, 82, 461–471.

Weber, M. (1958a). Class states, party. In H. D. Stein & R. A. Cloward (Eds.), *Social Perspectives on Behavior* (pp. 351–362). New York: Free Press.

Weber, M. (1958b). The essentials of bureaucratic organization. In H. D. Stein & R. A. Cloward (Eds.), *Social Perspectives on Behavior* (pp. 564–571). New York: Free Press.

6

A Social Constructionist Approach
with Diverse Populations

Robert Blundo, Roberta R. Greene, and Paul Gallant

Man is an animal suspended in the web of significance he himself has spun, and culture is the name given to this web of meaning. (Geertz, 1973, p. 4)

Social constructionists are part of the postmodern movement, which devalues the search for universal laws and theories, emphasizes localized experiences, and recognizes differences (Fraser, Taylor, Jackson, & O'Jack, 1991; K. J. Gergen, 1999, 2006; Sands & Nuccio, 1992). Social constructionists suggest that local or personal understandings help reduce stereotypes and promote first-hand understanding. Furthermore, they believe that personal meanings and views of social reality grow out of interaction and discourse in daily life experiences (M. M. Gergen & Gergen, 2006). These theorists also recognize that individual and family meanings are "socially constituted within the context of the present sociopolitical juncture" (Lowe, 1991, p. 47). Therefore, social constructivist therapies have the potential "to relate to themes of justice, poverty, gender, politics, and power" (p. 47). Social constructionists also contend that their interest in multiple perspectives emphasizes communal belief systems, an emphasis that is useful in clinical practice with people with diverse group membership (Lax, 1992; McNamee & Gergen, 1992).

The social constructionist concept of culture is the expression of historically shared meanings of a community of people. The meanings emerge within the context of human interaction and are continually transformed during that transaction. Culture does not exist as an entity, even though people often speak of culture as if it has a permanent and unchangeable form. A social constructivist perspective recognizes "cultures as texts ... [that therefore are] differently read, differently construed, by men and women, young and old, expert and nonexpert, even in the least complex societies" (Keesing, 1987, p. 161).

Culture thus is not recognized as a monolithic stereotype of groups of people. Attempts to draw broad cultural pictures of peoples do injustice to any particular individual who does not match this stereotypical version of a culture. For example, although it might be said that Puerto Rican people inhabit the world of two spiritual belief systems—the Roman Catholic Church and *Botanicas* (i.e., the practice of visiting the *espiritistas*, or spiritist mediums, for health and personal problems)—it cannot be assumed that every individual would use either belief system as other members of the community might (Delgado, 1977; see Chapter 10 for a discussion of natural healers). Social constructionists recognize the importance of social workers working within these beliefs and values, especially in terms of the particular meaning for the client (Fong & Furuto, 2001). Depending on the significance of either system, social workers should be able to acknowledge and work with these values and beliefs in support of the work in which they and their clients are engaged. It is important to note that K. J. Gergen (1999) has described the greater threat of "cultural imperialism" when one presumes the Euro-American centric worldview espoused in traditional social work whereby everyone is evaluated by universal truths (p. 17).

Social Work Intervention: Changes in Scientific Paradigm

Science is the constellation of facts, theories, and methods collected in current texts. (Kuhn, 1962/1970, p. 1)

This chapter is the first in the text to emphasize the use of human behavior theory to guide social work intervention with diverse populations. Traditional interventions in social work generally are thought of as social treatment—a process in which the social worker uses selective methods and techniques to enhance social functioning. These interventions may encompass forming supportive relationships, exploring and clarifying feelings, confronting issues, educating, or mobilizing and restructuring support systems (Northen, 1982).

To understand the use of social constructionist theory as a guide to social work practice and its particular approach to intervention, it is first necessary to understand social work's interest in science and the scientific method. Thomas Kuhn (1962/1970) suggested that the history of the philosophy of the social sciences is marked by the reconstruction of prior theory—the reevaluation of prior fact—and therefore is "an intrinsically revolutionary process" involving changes in underlying scientific paradigm (p. 7). Because any particular scientific approach is taken for granted, changes in underlying paradigm are indeed revolutionary. For example, Nicolaus Copernicus destroyed time-honored ideas about terrestrial motion, Isaac Newton did the same in his explanation of gravity, and Albert Einstein rewrote the laws of classical physics.

The social and psychological sciences have undergone a similar change process. The history of the social work profession's relationship to the philosophy of social science centers around a theoretical approach to questions such as the following: What is social reality like? How do people come to know about this reality, and how is this knowledge transmitted? What is human nature basically like? What methodology do people use to study or observe social reality? (Burrell & Morgan, 1979; Martin & O'Connor, 1989).

Two perspectives on how to answer these questions have dominated the social sciences and have been infused into social work thinking. Burrell and Morgan (1979) suggested that most social sciences are either *subjectivist*, claiming that human consciousness exists primarily in the mind; or *objectivist*, believing that it has a real concrete existence. As an expression of Western culture and the era of science, social work presently reflects the faith in progress through systematic observation and analytic reasoning that, for example, has occurred in the study of the physical world and the technologies of medicine. Much of social work rests on the belief that through the discovery of "objective" facts and universal laws, technology will be designed to take care of personal and social ills.

Bertrand Russell (1956) expressed this belief in the possibilities of science and technology when he proclaimed that the social sciences would discover the mathematics of human behavior to be as precise as the underlying working of machines. The rationalists and empiricists proposed this fundamental belief that truth is based on reason and logic. The study of humankind was to be scientific and could thus be understood in the same logical terms as mechanical devices (Priest, 1990; Russell, 1956).

A steady commentary within social work has been concerned with the development of the knowledge base of social work, that is, the perspective through which the profession conceives the relationships of persons and their worlds. Much of this work has been part of a controversy over the implications of positivism or the scientific method and possible alternative perspectives (Bateson, 1979; Goldstein, 1981, 1986b; Gottschalk & Witkin, 1991; Gould, 1984; Haworth, 1984; Heineman, 1981, 1982; Imre, 1982). For example, Bernice Simon (1970) expressed concern that social work lacked the conceptual tools to produce a fundamental knowledge base encompassing the complexity of "man [*sic*] in movement with life" (p. 367). Germain (1970) asserted that this problem was a consequence of "our language, cultural habits of thought, and schooling," which prevented social workers from seeing the world in other than linear cause-and-effect ways (p. 19). Social constructionist and feminist theorists in particular addressed the issue of linear cause-and-effect thinking and questioned the notion of objective discovery and reductionistic cataloging of the human condition and clinical intervention. Instead, they proposed a different concept of reality, one based on the context and meaning for both clients and social workers (Bricker-Jenkins & Hooyman, 1986; Hare-Mustin, 1990; Ruckdeschel, 1985; Saleebey, 1989, 1992; Scott, 1989; Sexton & Griffin, 1997; Tice, 1990; Weick, 1981, 1983, 1987).

Clearly, the mechanistic metaphor of objectivism has dominated the social sciences and social work. As a consequence, social constructionist theorists believe that social work has reduced the complexity of persons living out their lives to either their intrapsychic malfunctions or social and societal causes. For example, Rodwell (1987) claimed that general systems theory is an example of objectivist thinking, which assumes that scientific inquiry can produce a body of universal assumptions and facts that, in turn, facilitate and explain all human behavior. The consequence, according to social constructionists, is that the environment may erroneously be seen as a separate entity that acts on the person or is acted upon by the person in simple linear, billiard-ball fashion. The scientific method goes a step further and assumes that the unique complexity of any single person can be discovered through scientific study.

Social constructionist theorists have tended to criticize the use of such classifications, categories, theories, and treatments (K. J. Gergen, 1982, 1985, 1999, 2006; Mahoney, 1991; Weick, 1983). Social constructionists suggest that a fundamental reality cannot exist independently of the complexity of people's lives as expressed through discourse. In addition, social constructionists have moved away from the objectivist idea that the social worker is an expert who has access to universal truths through which he or she interprets and intervenes in the life of the client. Although values, beliefs, and sociopolitical and ethical issues are assumed to be eliminated from the objectivist process of discovery through use of proper scientific control (Hudson, 1978, 1982), social constructionists believe such values and "subjectivities" are at the heart of the helping process. Social constructionists reject the premise of objectivity because they believe that it forgoes the diversity of individuals, families, and communities, and the interweaving of a particular gender, race, religion, age, socioeconomic position, sexual orientation, and life experience expressed through the discourse of practice.

The emerging alternative perspective to the notion of objectivity and scientific inquiry within social work has been referred to by such labels as *naturalistic, qualitative, heuristic, ethnographic, hermeneutic, phenomenological, postmodern, postpositivist, constructivist,* and *social constructionist*. Although this new body of work has reflected differing emphases, these emphases have had in common a more dynamic and nondeterministic way of thinking of the complexity of human life (Fisher, 1991). For example, Ann Weick (1983, 1986) and Dennis Saleebey (1989, 1992, 2005a, 2005b) have based their work on the fundamental notion that human behavior cannot be isolated into component parts and predicted.

Howard Goldstein (1981, 1983, 1986b, 1990a, 1990b) also proposed an orientation toward social work knowledge that is concerned with the constructs with which individuals define their place in the world. He suggested that the client's conceptualization of his or her life is contained within "the private metaphors and symbols used by the mind to explain the world as it is perceived" (1990b, p. 268). This is the basis for "starting where the client is," that is, for understanding the client's unique version of the world and his or her place in it. In addition, Carolyn Saari (1986a, 1986b, 1991) and Joseph Palombo (1992) incorporated a similar concept of meaning-making within human interaction into psychoanalytic and object-relations-oriented clinical theories.

However, there is no single theory of constructivism or social constructionism conceived by one individual or academic discipline. It was not until recently that various theories and conceptualizations started to coalesce into patterns of ideas shared by members of different disciplines. As understood presently, this perspective represents a convergence of theories, concepts, and research from many areas of study (linguistics, sociology, anthropology, cognitive psychology, ethnology, philosophy, hermeneutics, neurobiology, developmental psychology, epistemology, and biology).

Mahoney (1991) proposed viewing these diverse ideas as a "family of theories about mind and mentation" that share three basic commonalities, in that they

1. emphasize the active and proactive nature of all perception, learning, and knowing;
2. acknowledge the structural and functional primacy of abstract (tacit) over concrete (explicit) processes in all sentient and sapient experience; and
3. view learning, knowing, and memory as phenomena that reflect the ongoing attempts of body and brain to organize (and endlessly reorganize) their own patterns of action and experience (p. 95).

The constructionist perspective taken by K. J. Gergen (2006), Mahoney (1991), Guidano (1991), Hayek (1978), Weimer (1977), and others considers a personal reality to be a "co-creation" of the person and his or her social and physical worlds. The basic sense of a person's being emerges from and is an expression of his or her unique individual history within the dialogical context of the community of others and the physical world. Social constructionism focuses on the social realities as a communal process. As so aptly stated by Kenneth Gergen (2006), "Social constructionist dialogues challenge the individualistic tradition, and invite an appreciation of relationship as central to human well-being. It is not the individual mind in which knowledge, reason, emotion and morality reside, but in the relationship" (pp. 18–19).

This brief overview of the kinds of contributions to this family of theories referred to as *social constructionist* demonstrates the diverse nature of the development of social constructionist thought. Presently, emphasis is on viewing language use or discourse in the context of social interaction, including the interaction of social work intervention. The concern is with how, through language, each person weaves a unique narrative or story about his or her life in the context of others and societal constraints (Sarbin, 1986). For example, anthropologist Clifford Geertz (1973) presented culture as a social system of shared symbols or language that provides the context for meaning and structure expressed through language and other actions.

In light of these powerful ideas, many social work theorists and practitioners are undergoing a fundamental shift in thinking about what intervention entails and its implications for the diversity of individuals and groups with which it is concerned. The following section provides the basic premises that underlie a social constructionist perspective of social work intervention and issues of diversity.

Basic Assumptions

> *The First Wave in psychotherapy was pathology-based. The Second Wave was problem-focused or problem-solving therapy. The Third Wave was solution-focused or solution-oriented. The Fourth Wave is what is emerging now. Only no one has a good name for it yet. (W. H. O'Hanlon, 1993, p. 3)*

The social constructionist approach to social work practice draws on a multi-faceted conceptual base that addresses how people think about and organize their worlds (Berlin, 1980, 1983, 2002; Fisher, 1991; Mahoney, 1988). In general, social constructionists tend to make four assumptions:

1. The manner in which people study the world is based on available concepts, categories, and scientific or research methods; these categories are a product of language.
2. The various concepts and categories that people use vary considerably in their meanings and from culture to culture as well as over time.
3. The popularity or persistence of certain concepts and categories depends on their usefulness rather than on their validity; ideas tend to persist because of their prestige or congruence with cultural values.
4. The way in which people describe or explain the world is a form of social action that has consequences; for example, the consequences of theories built on male experiences may deny women's values and processes (K. J. Gergen, 1985; see Table 6.1).

Social constructionists have proposed that no final, true explanation of the world, or client lives, can be found (Sluzki, 1990). Rather, there are multiple realities, and the purpose of inquiry is to gather conceptualizations of these realities manifested and considered in the social worker–client encounter. These constructs reflect the context of the lives of both client and therapist. Jenkins and Karno (1992) noted that "cross-cultural psychiatric literature of the past several decades has documented substantial cultural differences in conceptions of psychosis, display of emotion, behavioral rules and norms" (p. 19). For example, the importance of the concept of *confianza* (trust) and the interpersonal space that reflects respect for some Puerto Rican clients must be understood by the social worker (Morales, 1992). Understanding must encompass an appreciation and recognition of communal processes and not classify client issues in an oppressive or pejorative manner (Fong & Furuto, 2001; Fruggeri, 1992).

The social constructivist perspective asserts that people are active creators of their experience through the medium of language and not merely passive recorders of an external world. The world does not consist of things out there to be passively seen, experienced, and learned. The experience of "out there"

Table 6.1
Constructivist Theory: Basic Assumptions

- People, as biological organisms, manifest a biological imperative to differentiate and categorize the stimuli they receive.
- People actively construct or create meaning over time through interaction with other people and action with the environment.
- Language is a particular form of action. Through language, people are able to contemplate and self-evaluate events and construct personal meanings.
- People are able to consider alternative meanings because those new versions of reality are less disruptive to their sense of personal integrity.
- Emotions and cognition are interrelated manifestations of personal meanings in the context of the person's life and the moment.
- The construction and reconstruction of the core of personal meanings is experienced by the person as a sense of self.
- The sense of self is reconstructed as the core of meanings or life narrative is rewritten.
- The formation of meaning and the use of language are forms of communal action. Therefore, people develop systems of meanings called culture. A sociocultural system is a meaning-processing system through dynamic social exchange.

is the result of a person's biological structure "bringing forth a world" though discourse (Maturana & Varela, 1987, p. 35).

From this perspective, there is no such thing as a single or universal view of reality, but a reality constructed as an outcome of the biological structure and as a manifestation of a person's system of beliefs and social context at the moment through such dialogical processes as the interview (Watzlawick, 1984; see Chapter 2). Within the uniqueness of personal constructs it must be recognized that "phenomenological day-to-day [contexts] of race, language, class, gender, and age" emerge in each individual's recognition of himself or herself and the individual's relationship with his or her world (Rivera & Erlich, 1992, p.7). Both social worker and client reflect in their actions the diversity of their respective experiences.

From their beginnings, people act on the world, creating distinctions out of the enormous complexity of biological stimuli its structure is capable of organizing. The distinctions and classifications that emerge from people's actions are known as knowledge (Efran, Lukens, & Lukens, 1990; Maturana & Varela, 1987). Knowledge and meaning participate in the emerging patterns of experience as they form the forever-evolving perspective or core meanings from which the sense of order and consistency of one's own self and world are created and maintained. A person construes himself or herself in the world in a particular way by selectively attending, perceiving, interpreting, and integrating stimuli as meanings are generated consistent with the evolving core of meanings. This core is the emerging sense of self in the world. It is within the context of this most central and dominant core of meanings, as the individual's personal reality is constructed, that thoughts, affect, and behavior arise. A fundamental consequence of this biological imperative is that each individual occupies a unique reality reflecting his or her own biological propensities, history of personal experience, and the myths and traditions of community.

Biological Propensities

Each person comes into the world with unique sensitivities or temperaments (Markus, 1977; Nisbett & Ross, 1980; Pepitone, 1949; Schacter, 1964; von Glaserfeld, 1984; Weimer, 1977). People are biologically "wired" differently (Mahoney, 1991). For example, one child may sleep through the night, respond with an inviting smile, and act at ease with contact, whereas another child may awaken during the night, act fretful or cry, and stiffen when approached. The parent or caretaker will have his or her own interactional style that will result in a unique encounter between him or her and the child. A particular caretaker may respond to the first child with satisfaction and intimacy but respond to the second child with less satisfaction and connectedness. Thus, the biological disposition may set the possibilities for the experience between the caretaker and the child, and the consequence will be a part of the evolving relationship between them and, later, others (Guidano, 1991).

Tiefer (1987) suggested that, in addition to caregiving behaviors, human sexuality is another behavior that can be examined from a social constructionist perspective. She contended that a universal norm or single social–historical context cannot be used to define or understand human sexuality. Rather, biological sexuality is the necessary precondition to a set of potentialities transformed by societies.

History of Personal Experiences

Humans cannot know the world except through the self-referential context of perceived distinctions or meanings (Guidano, 1991). It is through the "eyes" of constructed meanings that each person views himself or herself and the world. Meanings are founded on the distinctions each person makes of the stimuli he or she engages. As a consequence of the embedded nature of constructs in language and discourse, people take for granted the reality of the world as differentiated and expressed in language and thus perceived (A. J. Stewart, Franz, & Layton, 1988). It is difficult for people to imagine it otherwise. It is on the basis of meanings attached to these perceived differences that decisions are made and actions are taken that affect people. A significant example is a person's skin color. Rivera and Erlich (1992) provided a poignant example of the strength of constructs in limiting understanding and of their power to act on others:

Middle-class Asians, Latinos, or African Americans are still viewed as minorities because of a most easily identified characteristic: skin color. Good clothes and an elegant briefcase are not much help when you need a cab in the middle of the night in Chicago or Washington, D.C. (p. 6)

In a similar manner, a person can experience a complex social occurrence from his or her unique perspective and interpret its meaning differently than anyone else. The history of personal experiences evolves over time, creating a perspective of idiosyncratic expectancy based on the accumulated picture of one's self in relation to the world, that is, a perspective that should reflect the diversity of an individual's personal life history. The basic concepts that account for these processes and their consequences are meaning, language and narrative, and mind and knowing.

Meaning

A fundamental premise of constructivist thinking is the idea that people construct meaning out of the jangle and dissonant chords of stimuli impinging at every moment (K. J. Gergen, 1999, 2006; Gordon, 1964; Mahoney, 1988). Meaning denotes the implications, effect, tenor, and intent of its referent. In this sense, meaning represents a form of distinction (see Chapter 3 for a discussion of symbolic interactionism). Meaning thus represents a person's ability to separate out and characterize the world. In this way, the person structures his or her world and attributes significance to the makeup of that structure. Meaning making represents a fundamental process by which people engage in and experience their existence in the world. Kelly (1955) observed that "man [*sic*] creates his own way of seeing the world in which he lives, the world does not create [perceptions] for him" (p. 12).

Language and Narrative

Meanings about the self in the world occur through language—any means of conceptualizing, representing, and communicating experience. Metaphorical representations expressed in narrative form provide the means for organizing and structuring the person's life experience in language (Polkinghorne, 1988; Sarbin, 1986; Shotter, 1993). The story a person constructs about his or her existence provides that person with a coherent understanding or meaning of his or her life as lived and a context from which to view the present and future.

Schank and Abelson (1990) suggested that these stories or scripts are means of coherently organizing experience into personally meaningful conceptualizations of one's life. The person approaches the world through the eyes of the organization of previous experiences expressed in the form of the metaphorical narrative. A story or script is thematic in that it contains not only content but a relationship between the details. In this way, a story acts as the context for understanding a familiar situation by recalling similar content and understanding novel situations by matching both details and the thematic nature of the story.

Lakoff and Johnson (1980) stated that people will

> define [their] reality in terms of metaphors and then proceed to act on the basis of
> the metaphors. [They] draw inferences, set goals, make commitments, and execute
> plans, all on the basis of how [they] in part structure [their] experience, consciously
> or unconsciously, by means of metaphor. (p. 158)

Consider, for example, the emergent shift in African American conceptualization of understanding self in relation to an oppressive society, which has been reflected in the change from the use of *Negro* to *Black* and later to *African American*. These are not merely changes in words used but changes revealed through the experiences of resisting oppressive and discriminatory practices. These metaphors represent an emergent meaning out of a people's experience and provide a way of considering oneself in relation to others on one's own terms.

Mind and Knowing

The biological process called *mind* fills in and elaborates on the sensations available to a person. The mind enables a person to maintain a sense of consistency and steadiness in the midst of the shifting and changing world (Guidano, 1987). People are continually involved in the process of creating notions about their world to anticipate and predict its circumstances. A person can be thought to be continually constructing and reconstructing theories about his or her world (Weimer, 1977).

In turn, the theory or theories of the world form the context from which a person selects in order to see and interpret his or her world. From this perspective, knowing the self and the world is acting on the sensations encountered at any particular moment (Maturana & Varela, 1987). The person knows by organizing the stimuli based on their previous organizations, stories, or scripts within the context of the moment.

Myths and Traditions of the Community

Language expresses the mind's construction of a person's life in the world. Language is a communal act and reflects both human biology and the communal relationships between persons. People are born physically helpless and dependent on a caretaker, who in turn has come of age within a community of other people with whom he or she shares a language. Through relationships, an infant acquires not only the means of using the caretaker's language but the meanings embedded in that language. Language expresses the myths and traditions of the family and community of which the growing child is a part. As a result, language provides individuals with the means of organizing the world and their relationship with others in terms of the experiences of their shared community. What is called *culture* is shared experiences, values, and beliefs of the community, present and past, that are contained in the language and in the stories or traditions used by the person to understand himself or herself and the world in which he or she lives. Wentworth and Wentworth (1997) noted that from this perspective, culture is the "grammar that organizes the bits and pieces of life and thereby makes them into meaningful wholes" (p. 42).

Each person is continually constructing a life narrative reflective of both his or her own unique life experiences and the prevailing theories about possible lives that are a part of that person's communal traditions (Bruner, 1987; Schank & Abelson, 1990; Shotter, 1993). Each person lives a life that is original and yet is within the broadest boundaries of the community of shared possibilities of a life to be lived. Although the context of an individual's life or culture can thus constrain change, people also bring about change through social discourse and a reconstruction of ideas and beliefs (Gelfand & Fandetti, 1986; Malinowski, 1954; Myerhoff, 1978).

Change and Intervention

The narrative view holds that it is the process of developing a story about one's life that becomes the basis of all identity and thus challenges any underlying concept of a unified or stable self. (Lax, 1992, p. 71)

The Self and Change

The social work profession's attempt to understand the consequences of the practitioner intervention or client change has had at its core the traditions of a mechanistic scientific theory. This perspective assumes, as noted earlier, that there is a reality that can be objectively measured, tested, and verified independent of the observer and context. Underlying varied methodologies and techniques is the assumption that interventions are concrete entities that somehow exist independently of a particular encounter or context. Problems exist as if they are entities to be discovered, identified, and measured through objective investigation and testing. Once a problem is objectively studied and understood, then the correct solution can be applied.

Schon (1983) referred to this basic premise as the myth of technical rationality. A consequence of this scientific perspective is that it fails to provide a body of knowledge for understanding the processes involved in what transpires during the encounter between the social worker and the client (Gordon, 1983; Stiles, 1988). Schon's work has demonstrated that applying expert technical understanding (i.e., methodology) can result in misunderstanding the essence of the client's situation. It was the contention of Rice and Greenberg (1984) that this "preoccupation with the role of the therapist and theoretical orientation used has led to ... losing sight of the mechanisms of change with the client. It is the client who changes" (p. 18). To understand the change processes, a social worker must concern himself or herself with the client's conceived world.

A consistent theme in the literature is that change necessitates transformations of meaning about the self and the world, although the theories of explanation and methodology differ. For example, Rogers and Dymond (1957) described change as the "emergence into awareness of new perspectives of self" (p. 425). Sanville (1987) contended that change is the creation and recreation of the self throughout one's life, and intervention is the vehicle for freeing this process in the client. In her text on clinical social work treatment, Saari (1986a) stated that intervention involves the client's "organizing of old meanings into newly constructed consciousness [or] new meanings" (p. 27).

Significant changes within the person are the consequence of transformations in the fundamental core of meanings about the self in relationship to others and within the context of one's life. The person experiences himself or herself as the same person in encounters from day to day and over a lifetime. At the same time, the context of that person's life is in constant flux, as each forthcoming encounter has yet to be experienced. To alter the fundamental core of meanings is to alter the person's felt experience of what it is to be himself or herself and to be in his or her world. Alternative versions of how a person should be or how that person should live a life challenge the individual's experience of a sense of self and reality.

Language is not only a means to change: It is the means by which persons categorize, explain, and predict their world. Therefore, from this point of view, the client's hesitation, reluctance, or uncertainty to take on the social worker's perspective is not resistance but client maintenance of the continuity of experience.

Language is also an action and, in many instances, contains power differentials between people. For example, Elliot Liebow's (1967) work *Tally's Corner* challenged the dominant culture's belief that the poor demonstrate an inability to defer gratification. Liebow demonstrated that this statement, although viewed as an important sociological "fact," does not reflect the issues of poverty or the lives of any particular people. Rather, this sociological language of the dominant culture blames the poor for their plight.

In fact, according to Lee (1980), language use by social workers can be an aggressive and demeaning act toward their clients. She commented that "how we talk and think about a client or, perhaps more important, a 'class' of clients, determines how we act toward the client" (p. 580). It is not unusual for social workers in community mental health settings to use professional jargon in referring to clients who do not cooperate with the rules and process of treatment. Such clients often are described as "resistant," "uncooperative," "not ready for treatment," or "borderline," as seen in the following case study:

> During a clinical conference in a mental health clinic in a large city in the Northeast, social workers were insistent that a particular female client was definitely a "passive-dependent personality and resisting treatment" because she would not recognize the importance of taking specific assertive actions the social worker had decided were needed. All the social workers at the meeting knew that these actions were the "healthy" thing for her to do and concurred with her pathology. Then, one social

worker pointed out that she was from a small rural town in the South and had lived there for 30 years before moving. This social worker, having lived in a town similar to that of the client, pointed out that the client and her family might view what was being asked of the client as being "uppity" and therefore unacceptable. The social worker was able to identify this issue with the client and their work took a different turn. Later, the client talked about her sessions, and confided that she had felt both pressured and stuck during the earlier part of their work together.

It is evident from this discussion that it is not only the client's construction of meaning but the social worker's personal and professional meanings that must be revealed if a truly collaborative exchange is to occur.

Interventions: Changed Meanings

White and Epston (1990) noted that "persons who seek therapy frequently experience an incapacity to intervene in a life that seems unchanging; they are stymied in their search for new possibilities and alternative meanings" (p. 36). An acceptable outcome of intervention would be the generation of alternative narratives that "enable [a person] to perform new meanings, bringing with them desired possibilities—new meanings that [the person] will experience as more helpful, satisfying, and open-ended" (p. 15).

According to Shafer (1983), psychoanalysts are "people who listen to the narrations of analysands and help them to transform these narrations into others that are more complete, coherent, convincing, and adaptively useful than those they have been accustomed to constructing" (p. 240). That is, therapists coauthor a new version of the original story, also known as *restorying*. The social worker's role is to ask questions that bring forth "alternative landscapes" and facilitate the "reauthoring" process (White, 1993, p. 41). All interventions are a variation on this process.

The social constructionist approach requires that practitioners adopt a "not-knowing position" (H. Anderson & Goolishian, 1992, p. 29). A practitioner must be diligent about his or her own assumptions about the client. Although the social worker must be aware of preconceived theoretical positions, he or she should rely on the client's views and explanations. This perspective is particularly congruent with empowerment models of cross-cultural practice (Fong & Furuto, 2001; Greene, 2008; Lum, 2007). Practitioners should not place people in predetermined social categories but must take the stance of learner to achieve cultural congruence with clients.

The constructivist perspective views intervention, then, as an opportunity for the social worker and client to explore together the narratives the client has evolved to give meaning to his or her life. The social worker must appreciate that his or her own understanding about the client reflects personal narratives or contexts. It is through language that collaboration is expressed in personal meanings and exchanged in conversation. From this perspective, intervention is not a treatment as much as it is a dialogue in which multiple meanings are shared and from which cultural meanings are drawn from both client and social worker. Change, then, is a rewriting of the personal narrative so that a person sees himself or herself and the world from a different perspective. This conversation is taking place through language reflective of the diversity of each participant. Each client's cultural diversity and social differences come to light in the client–social worker dialogue.

At times, the client seeks assistance because he or she has identified a personal struggle ensuing from living, for instance, a bicultural life. Such was the situation for a twenty-year-old Puerto Rican woman attending college. She had attempted to come to terms with her family and their opposition to her decision to move out of the neighborhood and start a career. The issue was not one of autonomy and individuality, which the dominant culture had decided was the "natural" order of things, nor was it what was best for her or who was right or wrong. Rather, the struggle was how to maintain what was important to her about her family and culture and, at the same time, express different values she had come to embrace while growing up in the United States. Issues of dating, marriage, and living on her own were only a few with which she had to come to terms in her efforts to maintain good relations with her family and also live a life that differed from her family and community's expectations. The issue for the social worker is that of appreciating and understanding the client's struggle in the language of the client. In this example, the social worker participated with the client as the client re-authored her cultural context as she had lived it and as she may live it in her present and future life.

Restoring People's Lives

Social constructionists have suggested that it is important to value a client's experiences "without trying to rid clients of those [seemingly negative] experiences directly" (W. H. O'Hanlon, 1993, p. 14). The focus is on client ideas, beliefs, frames of reference, and language and how these relate to the presenting issue. Clients are urged not to blame themselves but to change their stance toward the problem (T. Anderson, 1991; Auerswald, 1986; Durrant & Coles, 1991; Goldstein, 1986a, 1986b).

One way of restorying (i.e., developing new meanings) is through deconstruction (Derrida, 1976, 1978). *Deconstruction* is a technique in which the practitioner disrupts typical frames of reference, listens for multiple meanings, and reconstructs new meanings with the client (White, 1993, p. 34). Feminist therapists Hare-Mustin and Marecek (1988) contended that practitioners must challenge dominant norms related to gender through nontraditional forms of intervention such as deconstruction. In addition, Laird (1989), a family-focused theorist who wrote about restorying women's self-constructions, contended that, generally, women's stories have not been told by women but have been defined by men. The deconstruction of and retelling of women's lives is at the heart of the feminist movement (see Chapter 11). Similarly, Taggart (1989) argued that the struggle by women to define themselves has been held back by "the standard theories [that] routinely construct" the female position (p. 100). He believed that limited socially constructed knowledge about women, particularly women's roles in families, needs to be addressed in family therapy approaches (see Chapter 8).

An example of deconstruction is a cartoon of the Holocaust drawn by Spiegelman (1991) titled *Maus*. In the cartoon, which portrays Nazis as cats and Jewish people as mice, Spiegelman shocks the reader out of any sense of familiarity with the events described. Instead, he approaches the unspeakable through the diminutive; thus, externalizing events generates what might be thought of as "counter-language" (White, 1993, p. 39).

Knowledge and Power

Client stories generally tend to be directed by the knowledge of the dominant culture and may describe oppressive experiences (Polanyi, 1958; White, 1993). The way in which such knowledge is construed may give some individuals and groups power to dominate others (Foucault, 1965, 1978, 1980). According to Poster (1989), "To begin a discourse is to enter into a political world" (p. 50). One such argument about the political nature of knowledge concerns the revised third edition of the *Diagnostic and Statistical Manual of Mental Disorders* (*DSM–III–R*) published by the American Psychiatric Association (1987). Carolyn Cutler (1991) contended that *DSM–III–R* reflects the differential power-based relationship between the social worker and the client. She stated that this differential relationship is "based on the clinician's desire to see clients as other than themselves" (p. 157). Consequently, the client so labeled often becomes depersonalized and powerless (Rosenhan, 1984).

Tomm (1990) argued against pathologizing people through labeling and segregating. It is important that when considering the labeling of clients, practitioners remember that "truth" is often historical and can not stand apart from culture. For example, use of the term *learning disabled* invites a person who is so labeled to view himself or herself as less than whole and avoids an examination of contextually oriented interventions (B. Stewart & Nodrick, 1990).

How a practitioner defines truth or insight supports particular social/political arrangements (Efran et al., 1990; Kleinman, 1973). When knowledge is seen as universal or essentialist, it can be institutionalized in oppressive ways (Lowe, 1991; Lum, 2007; Saleebey, 2005a). The practitioner listens within his or her own "convictions, and puts them in a cultural context.... [Therefore, the helping process always] stems from the therapist's personal history, cultural context, and theoretical orientation" (Cecchin, 1992, p. 93). Hence, therapists must "become responsible for their own actions and opinions ... to dare to use their resources to intervene, to construct rituals, to reframe situations, behaviors, and ideas for both the client and themselves" (pp. 92–93).

For example, de Amorin and Cavalcante (1992) used a combination of constructionist narrative and puppet drama to counter the stories of stigmatized individuals—developmentally disabled adults—who faced myths of deficiency:

> Using a social constructionist perspective in our work we have encouraged persons labeled as "developmentally disabled" to reconstruct their personal narratives, socially re-examining the misconceptions and/or myth-conceptions that have caused their segregation. (p. 149)

The Social Worker's Role

Social constructionist theory is not a theory of universal stages, such as Erikson's (1974). Stage theories are considered static insofar as they tend to represent the attitudes and beliefs of a culturally derived way of conceiving of human development at a particular time in social history. In contrast, social constructionist theory does not impose a cultural- or temporal-bound model of human development. Rather, the theory provides the social worker with a seemingly homogeneous group (ethnic, religious, geographical, political, etc.), that is, a means to understand a particular individual within his or her sociocultural context (see Table 6.2).

The social worker listens to the client's story with curiosity and openness, acknowledges his or her own assumptions and beliefs, and attempts to refrain from quickly interpreting the client's story. In addition, the social worker does not assume that he or she knows what the client means. This form of sensitivity protects the social worker from potentially stereotyping the client's culture. This intervention approach stems from the perspective that any time practitioners set up predetermined assumptions about a group, they are evaluating those particular clients on the basis of an artificial stereotype—not all Italians are the same, not all Blacks are the same. Familiarity, even if based on the latest descriptions of a particular culture, holds the danger of becoming a template by which clients are measured.

Social constructionists appreciate differences, but in terms of the particular meanings expressed by the clients. Contained in the meaning is a particular person's experiences of gender, race, socioeconomic and religious background, and so forth, lived within the context of all levels of social structure: family, neighborhood, community, region, and country. Understanding client meaning also includes understanding the client's relationships with other groups and social systems.

The social worker starts where the client is and remains open to the client's story. In addition, the social worker is a collaborator, learning anew with each client what it is like to be, for example, this African American man, this American Indian woman, this southern White woman, this northern Jewish man, or this White Methodist man. The uneasy task is to initially take a learning stance with the client rather than portraying oneself as an expert who knows all about

Table 6.2
Guidelines for Social Workers Using a Constructionist Approach

- The social worker takes a stance of unconditional respect for the uniqueness of each client and the context of the client's life. The social worker recognizes that both he or she and clients respond to situations in idiosyncratic ways that reflect their experiential history, biological propensities, and the community of shared meanings embedded in the language of their day-to-day lives.
- The social worker makes an effort to be aware of his or her preconceived ideas (both personal and theoretical) about who the client is, what the problem is, and how the client should be helped, and refrains from imposing those ideas on the client. The social worker takes the stance of open curiosity and interest in the client's life narrative and the issue as perceived by the client.
- The social worker acknowledges that the context of the therapeutic setting by its very structure and procedures reflects the values and beliefs of the community sanctioning the work to be done.
- The social worker respects the client's personal reality and the maintenance of this reality as a means of strengthening client integrity and the world as the client knows it.
- The social worker appreciates that the issues will be resolved as a result of a collaborative understanding, shared meanings, and the generation of alternative meanings. The social worker does not support unjust and prejudicial interpersonal or institutional actions. In these instances, the social worker seeks alternative meanings to alleviate a negative condition.
- Therapy involves an ongoing exchange of client–social worker meaning that shifts as new information is added. Meaning is generated through this communication.
- To help people with interpersonal functioning, it is important to assist them in taking the perspective of the other person.
- The process of social work interventions is to provide a situation conducive for alternative meanings to be shared, understood, and used by the client and the social worker. Client-defined problems can be resolved as alternative meanings or perspectives emerge.

diversity and what the problem is. This task can be uncomfortable until the practitioner recognizes that it is his or her responsibility to hear the client's story. The social worker's ability lies in enabling the communication to inform him or her about who the client is and how the client understands himself or herself in the particular context of systems or community. The collaboration continues as the social worker and the client reassure themselves that there is a mutual level of understanding of how the client lives his or her life and what work might need to be done to meet the client's needs. The practitioner not only respects the client's construction of the world but emphasizes the client's ideas as to possible outcome goals and means of bringing forth these solutions (De Jong & Berg, 2002; B. O'Hanlon & Rowan, 1999).

Overall, social constructionists address the fundamental issues of diversity as it is expressed in the life of a particular person or group of persons with whom the social worker is engaged in work. It is diversity as it is lived, reflecting the temporal and contextual meanings for a particular client or client group. Social constructionists recognize that the agency, its structure, and its organizational values and goals may not necessarily reflect the needs of the client. Agencies, polices, and theoretical perspectives reflect the value-laden social scripts of how and where to get help. The structures of time, physical setting, and proper procedures all represent a fundamental belief in what is the "normal" or "right" way to live a life. Those who are a part of the dominant culture or those who successfully function within that culture do not recognize the embedded values as anything but reality.

A social constructionist perspective challenges the social worker to move away from the comfort of knowing and from technique to join with clients in discovering meanings and beliefs that the social worker, client, or both have assumed to be the only way to live. Diversity is an important and compelling example of the significance of difference. As each person respects another's version of life, he or she can recognize that there are multiple perspectives by which one can live.

References

American Psychiatric Association. (1987). *Diagnostic and Statistical Manual of Mental Disorders* (3rd ed., rev.). Washington, DC: Author.

Anderson, H., & Goolishian, H. (1992). The client is the expert: A not-knowing approach to therapy. In S. McNamee & K. J. Gergen (Eds.), *Therapy as Social Construction* (pp. 25–39). Newbury Park, CA: Sage.

Anderson, T. (1991). *The Reflecting Team: Dialogues and Dialogues about the Dialogues.* New York: Norton.

Auerswald, E. H. (1986). Thinking about thinking in family therapy. In H. C. Fishman & B. L. Rosman (Eds.), *Evolving Models for Family Change* (pp. 13–27). New York: Guilford Press.

Bateson, G. (1979). *Mind and Nature: A Necessary Unity.* New York: Bantam Books.

Berlin, S. (1980). A cognitive-learning perspective for social work. *Social Service Review*, 54, 537–555.

Berlin, S. (1983). Cognitive-behavioral approaches. In A. Rosenblatt & D. Waldfogel (Eds.), *Handbook of Clinical Social Work* (pp. 1095–1119). San Francisco: Jossey-Bass.

Berlin, S. (2002). *Clinical Social Work Practice: A Cognitive Integrative Perspective.* New York: Oxford University Press.

Bricker-Jenkins, M., & Hooyman, N. (1986). *Not for Women Only: Social Work Practice for a Feminist Future.* Silver Spring, MD: NASW Press.

Bruner, J. (1987). Life as narrative. *Social Research*, 54(1), 11–22.

Burrell, G., & Morgan, G. (1979). *Sociological Paradigms and Organisational Analyses.* London: Heinemann.

Cecchin, G. (1992). Constructing therapeutic possibilities. In S. McNamee & K. J. Gergen (Eds.), *Therapy as Social Construction* (pp. 86–95). Newbury Park, CA: Sage.

Cutler, C. (1991). Deconstructing the *DSM III. Social Work*, 36, 154–157.

de Amorin, A., & Cavalcante, G. F. (1992). Narrations of the self: Video production in a marginalized subculture. In S. McNamee & K. J. Gergen (Eds.), *Therapy as Social Construction* (pp. 149–165). Newbury Park, CA: Sage.

De Jong, P., & Berg, I. K. (2002). *Interviewing for Solutions* (2nd ed.). Monterey, CA: Brooks/Cole.

Delgado, M. (1977). Puerto Rican spiritualism and the social work profession. *Social Casework*, 58, 451–458.

Derrida, J. (1976). *Of Grammatology to G. C. Spivak*. Baltimore: Johns Hopkins University Press.

Derrida, J. (1978). *Writing and Difference*. Chicago: University of Chicago Press.

Durrant, M., & Coles, D. (1991). Michael White's cybernetic approach. In T. C. Todd & M. D. Selekman (Eds.), *Family Therapy Approaches with Adolescent Substance Abusers* (pp. 137–174). Boston: Allyn & Bacon.

Efran, J. S., Lukens, M. D., & Lukens, R. J. (1990). *Language Structure and Change: Frameworks of Meaning in Psychotherapy*. New York: Norton.

Erikson, E. H. (1974). *Dimensions of a New Identity*. New York: Norton.

Fisher, D. D. V. (1991). *An Introduction to Constructivism for Social Workers*. New York: Praeger.

Fong, R., & Furuto, S. (Eds.). (2001). *Culturally Competent Practice: Skills, Interventions, and Evaluations*. Boston: Allyn & Bacon.

Foucault, M. (1965). *Madness and Civilization*. New York: Vintage.

Foucault, M. (1978). *The History of Sexuality: Volume 1. An Introduction*. New York: Vintage Books.

Foucault, M. (1980). *Power/Knowledge: Selected Interviews and Other Writings, 1972–1977*. New York: Pantheon Books.

Fraser, M., Taylor, M. J., Jackson, R., & O'Jack, J. (1991). Social work and science: Many ways of knowing. *Social Work*, 27, 5–15.

Fruggeri, L. (1992). Therapeutic process as the social construction of change. In S. McNamee & K. J. Gergen (Eds.), *Therapy as Social Construction* (pp. 40–53). Newbury Park, CA: Sage.

Geertz, C. (1973). *The Interpretation of Cultures*. New York: Basic Books.

Gelfand, D. E., & Fandetti, D. V. (1986). The emergent nature of ethnicity: Dilemmas in assessment. *Social Casework*, 67, 542–550.

Gergen, K. J. (1982). *Toward Transformation in Social Knowledge*. New York: Springer.

Gergen, K. J. (1985). The social constructionist movement in modern psychology. *American Psychologist*, 40, 266–275.

Gergen, K. J. (1999). *An Invitation to Social Construction*. Thousand Oaks, CA: Sage.

Gergen, K. J. (2006). *Therapeutic Realities: Collaboration, Oppression and Relational Flow*. Chagrin Falls, OH: Taos Institute Publications.

Gergen, M. M., & Gergen, K. (2006). Narratives in action. *Narrative Inquiry*, 16(1), 112–121.

Germain, C. B. (1970). Casework and science: A historical encounter. In R. Roberts & R. Nee (Eds.), *Theories of Social Casework* (pp. 3–32). Chicago: University of Chicago Press.

Goldstein, H. (1981). *Social Learning and Change: A Cognitive Approach to Social Services*. Columbia: University of South Carolina Press.

Goldstein, H. (1983). Starting where the client is. *Social Casework*, 64, 267–275.

Goldstein, H. (1986a). A cognitive humanistic approach to the hard-to-reach client. *Social Casework*, 7, 27–36.

Goldstein, H. (1986b). Toward the integration of theory and practice: A humanistic approach. *Social Work*, 31, 352–357.

Goldstein, H. (1990a). The knowledge base of social work practice: Theory, wisdom, analogue, or art? *Families in Society*, 71, 32–43.

Goldstein, H. (1990b). Strength of pathology: Ethical and rhetorical contrasts in approaches to practice families in society. *Families in Society*, 71, 267–275.

Gordon, W. (1964). Notes on the nature of K. In H. Bartlett (Ed.), *Building Social Work: A Report of a Conference* (pp. 1–15). New York: NASW Press.

Gordon, W. (1983). Social work revolution or evolution? *Social Work*, 28, 181–185.

Gottschalk, S. S., & Witkin, S. L. (1991). Rationality in social work: A critical examination. *Journal of Sociology and Social Welfare*, 18(4), 121–135.

Gould, K. H. (1984). Original works of Freud on women: Social work references. *Social Casework*, 65, 94–101.

Greene, R. R. (Ed.). (2008). *Human Behavior Theory and Social Work Practice*. New Brunswick, NJ: Aldine Transaction.

Guidano, V. F. (1987). *Complexity of the Self*. New York: Guilford Press.

Guidano, V. F. (1991). *The Self in Process: Toward a Post-Rationalist Cognitive Therapy*. New York: Guilford Press.

Hare-Mustin, R. T. (1990). Sex, lies and headaches: The problem is power. In T. J. Goodrich (Ed.), *Women and Power: Perspectives for Family Therapy* (pp. 61–83). New York: Norton.

Hare-Mustin, R. T., & Marecek, J. (1988). The meaning of difference: Gender theory, postmodernism and psychology. *American Psychologist*, 43, 445–464.

Haworth, G. (1984). Social work research, practice and paradigms. *Social Service Review*, 58, 343–357.

Hayek, F. A. (1978). *New Studies in Philosophy, Politics, Economics and the History of Ideas*. Chicago: University of Chicago Press.

Heineman, M. B. (1981). The obsolete scientific imperative in social work research. *Social Service Review*, 55, 371–397.

Heineman, M. B. (1982). Author's reply. *Social Service Review*, 56, 312.

Hudson, W. W. (1978). First axioms of treatment. *Social Work*, 23, 65–66.

Hudson, W. W. (1982). Scientific imperatives in social work research and practice. *Social Service Review*, 56, 242–258.

Imre, R. W. (1982). *Knowing and Caring: Philosophical Issues in Social Work*. Lanham, MD: University Press of America.

Jenkins, J. H., & Karno, M. (1992). The meaning of expressed emotion: Theoretical issues raised by cross-cultural research. *American Journal of Psychiatry*, 149, 9–21.

Keesing, R. M. (1987). Anthropology as interpretive quest. *Current Anthropology*, 28, 161–176.

Kelly, G. A. (1955). *The Psychology of Personal Constructs*. New York: Norton.

Kleinman, A. M. (1973). Medicine's symbolic reality on a central problem in the philosophy of medicine. *Inquiry*, 16, 206–213.

Kuhn, T. S. (1970). *The Structure of Scientific Revolutions*. Chicago: University of Chicago Press. (Original work published 1962)

Laird, J. (1989). Women and stories: Restoring women's self-constructions. In M. McGoldrick, C. M. Anderson, & F. Walsh (Eds.), *Women in Families: A Framework for Family Therapy* (pp. 427–450). New York: Norton.

Lakoff, G., & Johnson, M. (1980). *Metaphors We Live By*. Chicago: University of Chicago Press.

Lax, W. D. (1992). Postmodern thinking in a clinical practice. In S. McNamee & K. J. Gergen (Eds.), *Therapy as Social Construction* (pp. 69–85). Newbury Park, CA: Sage.

Lee, J. A. B. (1980). The helping professional's use of language in describing the poor. *American Journal of Orthopsychiatry*, 50, 580–584.

Liebow, E. (1967). *Tally's Corner*. Boston: Little, Brown.

Lowe, R. (1991). Postmodern themes and therapeutic practices: Notes towards the definition. *Dulwick Centre Newsletter*, 3, 41–53.

Lum D. (2007). *Culturally Competent Practice: A Framework for Understanding Diverse Groups and Justice Issues* (3rd ed.). Monterey, CA: Brooks/Cole.

Mahoney, M. J. (1988). The cognitive sciences and psychotherapy: Patterns in a developing relationship. In K. S. Dobson (Ed.), *The Handbook of Cognitive-Behavioral Therapies* (pp. 357–386). New York: Guilford Press.

Mahoney, M. J. (1991). *Human Change Processes: The Scientific Foundations of Psychotherapy*. New York: Basic Books.

Malinowski, B. (1954). *Magic, Science and Religion*. New York: Doubleday.

Markus, H. (1977). Self-schemata and processing information about the self. *Journal of Personality and Social Psychology*, 35, 63–78.

Martin, P. Y., & O'Connor, G. G. (1989). *The Social Environment: Open Systems Applications*. New York: Longman.

Maturana, H., & Varela, F. (1987). *The Tree of Knowledge*. Boston: New Science Library.

McNamee, S., & Gergen, K. J. (Eds.). (1992). *Therapy as Social Construction*. Newbury Park, CA: Sage.

Morales, J. (1992). Community social work with Puerto Rican communities in the United States: One organizer's perspective. In F. G. Rivera & J. L. Erlich (Eds.), *Community Organization in a Diverse Society* (pp. 91–112). Boston: Allyn & Bacon.

Myerhoff, B. (1978). *Number Our Days*. New York: Dutton.

Nisbett, R., & Ross, L. (1980). *Human Inference: Strategies and Shortcomings of Social Judgment*. Englewood Cliffs, NJ: Prentice Hall.

Northen, H. (1982). *Clinical Social Work*. New York: Columbia University Press.

O'Hanlon, B., & Rowan, T. (1999). *Solution-Oriented Therapy for Chronic and Severe Mental Illness*. New York: Norton.

O'Hanlon, W. H. (1993). Possibility therapy: From iatrogenic injury to estrogenic healing. In S. Gilligan & R. Price (Eds.), *Therapeutic Conversations* (pp. 3–17). New York: Norton.

Palombo, J. (1992). Narratives, self-cohesion, and the patient's search for meaning. *Clinical Social Work Journal*, 20, 249–270.

Pepitone, A. (1949). Motivation effects in social perception. *Human Relations*, 3, 57–76.

Polanyi, M. (1958). *Personal Knowledge*. Chicago: University of Chicago Press.

Polkinghorne, D. E. (1988). *Narrative Knowing and the Human Sciences*. Albany: State University of New York Press.

Poster, M. (1989). *Critical Theory and Poststructuralism: In Search of a Context*. Ithaca, NY: Cornell University Press.

Priest, S. (1990). *The British Empiricists*. New York: Penguin Press.

Rice, L. N., & Greenberg, L. S. (Eds.). (1984). *Patterns of Change: An Intensive Analysis of Psychotherapy Process*. New York: Guilford Press.

Rivera, F. G., & Erlich, J. L. (1992). Introduction: Prospects and challenges. In F. G. Rivera & J. L. Erlich (Eds.), *Community Organization in a Diverse Society* (pp. 1–26). Boston: Allyn & Bacon.

Rodwell, M. K. (1987). Naturalistic inquiry: An alternative model for social work assessment. *Social Service Review*, 59, 231–246.

Rogers, C. R., & Dymond, R. F. (Eds.). (1957). *Psychotherapy and Personality Change*.

Chicago: University of Chicago Press.

Rosenhan, D. L. (1984). On being sane in insane places. In P. Watzlawick (Ed.), *The Invented Reality: Contributions to Constructivism* (pp. 250–258). New York: Norton.

Ruckdeschel, R. A. (1985). Qualitative research as a perspective. *Social Work Research and Abstracts*, 21, 17–21.

Russell, B. (1956). *Logic and Knowledge.* London: Allen & Unwin.

Saari, C. (1986a). *Clinical Social Work Treatment: How Does It Work?* New York: Gardner Press.

Saari, C. (1986b). The created relationship: Countertransferences and the therapeutic culture. *Clinical Social Work Journal*, 14(1), 39–51.

Saari, C. (1991). *The Creation of Meaning in Clinical Social Work.* New York: Guilford Press.

Saleebey, D. (1989). The estrangement of knowing from doing: Profession in crisis. *Social Work*, 70, 556–563.

Saleebey, D. (1992). Introduction: Power to the people. In D. Saleebey (Ed.), *The Strengths Perspective in Social Work Practice* (1st ed., pp. 3–17). New York: Longman.

Saleebey, D. (2005a). The strengths approach to practice. In D. Saleebey (Ed.), *The Strengths Perspective in Social Work Practice* (4th ed., pp.77–92). Boston: Allyn & Bacon.

Saleebey, D. (2005b). *The Strengths Perspective in Social Work Practice* (4th ed.). Boston: Allyn & Bacon.

Sands, R. G., & Nuccio, K. (1992). Post-modernization feminist theory and social work. *Social Work*, 37, 489–502.

Sanville, J. (1987). Creativity and constructing of the self. *Psychoanalytic Review*, 74, 263N279.

Sarbin, T. R. (1986). *Narrative Psychology.* New York: Praeger.

Schacter, S. (1964). The interaction of cognitive and physiological determinants of emotional state. In L. Berkowitz (Ed.), *Advances in Experimental Social Psychology* (Vol. 1). New York: Academic Press.

Schank, R. C., & Abelson, R. P. (Eds.). (1990). *Scripts, Plans, Goals and Understanding.* Hillsdale, NJ: Erlbaum.

Schon, D. (1983). *The Reflective Practitioner: How Professionals Think in Action.* New York: Basic Books.

Scott, D. (1989). Meaning construction and social work practice. *Social Service Review*, 63, 39–51.

Sexton, T. L., & Griffin, B. L. (Eds.). (1997). *Constructivist Thinking in Counseling Practice, Research, and Training.* New York: Teachers College Press.

Shafer, R. (1983). *The Analytic Attitude.* New York: Basic Books.

Shotter, J. (1993). *Conversational Realities: Constructing Life through Language.* Thousand Oaks, CA: Sage.

Simon, B. (1970). Social casework theory: An overview. In R. Roberts & R. Nee (Eds.), *Theories of Social Casework* (pp. 353–394). Chicago: University of Chicago Press.

Sluzki, C. E. (1990). Negative explanations drawing distinctions, raising dilemmas, collapsing time externalization of problems: A note on some powerful conceptual tools. *Residential Treatment for Children and Youth*, 7(3), 33–37.

Spiegelman, A. (1991). *Maus.* New York: Pantheon Books.

Stewart, A. J., Franz, C., & Layton, L. (1988). The changing self: Using personal documents to study lives. *Journal of Personality*, 56(1), 41–73.

Stewart, B., & Nodrick, B. (1990). The learning disabled lifestyle: From reification to liberation. *Family Therapy Case Studies*, 5(1), 60–73.

Stiles, W. B. (1988). Psychotherapy process-outcome correlations may be misleading.

Psychotherapy, 25, 27–35.

Taggart, M. (1989). Epistemological equality as the fulfillment of family therapy. In M. McGoldrick, C. M. Anderson, & F. Walsh (Eds.), *Women in Families: A Framework for Family Therapy* (pp. 97–106). New York: Norton.

Tice, K. (1990). Gender and social work education: Directions for the 1990s. *Journal of Social Work Education*, 26, 134–144.

Tiefer, L. (1987). Social constructionism and the study of human sexuality. In P. Shaver & C. Hendrick (Eds.), *Sex and Gender* (pp. 70–93). Newbury Park, CA: Sage.

Tomm, K. (1990). A critique of the *DSM*. *Dulwich Centre Newsletter*, 3, 5–8.

von Glaserfeld, E. (1984). An introduction to radical constructivism. In P. Watzlawick (Ed.), *The Invented Reality: Contributions to Constructivism* (pp. 18–30). New York: Norton.

Watzlawick, P. (1984). *The Invented Reality: How Do We Know What We Believe We Know?* New York: Norton.

Weick, A. (1981). Reframing the person-in-environment perspective. *Social Work*, 26, 140–143.

Weick, A. (1983). Issues in overturning a medical model of social work practice. *Social Work*, 28, 467–471.

Weick, A. (1986). The philosophical contest of a health model of social work. *Social Casework*, 67, 551–559.

Weick, A. (1987). Reconceptualizing the philosophical perspective of social work. *Social Service Review*, 61, 218–230.

Weimer, W. B. (1977). A conceptual framework for cognitive psychology: Motor theories of the mind. In R. Shaw & J. Bransford (Eds.), *Perceiving, Acting, and Knowing* (pp. 267–311). Hillsdale, NJ: Erlbaum.

Wentworth, W. M., & Wentworth, C. M. (1997). The social construction of culture and its implications for the therapeutic mind-self. In T. L. Sexton & B. L. Griffin (Eds.), *Constructivist Thinking in Counseling Practice, Research, and Training*. New York: Teachers College Press.

White, M. (1993). Deconstruction and therapy. In S. Gilligan & R. Price (Eds.), *Therapeutic Conversation* (pp. 22–61). New York: Norton.

White, M., & Epston, D. (1990). *Narrative Means to Therapeutic Ends*. New York: Norton.

7

Risk, Resilience, and Resettlement

Rowena Fong and Roberta R. Greene

Crisis is the turning point at which things will either get better or get worse.... In Chinese, the word "crisis" is made up of characters for "danger" and "opportunity." Resettlement is such a risk and opportunity. (Hulewat, 1996)

This chapter explores concepts of risk and resilience theory as applied to the refugee and immigrant experience. Because risk and resilience theory—its terms and basic assumption—so well describe clients' experiences as they arrive and rebuild their lives in America, the theory has important implications for social work practice (Greene, 2007).

Immigration and resettlement can offer enormous opportunities while presenting life crises (Hulewat, 1999). Those who resettle in the United States, whether immigrants or refugees, have left behind a country, language, and culture familiar to them, resulting in varying levels of distress. Feelings of loss and depression are common (Mui & Kang, 2006), as is the stress that arises from living in a bicultural environment (Romero & Roberts, 2003). Refugees may be recovering from the effects of civil war and violence. Their new host countries form part of a global trend of population movements and multiculturalism, challenging existing political, social, and cultural orders (Lifton, 1999; Orum, 2005; Verkuyten, 2005).

Although resettlement tests peoples' coping capacities, researchers have identified several protective factors, such as a strong mother–child bond, that allow people to retain their psychosocial competence or resilience (Melville & Lykes, 1992; Zea, Diehl, & Porterfield, 1996; Zuniga, 2002). Preserving cultural values from home countries and promoting ethnic pride also serve as protective factors, providing strength and resilience for Asians and Pacific Islanders who migrate to new environments (Fong, 2004; Mokuau, 1991).

Resilience is a universal capacity that permits an individual, group, or community to prevent, minimize, or overcome adversity. Resilience may transform or promote growth among those who have faced risks and the damaging effects of stress (Grotberg, 1995). Risk and resilience theory stems from a wellness philosophy that holds that people have the capacity for self-healing, builds on the ecological perspective, and incorporates concepts from various theoretical schools of thought familiar to social workers (Greene, 2008). A resilience-enhancing philosophy embodies a strengths-based approach to human behavior content, affording "ways to think about individual and collective assets" (Saleebey, 1997, p. 21). An integration of risk and resilience factors into practice interventions offers social workers a means to build strengths-based adaptive strategies for their clients, enabling these clients to better handle possible adverse consequences of resettlement.

Resilience: Research Background

An understanding of the phenomenon of resilience emerged from research on children at risk (Bogenschneider, 1996; Hawkins, Catalano, & Miller, 1992; Werner & Smith, 1982, 1992). Researchers were interested in how children dealt with high-risk situations—such as abuse, poverty, violence, and war—and then became competent adults. International research projects, such as those sponsored by the University of Alabama Civitan International Research Center, explored child well-being in numerous countries, attempting to identify the proportion of child populations at risk that might experience problems in the future. These studies revealed that although some children might have adverse reactions to negative or traumatic experiences, adverse events in childhood do not inevitably lead to adult pathology (Grotberg, 1995).

Robert Coles (1986), a renowned researcher of children who have overcome adversity, studied Cambodian refugee children and their parents. He and other researchers found that many survivors of the thirty-year Cambodian civil war and concentration camps suffered posttraumatic stress, experiencing symptoms that included avoidance, hyperactive startle reactions, emotional numbness, intrusive thoughts, and nightmares (Boehnlein, 1987; Carlson & Rosser-Hogan, 1993; Eisenbruch, 1984; Kinzie, Fredrickson, Ben, Fleck, & Karls, 1984; Lee & Lu, 1989). Nonetheless, Coles concluded that despite the terrible experiences these children had under the Khmer Rouge, "I have never seen a group of children, in all the years of my work, who are more resilient and perceptive" (p. 266). He attributed their successful adaptation to caring mothers and fathers. Masten and Coatsworth (1998) also commented on these young people's success, saying "they are absolute, living testimony to the human capacity for resilience" (p. 206).

Carranza (2007), who studied thirty-two Salvadoran mothers and daughters who had settled in Canada, provided further documentation of how parents can foster resilience and resistance to racism and discrimination. Salvadoran mothers taught their daughters strategies to resist prejudice, focusing on consciousness raising, stressing ethnic pride, and continuing to speak their native tongue of Spanish. The result was the daughters feeling a sense of belonging and pride in their Salvadoran roots. This allowed them "to carry sources of strength and resilience" (Carranza, 2007, p. 398).

The American experience suggests that when immigrants and refugees settle into the United States, they may lose their sense of ethnic pride and social support and become more vulnerable to poor mental and physical functioning. Ruben Rumbaut and John Weeks (1999) researched whether Americanization is hazardous to infant health. They found an "infant health paradox" among new immigrants to the United States (i.e., that "high risk groups, particularly low income immigrants from Mexico and Southeast Asia showed unexpectedly favorable perinatal outcomes and seemed to be 'superior health achievers'" [p. 160]). In their study of 1,464 pregnancies of women (80 percent of whom were born outside of the United States, predominantly in Mexico or Asia) who delivered their babies at the University of California, San Diego, Medical Center during 1989 to 1991, Rumbaut and Weeks found that the best infant health outcomes were among an Asian immigrant group (the Indochinese, who were the least educated), but the worst outcomes for the Middle Easterners, the most educated. And immigrants did indeed do better than the native-born U.S. babies overall; the most assimilated immigrants, White Europeans and Canadians, did worse than the U.S.-born Asians, Hispanics, and Blacks. The study found that immigrants initially did better than native-born Americans, but as the immigrants assimilated they tended to fare more poorly than the U.S.-born Asian, Black, and Hispanic populations. This might lead one to wonder if immigrant groups become less resilient over time if they have less social support and resources to overcome adversity during their acculturation process.

Definitions Applied to Resettlement

Risk and resilience is a multitheoretical framework that helps social workers understand how people maintain well-being despite adversity (Fraser, 1997; Greene, 2002, 2007; table 7.1). Although *resilience* refers to a wide array of adaptive behaviors (Gordon & Song, 1994), it generally is considered "a pattern over time, characterized by good eventual adaptation despite developmental risks, acute stressors, or chronic adversity" (Masten, 1994, p. 5). Webb (2007) stated that "the term 'resilient' has been used to describe children who demonstrate successful adaptation despite high-risk status, chronic stress, or prolonged and severe trauma" (p. 16). However, there is no consensus or agreement about the definition of resilience. The next sections provide various theorists' definitions, each of which offers a means of understanding the resettlement experience.

Facing Disruptive Change

The term *resilience*, often used interchangeably with *persistence* or *successful coping*, is commonly thought of as referring to a good track record of success in the face of disruptive change (Werner & Smith, 1992). For example, Christopher (2000) wrote, "Immigration disrupts every aspect of an individual's life resulting in the need to restructure one's way of looking at the world and one's plans for living in it" (p. 123). She studied 100 Irish immigrants to determine "if the psychological well-being among immigrants is independently associated with being married, educated, employed, residing longer in the United States, possessing higher resilience, and having greater life satisfaction" (p. 126). Her research corroborated other studies that had found that "overall life satisfaction is a strong predictor of psychological well-being" (p. 136). But not all immigrants or refugees report a satisfaction with life, especially unaccompanied asylum-seeking minors who have experienced traumatic and disruptive changes. Many of them are living parents and may have been tortured in their flight to safety. Almost all of them have experienced mental health problems or have had difficulties in coping with daily living because of the past disruptive changes in their lives.

In 2002, the United Kingdom set up a project funded by the European Commission and the Princess Diana of Wales Memorial Fund for unaccompanied minors seeking asylum (Kohli & Mather, 2003). This project had four purposes:

1. to help young people make sense of what happened to them in the past;
2. to help them identify and use their own capabilities and skills in integrating into their new environments;
3. to provide opportunities to learn new skills to assist them to find emotional and practical stability, either in the United Kingdom or upon return to their countries of origin; and
4. to connect them to helpful people within their informal and formal networks of care so that they are not isolated and can be accompanied in their journeys toward settlement. (p. 202)

Refugee children, such as the unaccompanied minors served by this project, demonstrate several definitions of resilience. According to Kohli and Mather (2003), these children have overcome the odds, are successful despite exposure to high risk, sustain competence under pressure, adapt to high risk, recover from trauma, and adjust successfully to negative life events.

Successfully Adapting after an Adverse Event

Resilience is often referred to as markedly successful adaptation following an adverse event (Rutter, 1987). Natural disasters such as earthquakes, tsunamis, floods, hurricanes, and famines are adverse events that occur worldwide. Immigrants and refugees fortunate enough to survive such natural disasters are often in need of counseling (table 7.2). Baggerly (2007) wrote about principles and preparation for deployment after a natural disaster. She said that mental health professionals need to understand disaster relief principles that

- follow the incident command structure,
- discern phases of disaster,
- expect children's normal recovery,

- implement the 6 Cs of mental health (calmness, common sense, compassion, collaboration, communication, and control of self),
- maintain hardiness and flexibility,
- utilize developmentally appropriate approaches of play, and
- gain information about the specific natural disaster and country. (p. 364)

The principle "to maintain an expectation that children and their families will have a normal recovery" (p. 351) reflects a resilience-based attitude. In *International Interventions and Challenges Following the Client Crisis of Natural Disasters*, Baggerly (2007) applied the principle of expecting children to recover to the Tamil children in Sri Lanka who had been orphaned by a civil war and then experienced a tsunami. She exhorted mental health practitioners to follow the principle of expecting children to recover "so that they can be global citizens in a global village that helps children recover from international disasters" (p. 364).

Showing the Power of Recovery

As already stated, resilience involves the power of recovery and the ability to return once again to those patterns of adaptation and competence that characterized the individual before the episode of extreme stress (Garmezy, 1993). Immigrant or refugee women who are victims of human trafficking often show great resiliency in their power to recover from being forced to work in the sex industry, a modern form of slavery. Victims of human trafficking and sexual slavery are usually women and children from less developed countries who lack education and employment opportunities. They are often deceived with promises of legitimate work and are transported from their home countries to unknown destinations, including foreign countries. Upon arriving at their destination, they are forced by rape; physical or mental torture; starvation; threats to family members; and imprisonment in confined, unhealthy environments to involuntary servitude in the sex or labor industry. If the victim agrees to cooperate with law enforcement to prosecute her trafficker, she is better able to concentrate on the social services that are offered to her to help her recover from her horrific ordeal.

An evaluation of the Central Texas Coalition Against Human Trafficking found that victims felt safe and protected and trusted the services of providers who went beyond perfunctory service delivery (Busch, Fong, Heffron, Faulkner, & Mahapatra, 2007). A trafficked victim reported as follows:

They [the service providers] haven't just helped us with getting documents and all this, they also helped me morally. Not just physically, but morally because I came practically destroyed from that place [where the trafficked victim was held involuntarily]. I was accustomed to a different environment and I really wanted to get out of that. (as cited in Busch et al., 2007, p. 32)

These victims showed great resiliency in pursuing their road of survivorship and recovery and in reclaiming their lives.

Maintaining One's Narrative through Adversity

Because narrative therapy helps survivors to maintain the continuity of their personal narrative (Borden, 1992), it may be used with immigrants and refugees to recount and process traumatic events. Goodman (2004) wrote about Balkan refugees that "giving testimony or telling one's story has been a powerful therapeutic tool among oppressed people.... The stories told 'are powerful because they determine what people will notice and remember'" (p. 283).

Narrative therapy, according to private practitioner Dr. Ann Cattanach (2007), is a process of storying and restorying experiences. She stated, "Narrative frameworks are constructed that allow a child begin to sequence, order, predict, and make sense of complex feelings that can exist as a result of abuse or other trauma" (p. 429). She emphasized that refugee children and families do not have continuity of culture. Thus, the use of narrative play therapy for children allows them to tell and play out stories, which may help them regain power and control and some sense of continuity, resulting in the rebuilding of resiliency.

Preservation of self and culture is crucial across the entire life course. For older adults, leisure activities serve the function of preserving one's history and cultural narrative. In a qualitative study on older Korean Americans, leisure-based activities were found to have a bidirectional effect on the older adults (Kim, Kleiber, & Kropf, 2001). Some leisure pursuits, such as watching Korean videos, being involved in Korean singing activities, or participating in *kye* (a social gathering that provides both financial and social support), solidified their ethnic and social heritage. Other pursuits, however, provided opportunity for assimilating into their new culture or "dancing between the old and the new" (p. 124). Some of the participants enjoyed watching American television programs or branching into new food choices. Clearly, these older adults were structuring their leisure experiences in ways that had multiple meanings within their self-narrative.

Demonstrating Competence Following Risks

Masten (1994) suggested that resilience is a developmental process linked to *demonstrated competence*, the learned capacity to interact positively with the environment and to complete tasks successfully. In a study of successful refugee entrepreneurs who had come to the United States, many of whom had experienced severe hardships and traumas, Fong, Busch, Armour, Heffron, and Chanmugam (2007) found that survivors first therapeutically worked through their risky experiences during migration journeys. Those who became entrepreneurs had positive experiences owning and running businesses:

> Refugee entrepreneurs ... have leadership and innovation skills, or the ability to independently institute original and creative ideas. This includes a proactive, engag-

ing outlook and a high level of resourcefulness in identifying solutions to barriers. (p. 136)

Zhou and Bankston (1998) also found that achieving competence following an adverse event can contribute to competence. Their study of Vietnamese immigrant children revealed that the children

> adapted surprising (sic) well to the American educational system in a relative (sic) short period of time. Over the last ten years or so, Vietnamese children have come to excel academically not only by the standards expected of a new refugee group but also by comparison with segments of the established population. (p. 130)

Thus, academic competence and excellence after enduring the risks involved in assimilating to a new educational system and society are indicators of resilience.

Addressing Client Assets

Benard (1993) argued that the concept of resilience should stand alone (without the consideration of risk) as a means of positively addressing client assets. She agreed with Garmezy that, in this way, the practitioner can truly foster a client's "natural self-righting tendencies" (Garmezy, 1993, p. 129). Many of the personal assets of immigrants and refugees get forgotten during their migration journeys and after their adjustment to the new host country. In their interviews with successful refugee entrepreneurs, Fong and colleagues (2007) found that individual and family success factors that contributed to refugees' resilience included personal characteristics and attitudes, family–community orientation, prior experience with stress, clarity of purpose, language and communication, and access to capital.

Resiliency Terms: Exploring Resettlement

Risk

Risk is a factor that influences or increases the (statistical) probability of the onset of stress or negative outcomes following adverse events. Risk-related life events may include such things as childhood abuse, neighborhood disorganization, racism, civil war, or resettlement. Risks such as the need to resettle may occur at any time during a person's life course, and the events affect their lives at various system levels (Greene, 2002). In the trauma literature, Foster (2001) distinguished between first- and second-generation immigrant mental health investigations. She made the point that when conducting needs assessments, it is important to remember that life course events of first-generation immigrants differ from those of second-generation immigrants. She explained that there could be a "second language anxiety" and that "when speaking in their non dominant language, bilinguals perceive themselves as less intelligent and self-confident" (p. 164). She cautioned, "The monolingual clinician must take care not to misinterpret the halting quality, sparse words, and emotional preoccupation of the struggling bilingual as psychopathology" (p. 164).

Cumulative risk is the number of negative or stressful life events a person experiences in a lifetime. Assessing this information allows the social worker to identify clients as high risk or low risk (Gilgun, 1996). Those who have resettled have generally faced numerous risks. The population of Sudanese reported by Schweitzer, Melville, Steel, and Lacherez (2006) have a history of trauma due to civil war between the predominantly Islamic, Arabic north and African ethnic groups in the south who are Christian or Animist. As these researchers explained, "Before migration refugees have often been exposed to human rights violations, torture and systematic violence. The traumatic experience of refugees tend to be interrelated and cumulative, unlike single event trauma" (p. 187). According to these researchers, who studied the trauma, postmigration living difficulties, and social supports of Sudanese refugees, this refugee group "might be considered an extreme group in terms of pre-migration traumas, many have lived thorough extreme hardships on the way to resettlement in another country" (p. 180). Therefore, they will need more time and assistance to heal from the experience.

Risks Propel Resilient Behavior

Strumpfer (2002) proposed that the process of "resiling" starts when an individual perceives a risk threat, which acts as a catalyst to set goals and to take action. In this sense, people do not have (ongoing) resilience but exhibit it in six potentially risky situations:

1. exceptionally challenging experiences, for example, in a new job;
2. developmental transitions, including in the transition to parenthood;
3. individual adversity, such as in discrimination or persecution;
4. collective adversity, as in the aftermath of natural disaster or war;
5. organizational change, including with the use of technology; and
6. large-scale sociopolitical change, such as when the *glasnost*-era nuclear explosion in Chernobyl in the former Soviet Union caused alarm around the world and forced the resettlement of thousands.

Many immigrants and refugees have experienced all of these six risky situations. It is important for practitioners to take the time and assess the kind and degree of trauma experienced to determine when "resiling" started. It would be erroneous to assume that this process started once the immigrants and refugees arrived in their host country. Many refugees have spent years in refugee camps, when the process of "resiling" would have begun in order for them to survive.

Protective Factors

Protective factors are events and conditions that help individuals to reduce risk and enhance adaptation. They may be internal personal characteristics (such as good problem-solving skills) or external environmental factors (such as viable support networks that modify risks; Rutter, 1987). Social supports are also considered protective factors. Simich, Beiser, Stewart, and Mwakarimba (2005) found social supports for immigrants and refugees in Canada to be a "springboard" and not just a "safety net" in that they play a particularly important role during major transition periods by enhancing coping, moderating the impact of stressors and promoting health.

There are varying points of view on the interaction between risk and protective factors. Masten (1994) suggested that risk and protective factors are polar opposites, whereby competence decreases as stress increases. A model in which risk factors increase the probability of a negative outcome is called an *additive model*.

In contrast, Rutter (1987) contended that risk and protective factors interact to produce an outcome—when stress is low, protective factors are of less influence. This approach, in which risk and protective factors only work in conjunction with each other, is termed an *interactive model*. Protective factors of social support, psychosocial competence, and cognitive factors (Zea et al., 1996) are needed to counteract the risk factors of poverty, unemployment, language inadequacies, prejudice, and discrimination for most immigrants and refugees.

Basic Human Behavior Assumptions

Because risk and resilience theory is an integrated approach, some of its assumptions are derived from other familiar theory bases. For example, Fraser (1997) and Masten and Reed (2002) underscored the idea that risk and resilience must be understood as an ecological phenomenon.

Resilience as an Ecological Perspective

Risk and resilience is an ecological concept (Bronfenbrenner, Moen, & Garbarino, 1984; Fraser, 1997). It is a multisystemic approach encompassing small-scale microsystems, mesosystems, exosystems, and macrosystems (see Chapter 10). Several benefits stem from this ecological viewpoint: (a) An individual is understood within his or her relationships with other social systems; (b) resilience is viewed as affected by any system in the individual's life space; and (c) families, communities, and societies are perceived as having collective resilient properties.

An ecological perspective allows practitioners to understand how a person who has resettled must deal with his or her new environment and accompanying cultural, economic, health, and educational factors (Germain & Gitterman, 1996). Weaver, Hunt-Jackson, and Burns (2003) wrote about the challenges of asylum seekers along the U.S.–Canadian border and explained their challenges in leaving their homelands and seeking safety in a new environment without legal documents:

Table 7.1
Risk and Resilience Theory: Basic Assumptions

- People experience stress following adverse or traumatic events.
- People will naturally attempt to overcome the associated risks following an adverse event.
- People can experience natural stressors in everyday life, including difficult life transitions, unfavorable political and economic climates or historical events, and environmental pressures.
- Resilience is shaped by biopsychosocial and spiritual factors.
- Resilience develops throughout the life course and is concerned with individual competence in the face of adversity. An evaluation of competence may take into account whether an individual is adapting well to normative developmental tasks that are expected to occur at various stages of life. In contrast, competence may be viewed as a relative characteristic specific to a particular cultural context.
- The development of resilience is a dynamic process of person-in-environment exchanges over time, involving person–environment fit.
- An individual's resilient behavior is influenced/affected by the multiple systems in his or her life.
- Systems may be resilient in their own right.

Source. Adapted from Greene, R. R. (2002). *Resiliency: An Integrated Approach to Practice, Policy, and Research*. Washington, DC: NASW Press.

> Asylum seekers are often unable to obtain official travel documents before departure since they may not have legal means to get such documents. People without documents or forged ones can be denied entry to the U.S. and Canada, yet the very notion of "illegal departure" violates the right of every person to leave any country, including his or her own—a fundamental principle in the Universal Declaration of Human Rights. (p. 85)

The risk that asylum seekers endure without legal documents must be understood from the ecological perspective of the dire circumstances in their home countries that force them to seek safety elsewhere. This knowledge is necessary for practitioners to help asylum seekers adjust and find the resilient strengths that are part of their personhood.

Resilience from a Stress Perspective

Flow of family stress. Risk and resilience theorists have recognized that the stress that occurs with adverse events may be a deterrent to natural healing (Masten, 1994; Rutter, 1987). The influence of stress on everyday family life within the larger cultural context was discussed by Carter and McGoldrick (2005). They identified stressors associated with developmental events, such as life cycle transitions and migration; unpredictable events, such as the untimely death of a friend or family member, chronic illness, accident, or unemployment;

and historical events, such as war, economic depression, the political climate, and natural disasters. Macrolevel stressors might involve racism, sexism, classism, ageism, consumerism, poverty, disappearance of community, more work, less leisure, and inflexibility of the workplace. Stressors could also include more immediate factors such as little time for friends; family emotional patterns, such as myths, triangles, secrets, legacies, and losses; violence, addictions, ignorance, depression, and inadequate spiritual expression or dreams; and genetic makeup, abilities, and disabilities.

Family Stress over Time

Acculturation stress. Many immigrant and refugee families experience stress over time due to generational differences, language inadequacies, role reversals, and readjustments that need to be made in coping skills. Hsu, Davies, and Hansen (2004) addressed the mental health needs of Southeast Asian refugees, summarizing historical, cultural, and contextual challenges. They wrote:

> These traditional values of the Southeast Asian Refugees were affected by trauma endured in the native country and the migration to another country. The possible effects of trauma on a person can greatly impact an individual's ability to function in the family. Given the language barriers, and little or no formal Western education and vocational experiences, older adults lost their status within the family and the society. Due to the high rates of male deaths during the Cambodian traumas, family structures have often changed. Single mothers taking over the responsibility as the primary caregiver and raising a family became more common. Children's roles were also altered. Children became communication facilitators between their parents and the mainstream society, therefore reversing the traditional parent-child relationship. The transfer of authority from respected elders to the young disrupted traditional cultural values and roles within the family structure.

For these Southeast Asian families and other immigrant and refugee groups, these family stressors take their toll over time not only on the individual family but also on the collective families in the ethnic population.

Resilience as Adaptation

Risk and resilience theory addresses adaptiveness in several ways. First, it emphasizes a wellness perspective, focusing on how an individual maintains positive self-regard and continues to grow and reach self-realization despite high levels of risk (Ryff & Singer, 2002; Seligman, 2002). Risk and resilience theory also focuses on the power people have to recover following adversity or extreme stress that might threaten their basic assumptions about self-reliance. The idea that people continue to manage their own affairs, known as *self-efficacy*, is central to the risk and resilience approach. Gorman (2001) recounted Herman's (1992) view of the third stage of recovery from trauma to the time for reconnection when there is a reconciliation with oneself and the survivor "forge[s] a more resilient and enabling sense of identity. Respect for one's own 'traumatized victim self' is united with earned pride in the 'survivor self'" (p. 448). A sense of self-efficacy returns and the past is reembodied in the present, allowing for new developments in the sense of self.

Ability to Adapt to a New Culture

Resilience as Cross-Cultural

Miller and MacIntosh (1999) suggested that the capacity to transcend the risk of oppressive environments can be attributed in part to a family's "culturally unique protective factors" (p. 159). Specific family cultural forms contribute to a child's capacity to overcome the risks associated with discrimination and to withstand stress (Genero, 1998; Solomon, 1976).

Individualistic and Relational Cultures

Immigrant and refugee children and families make adjustments to cultures that are individual oriented (like that of the United States) rather than relationally oriented (like those of many Asian countries that are family oriented). Gorman (2001) warned that, with respect to refugees who have survived torture,

> when working across differences with respect, for example, to class, disability, ethnicity, race, national origin, sexual orientation, or religion, psychologists [and other practitioners] must be cognizant of and able to "bracket" their own culturally derived reactions, assumptions, and values. They need to maintain a phenomenological stance to appreciate the meaning of the clients' distinctive way of being in the world.... Knowledge must be gained in each instance from the client and from background sources about the historical, spiritual, and sociopolitical realities from which he or she comes. (p. 445)

Biculturalism

Biculturalism is the ability to develop knowledge of and a positive attitude toward two cultures simultaneously. It allows a child to learn about and take advantage of mainstream culture without compromising ethnic pride. For a child to be bicultural, the family needs to validate that it is acceptable to live in two communities and accept certain values from each (Genero, 1998). A child who is bicultural can communicate effectively across cultures. Thus, he or she feels effective and well grounded in both the ethnic and mainstream cultures, which contributes to the development of resilience (La Fromboise, Coleman, & Gerton, 1993). Suarez-Orozco and Suarez-Orozco (2001) discussed the "re-making identities" of immigrant children and described what it takes for them to be resilient and adapt:

> The experiences of the children offer us a particularly powerful lens through which to view the workings of identity. These children must construct identities that will

enable them to thrive in profoundly different settings such as home, schools, the world of peers, and the world of work. Immigrant children today may have their breakfast conversation in Farsi, listen to African American rap with their peers on the way to school, and learn about the New Deal from their social studies teacher in mainstream English. (p. 92)

In some instances immigrant and refugee children not only may be forced to be bicultural but may be multicultural, depending on the racial/ethnic composition of their family and the complexity of their migration journeys (where they may have lived in different cultures and social environments in refugee camps, and where they may have stayed for long periods of time and been immersed in the culture of those living situations).

Spirituality

Many immigrants and refugees have cultural and religious beliefs that were protective factors during their trauma and adjustments to the host country. The practice of integrating spirituality as a strength and resource has been documented in the literature on cultural competence (Fong, 2004; Lum, 2007; Morelli, 2001; Webb, 2001). Anne Fadiman (1998), author of the award-winning book *The Spirit Catches You and You Fall Down*, wrote about the important role of the spiritual healers or shamans in the Hmong culture. She described the shaman or *txiv neeb* as a necessary part of the Hmong culture: "Becoming a *txiv neeb* is not a choice, it is a calling.... *Txiv neeb* means 'person with a healing spirit'" (p. 21). The position of shaman is important in this and other Southeast Asian cultures because the shaman is a person of high moral character, is trained in the ritual techniques and chants, and is depended upon to save lives and heal individuals searching for their lost souls.

Interventions

Researchers who have witnessed the lives of children in danger around the world have deduced that children can maintain resilience under adversity if they have sufficient psychological and social resources, are attached to significant adults, develop cultural and spiritual resources, and have an ideology or activism about their situation (Garbarino, Dubrow, Kostelny, & Pardo, 1992). The benefit of these findings is that they remind professionals that, to foster resilience, it is wise to think beyond traditional interventions (Greene, 2007).

Resilience-enhancing models of social work practice, such as those proposed by Greene (2002, 2007), embody a philosophy of hope and instill positive expectations for the future. These models are based on the belief that people have an innate capacity to lead productive lives and the propensity to grow and heal. Resilience-enhancing model interventions help clients tell their narratives or stories and ascribe new, more positive meanings to adverse events (White & Epston, 1990). Effective interventions also draw on environmental resources to reduce the negative effects of the aftermath of adversity, ensuring that clients are safe and secure.

Family Interventions

Because systems may be resilient in their own right, an assessment of the resilience of social systems focuses on the collective. That is, understanding

Table 7.2
Guidelines for the Social Worker Practicing in the Risk and Resilience Tradition

Assessment
- Determine the client's relative balance between risk and adaptive strategies.
- Establish the source of stress, whether it be a life transition, traumatic life event, or environmental pressure.
- Examine the client's goodness of fit with other social systems. Ascertain what support is available from family, friends, community, organizations, and macrolevel entities.
- Address how the client has functioned over time, the timing of family life events, and the historical and cultural changes associated with them.
- Explore what risks the client has overcome in the past.
- Consider biopsychosocial spiritual functioning as complementary and explore how these factors contribute to risk and resilience.
- Differentiate the assessment process, learning about culturally sound solutions.

Interventions
- Provide basic resources for change, especially daily needs.
- Collaborate in client self-change, fostering his or her natural self-righting tendencies.
- Adopt an empathetic posture to acknowledge client stress, loss, and vulnerability.
- Use the client's narrative or story as a primary source of information.
- Direct the client's attention to future possibilities.
- Use strategies to promote hope, optimism, and other positive emotions.
- Establish that the adverse event is part of life's travails by stabilizing or normalizing the situation. Indicate that others in similar situations may feel troubled.
- Begin to seek possible solutions to help the client take control.
- Promote client self-efficacy by pointing out client successes.
- Attempt to strengthen problem-solving strategies.
- Listen to the client's narratives for opportunities to help him or her make meaning of critical events.
- Learn how the client is appraising the situation.
- Help the client find the potential benefits of the adverse event.
- Assist the client in transcending the immediate situation.
- Help the client discover a brighter future.

Source. Adapted from Greene, R. R., & Armenta, K. (2007). The REM model: Phase II—Practice strategies. In R. R. Greene (Ed.), *Social Work Practice: A Risk and Resilience Perspective* (pp. 67-90). Monterey, CA: Brooks/Cole.

family resilience requires an exploration of the functional capacity and the collective contribution of its members. For example, Walsh (1998a, 1998b) combined a risk and resilience philosophy with a systems theory approach to family resilience.

Her belief is that family systems break down under the pressures of changing roles within the family, losses, separations, and intergenerational conflicts. Delgado, Jones, and Rohani (2005) cited Falicov's list of the myriad ways in which families may sustain "daily rituals" from the homeland (including meals, greetings, dress, prayers, and folk medicines) in addition to the continued celebration of special holidays and rite of passage. She also described the evolution of "new rituals of connection" to family in the homeland in the form of regular communication, visits, and remittances, which help keep family members psychologically present even if physically absent. Such practices allow a sense of transnational or transcontinental family "intactness" (p. 60).

Conclusion: Influence of Host Countries

During the past four decades, millions of new Americans have immigrated to the United States. Most of the research and discussion of the well-being of those new immigrants has focused on how they have adapted to their new country or host society. Current researchers have suggested that a new generation of Americans has begun to have a dramatic influence on the nature of society (Orum, 2005). Although the issues of immigration and multiculturalism are beyond the scope of this chapter, it is clear that the cultural order of a society is affected by the introduction of differing political, ideological, and social views of newcomers (Verkeyten, 2005), hopefully enriching the lives of all.

References

Baggerly, J. (2007). International interventions and challenges following the client crisis of natural disasters. In N. B. Webb (Ed.), *Play Therapy with Children in Crisis: Individual, Group, and Family Treatment* (pp. 345–367). New York: Guilford Press.

Benard, B. (1993). Fostering resiliency in kids. *Educational Leadership*, 51(3), 44–48.

Boehnlein, J. K. (1987). Clinical evidence of grief and mourning among Cambodian refugees. *Social Science & Medicine*, 25, 765–772.

Bogenschneider, K. (1996). Family related prevention programs: An ecological risk/preventive theory for building prevention programs, policies, and community capacity to support youth. *Family Relations*, 45, 127–138.

Borden, W. (1992). Narrative perspectives in psychosocial intervention following adverse life events. *Social Work*, 37, 125–141.

Bronfenbrenner, U., Moen, P., & Garbarino, J. (1984). Family and community. In R. Parke (Ed.), *Review of Child Development Research* (Vol. 7, pp. 283–328). Chicago: University of Chicago Press.

Busch, N., Fong, R., Heffron, L., Faulkner, M., & Mahapatra, N. (2007). *Assessing the Need of Human Trafficking Victims: An Evaluation of the Central Texas Coalition Against Human Trafficking*. Austin: University of Texas at Austin, School of Social Work, Center for Social Work Research.

Carlson, E., & Rosser-Hogan, E. (1993). Mental health status of Cambodian refugees ten years after leaving their homes. *American Journal of Orthopsychiatry, 63,* 223–231.

Carranza, M. (2007). Building resilience and resistance against racism and discrimination among Salvadorian female youth in Canada. *Child and Family Social Work, 12,* 390–398.

Carter, B., & McGoldrick, M. (Eds.). (2005). *The Expanded Family Life Cycle: Individual, Family, and Social Perspectives* (3rd ed.). Boston: Allyn & Bacon.

Cattanach, A. (2007). Brief narrative play therapy with refugees. In N. B. Webb (Ed.), *Play Therapy with Children in Crisis: Individual, Group, and Family Treatment* (pp. 426–442). New York: Guilford Press.

Christopher, K. (2000). Determinants of psychological well-being in Irish immigrants. *Western Journal of Nursing Research, 22,* 123–143.

Coles, R. (1986). *The Political Life of Children.* Boston: Houghton Mifflin.

Delgado, M., Jones, K., & Rohani, M. (2005). *Social Work Practice with Immigrant Youth in the United States.* Boston: Pearson Education.

Eisenbruch, M. (1984). From post-traumatic stress disorder to cultural bereavement: Diagnosis of Southeast Asian refugees. *Social Science & Medicine, 33,* 673–680.

Fadiman, A. (1998). *The Spirit Catches You and You Fall Down: A Hmong Child, Her American Doctors, and the Collision of Two Cultures.* New York: Farrar, Straus, & Giroux.

Fong, R. (Ed.). (2004). *Culturally Competent Practice with Immigrant and Refugee Children and Families.* New York: Guilford Press.

Fong, R., Busch, N., Armour, M., Heffron, L., & Chanmugam, A. (2007). Pathways to self sufficiency: Successful entrepreneurship for refugees. *Journal of Ethnic and Cultural Diversity in Social Work, 16,* 127–159.

Foster, R. (2001). When immigration is trauma: Guidelines for the individual and family clinician. *American Journal of Orthopsychiatry, 71,* 153–170.

Fraser, M. W. (1997). *Risk and Resilience in Childhood.* Washington, DC: NASW Press.

Garbarino, J., Dubrow, N., Kostelny, K., & Pardo, C. (1992). *Children in Danger: Coping with Community Violence.* San Francisco: Jossey-Bass.

Garmezy, N. (1993). Children in poverty: Resilience despite risk. *Psychiatry, 56,* 127–136.

Genero, N. P. (1998). *Culture, resiliency, and mutual psychological development.* In H. I. McCubbin, E. A. Thompson, A. I. Thompson, & J. A. Futrell (Eds.), *Resiliency in African-American Families* (pp. 31–48). Thousand Oaks, CA: Sage.

Germain, C. B., & Gitterman, A. (1996). *The Life Model of Social Work: Advances in Theory and Practice.* New York: Columbia University Press.

Gilgun, J. F. (1996). Human development and adversity in ecological perspective, Part 1: A conceptual framework. *Families in Society, 77,* 395–402.

Goodman, M. (2004). Balkan children and families. In R. Fong (Ed.), *Culturally Competent Practice with Immigrant and Refugee Children and Families* (pp. 274–288). New York: Guilford Press.

Gordon, E. W., & Song, L. D. (1994). Variations in the experience of resilience. In M. C. Wang & E. W. Gordon (Eds.), *Educational Resilience in Inner-City America: Challenges and Prospects* (pp. 27–44). Hillsdale, NJ: Erlbaum.

Gorman, W. (2001). Refugee survivors of torture: Trauma and treatment. *Professional Psychology: Research and Practice, 32,* 443–451.

Greene, R. R. (2002). *Resiliency: An Integrated Approach to Practice, Policy, and Research.* Washington, DC: NASW Press.

Greene, R. R. (Ed.). (2007). *Social Work Practice: A Risk and Resilience Perspective.* Monterey, CA: Brooks/Cole.

Greene, R. R. (2008). Resilience. In T. Mizrahi & L. Davis (Eds.), *Encyclopedia of Social Work* (20th ed.). Silver Spring, MD: NASW Press.

Greene, R. R., & Armenta, K. (2007). The REM model: Phase II—Practice strategies. In R. R. Greene (Ed.), *Social Work Practice: A Risk and Resilience Perspective* (pp. 67-90). Monterey, CA: Brooks/Cole.

Grotberg, E. H. (1995, September). *The International Resilience Project: Research, Application, and Policy.* Paper presented at the Symposio Internacional Stress e Violencia, Lisbon, Portugal.

Hawkins, J. D., Catalano, R. F., & Miller, J. Y. (1992). Risk and protective factors for alcohol and other drug problems in adolescence and early adulthood: Implications for substance abuse prevention. *Psychological Bulletin, 112,* 64–105.

Herman, J. (1992). *Trauma and Recovery.* New York: Basic Books.

Hsu, E., Davies, C., & Hansen, D. (2004). Understanding mental health needs of Southeast Asian refugees: Historical, cultural, and contextual challenges. *Clinical Psychology Review, 24,* 193–213.

Hulewat, P. (1996). Resettlement: A cultural and psychological crisis. In P. Ewalt, E. Freeman, A. Fortune, D. Poole, & S. Witkin (Eds.), *Multicultural Issues in Social Work: Practice and Research* (pp. 669–678). Washington, DC: NASW Press.

Kim, E., Kleiber, D. A., & Kropf, N. P. (2001). Leisure activity, ethnic preservation, and cultural integration of older Korean Americans. *Journal of Gerontological Social Work, 36*(1/2), 107–129.

Kinzie, J. D., Fredrickson, R. H., Ben, R., Fleck, J., & Karls, W. (1984). Posttraumatic stress disorder among survivors of Cambodian concentration camps. *American Journal of Psychiatry, 141,* 645–650.

Kohli, R., & Mather, R. (2003). Promoting psychosocial well-being in unaccompanied asylum seeking young people in the United Kingdom. *Child and Family Social Work, 8,* 201–212.

La Fromboise, T. D., Coleman, H. L. K., & Gerton, J. (1993). Psychological impact of biculturalism: Evidence and theory. *Psychological Bulletin, 114,* 395–412.

Lee, E., & Lu, F. (1989). Assessment and treatment of Asian American survivors of mass violence. *Journal of Traumatic Stress, 2,* 93–120.

Lifton, R. J. (1999). *The Protean Self: Human Resilience in an Age of Fragmentation.* Chicago: University of Chicago Press. (Original work published 1993.)

Lum, D. (2007). *Culturally Competent Practice: A Framework for Understanding Diverse Groups and Justice Issues.* Monterey, CA: Brooks/Cole.

Masten, A. (1994). Resilience in individual development: Successful adaptation despite risk and adversity. In M. C. Wang & E. W. Gordon (Eds.), *Educational Resilience in Inner-City America: Challenges and Prospects* (pp. 3–25). Hillsdale, NJ: Erlbaum.

Masten, A., & Coatsworth, J. D. (1998). The development of competence in favorable and unfavorable environments. *American Psychologist, 53,* 205–220.

Masten, A., & Reed, M. (2002). Resilience in development. In C. R. Snyder & S. J. Lopez (Eds.), *Handbook of Positive Psychology* (pp. 74–88). New York: Oxford University Press.

Melville, M. B., & Lykes, M. B. (1992). Guatemalan Indian children and the sociocultural effects of government-sponsored terrorism. *Social Science & Medicine, 34,* 533–548.

Miller, D. B., & MacIntosh, R. (1999). Promoting resilience in urban African American adolescents: Racial socialization and identity as protective factors. *Social Work Research, 23,* 159–170.

Mokuau, N. (Ed.). (1991). *Handbook of Social Services for Asian and Pacific Islanders.* New York: Greenwood Press.

Morelli, P. (2001). Culturally competent assessment of Cambodian survivors of the killing fields: A tool for social justice. In R. Fong & S. Furuto (Eds.), *Culturally Competent Practice: Skills, Interventions, and Evaluations* (pp. 196–210). Boston: Allyn & Bacon.

Mui, A., & Kang, S.-Y. (2006). Acculturation stress and depression among Asian Immigrant elders. *Social Work*, 51, 243–255.

Orum, A. (2005). Circles of influence and chains of command: The social processes whereby ethnic communities influence host societies. *Social Forces*, 84, 921–939.

Romero, A. J., & Roberts, E. R. (2003). Stress within a bicultural context for adolescents of Mexican descent. *Cultural Diversity and Ethnic Minority Psychology*, 9(2), 171–184.

Rumbaut, R., & Weeks, J. (1999). Children of immigrants: Is Americanization hazardous to infant health? In H. Fitzgerald, B. Lester, & B. Zuckerman (Eds.), *Children of Color: Research, Health, and Policy Issues* (pp. 159–184). New York: Garland.

Rutter, M. (1987). Psychological resilience and protective mechanisms. *American Journal of Orthopsychiatry*, 57, 316–331.

Ryff, C. D., & Singer, B. (2002). From social structure to biology: Integrative science in pursuit of human health and well-being. In C. R. Snyder & S. J. Lopez (Eds.), *Handbook of Positive Psychology* (pp. 541–555). New York: Oxford University Press.

Saleebey, D. (1997). *The Strengths Perspective in Social Work Practice* (2nd ed.). New York: Longman.

Schweitzer, R., Melville, F., Steel, Z., & Lacherez, P. (2006). Trauma, post-migration living difficulties, and social support as predictors of psychological adjustment in resettled Sudanese refugees. *Australian and New Zealand Journal of Psychiatry*, 40, 179–187.

Seligman, M. E. P. (2002). Positive psychology, positive prevention, and positive therapy. In C. R. Snyder & S. J. Lopez (Eds.), *Handbook of Positive Psychology* (pp. 3–7). New York: Oxford University Press.

Simich, L., Beiser, M., Stewart, M., & Mwakarimba, E. (2005). Providing social support for immigrants and refugees in Canada: Challenges and directions. *Journal of Immigrant Health*, 7, 259–268.

Solomon, B. (1976). *Black Empowerment: Social Work in Oppressed Communities.* New York: Columbia University Press.

Strumpfer, D. J. W. (2002, September). *A Different Way of Viewing Adult Resilience.* Paper presented at the 34th International Congress on Military Medicine, Sun City, North West Province, South Africa.

Suarez-Orozco, C., & Suarez-Orozco, M. (2001). *Children of Immigration.* Cambridge, MA: Harvard University Press.

Verkuyten, M. (2005). Immigration discourses and their impact on multiculturalism: A discursive and experimental study. *British Journal of Social Psychology*, 44, 223–240.

Walsh, F. (1998a). Beliefs, spirituality, and transcendence: Keys to family resilience. In M. McGoldrick (Ed.), *Re-Visioning Family Therapy: Race, Culture, and Gender in Clinical Practice* (pp. 62–77). New York: Guilford Press.

Walsh, F. (1998b). *Strengthening Family Resilience.* New York: Guilford Press.

Weaver, H., Hunt-Jackson, J., & Burns, B. (2003). Asylum seekers along the U.S. Canada border: Challenges of a vulnerable population. *Journal of Immigrant and Refugee Services*, 1(3/4), 81–98.

Webb, N. (Ed.). (2001). *Culturally Diverse Parent-Child and Family Relationships: A Guide for Social Workers and Other Practitioners.* New York: Guilford Press.

Webb, N. (Ed.). (2007). *Play Therapy with Children in Crisis: Individual, Group, and Family Treatment.* New York: Guilford Press.

Werner, E., & Smith, R. S. (1982). *Vulnerable, but Invincible: A Longitudinal Study of Resilient Children and Youth.* New York: McGraw-Hill.

Werner, E., & Smith, R. S. (1992). *Overcoming the Odds: High Risk Children from Birth to Adulthood.* Ithaca, NY: Cornell University Press.

White, M., & Epston, D. (1990). *Narrative Means to Therapeutic Ends.* New York: Norton.

Zea, M. C., Diehl, V. A., & Porterfield, K. S. (1996). Central American youth exposed to war violence. In J. G. García & M. C. Zea (Eds.), *Psychological Interventions and Research with Latino Populations* (pp. 39–55). Boston: Allyn & Bacon.

Zhou, M., & Bankston, C. (1998). *Growing up American: How Vietnamese Children Adapt to Life in the United States.* New York: Russell Sage Foundation.

Zuniga, M. E. (2002). Latino immigrants: Patterns of survival. *Journal of Human Behavior and the Social Environment*, 5(3/4), 137–155.

8

A Systems Approach: Addressing Diverse Family Forms

Roberta R. Greene, Nancy Kropf, and Karen Frankel

> *The very concept of the family has been undergoing redefinition as tumultuous social and economic changes in recent decades have altered the landscape of family life. Amid the turmoil, couples [partners] have been forging new and varied arrangements as they strive to build caring committed relationships. (Walsh, 2003, p. 4)*

This chapter outlines the basic tenets of general systems theory as well as key concepts from select schools of family therapy. It then critiques how these assumptions and concepts have been used to serve diverse family forms. It specifically emphasizes human behavior principles that explain differences in family culture, composition, and developmental processes. The chapter also examines the literature that takes issue with or augments the family systems perspective of assessment and intervention, particularly the application of this perspective in certain family therapy approaches.

Since the 1960s, the structure and functioning of American families have undergone rapid and far-reaching changes. Social workers are increasingly practicing with single-parent households; gay and lesbian couples; remarried and dual-career families; and multiple generation, step, or blended families, among others.

The previous modal family form of the heterosexual, first-married, two-parent household has now given way to a multitude of structural and membership forms with the definition broadening (Erera, 2002). Given the variation in composition, a range of definitions has emerged regarding what constitutes a family, from the traditional family (a nuclear unit composed of blood relatives) to the self-defined family unit composed of individuals bound together by emotional relationships (Greene, 2008a). That is,

> a family consists of a domestic group of people (or a number of domestic groups), typically affiliated by birth or marriage, or by analogous or comparable relationships—including domestic partnership, cohabitation, adoption, and surname.... A family could also be people being joined by love and/or promises of commitment. (*http://en.wikipedia.org/wiki/Family*)

In some parts of the world, it is necessary to use the word *kinship* to describe the family, encompassing the *tribe*, *clan*, and one's *father's house*.

In addition to these various family forms, social workers are increasingly serving ethnic minority families. Although a family's culture influences how it defines a problem and the way in which it tends to seek help, the literature on family-centered approaches mainly uses a frame of reference centered around the white, middle-class U.S. family (Ho, Rasheed, & Rasheed, 2003). Only recently have ethnic differences been considered when developing therapeutic models (Alemàn, Fitzpatrick, Tran, & Gonzalez, 2000; McCubbin, McCubbin, Thompson, & Thompson, 1998; Walsh, 1996, 2003, 2006). Ho et al. suggested that this insensitivity is often a problem because some of these interventions diametrically oppose indigenous cultural beliefs and family structure.

Social workers must not only understand the role of culture and ethnicity in family life but be prepared to understand the developmental histories of client families (McCubbin, Thompson, Thompson, & Futrell, 1998; Pinderhughes, 1982, 1995). For example, Stewart (2004) pointed out that an African American family cannot be understood without addressing its African roots. In viewing the history of the family through an Afrocentric perspective (e.g., Billingsley, 1994; Schiele, 1996), Stewart proposed Afrocentric interventions to deal with some of the social problems that families are facing today. An Afrocentric perspective stresses the sense of connectedness between individual, family, community, and culture. Spirituality is an important part of this perspective as well and affirms "the interconnectedness of all living things" (p. 225). However, the importance of recognizing subgroups between African American families cannot be overlooked. Differences exist between African American families that are important dimensions of assessment and practice, including religious and spiritual belief systems, socioeconomic and educational levels, skin color, and levels of acculturation (Boyd-Franklin, 1995, 2003). To provide effective services to diverse families, social workers must be armed with a human behavior theory that can address each family's "persistent system of rules, predominant themes and patterns of behavior, and particular pattern of adaptation and change" (Hartman & Laird, 1983, p. 105).

Research has suggested that failure to address families in a manner sensitive their values and culture often leads to ineffective service (Doherty & Boss, 1992). For example, as a result of their research with the National Chicano Research Network, Rothman, Gant, and Hnat (1985) found that failure to identify family cultural characteristics in the design of intervention strategies resulted in less effective service delivery. They urged that research be used more extensively to derive culturally sensitive family social work techniques.

Beyond their work with a particular family, practitioners must work to alleviate forms of social oppression. Poverty is one such difficulty. "To work with the poor may be to contend with social issues about money, housing, crime-ridden neighborhoods, as well as racial, ethnic, and cultural discrimination" (Aponte,

1994, p. 13). In fact, "practitioners should know that unwillingness to challenge and address oppression in large societal systems is akin to aiding families in adjusting to their oppressors. Oppression can never be accepted as normal" (Hopps & Kilpatrick, 2006, p. 39).

Although a considerable body of theory informs family-focused social work practice, in many instances general systems theory has been used to better understand the reciprocal interactions among a system's members in many types of systems (Hepworth, Rooney, Larsen, Rooney, & Strom-Gottfried, 2005; Minuchin & Montalvo, 1971). Because general systems theory is a highly abstract model, it is viewed as being well suited for explicating the value orientation, culture, and developmental stage of a particular family, often within the context of other ecological systems (Fong & Furuto, 2001). For example, Greene (2008a) believes that systems theory's broad universal principles suggest the inclusion of cross-cultural content and have the potential to offer culture- and gender-fair assessment and intervention techniques. She argued that this theory is particularly useful in understanding the evolution of a culture and in appraising transactions between different cultural systems, thus permitting an understanding of various family forms.

Basic Assumptions: A Critique of Universality

In family groups, all members influence and are influenced by every other member, creating a system that has properties of its own and that is governed by a set of implicit rules, power structure, forms of communication, and ways of negotiating and solving problems. (Hepworth et al., 2005, p. 263)

General systems theory is a comprehensive model for analyzing the interaction and relational qualities between and among the components of a system. Its assumptions serve as a working hypothesis for explaining, predicting, and controlling phenomena. General systems theory, which came to the fore in the late 1960s and early 1970s, provides a multicausal context for understanding human behavior, emphasizes the interdependence and interactions among people, and considers the many systems in which people interact (Schriver, 2003). The theory, especially when combined with an ecological perspective (see Chapter 10), is a means of conceptualizing the mutual interrelatedness of individuals, families, social groups, communities, and societies. Systems theory is a way of thinking in an organized, integrated way about the interactions among system members (see Table 8.1).

A *social system* is a defined structure of interacting and interdependent persons that has the capacity for organized activity. As a social system develops over time, it takes on a unique character. Because of the high degree of interaction and interdependence among system members, systems theory proposes that a change in any one member of the system affects the social system as a whole.

Table 8.1
Systems Theory: Basic Assumptions

- A social system comprises interrelated members who constitute a unit or a whole.
- The organizational "limits" of a social system are defined by its established or arbitrarily defined boundaries and identified membership.
- Boundaries give the social system its identity and focus as a system.
- A systems environment is an environment that is defined as outside the system's boundaries.
- The life of a social system is more than just the sum of its participants' activities. Rather, a social system can be studied as a network of unique, interlocking relationships with discernible structural and communication patterns.
- There is a high degree of interdependence and internal organization among members of a social system.
- All systems are subsystems of other (larger) systems.
- There is an interdependency and mutual interaction between and among social systems.

Source. Greene, R. R. (2008a). General systems theory. In R. R. Greene (Ed.), *Human Behavior Theory and Social Work Practice.* New Brunswick, NJ: Aldine Transaction.

Systems theory also suggests a number of concepts that may be applied to diverse family forms. Perhaps its most important assumption is that each family has its own interlocking network of relationships with discernible structural and communication patterns. Minuchin (1974), one of the founders of structural family therapy, defined a family as a system that operates though repeated transactional patterns of how, when, and to whom members relate: "Family structure is the [resulting] invisible set of functional demands that organizes the way in which family members interact" (p. 51).

Another major assumption of the theory is that because each family has a history of working together and maintaining a sense of balance, its structure, energy exchange, and organization—or its system of relationships—vary. Through repetitive exchanges, each family develops distinctive patterns of *roles*, that is, differentiation of members by tasks. These patterns provide the family with cognitive maps about how to interact in reciprocal roles such as mother/daughter or husband/wife (Greene, 2008b; see Chapter 5 for a discussion of role theory).

Over time, family interaction also produces *subsystems*, components of a system that are themselves systems. Parent, sibling, or spouse family subsystems, for example, tend to follow an observable pattern based on the family's needs and culture. An example of a shift within the subsystems of a family is when, in later life caregiving, an adult child becomes the care provider for an older parent. Another example is when a father becomes a stay-at-home parent and the mother the primary breadwinner. Both of these situations can present possible disruptions within the family. As role shifts become necessary, there also may be a realignment with social systems in the environment. The practitioner needs to be aware of the consequences of these changes for the family as a whole, as well as for the individual members (Greene, 2008c).

Furthermore, family interactions create a *hierarchy*, a power structure or a means of distributing power in particular circumstances. Moreover, all families have *rules*—implicit and explicit agreements about duties, rights, and the range of appropriate and acceptable behaviors. Social workers can come to understand a family's rules because these rules are reflected in a family's *communication patterns*, the flow of information within and from outside the system. For example, Hepworth et al. (2005) argued that because a major rule in many cultural groups is a pattern of discouraging open communication, practitioners must seek culturally acceptable ways of gaining pertinent information.

Energy, which deals with a system's capacity to act and maintain itself, is another important property of a social system. Energy is a family's power to organize itself (to keep itself in working balance) and its ability to obtain sufficient resources from its environment. Social workers, who hope to see a family become adaptive, often set goals with families to obtain needed resources. The more *adaptive systems* use energy well and are able to keep relatively organized through effective communication, thus obtaining sufficient resources from the surrounding environment.

When energy is insufficient and communication poor, tension results in the family's internal organization. The literature suggests that these families are relatively *dysfunctional*, apt to be inflexible, less open to other social institutions, and therefore less effective (Goldenberg & Goldenberg, 2007). Families that are relatively more functional tend to be better organized, have effective communication, and allow for the development of individuals.

However, what constitutes functional and dysfunctional behavior is debatable. These terms are used to describe what is working or not working in a family and what may be the source of distress. Hepworth et al. (2005) suggested that practitioners view functional and dysfunctional behavior within the context of a family's culture. This concept, known as *cultural relativity*, means that behavior found unacceptable in one culture may be perceived as acceptable in another. This relative approach allows the practitioner to ask what is functional to what ends and for whom (Walsh, 2003). In contrast, some theorists believe that "there is indeed psychopathological behavior" and that a universal standard can be set (Trepper, 1987, p. xi). In a cultural climate of uncertainty about the future of societal norms and of the family, it can be expected that these various perspectives on family life will continue to be debated (Walsh, 2003).

Although the family systems perspective is often characterized as neutral, the approach has been criticized for placing insufficient attention on factors of culture, class, ethnicity/race, gender, or age. The remainder of the chapter examines this contention.

Family-Focused Social Work Interventions and Diversity

The boundaries between social work and family therapy are hard to draw because there is extensive overlap. (Hartman, 1995, p. 985)

Social work practice with families dates back to the inception of the profession. Today, most social work practice is family centered and reflects involvement with the family therapy movement, which has strong ties to general systems theory (Greene, 2008a). Family-centered social work, part of direct practice in social work that emphasizes adaptation among individuals, families, and groups and their environments, has come to include a broad spectrum of services and methods of intervention, such as marital and family therapies, problem-solving guidance, environmental intervention, and advocacy, as well as homemaker services, financial relief, or other tangible assistance (Greene, 2008c).

A major general systems theory theme in most family approaches is that in attempting to alleviate family difficulties, social workers attend to the impact of one family member's behavior on another's. Generally speaking, family-centered interventions are indicated when the family is unable to perform its basic functions. Practitioners also address how a family changes and use interventions designed to modify those elements of the family relationship system that are interfering with the life tasks of the family and its members.

Most family-centered social workers share the view that if an individual changes, the family context in which he or she lives will also change, and vice versa. Hence, the ultimate goal of most family-centered social work is to enhance the social functioning of all persons (Hartman 1995). Family-focused interventions tend to recognize that one family member's symptoms or problems usually bring a family for help, and so the focus of family approaches is altering family relationship patterns.

From a systems perspective, "problem behavior" is seen as not exclusively influenced by personality and past events. Rather, behaviors are influenced by current patterns of interaction between family members and between the family and its environments. Family theorists suggest that when problem behavior persists, the resolution of the problem usually requires an appropriate change in behavior within the family interaction system (Hartman, 1995; Hartman & Laird, 1987; Herr & Weakland, 1979).

Family social work, then, may be defined as an interactional process of planned interventions in an area of family difficulty. The family is a self-regulating or rule-governed group with fairly consistent patterns over time. Interventions are aimed at the system as a whole, with the family's structure, organization, development, and openness to its environment as the targets of intervention. General systems theorists argue that the impetus for change rests with the family members, particularly in making adjustments in their daily lives (Hartman & Laird, 1987). The idea that the family comprises individuals who make up an entity, system, or group that is capable of solving its problems is at the center of general systems interventions.

Schools of Family Therapy

The degree of emphasis on these general systems principles varies within major schools of family therapy (Hartman, 1995). The different methods of family treatment form a treatment continuum. At one end of the continuum, the concept of the family emphasizes emotional or affective relationships within the system. The therapist promotes health and growth through insight-oriented techniques and uses transference for therapeutic goals (Ackerman, 1972; see Chapter 2 for a discussion of transference). At the other end of the continuum, therapists aim to intervene in the structure and communication patterns of the family to improve an area of family dysfunction. The focus of family therapy, then, is to alter the structure of the family group and the functions, or roles, of individual family members (Bowen, 1971; Crawford, 1987; Haley, 1963; Minuchin, 1974).

The selection of family therapy techniques is influenced by the social worker's personal style and theoretical beliefs, characteristics of the family system, personalities of family members, the developmental stage of the family, the nature and severity of the presenting problem, particular family members present, and desired therapeutic goals (Goldenberg & Goldenberg, 2007). Variation exists in family-focused social work and family therapy approaches, styles, and techniques as well as in settings and specific client groups. Intervention goals also differ in emphasis and include restructuring the family (Minuchin, 1974), resolving intergenerational conflict (Bowen, 1971), renegotiating roles (Satir, 1967), and improving communication (Haley, 1976).

Families and Belief Systems

As social workers increasingly serve families of diverse forms and cultural backgrounds, it is imperative for them to use family-focused interventions sensitively and selectively and to address family patterns and belief systems (T. Anderson, 1991; Hepworth et al., 2005; Merighi & Grimes, 2000). A number of theorists have suggested that general systems theory has brought social work practice to a more value-free, if not more universal, orientation (Berger & Federico, 1982; Janchill, 1969; Meyer, 1973). Social workers have a framework for understanding the cultural context of how client families seek help. For example, McCubbin, Fleming, et al. (1998) offered a culturally sensitive resilience-based systems model for working with "at-risk" African American youth and their families. Iris HeavyRunner and Kathy Marshall (2003) developed a college-level program for native students that identifies cultural factors essential in preventing alcohol and drug abuse in American Indian families and communities. Based on their findings, HeavyRunner and Marshall developed the family education model to foster cultural resilience and to build college retention among students at tribal colleges. The program includes culturally specific family activities on campus, individual and family counseling, formal and informal mentoring, seminars and workshops on family life skills, networking, and an evaluation. They stated that natural helping systems may also be employed when helping Native families. Other theorists have incorporated helping strategies involving historical and cultural perspectives, such as attention to the sociopolitical trauma experienced by Native peoples (Yellow Horse Brave Heart, 2001).

Families, Social Justice, and Ethical/Value Orientations

Some theorists have argued that a general systems approach in family therapy has neither sufficiently made room for social justice and individual choice nor challenged the status quo (Aponte, 1994; Hoffman, 1990). For example, in a discussion of the problem of gender in family therapy, Hare-Mustin (1986, 1989) contended that the use of systems theory in family therapy has led to a microscopic examination of family interaction but ignores societal changes and the concern for equality within the family. She suggested that practitioners who consider differentiation and negotiation as the most important intervention goals ignore "differences in power, resources, needs, and interests among family members" (Hare-Mustin, 1989, p. 69). That is, practitioners alter the internal functioning of families without proper concern for political, economic, and social contexts (Carter & McGoldrick, 2005).

In addition, Hoffman (1985, 1990) proposed that practitioners should not act as experts who assess and describe family problems. She and other construction-ist theorists (Laird, 1993) have contended that giving people negative causal explanations of their problems serves only to maintain the family's problem and maintain negative power relationships. Instead, constructionist theorists suggest that descriptions of a family's problematic behavior be coconstructed with the family, paying ample attention to subjective ideas and exploring alter-native courses of action (Knei-Paz & Ribner, 2000; Mailick & Vigilante, 1997). This alternative approach to intervening in circular, patterned cycles of events is known as *second-order cybernetics* and is increasingly used in family treat-ment (Hoffman, 1992; Madanes, 1990, 1991; see Chapter 6 for a discussion of constructionism).

Margolin (1982) stated that family therapy has different, if not more complex, ethical questions than individual psychotherapy, such as the following: Who is the client? How is confidential information handled? Does each family member have an equal right to refuse treatment? What is the role of the therapist vis-à-vis conflicting values of family members? (p. 789). Ryders (1987) took the point a step further and argued that family therapists often bury their value stances in the jargon they use to describe families, such as *dysfunctional* or *marital satisfaction* (p. 136). Aponte (1994) argued that values are central to family therapy. He proposed that a practitioner's values are central to all social system operations and are therefore at the core of the therapeutic process. Therefore, social workers do not have the option of whether to deal with values in therapy but must figure out how well they can accomplish this task, especially when serving people in poverty.

Although family therapies may "appear to transcend the atomic individual," they are nonetheless "part of the American culture" or part of the mainstream of mental health practice (Doherty & Boss, 1992, p. 613). Therefore, the various family therapies follow other clinical professions and tend to ignore larger social, cultural, and political issues. According to Doherty and Boss, family therapy has tended to make family problems private matters rather than public concerns. How much should issues in the larger social sphere, such as gender and culture, be included in setting goals of therapy? To what extent should differentiation of self be considered a universal life goal suitable for therapy?

In another critique of the family systems perspective, Hare-Mustin (1978) suggested that "when we alter the internal functioning of the family without concern for the social, economic, and political context, we are in complicity with the society to keep the family unchanged" (p. 183). Likewise, Aponte (1979, 1987, 1994) argued that the relationship of societal forces to intrapsychic or mental distress has not been sufficiently addressed.

Inattention to the effects of such strains on family structure often is a barrier to family-centered interventions. To be effective, a family systems perspective must consider ethnicity and socioeconomic influences on family lifestyles as well as the way in which gender shapes role expectations, experiences, goals, and opportunities within the family (Goldenberg & Goldenberg, 2007).

Culture and the Family

Ethnicity and family life are two concepts which … go hand in hand. They are so en-twined that it is very difficult indeed to observe the one or even to reflect it seriously without coming to grips with the other. (Billingsley, 1976, p. 13)

For social workers to provide culturally sensitive assessment and treatment for families with ethnic and cultural backgrounds different from their own, it is necessary for them to understand the cultural aspects of family systems (Genero, 1998; Mailick & Vigilante, 1997; Tseng & Hsu, 1991). As family members inter-act with one another and the environment, they develop a set of shared meanings that serve as a social foundation for their culture (Norlin, Chess, Dale, & Smith, 2002). *Culture* refers to a group's way of life: those elements of a people's his-tory, tradition, values, and social organization that become implicitly or explicitly meaningful to the participants (Greene, 2002).

The family is often viewed as the basic sociocultural institution through which culture is transmitted. Societal culture is said to shape the cycle of growth of family systems members as well as the group's culture. The family maintains itself throughout its life by adhering to its own values and beliefs (Patterson &

Marsiglia, 2000; Walsh, 2006). Culture, then, is the symbolic image of a family's purpose that its members incorporate into daily living.

Castex (1993) cautioned, though, that ethnic groups are not static and must be understood as evolving interactional units that change over time. She warned that practitioners must shy away from the notion that there is a list of ethnic traits to describe any one family. This approach increases the risk of stereotyping and avoiding the effects of power relations on group behavior.

In a similar vein, Germain (1991) argued that social workers must be self-aware so that they can be more sensitive to the differences in behavior, expectations, and attitudes of diverse families. However, practitioners must be careful to distinguish between the general cultural traits, values, and norms attributed to a group, such as those found in some anthropological texts, and the unique features of a specific family group. James Green (1999) proposed an ethnographic approach to understanding specific families as a method of culturally sound understanding (see Chapter 1 for a description of this approach).

In a book dedicated to presenting a conceptual framework for family therapy with ethnic minority families, Ho et al. (2003) outlined the major features of culturally sensitive family therapy with ethnic minorities. They proposed that cross-cultural family practice

- recognizes that some of the assumptions of a particular human behavior theory may be antithetical to a particular cultural orientation;
- uses theory-based practice differentially;
- considers the family's sociopolitical history and present situation;
- is congruent with the family's belief system and ethical and value orientations;
- is accepting of the way in which a particular family defines its problem and expresses help-seeking behaviors;
- identifies and works within a particular family's form;
- is based on a culturally sound examination of family structure and communication patterns;
- may, at times, be delivered in a language other than English or by a social intermediary;
- recognizes the way in which culture shapes individual and family life experiences as well as developmental transitions;
- is sensitive to the influences of culture on a family's role differentiation and process of self-definition;
- selects skills and techniques differentially to achieve congruence with a family's culture;
- uses a multisystems approach;
- uses natural support systems and helpers, such as healers and religious leaders;
- selects goals culturally congruent with and mutually satisfactory to the family's goals; and
- is open to the family members' ideas about what is effective for them.

Class

Class and ethnicity may be distinguished from culture. *Social class* is based on differences in wealth, income, occupation, status, community power, level of consumption, and family background. Because the same people may belong to different social classes, ethnic groups, and cultures, seemingly similar groups may vary. For example, Logan (1990) cautioned that black culture should not be seen as "an 'underclass' world view, [that is,] that poverty and black culture are not to be viewed interchangeably" (p. 25). Rather, the issue of distinguishing class and culture is related to the controversy over why a group has a particular social and/or economic status (Chestang, 1972; Franklin, 1988; Freedman, 1990a; Hollingsworth, 1999; see Chapter 11 for a discussion of power factors in social work practice). *Ethnicity*, or the behavioral and cognitive participation in the symbolic communication of a group, usually involves a common language. Many ethnic groups or subcommunities, each with its own common history, ancestry, and status (or power position), exist in U.S. society. The idea is increasingly proposed that the United States is a multicultural society, a society in which "ethnic identities are not amalgamated ... [but] should remain a mosaic of separate, diverse, and equally proud identities" (Longres, 2000, p. 78).

Biculturalism

Biculturalism refers to membership in two cultural systems. The *dual perspective* assumes that "every individual is part of two systems: the small system of the client's immediate environment and the larger social system" (Greene, Taylor, Evans, & Smith, 2002, p. 243). There may be differences in acculturation (how much a person takes on the "mainstream" culture) among family members. For example, in Asian/Pacific families, children, in contrast to their parents, tend to be more receptive to Western culture. When children are more open to ideas of individualism and sexual freedom than are their parents, family dysfunction may occur (Ho et al., 2003).

For parents, socialization of children into two cultural systems involves insight and sensitivity. Children need to adapt to two styles of behavior or social roles, as well as master the ability to move back and forth between these two settings; for example, black parents must help their children function in both a black and a white society (McAdoo, 2006). Part of this quest is to help children learn to take advantage of resources and opportunities within the mainstream culture without compromising pride in their own heritage and identity. Promoting a dual-cultural perspective for children is a complex and involved task for parents. As Comer and Poussaint (1992) stated, "Many black parents question and have mixed feelings about passing on the values and ways of a society that says in so many ways, 'we do not value black men and women, boys and girls, as much as we do whites'" (p. 2).

Immigrant Families

Therapists need to be sensitive to the cultural transitions and cognitive changes that are often made as newly immigrant families become oriented to life in the United States. Matsuoka (1990) pointed out that there is usually a culture conflict when people migrate from one culture to another or when individuals in a pluralistic culture move from their ethnic community into the mainstream environment. He suggested that because there has been differential acculturation among Vietnamese refugees, there may be disruption in traditional age-related family roles. In particular, families that include older members may experience additional stresses as younger generations (e.g., school-aged children) acculturate quickly and older family members may cling to more traditional cultural patterns of behavior. This is especially complex in light of the numerous geopolitical changes that have occurred globally, as older immigrants may experience compound grief if their "homeland" no longer exists. Such is the case with older Russian immigrants who may experience grief, mourning, and a sense of loss for parts of their Soviet culture and identity that no longer exist (Kropf, Nackerud, & Gorokhovski, 1999).

Given the large numbers of immigrants to the United States who may seek assistance, social workers need to understand these possible cultural factors and disruptions. However, immigrants often exhibit signs of resilience and the ability to overcome difficult transitions. Clearly, culturally appropriate methods are needed, particularly for refugees in crisis or for those for whom the very concept of "social work" does not exist (Queralt, 1984; Timberlake & Cook, 1984; Weiss & Parish, 1989; see Chapter 7). In order that social workers might practice in a culturally competent way, several practice and intervention principles have been outlined to guide practitioners in working with immigrant clients and families (Damsky, 2000):

- Understand the historical context that has shaped the client's experience in the country of origin.
- Understand how the stress of immigration has had an impact on the client and the family.
- Be sensitive to issues of acculturation, loss, and grief. This is especially acute in those clients who have left their homeland because of political, ethnic, or religious persecution.
- Be mindful of family structure issues, including family values of individualism, communalism, authority, control, and personal fulfillment.

Structural Issues and Diverse Family Forms

Family structure and lifestyles vary, especially at this time in society when a variety of family forms is becoming more common.... Each of these family forms has its own particular strengths and vulnerabilities. (Chilman, Nunnally, & Cox, 1988, p. 9)

Roles

Socially recognized family roles tend to be those explicitly and implicitly defined by culture. For many decades, general U.S. society conceptualized the family as comprising a husband/father who worked to support the family, a wife/mother who raised the children full time, and their biological, dependent children (Parsons & Bales, 1955; see Chapter 5 on role theory). These roles generally were associated with traditional family functions, which included the legitimation of mating and sexual reproduction; the socialization of all members, particularly children; the economic maintenance of the group; the division of domestic labor; and the transmission of culture (Germain, 1991).

However, there is increasing debate about the way in which roles are defined as well as about the evolution of family organization, form, or structure. This debate stems largely from changing roles and forms of the U.S. family, including differences in role expectation by gender (Cinamon, 2006; Longres, 2000). For example, longitudinal research on married/cohabiting couples indicates that one partner's attitudes toward egalitarian roles within a relationship will shift over time to become similar to his or her partner's (Kalmijn, 2005). From a systems perspective, this finding reinforces the mutual and reciprocal influences within the relationship that shape the distribution of roles and tasks that are assumed by both individuals of the couple.

Practitioners must be aware that personal and family definitions vary widely (Duberman, 1975; Tseng & Hsu, 1991). For example, Hepworth et al. (2005) cautioned that each culture has different role expectations and distribution of labor in the family, particularly concerning male and female roles sometimes understood as rules (Jackson, 1965). Therefore, social workers must assess the extent to which there is a goodness of fit between individual roles and the needs of family members.

Hepworth et al. (2005) provided the following assessment questions regarding family roles:

- To what extent are role assignments in the family made on the basis of gender rather than factors such as abilities, interests, and available time of individual members to perform various roles?
- How clearly are roles defined in the family?
- How satisfied are marital partners with their prescribed roles, and to what extent is each willing to consider adjustments when dissatisfaction is a key in family problems? How flexible is the entire family system in readjusting roles in response to everyday pressures and changing circumstances?
- How adequately do spouses (partners) perform in their designated roles as partner and/or parent?
- To what extent are pressures and stresses in the family caused by role overload, a state of affairs when partners play too many roles at home and at work for the time and energy they have available? (pp. 290–291)

Historical Differences in Family Definition Based on Structure

The family as a social institution exists in all societies. Yet there have been numerous approaches to the study of the family and typologies of family forms. Sociologists and anthropologists have distinguished between various family systems relating to such parameters as *marriage forms* (the number of spouses a person has at one time); *choice of mates* (the choice of partners inside or outside one's own kin group); *descent system* (the rights and obligations as seen in male kinship connections, female kinship connections, or both); *postmarital residence choice* (the patterns of residence based on whether it is a new place of one's own or near the husband's or wife's family); and *household structure* (persons who share living quarters and family functions).

Families also may vary according to how they allocate authority, power, and decision making, whether customarily relegated to the men, women, or both (Tseng & Hsu, 1991). In addition, family patterns must be understood in relation to historical, political, and economic variables (Coontz, 2005; Franklin, 1988). For example, to understand current African American families, according to Dodson (1988), it is necessary to examine multiple factors, such as the influence of African culture, the inherent strength of family networks, the oppressive racial conditions in American society, and the social class differences between and within groups.

Practitioners must be familiar with the sociocultural and historical conception of the family: Franklin (1988) contended that the strong family tradition among blacks survived "the slave system, then legal segregation, discrimination, and enforced poverty, and finally ... racially hostile governmental and societal practices, policies, and attitudes" (p. 25). Sudarkasa (1988) argued that to understand the African American family, it is necessary to avoid false dichotomies concerning explanations of Black family organization:

> Just as surely as Black American family patterns are in part an outgrowth of the descent into slavery, so too are they partly a reflection of the archetypical African institutions and values that informed and influenced the behavior of those Africans who were enslaved in America. (p. 27)

Sudarkasa suggested that Western or European cultures tend to follow conjugal patterns of family organization (i.e., *affinal kinship* created between spouses), whereas African families have traditionally been organized around *consanguineal cores* (i.e., biologically based kinship that is rooted in blood ties formed by adult siblings of the same gender).

Indeed, according to Longres, American family life is taking different forms. Such forms may include serial monogamy-repeated marriages one at a time after divorce or widowhood, the one-parent family, stepfamilies or reconstituted families, cohabiting couples, and gay and lesbian couples. Harry (1988) proposed that gay and lesbian families be defined as "a homosexual person tied by affectional and/or erotic needs to either another homosexual person or to children with whom they may cohabit" (p. 6). In addition, Cooper (1999) discussed social work practice with families who have a transgender child. Across these different family forms and concomitant issues, social work practitioners need to be sensitive to the experiences of the family members and the relationship of the family to the larger environmental context.

Family Boundaries and Family Forms

From a family systems perspective, a family may be defined as "two or more people in a committed relationship from which they derive a sense of identity as a family" (Chilman et al., 1988, p. 11). Hartman and Laird (1984) defined the family as consisting "of two or more people who have made a commitment to share living space, have developed emotional ties, and share a variety of family roles and functions" (p. 30). These definitions are broad enough to include many nontraditional family forms. Each family unit, then, has its own identity and focus as a system, distinguishable from other social systems by its *boundaries*, or organizational "limits." Boundaries are the permeable limits of a system that define who is inside or outside the system or who participates, and how.

From a systems point of view, people who join together and acknowledge family membership constitute a family and become the unit of social work attention. In addition, people within the systems boundaries have specific functions and roles or behavioral demands. Systems theory definitions are said to offer a means of understanding a family's cultural values and assessing their unique form, structured pattern of relationships, and communication style, as well as specific needs for intervention.

Lesbian Couples

With the advent of social changes facing gay and lesbian individuals, several modifications are taking place within these families (Laird, 2003). The literature increasingly offers research and theoretical constructs about the pattern of developmental processes and coherent personal identity of persons with a homosexual orientation (Brown, 1995; Fassinger & Miller, 1996; Herdt, 1992; Slater, 1999; Swann & Anastas, 2003). Too often, however, the literature on family interventions assumes that the family is a heterosexual unit.

Theorists who have offered suggestions for family therapy with lesbian couples have suggested a redefinition of the family to include factors such as continuity of commitment by members over a significant period of time, mutual obligation, economic and domestic interdependence, and performance of daily family functions (Poverny & Finch, 1988). Definitions are seen as having important implications for policy and practice.

From a systems perspective, the broader definition suggests that practitioners aim to understand the way in which lesbian couples tend to be oppressed by general society. Furthermore, Laird (1996) described the intersection of gender identity and socialization that takes place within lesbian couples and that requires redefinition of social roles and relational and intimacy styles. In addition, she also proposed that societal oppression makes the family-building process more difficult for lesbians than for the heterosexual family. Harry (1988) contended that forgoing concealment by homosexual couples may be "fraught with dangers" and may produce "permanent or long-term rejection" (p. 6).

When practitioners examine their own notions of the family and expand their definitions, they are better able to identify significant members of the client system as well as the issues they face (Crawford, 1988). For this reason, Laird (1996) advocated for a theoretical and intervention model that uses a constructionist approach to focus on client narratives rather than dominant theories. Practitioners who are conversant with a systemic approach to helping lesbian families have suggested that problems be explored in such a way as to expand the family's ideas and beliefs about themselves, thereby seeking a greater number of possible solutions.

Single Parents

Since the 1970s, the number of single-parent families has increased dramatically. In 1970, there were about 3 million mother-headed families, but by 2003, this number had grown to about 10 million (U.S. Census Bureau, 2004). Despite the increasing number of one-parent families over the decades, family therapists have not focused much attention on this form; instead, the literature has concentrated on the parental or marital subsystem, the parent–child subsystem, and the sibling subsystem (Westcot & Dries, 1991). Kissman (1991) urged that social work with single-parent families "redefine the boundaries of 'functional' family norms" and not use "negative comparisons with 'intact' families" (pp. 23–24).

Family therapy is a psychotherapeutic approach that concentrates on changing interactions between family members and between families and other interpersonal systems in a way that improves the dynamics of the family, the subsystems, and the individual members (Greene, in 2008b). Although this definition does not preclude work with single-parent families, it does not focus on the particular needs of these families, such as the way in which single-parent status was acquired (e.g., a child born to a single woman, divorce, death, or abandonment by a parent; Morawetz & Walker, 1984). Nearly a quarter of the nation's unmarried women become mothers. The social and political explanations for single parenthood are beyond the scope of this chapter and are a matter of heated debate among social scientists.

Nonetheless, most single parents face social stigmatization because they are seen as having a "broken home." Therefore, it is even more important for therapists not to view the single parent as having an emotional disability because he or she is living in a nontraditional family. If this stereotyping occurs, the treatment adds to the problem-generating cycle. In addition, the family therapy focus frequently is not on stressors (e.g., child maladjustment due to death or divorce of one parent, grief, loss, guilt, visitation rights, parenting functions, financial matters, and social life issues; Korittko, 1991).

Feminist-based social workers have argued that practitioners need to take a more holistic view of single-parent families (C. Anderson, 2003) and recognize and address the strengths of single-parent families. They have contended that interventions with single-parent families across the life cycle can be linked to important feminist social work tenets such as networking, awareness, support, and self-help.

Furthermore, theorists who have discussed the phenomenon of single parenthood in the African American community have suggested that, although the level of poverty among single-parent families is of great concern, to enhance quality of social and economic opportunities social workers need to understand the social and cultural contexts of early childbearing (Dore & Dumois, 1990; Logan, Freeman, & McRoy, 1990). One such exploration is a seminal study by Stack (1975), who lived for several years in a low-income Black community in the midwestern United States and described that community's adaptive response to childrearing. Stack's study discussed the community's cultural value of the inherent worth of each child as well as the way in which black fathers remained connected to their children through kinship networks.

Disproportionately, single parents head families of color. Contemporary social problems have challenged these families and communities and have also caused a number of shifts in childrearing forms. However, single parenting is not by itself a risk factor for children (Kesner & McKenry, 2001). Structural issues, such as poverty and access to adequate resources such as health care and education, are crucial to children's development in these families (and any others). In addition, the involvement of nonresidential fathers is another factor that is crucial to development of children (Leite & McKenry, 2006).

Single-parent families may also be headed by a custodial grandparent who is raising one or more grandchildren. As with other caregiving roles, women greatly outnumber men when it comes to raising grandchildren, with estimates of grandmothers among custodial grandparents ranging from 77 percent to 86 percent (Fuller-Thomson, Minkler, & Driver, 1997; Hayslip, Shore, Henderson, & Lambert, 1998). A significant number of these families are maintained solely by a grandparent without a partner present (Bryson & Casper, 1999). As the number of single-parent households grows, practitioners need to be aware that a number of grandparents are also raising their grandchildren.

As in other family treatment approaches, applying a systemic perspective to family therapy with single-parent families means viewing symptoms other than in linear cause-and-effect terms (McLeod, 1986). Rather, systemic family therapists may conceptualize problems by considering the family system to include not just the nuclear family, but also the larger system of extended family members and friends (Madanes, 1991). Sider and Clements (1982) suggested that therapists decide at what level or levels of system to intervene, because there are times when intervening at one system level may interfere with or alter the functioning of the system at another level. In addition, problems encountered by clients may result from relationships in their families of origin (Minuchin, 1974). Therefore, therapists must look at the larger kin network.

Minuchin's approach, called *strategic family therapy*, appears to be the most popular for use with single-parent families (Grief, 1987). By engaging in direct teaching with the family using techniques such as role play, teaching of communication skills, discussion of limit setting, and assertiveness training, practitioners can teach family members to relate differently to one another and to gain insight into their own behavior or role in the single-parent family system.

Another family treatment approach, Bowen's (1976, 1978) extended family systems therapy, has been used to establish a supportive social network for low-income single-parent families. This network includes family, former spouses, mother's siblings, mother's parents, friends, and relatives (Speck & Attneave, 1971; Westcot & Dries, 1991). The reciprocal support of a social network helps single parents function at a more optimal level. Another structural family therapist has instructed practitioners to assist fathers in improving their adjustment to life as single people (Grief, 1987). Social workers might provide vocational counseling for finance and employment issues or discussions to help families adapt to different life schedules, might involve former spouses with children in discussions regarding boundaries, and might develop viable boundaries of parent–child subsystems.

Although the family therapy literature offers established systems of family therapy, it does not make a clear enough distinction between transitional single-parent systems and those more stabilized in a single-parent family unit. Therapists who are working with single-parent families, therefore, must look at the different strengths and risks of each individual family to develop the kind of therapeutic intervention that fits that family (Miller, 1987).

Diversity of Family Developmental Tasks

The family is a social unit that faces a series of developmental tasks. These differ along the parameters of cultural differences, but they have universal roots. (Minuchin, 1974, p. 16)

General systems theory has served as a conceptual model for examining the family group as a developmental unit (Rhodes, 1977, 1980). The developmental approach to the family suggests that the family unit passes through normal, expected life stages that test the group's adaptive capacity usually in terms of landmarks such as getting married as well as bearing, raising, and launching children. Each change brings about a new set of circumstances to which the family must adapt (Greene, 2008a). Rhodes (1980) suggested that the family is a social system that evolves over time, with shifts in family composition at different points in the life cycle. However, failure to meet life transitions may lead families to seek mental health services (Minuchin, 1974).

The stages of the life cycle have tended to be defined for intact nuclear families in contemporary Western societies (Tseng & Hsu, 1991). These stages have tended to include the unattached young adult, the formation of the dyadic relationship, the family with young children, the family with adolescents, the family launching children, the family with older members, and the family in later years (Carter & McGoldrick, 2005; Goldenberg & Goldenberg, 2007). Some theorists, though, have addressed how the structure and development of the family may vary with diverse needs and interests—for example, the adaptability of families that have adopted special-needs children (Dewees, 2004; Groze & Rosenthal 1991), the multiple role and caregiving experiences of women (Reid & Hardy, 1999), and the normative family crisis of confronting dementia (Kuhn, 1990).

Roth (1989) cautioned that although all couples are unique, lesbian couples often have no markers of critical developmental events, such as the change in status from a dating couple to a married couple. The addition of children further complicates separation and differentiation from each partner's families of origin as well as presents issues of public acceptance. Because rituals and ceremonies are central features of family life, these situations often produce stress for the lesbian couple.

However, same-sex families are becoming more diverse in terms of parenting children as well as caregiving for partners and older parents (Cohen & Murray, 2007). Because of homophobia and secrecy about sexual orientation, gay and lesbian couples historically often kept the true nature of their emotional bond from their children, other family members, or friends and coworkers (Dahlheimer & Feigal, 1991; Hash & Cramer, 2003). These "secret selves" create problems for the gay and lesbian individuals when the private experiences of their sexual orientation come into conflict with the more public aspects of parenting or caregiving roles. In spite of the challenges associated with raising children, a review of the literature on lesbian parenting indicated that children raised in same-sex households show positive behavioral and emotional development (Fitzgerald, Steinmetz & Peterson, 1999).

Studies of the family life cycle also should consider the effects of cultural variables such as social class, ethnicity, cultural context, and religion (Falicov & Karrer, 1980; Vandergriff-Avery, Anderson, & Braun, 2004). In applying this perspective to family assessment, it therefore would be more appropriate to think of several "typical" family life cycles. For example, although women play a central role in families, the idea that women may have a "life cycle apart from their roles as wife and mothers" (McGoldrick, 1989, p. 200) is fairly recent.

These family life cycles vary among families of different cultural backgrounds, according to Tseng and Hsu (1991):

- In addition to marriage and the bearing and rearing of children, many other milestone factors relate to family system and structure. These factors may include the pattern of getting married, ways to bear and adopt a child, and cohabiting with members in the household, all of which affect the total configurational pattern of the family life cycle.

- Due to numerous variations (such as differences in premarital experience, patterns of childbearing, the life span of parents, and the structure of the household), the rhythm of family development may vary; the transition between phases may be clear cut or blurred; and each stage may be short, long, or even absent.
- Associated with the different cultural implications of critical issues concerning developmental milestones (such as the formal marital union, dissolution of marital relations, launching of children from the home, and widowhood), the impact of such milestones of family development on the family members has different meanings and effects. Therefore, it is necessary to examine the meaning of family development in the context of cultural background. (p. 46)

Family developmental patterns also may be affected by the geographical origin and birthplace of individual members and where they are in the cycle of acculturation to mainstream U.S. society. Ho et al. (2003) proposed that practitioners need to be aware that behaviors differ depending on whether a family and its members are foreign born or native born and the degree to which they are bicultural. He suggested that the process of immigration and cultural transition delivers a severe blow to many Asian/Pacific American families. Therefore, practitioners may need to assist with factors including economic survival, American racism, loss of extended family and support systems, vast cultural conflicts, and cognitive reactive patterns to a new environment.

The life cycle unfolds within a context of culture and significant life events, a process social workers must understand (Freeman, 1990). In addition, social workers must acknowledge the differences and similarities in the life cycle of black families and in that of other minority and majority families. According to Freeman, black families adapt in three major areas as a result of a history of oppression, institutional racism, and a general degree of economic deprivation: (a) fluidity of roles, (b) the value placed on education, and (c) the dual perspective. She traced the fluidity of roles observed in many black families to the African family patterns of extended families, joint decision making, ownership of property, and the socialization of children by the extended family group. This pattern of including "pseudo-family members and other relatives in family roles continues among many black families today" and sometimes referred to as fictive kin (p. 75).

The value of education also is linked to external conditions that often thwart gainful employment. Barriers to education may lead many African American youths to feel that they have missed the opportunity to better their lives. Furthermore, the dual perspective, a conflict between expectations of the larger society and those of one's own group, has a strong impact on the life cycle of the black family (Logan et al., 1990). Black parents frequently must struggle with how to socialize children to have a positive self-image, maintain their cultural strengths, and meet general societal expectations.

Social workers are perhaps more likely to ensure culturally specific interventions across cultures when using a strengths perspective. In the late 1990s and the beginning of the twenty-first century, theorists developed new resiliency-based models based on a family systems approach that may foster a strengths-based perspective (Greene, 2002, 2007; Walsh, 1996, 2003, 2006). For example, Walsh (2003) developed a metaframework based on the concept of family relational resilience that suggests that severe challenges influence the whole family. Interventions are designed to respond to crisis events, emphasize how a family has developed over time, foster the family relationship network, and employ multiple systems interventions. The practitioner focuses on the following three key domains of family functioning:

1. family belief systems: learning what meaning a family gives to the crisis,
2. organizational patterns: exploring the family's structure and supports, and
3. communication processes: enhancing a family's problem-solving ability (see Table 8.2 for more details).

Social Work Interventions: Issues with Diverse Families

Social work practice is guided first and foremost by a profound awareness of, and respect for, clients' positive attributes and abilities, talents and resources, desires and aspirations. (Saleebey, 1992, p. 6)

Assessment: A Strengths Perspective

Social work theorists have long sought a strengths perspective (Early, 2001; Freedman, 1990a, 1990b; Saleebey, 1992). The practitioner who uses a strengths perspective examines each family's particular attributes and needs, respects a family's cultural patterns, and avoids using negative labels. Many poor and minority families face economic and social stressors. Many families may be "crushed by the effects of poverty, and a legacy of racism" (Aponte, 1991, p. 24). Dodson (1988) argued that to achieve a strengths perspective with a black family, the social worker must make an acceptable conceptualization of the family, one that suggests that family patterns possess a degree of integrity.

Goals of Family Intervention

The goals of family intervention vary with the conceptual approach. For example, the structural approach to family intervention is based on the idea that the family "is more than the individual biopsychodynamics of its members" (Minuchin, 1974, p. 89). Families are viewed as social structures with behavioral

Table 8.2
Key Processes in Family Resilience

Belief Systems

Making meaning of adversity
- Affiliative value: resilience as relationally based
- Family life cycle orientation: normalizing, contextualizing adversity and distress
- Sense of coherence: crisis as meaning, comprehensible, manageable challenge
- Appraisal of crisis, distress, and recovery: facilitative versus constraining beliefs

Positive outlook
- Active initiative and perseverance
- Courage and en-courage-ment
- Sustaining hope, optimistic view: confidence in overcoming odds
- Focusing on strengths and potential
- Mastering the possible; accepting what can't be changed

Transcendence and spirituality
- Larger values, purpose
- Spirituality; faith, communion, rituals
- Inspiration: envisioning new possibilities, creativity, heroes
- Transformation: learning and growth from adversity

Organizational Patterns

Flexibility
- Capacity to change: rebounding, reorganizing, adapting to fit challenges over time
- Counterbalancing by stability: continuity, dependability through disruption

Connectedness
- Mutual support, collaboration, and commitment
- Respect for individual needs, differences, and boundaries
- Strong leadership: nurturing, protecting, guiding children and vulnerable members
- Varied family forms: cooperative parenting/caregiving teams
- Couple/coparent relationship: equal partners
- Seeking reconnection, reconciliation of troubled relationships

Social and economic resources
- Mobilizing extended kin and social support; community networks
- Building financial security; balancing work and family strains

Communication Processes

Clarity
- Clear, consistent messages (words and actions)
- Clarification of ambiguous situation; truth-seeking/truth-speaking

Table 8.2 (cont.)

Open emotional expression
• Sharing range of feelings (joy and pain; hopes and fears)
• Mutual empathy; tolerance for differences
• Responsibility for own feelings, behavior: avoid blaming
• Pleasurable interactions: humor

Collaborative problem solving
• Creative brainstorming; resourcefulness
• Shared decision making: negotiation, fairness, reciprocity
• Conflict resolution
• Focusing on goals: taking concrete steps, building on success, learning from failure
• Proactive stance: preventing problems, crises; preparing for future challenges

---

Source. Walsh, F. (1998). *Strengthening Family Resilience* (1st ed., p. 133). New York: Guilford Press.

patterns discernible to social workers. Each person in a family is seen as carrying out multiple roles based on what that particular family expects, permits, or forbids (Jackson, 1965).

This school of thought, which emphasizes family roles, was influenced by sociologists who believed that roles are assigned on the basis of legal or chronological status and gender (see Chapter 5 on role theory). In this traditional view, men are seen as the more aggressive wage earners, and women as the more expressive and nurturing figures. For example, Minuchin (1974) stated that by joining the family to make a structural diagnosis, the practitioner observes how family members relate. Questions of concern include the following: Who is the family spokesperson? If the father is acting as spokesperson, what does this mean? Is the mother "ceding her power temporarily to the father because of some implicit rule about the proper role of men"? (Minuchin, 1974, p. 89).

The observation of the family by structural family therapists results in a family map that serves as an organizational scheme to understand the family and to set therapeutic goals. According to structural theorists, no family model "is inherently normal or abnormal, functional or dysfunctional. A family's differentiation [is thought to be] idiosyncratic, related to its own composition, developmental stage, and subculture" (Minuchin, 1974, p. 95). Practitioners also accommodate a particular family's style and affective range.

Family-focused therapies also emphasize the differentiation of self, which refers to a family's ability to accept its members as autonomous and to encourage them to be this way. Several schools of family therapy suggest that practitioners explore how much "connectedness" or "separateness" each family member has achieved (Hartman & Laird, 1983). Yet feminist theorists have suggested that concepts often addressed in family therapy, such as separateness, power, and control, negate female values of intimacy and connectedness (Germain, 1991; Hare-Mustin, 1978).

In a similar vein, Falicov and Karrer (1980) indicated that, in contrast to other Anglo-American values, identity seeking or "finding oneself" often is not a primary concern of Mexican American young adults. In fact, the importance of finding connection to the larger community and cultural group is critical (Delgado & Barton, 1998). Forming a marital system with common goals and negotiated values usually has precedence over the impetus for individuation. Similarly, Ho et al. (2003) pointed out that because most Asian-/Pacific American families do not stress individuality, and members expect parents, grandparents, and extended kin to be part of shaping their lives, this principle is ineffective. Therefore, it is important for social workers to remember that there needs to be an eclectic selection of techniques that are congruent with the client system's culture (Red Horse, 1980).

The Role of the Social Worker

Social workers in family-focused interventions generally use techniques that restructure dysfunctional family interaction patterns (see Table 8.3). Perhaps the most debated technique to achieve this end is the use of the paradoxical intervention. Through *paradoxical interventions*, practitioners explain a family's problems in counterintuitive ways, deliberately escalate the symptoms of a member, or redirect symptoms into new or different contexts (e.g., "I want you and your mother to plan four eating binges this week"; Doherty & Boss, 1992, p. 618). Concerns associated with the use of paradoxical interventions include manipulation, client self-determination, and client control and empowerment.

The extent to which individuals are seen as relatively autonomous persons or strongly connected to their family is a major theme in family-centered approaches (Cross, 1998). Possible conflict exists between individual and family goals, as well as the potential for practitioner gender bias in therapy. Because the pursuit of family-level goals may conflict with individual goals, different family members are unlikely to benefit equally from therapy (Hare-Mustin, 1990; Hare-Mustin & Marecek, 1988). In addition, because women tend to struggle with personal growth in addition to their roles as caretakers, they may need help in therapy in balancing their own personal needs with those of family members (Gluck, Dannefer, & Milea, 1980).

By providing culturally sensitive services, the social work practitioner can enhance the family's sense of resilience. For example, a practitioner may need to engage *natural helpers* that are integral parts of a family's sense of identity and hold a major role in helping the family with enhancing functioning or healing (Greene et al., 2002). In addition, the family's spirituality can also be a protective force in dealing with challenges such as drug abuse, poverty, or violence.

Table 8.3
Systems Theory Guidelines for Assessment and Intervention
in Family Social Work

- Assume the family is a system with a unique structure and communication patterns that can be examined. The purpose of assessment is to work with the family to determine what is bringing about its dysfunction.
- Define the boundaries of the family system by working with the family to ascertain membership. Observe functions and behaviors, and be cognizant of cultural forms.
- Assess the properties related to relative openness or closed boundaries by observing and asking about the extent of exchange the family has with larger societal systems.
- Determine how well the family system fits with its environment. Review what additional resources need to be obtained or accessed to improve the family system–environment fit.
- Develop a picture of the family structure through an understanding of its organization.
- Explore socialization processes, how subsystems are created, the nature of their hierarchy(ies), and the way in which roles are and continue to be differentiated. Learn from the family how its culture influences organizational structure.
- Examine the family's communication patterns. Follow the transfer of information and resources in and between the system and its environment. Assess the relative nature of the system's feedback processes. Determine how this relates overall to patterns of interaction.
- Ask if the family can describe its rules. Work with the family to identify dysfunctional triangulation in communication. Ask family members about their specific cultural communication clues.
- Determine how responsive the family is to stress. Work with family members to identify elements in their structure and communication patterns that contribute to entropy, synergy, or achieving a steady state. Explore ways the system can decrease stress and move to a new level of adaptation, possibly by restructuring.

Source. Greene, R. R. (2008a). General systems theory. In R. R. Greene (Ed.), *Human Behavior Theory and Social Work Practice*. New Brunswick, NJ: AldineTransaction.

When attempting to resolve whether a clinician's loyalties are to the individual or the group, it should be kept in mind that there are general culture differences (Greene, in press-c). Western medicine has tended to view responsibility to the individual as greater, whereas Eastern cultures have tended to place the practitioner's first responsibility to the group. Sider and Clements (1982) addressed the problem of how practitioners resolve the issue of loyalty and ethics when choosing among therapeutic modalities and techniques. They suggested that, although the resolution of this dilemma is difficult, the practitioner should make explicit statements to the family about possible conflicting loyalties.

The Family and Other Social Institutions

[The focus of family-centered practice is the] family–environment interface, as the
social worker and family examine the fit or lack of fit between the family and its
"surround." (Hartman & Laird, 1987, p. 582)

Studies and conceptualizations of human development are increasingly using an
ecological systems approach that examines how intrafamilial processes are influenced
by the external environment (Auerswald, 1971; Bronfenbrenner, 1986; Germain,
1991; Holland & Kilpatrick, 2006). Although the family continues to be the principal
context for human development, it is recognized that development is affected by the
other environments with which families interact. For example, even though children
may never physically enter a work setting, their psychological development is affected by the work settings in which their parents spend their lives.

Culturally sensitive social work practice with ethnic and racial minorities
often uses an ecological systems approach involving and accessing other social
systems on behalf of the family (Aponte, 1987; Ho et al., 2003; Sotomayor, 1971;
Wright, Kail, & Creecy, 1990). This approach examines the family within the
context of the wider social context in which families must interact. The family–larger systems interface often involves work systems, school and religious
institutions, and health care systems. For some families, it may include welfare
agencies, mental health clinics, or components of the criminal justice system,
such as courts (Imber-Black, 1991).

Many theorists have suggested that it is important for practitioners to conduct
a family–larger system assessment when engaging in family systems interventions (Dewees, 2004; Hartman & Laird, 1983; Ho et al., 2003; Imber-Black,
1991; Speck & Attneave, 1973). This process examines the interdependence
between people and resources and may be achieved through pencil-and-paper
simulations or *ecological mapping*. Both techniques involve asking the family
to describe and draw a simulation of their interaction with other social systems,
such as educational, religious, health, recreational, political, and economic systems. It also may include asking the family about the agencies and institutions
with which they are involved as well as from which members are most likely
to seek outside help. By examining the macrosystem for possible definitions of
the problem and solutions, the practitioner is better able to effect change (see
Chapter 10 on natural support networks).

Language is another particular family and ethnic group feature that becomes
even more important when moving outside the family's boundaries. For bilingual people, for example, the choice of language in certain circumstances has
symbolic meaning (Draper, 1979). Practitioners who do not speak the same
language as their client family may want to consider collaborating with a natural
or community helper.

Many minority group members hesitate to seek mental health services from
formal agencies. Instead, they may rely heavily on the mutual aid of extended

family members and religious leaders (Farris, 2007; Pinderhughes, 1983). Often natural helpers may be asked to work in conjunction with social workers. For example, a family-centered approach that is common in native Hawaiian culture, called *ho'oponopono*, is a spiritual family conference that works to assess, prioritize, and resolve problems (Mokuau, 1990). *Ho'oponopono* serves as a means of affirming native Hawaiian culture and history.

Finally, family functions, such as participation within society, need to be examined in light of institutional racism. Because societal institutions promote the "melting pot concept" with its "individualistic, competitive achievement," many Mexican American families, whose values are in conflict with this theory, are excluded from full participation (Sotomayor, 1971, p. 317). For this reason, the ecological systems approach that views a family's social supports as "an inextricable component of an overall helping strategy" may provide the most inclusive model (p. 318).

References

Ackerman, N. (1972). Family psychotherapy-theory and practice. In G. D. Erikson & T. P. Hogan (Eds.), *Family Therapy: An Introduction to Theory and Technique.* Monterey, CA: Brooks/Cole.

Alemàn, S., Fitzpatrick, T., Tran, T. V., & Gonzalez, E. W. (Eds.). (2000). *Therapeutic Interventions with Ethnic Elders: Health and Social Issues.* New York: Haworth Press.

Anderson, C. (2003). The diversity, strength, and challenges of single-parent households. In F. Walsh (Ed.), *Normal Family Processes: Growing Diversity and Complexity* (pp. 121–152). New York: Guilford Press.

Anderson, T. (1991). *The Reflecting team: Dialogues and Dialogues about the Dialogues.* New York: Norton.

Aponte, H. J. (1979). Diagnosis in family therapy. In C. B. Germain (Ed.), *Social Work Practice: People and Environments* (pp. 107–149). New York: Columbia University Press.

Aponte, H. J. (1987). The treatment of society's poor: An ecological perspective on the underorganized family. *Family Therapy Today*, 2, 1–7.

Aponte, H. J. (1991). Training on the person of the therapist for work with the poor and minorities. *Journal of Independent Social Work*, 5(3/4), 23–30.

Aponte, H. J. (1994). *Bread and Spirit: Therapy with the New Poor: Diversity of Race, Culture, and Values.* New York: Norton.

Auerswald, E. H. (1971). Families, change and the ecological perspective. *Family Process*, 10, 263–280.

Berger, R. M., & Federico, R. (1982). *Human Behavior: A Social Work Perspective.* New York: Longman.

Billingsley, A. (1976). *The Family and Cultural Pluralism.* Address at the Baltimore Conference on Ethnicity and Social Welfare, Institute on Pluralism and Group Identity, New York.

Billingsley, A. (1994). *Climbing Jacob's Ladder.* New York: Simon & Schuster.

Bowen, M. (1971). Aging: A symposium. *Georgetown Medical Bulletin*, 30(3), 4–27.

Bowen, M. (1976). Theory and practice of psychotherapy. In P. Guerin (Ed.), *Family Therapy: Theory and Practice* (pp. 42–90). New York: Garden.

Bowen, M. (1978). *Family Therapy in Clinical Practice.* New York: Aronson.

Boyd-Franklin, N. (1995). Therapy with African American inner-city families. In H. Mikesell, D. D. Lusterman, & S. H. McDaniel (Eds.), *Integrating Family Therapy: Handbook of Family Psychology and Systems Theory* (pp. 357–374). Washington, DC: American Psychological Association.

Boyd-Franklin, N. (2003). Race, class, and poverty. In F. Walsh (Ed.), *Normal Family Processes: Growing Diversity and Complexity* (pp. 260–279). New York: Guilford Press.

Bronfenbrenner, U. (1986). Ecology of the family as a context for human development: Research perspectives. *Developmental Psychology*, 32, 723–742.

Brown, L. (1995). Lesbian identities: Concepts and issues. In A. R. D'Augelli & C. Patterson (Eds.), *Lesbian, Gay, and Bisexual Identities over the Lifespan* (pp. 3–23). New York: Oxford University Press.

Bryson, K., & Casper, L. M. (1999). *Coresident Grandparents and Grandchildren*. Retrieved June 12, 2007, from *http://www.census.gov/prod/99pubs/p23-198.pdf*.

Carter, B., & McGoldrick, M. (Eds.). (2005). *The Expanded Family Life Cycle: Individual, Family, and Social Perspectives* (3rd ed.). Boston: Allyn & Bacon.

Castex, G. (1993, February). *Using Diversity in the Classroom to Understand Diversity: Challenges and Techniques*. Paper presented at the 39th Annual Program Meeting of the Council on Social Work Education, New York, NY.

Chestang, L. (1972). *Character Development in a Hostile Environment* (Occasional Paper No. 3). Chicago: University of Chicago, School of Social Service Administration.

Chilman, C., Nunnally, E. W., & Cox, F. M. (Eds.). (1988). *Variant Family Forms*. Newbury Park, CA: Sage.

Cinamon, R. G. (2006). Anticipated work-family conflict: Effects of gender, self efficacy, and family background. *Career Development Quarterly*, 54, 202–215.

Cohen, H. L., & Murray, Y. (2007). Older lesbian and gay caregivers: Caring for families of choice and caring for families of origin. In R. R. Greene (Ed.), *Contemporary Issues of Care* (pp. 275–298). New York: Haworth Press.

Comer, J. P., & Poussaint, A. F. (1992). *Raising Black Children*. New York: Penguin Press.

Coontz, S. (2005). *Marriage, a History: From Obedience to Intimacy or How Love Conquered Marriage*. New York: Viking.

Cooper, K. (1999). Practice with transgendered youth and their families. *Journal of Gay & Lesbian Social Services*, 10(3/4), 111–129.

Crawford, S. (1987). Lesbian families: Psychosocial stress and the family-building process. In *Boston Lesbian Psychologies Collective Edition* (pp. 195–214). Champaign-Urbana: University of Illinois Press.

Crawford, S. (1988). Cultural context as a factor in the expansion of therapeutic conversation with lesbian families. *Journal of Strategic and Systemic Therapies*, 7(3), 2–10.

Cross, T. (1998). Understanding family resiliency from a relational world view. In H. I. McCubbin, E. A. Thompson, A. I. Thompson, & J. E. Fromer (Eds.), *Resiliency in Native American and Immigrant Families* (pp. 143–158). Thousand Oaks, CA: Sage.

Dahlheimer, D., & Feigal, J. (1991, January/February). Gays and lesbians in therapy: Bridging the gap. *Networker*, 44–49.

Damsky, M. (2000). Views and visions: Moving toward culturally competent practice. In S. Alemàn, T. Fitzpatrick, T. V. Tran, & E. W. Gonzales (Eds.), *Therapeutic Interventions with Ethnic Elders* (pp. 195–208). New York: Haworth Press.

Delgado, M., & Barton, K. (1998). Murals in Latino communities: Social indicators of community strengths. *Social Work*, 43, 346–356.

Dewees, M. (2004). Disability in the family: A case for reworking our communities. *Journal of Social Work in Disability & Rehabilitation*, 3(1), 3–20.

Dodson, J. (1988). Conceptualizations of black families. In H. P. McAdoo (Ed.), *Black Families* (2nd ed., pp. 77–90). Newbury Park, CA: Sage.

Doherty, W. J., & Boss, P. G. (1992). Values and ethics in family therapy. In A. D. Gurman & D. P. Kniskern (Eds.), *Handbook of Family Therapy* (pp. 606–637). New York: Brunner/Mazel.

Dore, M., & Dumois, A. O. (1990). Cultural differences in the meaning of adolescent pregnancy. *Families in Society*, 71, 93–101.

Draper, B. (1979). Black language as an adaptive response to a hostile environment. In C. B. Germain (Ed.), *Social Work Practice: People and Environments* (pp. 267–281). New York: Columbia University Press.

Duberman, L. (1975). *The Reconstituted Family: A Study of Remarried Couples and Their Children.* Chicago: Nelson Hall.

Early, T. J. (2001). Measures for practice with families from a strengths perspective. *Families in Society*, 82, 225–232.

Erera, P. I. (2002). *Family Diversity: Continuity and Change in the Contemporary Family.* Thousand Oaks, CA: Sage.

Falicov, C. J., & Karrer, B. M. (1980). Cultural variations in the family life cycle: The Mexican-American family. In E. A. Carter & M. McGoldrick (Eds.), *The Family Life Cycle* (pp. 383–426). New York: Gardner Press.

Farris, K. D. (2007). The role of African-American pastors in mental health care. In R. R. Greene (Ed.), *Contemporary Issues of Care* (pp. 159–182). New York: Haworth Press.

Fassinger, R. E., & Miller, B. A. (1996). Validation of an inclusive model of sexual minority identity formation on a sample of gay men. *Journal of Homosexuality*, 32(2), 53–78.

Fitzgerald, B., Steinmetz, S. K., & Peterson, G. W. (1999). Children of lesbian and gay parents: A review of the literature. *Marriage & Family Review*, 29(1/2), 57–75.

Fong, R., & Furuto, S. (Eds.). (2001). *Culturally Competent Practice: Skills, Interventions, and Evaluations.* Boston: Allyn & Bacon.

Franklin, J. H. (1988). A historical note on black families. In H. P. McAdoo (Ed.), *Black Families* (2nd ed., pp. 23–26). Newbury Park, CA: Sage.

Freedman, E. (1990a). The black family's life cycle: Operationalizing a strengths perspective. In S. M. L. Logan & R. G. McRoy (Eds.), *Social Work Practice with Black Families: A Culturally Specific Perspective* (pp. 55–72). New York: Longman.

Freedman, E. (1990b). Fear of feminism? An interview with Estelle Freedman. *Women's Review of Books*, 7(5), 25–26.

Freeman, M. L. (1990). Beyond women's issues: Feminism and social work. *Affilia*, 5(2), 72–89.

Fuller-Thomson, E., Minkler, M., & Driver, D. (1997). A profile of grandparents raising grandchildren in the United States. *The Gerontologist*, 37, 406–411.

Genero, N. P. (1998). Culture, resiliency, and mutual psychological development. In H. I. McCubbin, E. A. Thompson, A. I. Thompson, & J. A. Futrell (Eds.), *Resiliency in African-American Families* (pp. 31–48). Thousand Oaks, CA: Sage.

Germain, C. B. (1991). *Human Behavior and the Social Environment: An Ecological View.* New York: Columbia University Press.

Gluck, N. R., Dannefer, E., & Milea, K. (1980). Women in families. In E. A. Carter & M. McGoldrick (Eds.), *The Family Life Cycle* (pp. 295–327). New York: Gardner Press.

Goldenberg, H., & Goldenberg, I. (2007). *Family Therapy: An Overview* (7th ed.). Monterey, CA: Brooks/Cole.

Green, J. W. (1999). *Cultural Awareness in the Human Services: A Multi-Ethnic Ap-*

proach. Boston: Allyn & Bacon.

Greene, R. R. (2002). *Resiliency: An Integrated Approach to Practice, Policy, and Research.* Washington, DC: NASW Press.

Greene, R. R. (Ed.). (2007). *Social Work Practice: A Risk and Resilience Perspective.* Monterey, CA: Brooks/Cole.

Greene, R. R. (2008a). General systems theory. In R. R. Greene (Ed.), *Human Behavior Theory and Social Work Practice.* New Brunswick, NJ: Aldine Transaction.

Greene, R. R. (Ed.). (2008b). *Human Behavior Theory and Social Work Practice.* New Brunswick, NJ: Aldine Transaction.

Greene, R. R. (2008c). *Social Work with the Aged and Their Families* (3rd ed.). New Brunswick, NJ: Aldine Transaction.

Greene, R. R., Taylor, N. J., Evans, M. L., & Smith, L. A. (2002). Raising children in an oppressive environment. In R. R. Greene (Ed.), *Resiliency: An Integrated Approach to Practice, Policy and Research* (pp. 241–276). Washington, DC: NASW Press.

Grief, G. (1987). A longitudinal examination of single custodial fathers: Implications for treatment. *American Journal of Family Therapy,* 15, 253–260.

Groze, V., & Rosenthal, J. A. (1991). A structural analysis of families adopting special-needs children. *Families in Society,* 72, 469–482.

Haley, J. (1963). *Strategies of Psychotherapy.* New York: Grune & Stratton.

Haley, J. (1976). *Problem-Solving Therapy: New Strategies for Effective Family Therapy.* San Francisco: Jossey-Bass.

Hare-Mustin, R. T. (1978). A feminist approach to family therapy. *Family Process,* 17, 181–194.

Hare-Mustin, R. T. (1986). The problem of gender in family therapy. *Family Process,* 26, 15–27.

Hare-Mustin, R. T. (1989). The problem of gender in family therapy theory. In M. McGoldrick, C. M. Anderson, & F. Walsh (Eds.), *Women in Families: A Framework for Family Therapy* (pp. 61–77). New York: Norton.

Hare-Mustin, R. T. (1990). Sex, lies and headaches: The problem is power. In T. J. Goodrich (Ed.), *Women and Power: Perspectives for Family Therapy* (pp. 61–83). New York: Norton.

Hare-Mustin, R. T., & Marecek, J. (1988). The meaning of difference: Gender theory, postmodernism, and psychology. *American Psychologist,* 43, 445–464.

Harry, H. L. K. (1988, Spring). Will your daughter marry one? *UCLA Social Welfare,* 1, 5–6.

Hartman, A. (1995). Family therapy. In R. Edwards (Ed.-in-Chief), *Encyclopedia of Social Work* (19th ed., pp. 983–996). Washington, DC: NASW Press.

Hartman, A., & Laird, J. (1983). *Family-Centered Social Work Practice.* New York: Free Press.

Hartman, A., & Laird, J. (1984). *Working with Adoptive Families beyond Placement.* New York: Child Welfare League of America.

Hartman, A., & Laird, J. (1987). Family practice. In A. Minahan (Ed.-in-Chief), *Encyclopedia of Social Work* (18th ed., pp. 575–589). Silver Spring, MD: NASW Press.

Hash, K., & Cramer, E. P. (2003). Empowering gay and lesbian caregivers and uncovering their unique experiences through the use of qualitative methods. *Journal of Gay & Lesbian Social Services,* 15(1/2), 47–63.

Hayslip, B., Shore, J., Henderson, C. E., & Lambert, P. R. (1998). Custodial grandparenting and the impact of grandchildren with problems on role satisfaction and role meaning. *Journal of Gerontology: Social Sciences, 53B,* S164–S173.

HeavyRunner, I., & Marshall, K. (2003). Miracle survivors: Promoting resilience in Indian students. *Tribal College Journal,* 14(4), 14–19.

Hepworth, D. H., Rooney, R. H., Larsen, J., Rooney, G. D., & Strom-Gottfried, K. (2005). *Direct Social Work Practice: Theory and Skills* (7th ed.). Belmont, CA: Wadsworth.

Herdt, G. (1992). *Gay Culture in America: Essays from the Field*. Boston: Beacon Press.

Herr, J. J., & Weakland, J. H. (1979). *Counseling Elders and Their Families*. New York: Springer.

Ho, M. K., Rasheed, J. M., & Rasheed, M. N. (2003). *Family Therapy with Ethnic Minorities* (2nd ed.). Thousand Oaks, CA: Sage.

Hoffman, L. (1985). Beyond power and control: Toward a 'second order' family systems theory. *Family Systems Medicine*, 3, 381–396.

Hoffman, L. (1990). Constructing realities: An art of lenses. *Family Process*, 29, 1–12.

Hoffman, L. (1992). A reflective stance for family therapy. In S. McNamee & K. J. Gergen (Eds.), *Therapy as Social Construction* (pp. 7–24). Newbury Park, CA: Sage.

Holland, T. P., & Kilpatrick, A. C. (2006). An ecological systems–social constructionism approach to family practice. In A. C. Kilpatrick & T. P. Holland (Eds.), *Working with Families: An Integrative Model by Level of Need* (4th ed., pp. 15–34). Boston: Pearson.

Hollingsworth, L. D. (1999). Symbolic interactionism, African American families, and the transracial adoption controversy. *Social Work*, 44, 443–453.

Hopps, J. G., & Kilpatrick, A. C. (2006). Contexts of helping: Commonalities and human diversities. In A. C. Kilpatrick & T. P. Holland (Eds.), *Working with Families: An Integrative Model by Level of Need* (4th ed., pp. 36–51). Boston: Pearson.

Imber-Black, E. (1991). A family-larger system perspective. In A. S. Gurman & D. P. Kniskern (Eds.), *Handbook of Family Therapy* (pp. 583–600). New York: Brunner/Mazel.

Jackson, D. D. (1965). Family rules: Marital quid pro quo. *Archives of General Psychiatry*, 12, 589–594.

Janchill, M. P. (1969). Systems concepts in casework theory and practice. *Social Casework*, 15(2), 74–82.

Kalmijn, M. (2005). Attitude alignment in marriage and cohabitation: The case of sex-role attitudes. *Personal Relationships*, 12, 521–535.

Kesner, J. E., & McKenry, P. C. (2001). Single parenthood and social competence in children of color. *Families in Society*, 82, 136–144.

Kissman, K. (1991). Feminist-based social work with single-parent families. *Families in Society*, 72(2), 23–28.

Knei-Paz, C., & Ribner, D. S. (2000). A narrative perspective on "doing" for multiproblem families. *Families in Society*, 81, 475–482.

Korittko, A. (1991). Family therapy with one-parent families. *Contemporary Family Therapy*, 12, 625–639.

Kropf, N. P., Nackerud, L., & Gorokhovski, E. (1999). Social work practice with older Soviet immigrants. *Journal of Multicultural Social Work*, 7(1/2), 111–126.

Kuhn, D. R. (1990). The normative crises of families confronting dementia. *Families in Society*, 71, 451–460.

Laird, J. (Ed.). (1993). *Revisioning Social Work Practice*. New York: Haworth Press.

Laird, J. (1996). Family-centered practice with lesbian and gay families. *Families in Society*, 77, 559–572.

Laird, J. (2003). Lesbian and gay families. In F. Walsh (Ed.), *Normal Family Processes: Growing Diversity and Complexity* (pp. 176–209). New York: Guilford Press.

Leite, R., & McKenry, P. (2006). A role theory perspective on patterns of separated and divorced African-American nonresidential father involvement with children. *Father-*

ing, 4(1), 1–21.

Logan, S. M. L. (1990). Black families: Race, ethnicity, culture, social class and gender issues. In S. M. L. Logan, E. M. Freeman, & R. G. McRoy (Eds.), *Social Work Practice with Black Families: A Culturally Specific Perspective* (pp. 18–37). New York: Longman.

Logan, S. M. L., Freeman, E. M., & McRoy, R. G. (Eds.). (1990). *Social Work Practice with Black Families: A Culturally Specific Perspective*. New York: Longman.

Longres, J. F. (2000). *Human Behavior in the Social Environment* (3rd ed.). Belmont, CA: Wadsworth.

Madanes, C. (1990). *Sex, Love and Violence: Strategies for Transformation*. New York: Norton.

Madanes, C. (1991). *Strategic Family Therapy* (2nd ed.). San Francisco: Jossey-Bass.

Mailick, M. D., & Vigilante, F. W. (1997). The family assessment wheel: A social constructionist perspective. *Families in Society*, 78, 361–369.

Margolin, G. (1982). Ethical and legal considerations in marriage and family therapy. *American Psychologist*, 7, 789–801.

Matsuoka, J. K. (1990). Differential acculturation among Vietnamese refugees. *Social Work*, 35, 341–345.

McAdoo, H. (2006). *Black Families* (4th ed.). Thousand Oaks, CA: Sage.

McCubbin, H. L., Fleming, M. W., Thompson, A. I., Neitman, P., Elver, K. M., & Savas, S. A. (1998). Resiliency and coping in "at risk" African-American youth and their families. In H. I. McCubbin, E. A. Thompson, A. I. Thompson, & J. A. Futrell (Eds.), *Resiliency in African-American Families* (pp. 287–328). Thousand Oaks, CA: Sage.

McCubbin, H. I., McCubbin, M. A., Thompson, A. I., & Thompson, E. A. (1998). Resiliency in ethnic families: A conceptual model for predicting family adjustment and adaptation. In H. I. McCubbin, E. A. Thompson, A. I. Thompson, & J. E. Fromer (Eds.), *Resiliency in Native American and Immigrant Families* (pp. 329–352). Thousand Oaks, CA: Sage.

McCubbin, H. I., Thompson, E. A., Thompson, A. I., & Futrell, J. A. (Eds.). (1998). *Resiliency in African-American Families*. Thousand Oaks, CA: Sage.

McGoldrick, M. J. (1989). Women through the family life cycle. In M. J. McGoldrick, C. M. Anderson, & F. Walsh (Eds.), *Women in Families: A Framework for Family Therapy* (pp. 200–226). New York: Norton.

McLeod, M. (1986). Systemic family therapy. *Individual Psychology Journal of Adlerian Theory*, 42, 493–505.

Merighi, J. R., & Grimes, D. (2000). Coming out to families in a multicultural context. *Families in Society*, 81, 32–41.

Meyer, C. (1973). Direct services in new and old contexts. In A. Kahn (Ed.), *Shaping the New Social Work* (pp. 26–54). New York: Columbia University Press.

Miller, D. (1987). *Helping the Strong: An Exploration of the Needs of Families Headed by Women*. Silver Spring, MD: NASW Press.

Minuchin, S. (1974). *Families and Family Therapy*. Cambridge, MA: Harvard University Press.

Minuchin, S., & Montalvo, B. (1971). Techniques for working with disorganized low socio-economic families. In J. Halry (Ed.), *Changing Families* (pp. 202–211). New York: Grune & Stratton.

Mokuau, N. (1990). A family-centered approach in native Hawaiian culture. *Families in Society*, 71, 607–613.

Morawetz, A., & Walker, G. (1984). *Brief Therapy with Single-Parent Families*. New York: Brunner/Mazel.

Norlin, J., Chess, W., Dale, O., & Smith, R. (2002). *Human Behavior and the Social Environment*. Boston: Allyn & Bacon.

Parsons, T., & Bales, R. F. (1955). *Family Socialization and Interaction Process*. Glencoe, IL: Free Press.

Patterson, S. L., & Marsiglia, F. F. (2000). "Mi casa es su casa": Beginning exploration of Mexican Americans' natural helping. *Families in Society*, 81, 22–31.

Pinderhughes, E. (1995). Direct practice overview. In R. Edwards (Ed.-in-Chief), *Encyclopedia of Social Work* (19th ed., Vol. 1, pp. 740–751). Washington, DC: NASW Press.

Pinderhughes, E. B. (1982). Family functioning of Afro-Americans. *Social Work*, 27, 91–96.

Pinderhughes, E. B. (1983). Empowerment for our clients and for ourselves. *Social Casework*, 64, 331–338.

Poverny, L. M., & Finch, W. A. (1988). Gay and lesbian domestic partnerships: Expanding the definition of family. *Social Casework*, 69, 116–121.

Queralt, M. (1984). Understanding Cuban immigrants: A cultural perspective. *Social Work*, 29, 115–121.

Red Horse, J. G. (1980). Family structure and value orientation in American Indians. *Social Casework*, 25, 462–467.

Reid, J., & Hardy, M. (1999). Multiple roles and well-being among midlife women: Testing role strain and role enhancement theories. *Journal of Gerontology: Social Sciences, 54B*, S329–S338.

Rhodes, S. L. (1977). Contract negotiation in the initial stage of casework. *Social Service Review*, 51, 125–140.

Rhodes, S. L. (1980). A developmental approach to the life cycle of the family. In M. Bloom (Ed.), *Lifespan Development* (pp. 30–40). New York: Macmillan.

Roth, S. (1989). Psychotherapy with lesbian couples: Individual issues, female socialization and the social context. In M. McGoldrick, C. Anderson, & F. Walsh (Eds.), *Women in Families: A Framework for Family Therapy* (pp. 286–307). New York: Norton.

Rothman, J., Gant, L. M., & Hnat, S. A. (1985). Mexican-American family culture. *Social Service Review*, 59, 197–215.

Ryders, R. G. (1987). *The Realistic Therapist: Modesty and Relativism in Therapy and Research*. Newbury Park, CA: Sage.

Saleebey, D. (1992). Introduction: Power to the people. In D. Saleebey (Ed.), *The Strengths Perspective in Social Work Practice* (1st ed., pp. 3–17). New York: Longman.

Satir, V. (1967). *Conjoint Family Therapy*. Palo Alto, CA: Science and Behavior Books.

Schiele, J. H. (1996). Afrocentricity: An emerging paradigm in social work practice. *Social Work*, 41, 284–294.

Schriver, J. M. (2003). *Human Behavior and the Social Environment: Shifting Paradigms in Essential Knowledge for Social Work Practice* (4th ed.). Boston: Allyn & Bacon.

Sider, R. C., & Clements, C. (1982). Family or individual therapy: The ethics of modality choice. *American Journal of Psychiatry*, 139, 1455–1459.

Slater, S. (1999). *The Lesbian Family Life Cycle*. Urbana: University of Illinois Press.

Sotomayor, M. (1971). Mexican-American interaction with social systems. *Social Casework*, 51, 316–322.

Speck, R., & Attneave, C. L. (1971). Social network intervention. In J. Haley (Ed.), *Changing Families* (pp. 312–332). New York: Grune & Stratton.

Speck, R., & Attneave, C. L. (1973). *Family Network*. New York: Vintage.

Stack, C. (1975). *All Our Kin: Strategies for Survival in a Black Community*. New York: Harper & Row.

Stewart, P. E. (2004). Afrocentric approaches to working with African American families. *Families in Society*, 85, 221–228.

Sudarkasa, N. (1988). Interpreting the African-American family organization. In H. P. McAdoo (Ed.), *Black Families* (2nd ed., pp. 27–43). Newbury Park, CA: Sage.

Swann, S. K., & Anastas, J. W. (2003). Dimensions of lesbian identity during adolescence and young adulthood. *Journal of Gay & Lesbian Social Services*, 15(1/2), 109–125.

Timberlake, E. M., & Cook, K. O. (1984). Social work and the Vietnamese refugee. *Social Work*, 29, 108–112.

Trepper, T. (1987). Senior editor's comments. In W. S. Tseng & J. Hsu (Eds.), *Culture and Family Problems and Therapy* (pp. xi-xii). New York: Haworth Press.

Tseng, W. S., & Hsu, J. (1991). *Culture and Family Problems and Therapy*. New York: Haworth Press.

U.S. Census Bureau. (2004). *America's Families and Living Arrangements: 2003*. Retrieved June 22, 2007, from *http://www.census.gov/prod/2004pubs/p20-553.pdf*.

Vandergriff-Avery, M., Anderson, E. A., & Braun, B. (2004). Resiliency capacities among rural low-income families. *Families in Society*, 85, 562–570.

Walsh, F. (1996). Strengthening family resilience: Crisis and challenge. *Family Process*, 35, 261–281.

Walsh, F. (1998). *Strengthening Family Resilience* (1st ed.). New York: Guilford Press.

Walsh, F. (2003). *Normal Family Processes: Growing Diversity and Complexity*. New York: Guilford Press.

Walsh, F. (2006). *Strengthening Family Resilience* (2nd ed.). New York: Guilford Press.

Weiss, B. S., & Parish, B. (1989). Culturally appropriate crisis counseling: Adapting an American method for use with IndoChinese refugees. *Social Work*, 34, 252–254.

Westcot, M., & Dries, R. (1991). Has family therapy adapted to the single-parent family? *American Journal of Family Therapy*, 18, 363–371.

Wright, R., Kail, B. L., & Creecy, R. F. (1990). Culturally sensitive social work practice with black alcoholics and their families. In J. M. L. Logan, E. M. Freeman, & R. G. McRoy (Eds.), *Social Work Practice with Black Families: A Culturally Specific Perspective* (pp. 203–222). New York: Longman.

Yellow Horse Brave Heart, M. (2001). Culturally and historically congruent clinical social work interventions with native clients. In R. Fong & S. Furuto (Eds.), *Culturally Competent Practice: Skills, Interventions, and Evaluations* (pp. 285–298). Boston: Allyn & Bacon.

9

Small-Group Theory and Social Work: Promoting Diversity and Social Justice or Recreating Inequities?

Beth Glover Reed, Robert M. Ortega, and Charles Garvin

Groups remain the context for most social activities. Of the billions of people populating the world, all but an occasional recluse or exile belong to a group.... The impact of these groups on individuals, their communities, and their cultures is enormous. Thus, to understand individuals, we must necessarily understand their groups. (Forsythe, 1999, p. 2)

People live and work in groups in all social institutions—families, peer groups, work, and social and membership groups of various kinds. Groups provide meaning and support, and most social work occurs through groups. *Small groups* are usually defined as "two or more persons [up to a membership of about 20] who are interacting with one another in such a manner that each person influences and is influenced by each other person" (Shaw, 1976, p. 11). Essential to the meaning of groups is the interdependence of their members (Lewin, 1948). Groups can meet one time or continue to meet over a long period of time; they can have a stable membership or a fluid or changing membership.

In this chapter, we review the relevant research and knowledge about small groups with an emphasis on those factors that increase a group's ability to accomplish its goals and promote social justice. Social work has long had a commitment to furthering social and economic justice as well as reducing oppression. Social workers should be vigilant about social justice issues as participants and facilitators in small groups, whatever other purposes the groups may have. Building on the talents of diverse members is necessary but not sufficient for effective groups to further social justice and challenge the mechanisms and forces that sustain injustice.

Anti-oppression, civil rights, and other forms of social justice activism in the United States have challenged many of the most overt means of sustaining inequality (e.g., legal segregation, exclusion from types of work, hate crimes).

Current theories about social justice and forms of injustice illuminate subtle and less easily recognized barriers to justice and supports of injustice that are furthered, recreated, or sustained through small groups (Acker, 2006; Martin, 2004; Ridgeway, 2006; Rowe, 1990; Schippers, 2008).

The structures, cultural mechanisms, processes, interpersonal interactions, and leadership that are necessary to create and sustain stability, identity, belongingness, meaning, and effectiveness in small groups can also create and sustain inequities unless they are continuously monitored, influenced, and challenged. The chapter outlines and illustrates different ways of defining and negotiating differences and describes other domains that are important in small groups, especially for social justice practice. Key small group concepts and resources for additional learning are also presented.

Sources of Knowledge and Different Types and Functions of Small Groups

All of the social science disciplines and many professions have contributed to the development of theory and knowledge about small groups. Table 9.1 notes the wide range of topics related to small groups that have been researched in different fields and the many practice arenas in which small groups are important.

Social work's interest in practice with groups dates back to the earliest period of its history (Andrews, 2001). Social work views group work as a tool for individual, interpersonal, and/or larger system change across a wide range of populations and issues. Groups can be used to negotiate across interpersonal, societal, cultural, community, and organizational boundaries and to work toward social change goals in many venues. Table 9.2 illustrates some functions that different types of groups can serve. Although specifics about all of these types of groups are not included in this chapter, concepts and examples are used that apply across a number of contexts.

Some of the benefits and purposes listed in Table 9.2 are explicitly focused on creating change toward social justice goals or on learning about differences and barriers to justice. Most groups, however, have many other purposes. The chapter presents knowledge about common elements of small groups, how these elements are necessary and useful for achieving a group's goals, some ways in which they may contribute to furthering justice or injustice, and some implications for practice.

Social Justice Dimensions for Social Work Groups

Four major dimensions that link diversity and social justice to group concepts, performance, and outcomes: (a) group tasks and functions; (b) cohesiveness and diversity; (c) negotiation of differences and groupthink; and (d) power, social categories, and their manifestations. Then six components of small groups with key concepts in each are defined, and how each can contribute to furthering justice or to reifying privilege and oppression is discussed.

Table 9.1
Social Science and Professional Contributions to the Study of Small Groups

Discipline	Relevant Areas of Interest
Anthropology	Cultural development, social norms and customs, social and collective identity development, acculturation, assimilation and transnationalism, cross-cultural conflict
Economics	Interest groups, consensus modeling, small-group reform, competitive analysis, market influences, social exchange, group learning and performance
Psychology/Social psychology	Similarity/attraction, social categorization, social influence, social facilitation, social cognition, equity, interpersonal relationships
Sociology	Social influence, social stratification, social class and status differences, roles and role relations, norms, social structures, deviance, power and privilege, race relations
Political science	Leadership, international relations, group decision making, power and political influence, intergroup conflict
Business	Team building, motivational behavior and productivity, diversity, organizational culture and climate, organizational behavior, group decision making
Counseling and clinical psychology	Group psychotherapy and therapeutic change, group curative (therapeutic) factors, self-help, mutual aid, sensitivity training, social influence
Education	Group methods of instruction, performance and study groups, group workshop and training outcomes, team teaching, classroom composition
Health/Mental health	Recovery, grief counseling, disaster relief, phobia desensitization, habit cessation, rehabilitation, remediation, growth, social support
Social work	Couples, families, small groups, organizations, neighborhoods, communities, society, cultures, leadership, power and influence, conflict, diversity, consciousness raising, social policies

Group Tasks and Functions

Members of every group must work together to accomplish the group's stated purposes while also ensuring that the group becomes and remains a well-functioning entity that is of value to its members and sponsors. This involves assuming multiple tasks and roles over time. Small-group theories typically describe two types of major functions of the small group, both of which are important if the group is to be effective in accomplishing its purposes: (a) those associated with

Table 9.2
Functions of Different Types of Groups

Benefit or Purpose	Example
Help shape personal identity, feelings of belongingness, a sense of meaning and purpose	Families, peer groups, affinity groups (share a common interest or value), ethnic groups, some neighborhoods
Help socialize people (i.e., help people learn societal or organizational norms and customs, and decide on and fulfill new roles)	Peer groups, affinity groups, families, educational groups
Help people to change and grow; support them through difficult times	Mutual aid groups, support groups, therapeutic or psychoeducational groups
Facilitate planning, decision making, and problem solving in many settings (for policy, in organizations, and in communities); be a vehicle for getting work done	Work groups and teams (in communities, organizations, and government), task forces, boards of directors, committees, town hall meetings, volunteer groups work done (e.g., parent–teacher organizations), advisory groups
Be a vehicle for those with varying degrees of power to join together, plan, and stimulate and guide social change (including challenging injustice and working for justice)	Groups for social planning and social action, political advocacy groups, neighborhood advocacy groups
Allow members who cross organizational and group boundaries to coordinate goals, activities, and services in complex environments	Multidisciplinary and professional teams, steering committees, community coalitions and collaboratives
Help people learn about social categories, communication, privilege, oppression, and what is needed to work for justice	Groups for consciousness raising and dialogue, groups as part of diversity trainings and/or that allow people to negotiate differences

the explicit purposes for which the group was formed, its goals and desired outcomes, or the *overt* agenda a group is assigned or elects to accomplish; and (b) those associated with the tasks and activities important for the group to develop so that members work well together. The group uses the resources members can contribute, and the group is supportive of and meaningful for its members.

The authors believe that social justice issues are important within *each* of these sets of functions. For instance, Barusch (2006) reviewed many of the definitions of social justice applicable to social work and divided them into two types: (a) those that focus on end goals (e.g., desirable end states and criteria to assess a socially just situation); and (b) those that emphasize the processes of defining and moving toward justice, or components of the struggle for justice.

The first set is relevant for the group's purpose and the second for all of the interactions and elements relevant for creating and sustaining the group. Thus, a major reason for incorporating social justice into the agenda of small groups is that both product (i.e., the group's purpose, goals, and desired outcomes) and processes (i.e., the ways in which the group organizes itself and its members act together to become and sustain the group) should be valued equally. This includes incorporating social justice goals and using socially just processes and procedures, plus being vigilant about monitoring to prevent and reduce forces that may further injustice and unearned privilege.

Cohesiveness and Diversity

Cohesiveness, typically defined as all of the forces acting on members to remain in the group (Festinger, 1950)—or, more narrowly, as how much members are attracted to a group—is an important element for building and sustaining a viable group. Early research on similarity/attraction in groups and theories related to social identification and social facilitation focused on the value of homogeneity in increasing cohesiveness and group performance. This research suggested that people who hold similar values and attitudes to one another provide reassurance that their beliefs are valid and accurate and that future interactions will likely be free of conflict; thus, this similarity offers an immediate sense of unity (Arkin & Burger, 1980; Insko & Schopler, 1998; Newcomb, 1960). The literature also suggests that people are more likely to identify with groups that reflect positively on themselves as members and thus are drawn to groups seen as prestigious, high status, or high performing or that have an otherwise attractive image. This can be related to having members who are high status outside the group.

Other studies have challenged the notion that the subjective value of the group is higher for more homogeneous groups. In their research linking diversity to effective work groups, van Knippenberg, Haslam, and Platow (2007) drew upon group (social) identification theory and proposed that sometimes diversity rather than homogeneity fosters greater group identification; this occurs especially when people perceive the value of diversity for successful group performance and are thus likely to respond favorably to diverse work groups "precisely because of their diversity" (p. 208).

Beyond performance, group studies that have examined the impact of diversity on organizational climate and culture have underscored the fact that when diversity is perceived to increase group performance, it is likely to be embraced rather than viewed as aversive, especially when group members believe that there is greater value in diversity than homogeneity (van Knippenberg et al., 2007). Subjective value, as these studies suggest, may be higher for more diverse groups (Curseu, Schruijer, & Boros, 2007; Homan, van Knippenberg, Van Kleef, & De

Dreu, 2007; van Knippenberg et al., 2007). The literature is contradictory and the relationships complex. For instance, Sargent and Sue-Chan (2001) in an experimental study of diversity and performance found complex interactions between the degree of task interdependence among members and group diversity as mediators of cohesion.

Types of diversity/differences. Group diversity focuses on the ways in which group membership differs along specific dimensions. Research suggests that different types of diversity have different effects on the group's ability to achieve goals and complete tasks and members' ability to work together in an effective manner (Curseu et al., 2007). Group outcomes benefit from diversity to the extent that group performance is able to build on those diversity dimensions most relevant for the group's achievement of its goals (Curseu et al., 2007; Harrison & Klein, 2007).

Harrison and Klein's (2007) taxonomy of membership differences distinguished diversity along three dimensions: separation, variety, and disparity. *Separation* refers to differences in location on *one* dimension within a group (e.g., types of opinions among group members; approaches to the group's tasks; key values, beliefs, or attitudes). This perspective draws on theories of similarity/attraction-selection-attrition and social categorization. If these differences can be bridged, they can enrich group decision making. If they cannot, they can lead to reduced cohesion, increased interpersonal conflict, distrust, and decreased task performance.

Variety refers to differences in the kind, source, or category of relevant knowledge, perspective, or experience among group members. Jackson and Ruderman (1995) identified sources of variety as psychological characteristics, demographic differences, and attributes related to occupation or organizational location (unit level in the hierarchy). This perspective draws on theories about information processing, law of requisite cognitive and experiential variety, variation, selection, and retention. In situations in which unique or distinctive information is valued, groups with more variety can exhibit greater creativity and innovation, higher quality decisions, more task conflict, and increased unit flexibility (Page, 2007). Greater variety creates more complexity that must be negotiated, which can lead to more tension, even when differences are valued.

Disparity refers to differences among group members in socially valued assets or resources held. This perspective draws on theories of distributive justice and equality, status hierarchy, and social stratification. These differences are most relevant for social justice issues, although difficult negotiations related to other types of diversity can also contribute to injustice. Likely consequences for groups in the presence of disparity include more within-group competition, resentful deviance (people being unfairly marginalized and becoming resentful), reduced member input, and withdrawal (Harrison & Klein, 2007, p. 5).

Homan et al. (2007) examined instances in which different dimensions of diversity converge, resulting in *diversity faultlines*. These faultlines occur when subgroup categorizations or emerging power and status differentials influence or disrupt group processes such as decision making using criteria other than the best knowledge and skills about how best to proceed. For example, faultlines may undermine member trust and willingness to cooperate when certain privileges or priorities are given to some members because of their gender, age, or other social identity without acceptable rationale or justification. This increases tensions and conflict among group members and decreases communication.

Thus, although diversity can stimulate or undermine group performance, decreases in performance are most likely when dimensions of diversity converge to create diversity faultlines through subgroup social categorization processes. According to Homan and colleagues (2007), the group dynamics and processes that lead to positive performance outcomes in diverse groups can also result in disadvantage and exclusion when diversity encourages separation and fails to address power and status disparities.

Negotiation of Differences and Groupthink

If they are to be effective, all groups must develop ways to negotiate and build on differences among members, who can then make decisions and work together. Even in situations in which variety and diverse perspectives are sought and valued, groups must develop ways to identify and use differences. If groups cannot do this, they can not take advantage of the talents and perspectives of those who bring a range of knowledge, skills, and standpoints to the group.

In fact, there is a body of knowledge about how groups that suppress differences can engage in a set of phenomena known as *groupthink*. Groupthink is a mode of thinking in which people engage when they are deeply involved in a cohesive in-group in which "the members' striving for unanimity overrides their motivation to realistically appraise alternative courses of actions" (Janis, 1982, p. 9). In a groupthink condition, a group does not systematically gather and examine the knowledge and options available to it due to both positive and negative factors such as a strong allegiance to the group and great respect for its members, the dominance of the views of one person or a subgroup, strong norms for conformity, or a climate that ridicules or otherwise suppresses divergent views or behaviors (Esser, 1998). A group can make badly informed and reasoned decisions under these conditions, sometimes with major negative consequences.

Soliciting differences, surfacing and embracing conflict as a positive force, and other strategies have emerged as ways to prevent groupthink and to build on differences. Conflict can be a positive, negative, or neutral force in small groups, but all types are important within and between groups, especially if one is concerned about working both for social justice and with groups to reach desired goals.

Power, Social Categories, and Their Manifestations

Although these forms of difference have many implications for effective groups, most relevant for social justice practice are those associated with societal categories and unequal power. People occupy multiple social categories with different degrees of societal status and power. One set of differences especially relevant for social justice is those associated with different *positionalities* in society. People who occupy different positionalities develop different knowledge and worldviews (*standpoints*) informed by their social category locations. Recognizing and harnessing these different views and sources of knowledge are critical for incorporating social justice into small groups, as those with different standpoints will be able to recognize different forces that create inequities.

Power is often defined as the influence and resources needed to accomplish desired goals. Harnessing power is necessary for creating change and working for social justice. Feminist scholars and activists, especially, have urged those concerned about creating change for social justice to strive to use collaborative forms of power (i.e., having power *with* others by working together) versus using power to dominate or control others (e.g., Townsend, Zapata, Rowlands, Alberti, & Mercado, 1999). At the individual level, French and Raven (1960) defined five types of power: expertise (*expert*), control of resources (*reward*), control of punishments (*coercive*), power related to a person's structural position or role in a social system (*legitimate*), and power gained because people admire someone and aspire to be like him or her (*referent*). Many other forms of power derive from social structures and how groups and organizations work.

Knowledge is growing about how different types and sources of power combine to contribute to the creation and maintenance of privilege and oppression. These are barriers to social justice that lead to unearned advantages and multiple types of disadvantages, including threats to survival if these barriers are not repeatedly challenged and reduced. Especially relevant here are the concepts of earned and ascribed status.

The term *status* indicates stable differences in the power and influence among group members. Some positions of status are earned (e.g., educational degrees, promotions in the workplace), but other types of status are associated with the social categories one occupies. Social categories that are commonly associated with different forms of ascribed status include ability, age, class, culture, ethnicity, family structure, gender (including gender identity and gender expression), marital status, national origin, geographic location (e.g., rural, suburban, urban), race, religion or spirituality, sex, and sexual orientation.

Having higher ascribed status usually makes it more likely that a person will be able to acquire greater earned status. In social justice work, the consequences of having more or less ascribed power are frequently described as *having privilege* or *experiencing oppression*. People bring these experiences with them into groups and recreate them within groups in ways that are often not recognized.

Privilege is defined as unearned advantages that are associated with social categories (positionalities) that have a higher status in society (e.g., Whiteness, masculinity, higher economic class, heterosexuality, dominant religion; Johnson, 2003). P. McIntosh (1988) defined two types of privilege: those desired states that should be accorded to everyone, and those that create disadvantage for others that society needs to work to eliminate. Those with privilege frequently are unaware of the disparities between them with their sources of power and those who lack this power (Goodman, 2001).

Oppression refers to the ways in which people experience barriers to participation in society, such as by exercising their rights and taking advantage of opportunities. Mechanisms that create and sustain oppression are multiple, work together, and are often not recognized even by those affected by them. Young (1990) classified five types: powerlessness, marginalization, exploitation, cultural hegemony, and violence. People can have multiple responses to their own experiences with oppression (Mullaly, 2007). Some internalize their oppression and experience lower self-esteem and efficacy as a result. Others actively resist oppressive forces, often in concert with others.

Small-Group Components and Theory

> The small group is a social microcosm of the wider society in which it is located. Patterns of social oppression will be repeated in social group work practice unless active steps are taken to counteract these tendencies and replace them with a culture of empowerment. (A. Brown & Mistry, 1994, p. 133)

Earlier theories of injustice and justice, of society, and of stability and change tended to focus on group and societal *structures* and their functions and impacts, how *meanings* are developed and sustained (ideologies, symbols), or on individual and group "agency" (actions and behaviors—the *social-psychological* level). Other sets of theories focused on the functions and sources of *conflict* in the context of social injustice and inequities (e.g., Karl Marx; Harper & Leicht, 2007). All of these approaches can also be found in small-group theory and knowledge.

Multiple foci and methods of research on small groups and in organizations are increasingly documenting both the importance of small-group interactions in creating and sustaining inequities and strategies that reduce these inequities. The research uses formal system modeling, controlled laboratory studies, ethnomethodological and other observational strategies, surveys, and interviews. There is a large body of work on gender in small groups and less on race or ethnicity, although there is some attention to economic class and other social categories. Most research focuses primarily on one category (e.g., gender or race), but some is beginning to examine several social categories simultaneously. Some of the theorizing emphasizes multiple status categories, documenting similarities and differences across types of categories.

The inclusion of social justice must focus on both "product" (purposes) and other interactions within groups. Thus, in addition to its purposes and goals, consideration should be given to the work necessary to influence how a group is composed, organizes itself, conducts its work within the group and with its environments, conceptualizes and understands issues, uses language, enables people to interact and support one another, and fosters the growth of individual members.

Relationships with the Larger Environment

Inequalities in the distribution of resources in a population are translated into greater or lesser levels of consensus via social interaction in small groups. (Ridgeway & Balkwell, 1997, p. 14)

In Figure 9.1, larger environments are indicated by the two left-hand boxes: Socio-Cultural-Historical-Political Contexts, and Organizational and Community Contexts. The larger societal level influences how communities are organized and the procedures they use to operate. Communities are populated by organizations of different types, within sectors and neighborhoods. Members of small groups live and work within larger environments and are influenced by popular culture and the structures, ideologies, and practices that exist in these larger domains.

The boundaries around small groups are permeable to a greater or lesser degree. Group members bring values, assumptions, behaviors, and experiences from these larger environments into the small groups, and the members and the group itself are also likely to have multiple transactions with the larger environment during the life of the group.

The most immediate environment is the place in which the group meets and the resources it draws from its immediate sponsors. Frequently a group's charge comes from an external source, a group may communicate regularly with entities in its environment, and people may join or leave the group.

The group's purpose (Box A) is likely to be influenced by knowledge and perspectives from the larger environment, and members bring to the tasks of the group assumptions about social justice that are influenced by larger societal values and approaches to justice. These may include definitions of human well-being, values about the human condition, rights and responsibilities, and assumptions about conflict and community. In terms of group structures (C1), the larger political economy and its organizational forms and policies are likely to shape what members view as possible and how they believe a group should be organized and conducted. Laws and policies shape resources available to a group and how justice can be pursued in a community.

Similarly, societal beliefs and values, key symbols, rituals, and ideals (C2) influence what members value and define as acceptable and how they understand and draw meaning from their lives and interactions. Group processes (C3) are influenced by societal socialization practices and assumptions about everyday interactions, including the multiple ways in which people monitor themselves and one another to maintain order and ensure that behaviors and thoughts fall within acceptable limits. Finally, intra- and interpersonal elements (C4) are composed of all of the beliefs, attitudes, values, skills, and knowledge that individual people bring to their relationships and interactions from the larger environment.

Groups operate through multiple interactions among their members that are shaped by the individuals' experiences and the collective sense they make of them. These transactions and individual thoughts, feelings, and corresponding actions can shape alternative visions of justice or can recreate the multiple, often unrecognized micro-inequities that produce cues that maintain status differences and that marginalize certain thoughts, feelings, and behaviors.

Components within a Group

Structural factors. Social structure (C1) refers to how a group is organized, including such factors as group composition; roles and division of labor; division of resources; formal procedures and rules, including decision making; power and status hierarchies; communication and affectional patterns; and internal divisions, such as subgroups. These structures may either enhance social justice or impede it.

Previous sections have outlined some ways that the group's composition may involve diversity. *Group composition* is defined as the pattern that exists in the group related to the personal characteristics of the members or its degrees of homogeneity or heterogeneity. Groups can be composed of people who are similar on a dimension of concern (e.g., all women, all African Americans, all gays or lesbians), who are selected to represent different characteristics (e.g., a group composed of women and men in equal numbers), or who randomly represent differences on some characteristic. Each of these types of composition presents opportunities and challenges with regard to promoting diversity and social justice. We focus here primarily on social categories associated with differential status in society.

A growing body of literature has documented the consistent but complex effects of gender composition on a wide array of group conditions: dominance (Ridgeway & Diekema, 1989), legitimacy and status (Ridgeway, Diekema, & Johnson, 1995), communication patterns/interruptions (Karakowsky, McBey, & Miller, 2004; Smith-Lovin & Brody, 1989), and approaches to tasks. The salience of the social category is important (Randel, 2002), as is diversity in values (Rodriguez, 1998). These effects also depend on the nature of the task, environmental conditions, and a variety of other factors. In general men appear to be more engaged in dominance behaviors than women, whether they are in the minority or majority, although this is influenced by gender composition and the nature of the task (Smith-Lovin & Brody, 1989).

In studies focusing on race and cross-race interactions, race-related expectations have shaped emotional responses (Butz & Plant, 2006) and participation

(Li, Karakowsky, & Siegel, 1999), and some studies have found different patterns than those one might expect if one were generalizing from studies that focused primarily on gender (Craig & Rand, 1998). These studies combined suggest that the intersection of race and gender requires additional thought and attention to social justice matters in small groups.

Some group theories stress status structures and their development (i.e., stable differences in the patterns of power and influence among group members). The group is also affected by status characteristics outside the group that influence how people are perceived within the group as well as power and influence structures within the group. Group members should be prepared to challenge those power and status dynamics that appear to recreate gender-, race-, or other social-identity-based inequities as well as other societal injustice within the group.

Gender, race, ethnicity, and other diversity factors are strong determinants of the structure of every group (e.g., when men sit with men and women with women) and influence subgroup and communication patterns. We noted earlier that power structure consists of the degree to which members can influence the behavior of others by virtue of their position in the group, their ability to reward or punish others, their expertise, or their degree of attractiveness to others. A subset of members will likely attain or possess more power than other members by virtue of ascribed status (e.g., gender, social class, or ethnicity) and external roles. These power hierarchies can marginalize members with important knowledge and skills and create patterns of injustice in the group. Ideally, all members should be assisted to attain the power required to accomplish tasks they undertake and utilize the expertise they develop through group experience.

The *division of labor* in groups refers to the task-focused patterns of action undertaken by members on behalf of the group to assist it in accomplishing its purpose. Ideally, members assume tasks for the group based on ability and interest rather than status. Division of labor should encourage and support task assignments that open new opportunities for members who have been oppressed or denied opportunities to contribute to group progress.

Group task, which group workers often refer to as *program*, consists of the activities in which members engage together. Is the group attending to the ways that some tasks are preferred or rejected by people from different cultural groups or genders? Do members of various groups bring different assumptions and working styles to the tasks?

Internal boundaries defines the degree to which membership in and access to subgroups is easy or difficult to attain. Permeable boundaries allow members to build social connections within new subgroups or reconstitute subgroups based on individual and group need. When permeable boundaries exist, communication is open among all subgroups. With rigid boundaries, members are locked in to existing subgroups and communication is limited among subgroups. Such boundary patterns often ensue from issues of power and privilege and place barriers on the fulfillment of member and group needs.

Structural boundaries can also create insiders and outsiders—those within a subgroup derive support and status from other members, and those not included can be marginalized with less power and satisfaction. Hierarchies that develop and their potential to replicate external power structures can lead to patterns of exploitation and exclusion in the group.

For social work, this discussion emphasizes the importance of assessing visible or explicit and informal structures within the group and its environment, especially in relation to how power is created and manifested and whether this replicates external power structures. This can include evaluating formal policies and procedures that affect the group's work, as well as those that evolve in the group, in terms of how well they address issues of social justice (e.g., how power and authority are defined, who is included or excluded, the relevance of the group's actions toward purposes and goals). Assessment should also include important boundaries that must be negotiated outside and within the group.

Group culture. Culture is defined as the shared beliefs and traditions that exist among the members of the group and the ways in which group members create meaning within the group. Some aspects of a group culture may be very conscious, overt, and obvious to group members (e.g., explicit rituals or rules for behavior), whereas others are more subtle. Cultural elements can also include the theories or intervention models being employed in a group.

Key cultural elements include norms, symbols and rituals, taken-for-granted assumptions that explain key group phenomena, and the words used to signify these. *Norms* refers to expectations members have as to how other members should behave or refrain from behaving. These norms are shaped by societal assumptions (Ridgeway, 1991, 2001) in which beliefs about societal status create a network of restraining expectations that then shape people's behaviors. Members are frequently rewarded or punished if they follow or violate key shared expectations, sometimes overtly by being expelled from the group or explicitly sanctioned. Often, however, not fitting in leads to gradually having less influence and connections in a group.

Unjust or inflexible norms can lead to scapegoating and marginalizing and can leave some members more central than others in terms of power and status. This may be related to gender, ethnicity, age, social class, or other demographic characteristics and related behavioral expectations.

Many of these meaning-making processes can be very subtle—what Martin (2003) called *liminal*, meaning beyond the awareness of most participants. One might also call them *tacit*, meaning not articulated or recognized, maintained in the day-to-day interactions and thoughts that are taken for granted. Often these processes become difficult to change, especially when left unattended. Status-creating behaviors, for instance, are frequently legitimated by member assumptions about competency that are associated with their conceptual schemas about social categories (Ridgeway, 2006). Often not recognized, they are very resistant to change and shape behaviors in many ways that may not be obvious to group members, except maybe by the most marginalized group members who may be more aware of group forces because of their standpoints. Frequently, however, the group dynamics are not visible to anyone, and those who end up being marginalized often attribute their experiences in a group to personal deficits (Ridgeway & Johnson, 1990).

What creates legitimacy also has cultural elements. C. Johnson, Dowd, and Ridgeway (2006) described how legitimacy is shaped by beliefs and then, in turn, secures compliance with the existing social order that is embedded in shared and accepted (or at least not questioned) beliefs, norms, and values. They described some ways to disrupt these shared assumptions. For instance, group members can regularly critique the knowledge, values, research, theories, and practice methods/actions being used in the group in terms of underlying paradigms and the assumptions they represent, illuminate, or obscure.

A growing literature discusses steps and processes for surfacing and "de-centering" underlying paradigms and assumptions (Mann & Huffman, 2005; Narayan & Harding, 2000; Singleton & Linton, 2006; Yarbro-Bejarano, 1994). These include examining phenomena and options through the eyes of those from different standpoints, especially marginalized positions, and systematically considering the implications of different points of view.

Exploring phenomena being articulated as dichotomies is especially important. These can create false distinctions and obscure options not recognized (e.g., between the individual and the group, the outcome and the processes of the group), different goals and options that may be perceived as mutually exclusive (e.g., men and women, whites and people of color, right and wrong). Decentering the meanings of words, group symbols, norms, and values can identify dominant assumptions and ideologies that may marginalize some group members and increase the influence of others. It may be necessary to take the time to clarify how different people understand and interpret various group features. May (2007), for example, produced an overview of a collection of articles that problematized concepts of race.

Group processes and surveillance. Group process refers to how the group changes from moment to moment or over longer periods of time, often through member interactions or the enactment of procedures and tasks in the group. These interactions include communications, affects, conflicts, and the patterns among these as the group begins and, over time, seeks to accomplish its purposes and ends (referred to as *group development*). Processes such as how decisions are made or how a conversation unfolds among several people are also strongly affected by culture, gender, and other status issues. Are members attending to these aspects of group processes? For instance, men or women communicate quite differently in every culture (e.g., Tannen, 1990). People with higher status often talk more, express themselves differently, and interrupt others more than do those with less status, and there are marked differences across cultures as well (Karakowsky et al., 2004; Smith-Lovin & Brody, 1989).

Communication patterns, affectional factors, and conflict are especially important in this area. The pattern of positive and negative emotions that members direct at other members helps to shape subgroups and the climate of the group. Research suggests that over time negative emotions are suppressed in groups and positive ones enhanced, which increases cohesiveness but may lead to the suppression of important differences (Ridgeway & Johnson, 1990). These differences are usually accompanied by varying degrees of negative emotions. Engaging with conflict and disagreements is an important element in socially just groups and requires regular and special attention to maintain.

Multiple theories are now focusing explicitly on these types of day-to-day interactions and activities as major ways in which power is transacted and through which societal structures and ideologies are sustained and reinforced, or challenged and changed. For instance, Ridgeway and her colleagues (Ridgeway, 2006; Ridgeway, Boyle, Kuipers, & Robinson, 1998; Ridgeway & Erickson, 2000) articulated how assumptions about status are enacted through member transactions, often in unrecognized ways. Of particular importance are those transactions that support status hierarchies and dominant norms and values and that suppress member differences and agency.

Foucault (1975/1995) articulated how being observed and monitored by others (experiencing and participating in surveillance) leads people to constrain their own behaviors and to constrain the behavior of others. Although groups need routines and procedures to accomplish their tasks, these can quickly constrain innovation and lead to censoring as they become more embedded in group traditions and procedural mechanisms.

Becoming aware of and disrupting these forms of power is especially difficult and requires regular and ongoing collective reflection that many outcome-oriented group members will resist. It is also very difficult to keep attending to these issues over and over again. Research suggests that it is important to assess whose views and values are being represented in the group's activities and decisions and to identify some of the reciprocal ways that group members may be recreating power differences among members. Attending to the entire group network is important in this work, as everyone is involved in sustaining these; even when some members are the primary protagonists, bystanders play important roles in sustaining or challenging these dynamics (Ridgeway & Diekema, 1989).

Intra-and Interpersonal Factors and Micro-Inequities. Group members bring their attitudes, experiences, ways of thinking, and behaviors into their group interactions, and all of these are ultimately sustained by the individual and collective feelings, thoughts, and actions of members. Members enact patterns from the larger society, and it may take considerable effort to sort out individual factors from those reflecting larger forces. This is reflected in the social justice principle "the personal is political," which means that much that occurs at the personal level is related to societal factors. Thus, personal change should occur within an understanding of the societal and cultural contexts, and the fact that a member's status must address both psychological and sociocultural effects. Conversely, the experiences of members should always be examined for both their individual components and how they reflect larger cultural patterns.

The concept of *micro-inequities* is important at the interpersonal level. Rowe (1990) defined these as subtle slights that over time wear away at self-esteem and contribute to maintaining structural hierarchies and marginalizing dynamics. Members can learn about various types of micro-inequities, create ways to assess the group as to whether and how these are occurring, and develop ways to identify and stop them as they recur.

Becoming aware of and building on multiple positionalities and standpoints is especially important at the interpersonal level. These work together to create opportunities for learning (or barriers to justice if not recognized). Becoming aware of and building on multiple positionalities includes recognizing how dimensions of power, privilege, oppression, and differences associated with positionalities influence peoples' actions, perceptions, choices, and consequences; group, organizational, and community structures and processes; risk and protective factors; and assets and challenges.

Considerable knowledge now exists about different ways of knowing and learning, and ways that people respond to different types of opportunities depending on their backgrounds and cultural styles (e.g., Goodman, 2001. Having opportunities to share relevant histories and experiences can help members learn to interpret one another's behaviors and support one another. Those with significant unearned privilege must learn to recognize this and use their power to create change. Group members who have experienced marginality and historical trauma may be distrustful or impatient for change. Research suggests that it is useful to assist everyone to examine how they have internalized oppression and to learn skills for empowerment (individual, consciousness, group connections, taking action with others).

How Group Components Work Together to Create Order and Meaning and to Construct and Reconstruct Status and Inequities

Box D in Figure 9.1 outlines the fact that these group components operate together either to move toward justice or to sustain injustice. These components are evident in all group work texts and parallel remarkably well a number of integrative theories emerging in the social justice literature to describe and explain how inequalities and oppression are created, recreated, and maintained. Examples can be found in Collins's (2000) discussion of domains of power, Acker's (2006) depiction of inequality regimes, West and Fenstermaker's (1995) "doing difference" (summarized in Wickes & Emmison, 2007; Schippers, 2008), and Ridgeway and colleagues' formulations of status construction and legitimizing functions. Collins, for instance, stated that the *structural domain* organizes oppression through hierarchies, policies, and societal boundaries, whereas the interpretive (*cultural domain*) justifies oppression through hegemonic (dominant, frequently unconscious) explanations for power differences that provide alternative views of why and how these occur. The *disciplinary* or surveillance domain (called *group processes*) manages oppression through day-to-day interactions and exchanges of power that suppress differences and conflict and maintain order, whereas *intra- and interpersonal* cognitions, values, and behaviors perpetuate micro-inequities through transactions that signal and maintain patterns of privilege and inequities through the feelings, thoughts, and behaviors of group members.

Ridgeway and colleagues similarly described status construction processes, in which structures create status differences and conceptual schemas explain them and set up expectations as to how people occupying different statuses should behave (Ridgeway, 2006). These expectations then constrain behaviors when people interact and shape people's perceptions and interpretations of those interactions, which then reinforces the status hierarchies.

A number of studies have also demonstrated that those not directly affected by these transactions nevertheless learn the schemas by watching the interactions, and thus the expectations and subsequent behaviors spread and are sustained (Ridgeway & Erickson, 2000). Martin (2004) argued that the social categories associated with privilege and oppression are societal institutions similar to the government and law, and Acker (2006) has begun to discuss how structural, cultural, and interactional forces within organizations sustain what she has called *inequality regimes.*

We are encouraged by research that is beginning to document ways in which these forces can be disrupted and changed. For instance, Ridgeway and Correll (2006) found that even slight challenges by bystanders to the validating consensus weakened participants' status beliefs and the behaviors associated with them. Deutsch (2007), in a paper focused on gender, argued that instead of studying the "doing" of gender, researchers should study the "undoing" of gender so that they learn more about how not to reify status hierarchies and schemas and the inequities that result from them.

Infusing Social Justice into Group Components

One way to identify structural sources of injustice is to engage in *critical structural analyses* using theory and various types of assessments to illuminate how societal forces are being manifested and reinforced in small groups. We described earlier the importance of *decentering* and becoming aware of and challenging *micro-inequities* at the interpersonal level. All of these involve being skeptical about taken-for-granted features and working with others who have different standpoints and types of knowledge to help one another to recognize and name usually less visible forces. Once these forces are visible, it is considerably easier to challenge and change them. As alluded to earlier, addressing conflict is important across all of the group components.

Importance of Conflict and Negotiating Differences

Conflict is important in the knowledge and theory of groups in at least three ways: (a) as a component in group development and maintenance, (b) as a necessary element when negotiating and building upon differences among members, and (c) as a consequence of coming together across organizational interfaces or group boundaries. The most difficult conflicts to negotiate are those that occur around the faultlines described earlier, in which differences are polarized, differences are associated with patterns of distrust and power, and/or when multiple types of differences coincide.

Especially when groups form, group members must figure out how they will work together to accomplish their goals, discover and build on the talents and perspectives of group members, and negotiate members' different goals and ambitions. Earlier literature on how groups develop, in fact, defined *conflict* as a necessary and important phase during which norms, procedures, and member roles and rankings are established. In an ongoing group, many of these issues will resurface and need to be renegotiated when a group's membership, goals, or environment changes or when it must transition to different sets of challenges and tasks. These are critical periods in which many aspects of groups can be reexamined and renegotiated.

Figure 9.2 depicts three different configurations and sources of conflict in groups. All of them involve negotiating differences among group members, but in Conditions B and C (i.e., in coalitions and intergroup situations), members also represent different groups, social or job categories, or constituencies, so group and organizational boundaries as well as member differences are present.

Condition A represents conflict as a necessary element in negotiating differences among members. The overlapping circles represent people who bring both connections and differences into a group. One can address differences in ways that further social justice through such means as intersectionality and cultural humility. These require people to recognize and rely on self-definitions of human differences that vary based on important personal and multiple experiences associated with social categories but that also create opportunities for people to recognize commonalities and the potential for allyship and collaboration within and across differences.

The term *intersectionality* was coined originally by authors and practitioners simultaneously occupying several subordinate statuses within society (e.g., women of color within discussions of race or gender-sensitive approaches; e.g., Collins, 2000; Crenshaw, 1995), noting that their issues were relegated to the background or ignored altogether when identity groups were discussed one at a time. They argued that people simultaneously occupy not just one but multiple positions (positionalities) within the socio-cultural-political and structural fabric

Figure 9.2
Intra- and Intergroup Conflict

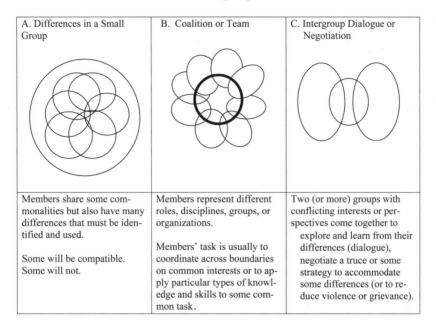

A. Differences in a Small Group	B. Coalition or Team	C. Intergroup Dialogue or Negotiation
Members share some commonalities but also have many differences that must be identified and used. Some will be compatible. Some will not.	Members represent different roles, disciplines, groups, or organizations. Members' task is usually to coordinate across boundaries on common interests or to apply particular types of knowledge and skills to some common task.	Two (or more) groups with conflicting interests or perspectives come together to explore and learn from their differences (dialogue), negotiate a truce or some strategy to accommodate some differences (or to reduce violence or grievance).

of society, and that these positions interact with each other (intersect) to create different sets of issues, resiliencies, and social contexts. For instance, people who occupy similar positions on race or ethnicity may experience substantial differences in age, economic status, religion, gender or sexual identity, and expression. People who are similar on several identity characteristics but differ in one may face very different issues, have access to alternative resources and supports, or perceive their situations, priorities, and options quite differently. "It is only when we examine identities as fields of intersection and therefore always of contestation that we can imagine possibilities other than … binaries …" (Sengupta, 2006, p. 632).

When we discuss differences comparatively, often as binaries (e.g., women and men, people of color and whites, differently abled and able-bodied people), our goal is often to illuminate characteristics related to oppression or those that differentiate the two groups. Although these approaches are one way to learn about important characteristics within a group, they frequently obscure differences *within* a group and make it more difficult to identify commonalities *across* groups. Intersectional approaches provide opportunities to look for both similarities and differences and to take multiple elements of someone's positionalities into account (Pyke & Johnson, 2003).

Moreover, because most people simultaneously occupy positions that are associated with higher or lower status (power and resources) within society, very few experience oppression or benefit from unearned advantage (privilege) in *all* aspects of their social identities. Thus, intersectional approaches incorporate an understanding of the impacts of multiple types of societal power and status—both the experiences of being marginalized, dominated, and otherwise disadvantaged in some ways, and of benefiting from unearned advantages in other arenas. Intersectional approaches consider multiple positionalities together, in terms of both their impacts on the people who live them and their consequences for social justice practice.

Not considering multiple positionalities creates problems for social justice work. Not recognizing a person's areas of privilege can block his or her ability to see oppression or to work as allies with others different from him or her. A person's experiences of oppression related to his or her position on one status dimension (e.g., religion) can help that person to recognize and empathize with people or groups who experience disadvantage related to their position on another dimension (e.g., race), or the person may be unable to see how he or she benefits from others' oppression or even recognize how those people are being oppressed because he or she is so focused on his or her own oppression. Considering multiple positionalities together is much more complex and difficult than taking them one at a time, but they do not occur separately in the world, and they need to be engaged together in practice.

Finally, intersectional approaches recognize the importance of social contexts. Different situations and environments make some aspects of peoples' identities more salient than others. For instance, people will experience race differently when surrounded by people who look more like themselves than they will in a racially diverse environment or in a group that is mostly of another race. It is noted earlier that men experience gender differently in a group of mostly women than they do with other men, and this will also differ if the environment is a social or a workplace setting. The characteristics, roles, and environments of the social work practitioner are part of the context for every practice situation and must be considered in preparing for and conducting socially just practice. Thus, a person's knowledge of himself or herself, the settings in which he or she practices, and how others experience him or her, including his or her multiple positionalities and experiences with oppression and privilege, become important components in intersectional practice frameworks.

Practicing intersectionally is not the same as treating everyone "as an individual," because it requires placing every individual within their larger group and societal contexts. The practitioner does take individual interests, goals, and lifestyles into account, but always in the context of understanding the impacts of a person's multiple group memberships and statuses in shaping who that person is and how he or she constructs the practices of daily life.

A *cultural humility* perspective is emphasized here to encourage a less deterministic, less authoritative approach to understanding diversity and social justice issues and their impact on group membership and participation. Such a perspective places more value on each member's own contributions (Tervalon & Murray-Garcia, 1998). A cultural humility perspective encourages participants to relinquish the role of expert in order to maximize the potential of all members while eliciting expertise that will most likely facilitate the group's movement toward its purpose. Members thus value both the expert and learner roles in ways that support each member's role of being a capable, contributing partner to the group's development and productivity.

Condition B in Figure 9.2 depicts the boundaries one might expect to see in a multidisciplinary team or a coalition. As shown in Table 9.2, one function of small groups can be to bring together people who represent different constituencies or different professions or skills, represented in Figure 9.2 by the circles surrounding the central group. A team or task force may bring together people with different perspectives, functions, and roles to coordinate or collaborate on a particular task or to bring together different sets of knowledge and skills to work on a common task (e.g., a case conference or grand rounds in a mental health setting). A coalition, coordinating group, or collaboration frequently brings together representatives of different elements within a community (e.g., interest groups, advocates, organizational members) to identify common issues and interests or to broker differences and find ways to work together.

L. D. Brown (1983) described conflict as inevitable at what he called *organizational interfaces*, or locations where members of different social units interact. These can be across units laterally, across organizational levels vertically, between members of different subcultures, or between organizations. As groups form and cohesiveness develops, members become committed to the group and develop preferences for ideas, practices, and people associated with their group. Belonging to one group can increase dislike and distrust for members and practices associated with other groups, thus creating conflict. If there are power differences and histories of distrust, as is often the case when group members have experienced disparities, the conflict may be high and difficult to address.

Condition C in Figure 9.2 illustrates a way of addressing cross-group conflicts in which members representing two (or more) groups are brought together to learn about each other's groups or to negotiate some grievance or dispute or solve some mutual problems. In the figure, two groups are represented in the ovals on either side, with the circle in the middle indicating the space in which representatives from these groups come together. The goal for this intergroup is frequently to negotiate, learn, or work together across differences. Intergroup relations units on many college campuses are one example of this type of conflict negotiation (Nagda, 2006a; Nagda, Kim, & Truelove, 2004). In one model, half of a group's members represent people with lower status on a particular social category, and the other half have access to unearned advantage on that category (e.g., African American and white, women and men, persons with disabilities and able-bodied persons). The goal is to share experiences, learn from one another about how privilege and oppression work, and join together to identify and work toward some common goals. Ideally, members discuss how their other social categories are also relevant (e.g., how gender affects one's experience of race). Other models are emerging that educate across multiple differences simultaneously or sequentially (Dessel, Rogger, & Garlington, 2006; Nagda, 2006b).

At a more macro level, this diagram can also represent the use of a group for negotiating conflicts, disputes, and different interests in an organization or the larger society. Such groups are used among unions and employers, gangs, nations, religious groups, or ethnic subgroups. International summits, for instance, frequently occur in small groups, with carefully developed protocols and skilled negotiators.

Within these groups, a facilitator needs to attend to emotional, cognitive, and behavioral issues and triggers so that people can develop (a) more positive feelings and thoughts about people who represent other social categories and (b) skills for communicating and working together across differences (Stephan, 2008). For intergroup negotiations, members and negotiators must help the protagonists to articulate their issues and views, explore the sources of these views, and search for common ground or exchanges that can be made (Alexander & Levin, 1998).

Working with Connections and Conflict

Dealing with different types and severities of conflict may require different approaches. Conflict, for instance, can be defined as an incompatibility or variance; a clash or divergence of opinions or interests; or as the act of contending, battling, or struggling for mastery (e.g., a hostile encounter). These different levels or intensity of conflicts may be related to different types and sources of differences. Working with and building on differences requires first that groups recognize them and consciously work with them, not avoiding the tensions and disputes but seeing them as opportunities to build on and negotiate differences. This is also essential if groups are to avoid marginalizing and exploiting some categories of members.

In some instances, one can carefully select group members to represent particular types of diversity, including people at multiple points on the distance continuum who can create bridges and mediate between two extremes. Whether or not a group composition can be selected to maximize desired diversity, every group can develop group norms and procedures that solicit, value, and systematically take into account the different approaches, knowledge and skill sets, and worldviews of members. Groups can value, work with, and build on differences; agree to disagree in some instances; compromise; or continue to work toward negotiating alternatives when people cannot agree. When factions are polarized with great distrust, many strategies are possible for finding common ground (e.g., developing overarching goals) or at least reducing some of the most negative consequences associated with conflict and connection that create inequities (e.g., R. J. Fisher, 2000; S. Fisher et al., 2000).

Leadership and Justice

> *If we agree that social conditions characterized by injustice, inequity, and discrimi-*
> *nation transcend cultural boundaries and that some kind of individual and collective*
> *action is required to change these conditions, then this means that we need some*
> *kind of leadership-like phenomenon.* (Tirmizi, 2005, p. 5)

A *leader* is broadly defined as an individual acting in ways that increase the effectiveness of a small group while working toward social justice. Although many groups have a designated leader or leadership team, either appointed by some external authority or emerging from the group, every group member can exert leadership by contributing to the evolution and accomplishments of a group. A social worker will participate in many types of groups and contribute leadership in many ways, not just when in formal leadership roles (e.g., chair, president, facilitator).

Anderson (1997) defined four major functions of leadership in small groups. Only one of these is directly related to the goal achievement function in groups, and even this includes some aspects more often associated with the development and maintenance of the group. Anderson described a *directing* function that incorporates the many elements necessary for completion of tasks such as managing time, pacing work, monitoring task completion, and creating and managing internal and external boundaries. In the *provider* function, leaders assist a group to develop relationships and a climate that facilitates its tasks.

The *processing* functions enables a group to develop the procedures, communication patterns, and decision-making protocols necessary to maintain and continue to develop the group, whereas the *catalyzing* function encourages member interactions and emotional expressions. Anderson suggested that more of the provider and processing functions contributes to better group functioning, whereas too little or too much of the directing or catalyzing functions can be problematic for group effectiveness. Regardless, working for social justice, challenging the forces that sustain inequalities, and valuing and building on the diversity of group members take consistent leadership of all types.

Leaders who occupy higher and lower power social status categories are perceived and reacted to differently by group members. Gender expectations continue to shape what is possible for women in leadership roles, although less so than they did earlier; women are now generally perceived to be as competent as men, although they elicit considerably more negative affect than men do (Carli & Eagly, 2001; Eagly, 2007; Koch, 2005). The situation for leaders in different racial categories is considerably less clear, with some studies suggesting they are perceived as less competent and others finding they are rated more favorably than whites in leadership (Ellis, Ilgen, & Hollenbeck, 2006; Kelsey, 1998; Pyke & Johnson, 2003).

Another factor that is important to consider is that those wishing to exert leadership represent all social categories. Just because one has experienced oppression does not automatically mean one has skills in working for justice. The literature is just beginning to address strategies useful for people of color in leadership positions (e.g., Marbley, 2004).

Critical Consciousness and Praxis

Critical consciousness is defined as regular examination of one's own positionalities within critical structural frameworks so that one is increasingly able to recognize one's own standpoints and continue to learn about how one's own life is being shaped by the forces of difference and constructed statuses (Suarez, Newman, & Reed, in press). This is a continuous process that works best in conjunction with the different experiences and standpoints of other people, in order that one may expand one's ability to understand how power works and is sustained.

Praxis, as defined by Freire, is one way to achieve critical consciousness, by engaging in iterative cycles of theorizing, acting, and then reflecting on those experiences in order to modify one's theories and frameworks and generate new questions and options for action. These cycles require (a) having the knowledge and skills for theorizing (critical structural and cultural analyses), (b) acting alone and with others, (c) engaging in strategies to create change, and (d) deepening one's own knowledge of oneself as an agent for change. Praxis helps a person put the parts together across structural, cultural, procedural, and interactional domains and sustain himself or herself so that he or she can continue to be a force for justice and not a perpetuator of injustice.

Summary

The very elements that can make living and working in groups such positive forces within society may also create conditions that disempower members, lead to inequities, and promote injustice. This is likely to occur unless group members and leaders are constantly vigilant about unintended consequences or else are willing to confront intentional acts that unjustifiably privilege differences among participants.

Definitions that focus on the struggle for justice describe a deep commitment to an ongoing engagement with and understanding of the dynamics and forms of privilege and oppression. Skills include working with people with diverse experiences, social locations, and perspectives toward socially just relationships, procedures, decision making, and environments.

Barriers to justice exist in mechanisms for privilege and oppression that must be understood and challenged as goals in themselves and as recurring processes in all social environments and systems. These barriers may be expressed in both the structures found in the group as well as in the interactions between the group and the larger society. All are associated with social categories/positions with and without power and influence and are maintained and can be challenged and changed through work in small groups.

References

Acker, J. (2006). Inequality regimes: Gender, class and race in organizations. *Gender and Society*, 20, 441–464.

Alexander, M. G., & Levin, S. (1998). Theoretical, empirical, and practical approaches to intergroup conflict. *Journal of Social Issues*, 54, 629–639.

Anderson, J. (1997). *Social Work with Groups*. New York: Longman.

Andrews, J. (2001). Group work's place in social work: A historical analysis. *Journal of Sociology and Social Work*. XXIV(3), 211-235.

Arkin, R. M., & Burger, J. M. (1980). Effects of unit relation tendencies on interpersonal attraction. *Social Psychology Quarterly*, 43, 380–391.

Barker, R. L. (2003). *The Social Work Dictionary* (5th ed.). Washington, DC: NASW Press.

Barusch, A. S. (2006). Social justice and social workers. In *Foundations of Social Policy: Social Justice in a Human Perspective* (2nd ed., pp. 3–23). Monterey, CA: Brooks/Cole.

Brown, A., & Mistry, T. (1994). Group work with "mixed membership" groups: Issues of race and gender. *Social Work With Groups*, 17, 133–148.

Brown, L. D. (1983). *Managing Conflict at Organizational Interfaces*. Reading, MA: Addison-Wesley.

Butz, D. A., & Plant, E. A. (2006). Perceiving outgroup members as unresponsive: Implications for approach-related emotions, intentions and behavior. *Journal of Personality and Social Psychology*, 91, 1066–1079.

Carli, L. L., & Eagly, A. H. (2001). Gender, hierarchy and leadership: An introduction. *Journal of Social Issues*, 37, 629–636.

Collins, P. H. (2000). Toward a politics of empowerment. In *Black Feminist Thought: Knowledge, Consciousness, and the Politics of Empowerment* (2nd ed., pp. 273–290). New York: Routledge.

Craig, K. M., & Rand, K. A. (1998). The perceptually "privileged" group member: Consequences of solo status for African Americans and Whites in task groups. *Small Group Research*, 29, 339–358.

Crenshaw, K. W. (1995). The intersection of race and gender. In K. Crenshaw, N. Gotanda, G. Peller, & K. Thomas (Eds.), *Critical Race Theory* (pp. 357–383). New York: New Press.

Curseu, P. L., Schruijer, S., & Boros, S. (2007). The effects of groups' variety and disparity on groups' cognitive complexity. *Group Dynamics: Theory, Research and Practice*, 11, 187–206.

Dessel, A., Rogger, M. E., & Garlington, S. B. (2006). Using intergroup dialogue to promote social justice and change. *Social Work*, 51, 303–315.

Deutsch, F. M. (2007). Undoing gender. *Gender and Society*, 21, 106–127.

Eagly, A. H. (2007). Female leadership advantage and disadvantage: Resolving the contradictions. *Psychology of Women Quarterly*, 31, 1–12.

Ellis, A. P. J., Ilgen, D. R., & Hollenbeck, J. R. (2006). The effects of team leader race on performance evaluations: An attributional perspective. *Small Group Research*, 37, 295–332.

Esser, J. K. (1998). Alive and well after 25 years: A review of groupthink research. *Organizational Behavior and Human Decision Processes*, 73(2/3), 116–141.

Festinger, L. (1950). Informal social communication. *Psychological Review*, 57, 271–282.

Fisher, R. J. (2000). Intergroup conflict. In M. Deutsch & P. T. Coleman (Eds.), *The Handbook of Conflict Resolution: Theory and Practice* (pp. 166–184). San Francisco: Jossey-Bass.

Fisher, S., Abdi, D. I., Ludin, J., Smith, R., Williams, S., & Williams, S. (2000). *Working with Conflict: Skills and Strategies for Action*. London: Zed Books.

Forsythe, D. (1999). *Group Dynamics* (3rd ed.). Monterey, CA: Brooks/Cole.

Foucault, M. (1995). *Discipline and Punish: The Birth of the Prison (A. Sheridan, Trans.)*. *New York: Vintage Books. (Original work published 1975.)*

French, J. P. R., Jr., & Raven, B. (1960). The basis of social power. In D. Cartwright & A. Zander (Eds.), *Group Dynamics: Research and Theory* (pp. 607–623). New York: Harper & Row.

Garvin, C. Reed, Reisch, B.G. & Yoshihama, M. (in press). *Doing Justice*. Cambridge, England: Oxford University Press.

Goodman, D. J. (2001). *Promoting Diversity and Social Justice: Educating People from Privileged Groups*. Thousand Oaks, CA: Sage.

Harper, C. O., & Leicht, K. T. (2007). *Exploring Social Change: America and the World* (5th ed.). Upper Saddle River, NJ: Pearson/Prentice Hall.

Harrison, D. A., & Klein, K. J. (2007). What's the difference? Diversity constructs as separation, variety or disparity in organizations. *Academy of Management Review*, 32, 1199–1228.

Homan, A. C., van Knippenberg, D., Van Kleef, G. A., & De Dreu, C. K. (2007). Bridging faultlines by valuing diversity: Diversity beliefs, information elaboration, and performance in diverse work groups. *Journal of Applied Psychology*, 92, 1189–1199.

Insko, C. A., & Schopler, J. (1998). Differential distrust of groups and individuals. In C. Sedikides, J. Schopler, & C. A. Insko (Eds.), *Intergroup Cognition and Intergroup Behavior* (pp. 27-44). Mahwah, NJ: Erlbaum.

Jackson, S. E., & Ruderman, M. N. (1995). *Diversity in Work Teams: Research Paradigms for a Changing Work Place*. Washington, DC: American Psychological Association.

Janis, I. L. (1982). *Groupthink: Psychological studies of Policy Decisions and Fiascos* (2nd ed.). New York: Houghton-Mifflin.

Johnson, C., Dowd, T. J., & Ridgeway, C. L. (2006). Legitimacy as a social process. *Annual Review of Sociology*, 32, 53–78.

Karakowsky, L., McBey, K., & Miller, D. (2004). Gender, perceived competence, and power displays: Examining verbal interruptions in a group context. *Small Group Research*, 35, 407–439.

Kelsey, B. L. (1998). The dynamics of multicultural groups: Ethnicity as a determinant of leadership. *Small Group Research*, 29, 602–623.

Koch, S. C. (2005). Evaluative affect display toward male and female leaders of task-oriented groups. *Small Group Research*, 36, 678–703.

Lewin, K. (1948). *Resolving Social Conflicts: Selected Papers on Group Dynamics*. New York: Harper & Row.

Li, J., Karakowsky, L., & Siegel, J. P. (1999). The effects of proportional representation on intragroup behavior in mixed-race decision-making groups. *Small Group Research*, 30, 259–279.

Mann, S. A., & Huffman, D. J. (2005). Decentering of second wave feminism and the rise of third wave. *Marxist-Feminist Thought Today*, 69(1), 56–91.

Marbley, A. F. (2004). His eye is on the sparrow: A counselor of color's perception of facilitating groups with predominantly White members. *Journal for Specialists in Group Work*, 29, 247–258.

Martin, P. Y. (2003). "Said and done" versus "saying and doing": Gendering practice, practicing gender at work. *Gender and Society*, 17, 342–366.

Martin, P. Y. (2004). Gender as social institution. *Social Forces*, 82, 1249–1273.

May, R. A. B. (2007). Introduction: Era(c)ing and (re)constructing race and the racialized self. *Symbolic Interaction*, 30, 293–295.

McIntosh, P. (1988). White privilege and male privilege: A personal account of coming to see correspondences through work in women's studies. In M. L. Anderson & P. H. Collins (Eds.), *Race, Class, and Gender: An Anthology* (pp. 70-81). Belmont, CA: Wadsworth.

Morris, P. M. (2002). The capabilities perspective: A framework for social justice. *Families in Society*, 83, 365–373.

Mullaly, B. (2007). *The New Structural Social Work* (3rd ed.). Don Mills, Ontario, Canada: Oxford University Press.

Nagda, B. A. (2006a). Breaking barriers, crossing borders, building bridges: Communication processes in intergroup dialogues. *Journal of Social Issues*, 62, 553–576.

Nagda, B. A. (2006b). Looking back as we look ahead: Integrating research, theory, and practice on intergroup relations. *Journal of Social Issues*, 62, 439–451.

Nagda, B. A., Kim, C., & Truelove, Y. (2004). Learning about difference, learning with others, learning to transgress. *Journal of Social Issues*, 60, 195–214.

Narayan, W., & Harding, S. (2000). *Decentering the Center: Philosophy for a Multicultural, Post Colonial, and Feminist world.* Bloomfield: Indiana University Press.

Newcomb, T. (1960). Varieties of interpersonal attraction. In D. Cartwright & A. Zander (Eds.), *Group Dynamics: Research and Theory* (pp. 104–119). New York: Harper & Row.

Page, S. (2007). *The Difference: How the Power of Diversity Creates Better Groups, Firms, Schools and Societies.* Princeton, NJ: Princeton University Press.

Pyke, K. D., & Johnson, D. L. (2003). Asian American women and racialized femininities: "Doing" gender across cultural worlds. *Gender and Society*, 17, 33–53.

Randel, A. E. (2002). Identity salience: A moderator of the relationship between group gender composition and work group conflict. *Journal of Organizational Behavior*, 23, 749–769.

Ridgeway, C. (1991). The social construction of status values: Gender and other nominal characteristics. *Social Forces*, 70, 367–386.

Ridgeway, C. L. (2001). Gender, status and leadership. *Journal of Social Issues*, 57, 637–655.

Ridgeway, C. L. (2006). Linking social structure and interpersonal behavior: A theoretical perspective on cultural schemas and social relations. *Social Psychology Quarterly*, 69(1), 5–16.

Ridgeway, C. L., & Balkwell, J. W. (1997). Group processes and the diffusion of status beliefs. *Social Psychology Quarterly*, 60(1), 14–31.

Ridgeway, C. L., Boyle, E. H., Kuipers, K. J., & Robinson, D. T. (1998). How do status beliefs develop? The role of resources and interactional experience. *American Sociological Review*, 63, 331–350.

Ridgeway, C. L., & Correll, S. J. (2006). Consensus and the creation of status beliefs. *Social Forces*, 85, 431–453.

Ridgeway, C., & Diekema, D. (1989). Dominance and collective hierarchy formation in male and female task groups. *American Sociological Review*, 54, 79–93.

Ridgeway, C. L., Diekema, D., & Johnson, C. (1995). Legitimacy, compliance, and gender in peer groups. *Social Psychology Quarterly*, 58(4), 298–311.

Ridgeway, C. L., & Erickson, K. G. (2000). Creating and spreading status beliefs. *American Journal of Sociology*, 106, 579–615.

Ridgeway, C., & Johnson, C. (1990). What is the relationship between socioemotional behavior and status in task groups? *American Journal of Sociology*, 95, 1189–1212.

Rodriguez, R. A. (1998). Challenging demographic reductionism: A pilot study investigating diversity in group composition. *Small Group Research*, 29, 744–759.

Rowe, M. P. (1990). Barriers to equality: The power of subtle discrimination to maintain unequal opportunity. *Employee Responsibilities and Rights Journal*, 3(2), 153–163.

Sargent, L. D., & Sue-Chan, C. (2001). Does diversity affect group efficacy? The intervening role of cohesion and task interdependence. *Small Group Research*, 32, 426–450.

Schippers, M. (2008). Doing difference/doing power: Negotiations of race and gender in a mentoring program. *Symbolic Interactionism*, 31(1), 77–98.

Sengupta, S. (2006). I/me/mine—Intersectional identities as negotiated minefields. *Signs: Journal of Women, Culture and Society*, 31, 629–639.

Shaw, M. E. (1976). *Group Dynamics*. New York: McGraw-Hill.

Singleton, G. E., & Linton, C. (2006). *Courageous Conversation about Race: A Field Guide for Achieving Equity in Schools*. Thousand Oaks, CA: Corwin Press.

Smith-Lovin, L., & Brody, C. (1989). Interruptions in group discussions. *American Sociological Review*, 54, 424–435.

Stephan, W. G. (2008). Psychological and communication processes associated with intergroup conflict resolution. *Small Group Research*, 39, 28–41.

Suarez, Z., Newman, P., & Reed, B. G. (in press). Critical consciousness and cross-cultural social work practice: A case analysis. *Families in Society*.

Tervalon, M., & Murray-Garcia, J. (1998). Cultural humility versus cultural competence: A critical distinction in defining physician training outcomes in multicultural education. *Journal of Health Care for the Poor and Underserved*, 9(2), 117–125.

Tirmizi, S. A. (2005, November). *Leadership for Social Justice: A Conceptualization and Model*. Paper presented at the 7th Annual International Leadership Association Conference, Amsterdam, The Netherlands.

Townsend, J., Zapata, E., Rowlands, J., Alberti, P., & Mercado, M. (1999). *Women and Power: Fighting Patriarchy*. London: Zed Books.

van Knippenberg, D., Haslam, S. A., & Platow, M. J. (2007). Unity through diversity: Value-in-diversity beliefs, work group diversity, and group identification. *Group Dynamics: Theory, Research, and Practice*, 11, 207–222.

West, C., & Fenstermaker, S. (1995). Doing difference. *Gender and Society*, 9, 8–37.

Wickes, R., & Emmison, M. (2007). They are all "doing gender" but are they all passing? A case study of the appropriation of a sociological concept. *Sociological Review*, 55, 311–330.

Yarbro-Bejarano, Y. (1994). Gloria Anzaldúa's Borderlands/La frontera: Cultural studies, "difference," and the non-unitary subject. *Cultural Critique*, 28, 5–28.

Young, I. M. (1990). *Justice and the Politics of Difference*. Princeton, NJ: Princeton University Press.

10

Working with Natural Social Networks: An Ecological Approach

Judith S. Lewis and Roberta R. Greene

The ecological focus on universal life processes reminds social workers that supporting people's strengths and reducing environmental barriers to growth and adaptation are their foremost concerns. (Germain, 1991, p. 331)

This chapter examines how the basic assumptions of the ecological perspective on human behavior have been applied in social work practice with diverse natural social networks. Evidence for such interventions is drawn from the social work literature on work with various client populations; particular attention is paid to factors of race, culture, gender, class, and age. The major assumptions of the ecological perspective are presented and their meaning for diverse populations discussed. The chapter concludes with a discussion of questions and challenges related to the historic social work commitment to improving client environments.

The ecological approach to social work practice examines conditions that support or interrupt the balance or goodness of fit between people and their environments. From this perspective, the focus of intervention is on identifying, supporting, and mobilizing the internal resources of the client (Greene & Watkins, 1998; Maluccio, 1979). The environment is viewed as a full-fledged mode of intervention, rather than as an ancillary means of interpersonal helping; that is, people's social networks are viewed as mutual-aid systems and affective resources (Gitterman & Shulman, 2005).

In a similar vein, Scott (2000), in a discussion of community rebuilding and family strengthening in Australia, made the helpful connection between individuals, families, and natural helping systems. She described what she called *microlevel community building*, or interventions aimed at creating natural helping networks around families and generating social capital for local neighborhoods. Scott argued that psychosocial problems may be prevented and/or reduced by targeting programs to deal with risks across ecological systems, including the individual, family, peer groups, schools, and the broader community environment.

When addressing problems holistically, individuals, organizations, and societal structures are brought together in partnerships (G. Cox & Powers, 1998).

Basic Assumptions: The Ecological Perspective

By offering the opportunity to relate to others and to exchange resources and social support, social networks have the potential for contributing to growth and adaptation. (Greene, 2008a, p. 200)

Drawing on concepts from ecology, general systems theory, ego psychology, anthropology, role theory, stress theory, and other bodies of knowledge, the assumptions of the ecological approach to human behavior provide a knowledge base for practice that addresses the degree of person-environment fit, the reciprocal exchange between person and environment, and the forces that support or inhibit that exchange (Greene, 2008a). Because of its broad theoretical base, the perspective permits multiple views of client situations. Furthermore, it provides a framework to address content on a client's culture, historical era, gender, ethnicity, and other diversity factors (Greene & Watkins, 1998).

According to Germain (1991), people's needs and problems are located in the interface between person and environment, and interventions are aimed at ameliorating maladaptive transactions within this life space (see Table 10.1). A major appeal of the ecological perspective is its relevance for the enhancement of both the psychological and social lives of the client as well as the environmental conditions and situations within which the client functions (Haynie, Silver, & Teasdale, 2006). Ecological approaches emphasize the connections between individuals at various system levels. For example, Bronfenbrenner (1979) conceptualized the nature of the ecological environment as "a set of nested structures, each inside the next, like a set of Russian dolls" (p. 22). The model also may be visualized as ever-widening concentric circles of environment that surround the individual, moving from the nearest to the most remotest as follows:

1. the *microsystem*, a pattern of activities and roles and interpersonal face-to-face relations in the immediate setting, such as the family;
2. the *mesosystem*, the linkages and processes occurring between two or more settings containing the (developing) person, such as the school and the family;
3. the *exosystem*, the linkages and processes that occur between two or more settings, at least one of which does not ordinarily contain the developing person, such as the workplaces of parents; and
4. the *macrosystern*, the overarching patterns of a given culture, or broader social context, such as an ethnic group system.

McGoldrick and Carter (2005) further described the environment in which people evolve to encompass a broader cultural context and greater diversity of family form. Each system is represented schematically as eight concentric circles from the inner self to the larger society. Evolving systems have two time dimensions: the historical and the developmental. This schema allows practitioners to visualize and address personal characteristics of clients such as their emotional makeup within a specific sociohistorical context, such as the Great Depression or the African American Great Migration North. The visualization of the "family moving through time" (p. 417) also helps the practitioner consider the meanings of life in a particular era, as well as a family's belief system. Moreover, by using an ecological metaphor to understand the family, practitioners can understand how patterns of power, privilege, and oppression affect well-being and stress.

Natural Social Networks

The interest in social support and networks was prompted by landmark studies in the 1970s that found strong connections between social support and physical and mental health (Berkman & Syme, 1979; Lin, Simeone, Ensel, & Kuo, 1979; Nuckolls, Cassel, & Kaplan, 1972). This research has continued to this day (Greenglass, Fiksenbaum, & Eaton, 2006; Haynie et al., 2006; Solomon, Martin, & Westerof, 2006). Social support and social networks are two distinct concepts. *Social support* generally refers to the structure and content of a person's social relationships. *Structure* includes the number, types, and interconnectedness of ties; and *content* describes the kind of assistance a person gives and receives.

Table 10.1
The Ecological Perspective: Basic Assumptions

- The capacity to interact with the environment and to relate to others is innate.
- Genetic and other biological factors are expressed in a variety of ways as a result of transactions with the environment.
- Person–environment forms a unitary system in which humans and environment mutually influence each other (form a reciprocal relationship).
- Goodness of fit is a reciprocal person–environment process achieved through transactions between an adaptive individual and his or her nurturing environment.
- People are goal directed and purposeful. Humans strive for competence. The individual's subjective meaning of the environment is key to development.
- People need to be understood in their natural environments and settings.
- Personality is a product of the historical development of the transactions between person and environment over time.
- Positive change can result from life experiences.
- Problems of living need to be understood within the totality of life space.
- To assist a client, the social worker should be prepared to intervene anywhere in the client's life space.

Source. Greene, R. R. (2008-a). The ecological perspective: An eclectic theoretical framework. In R. R. Greene (Ed.), *Human Behavior Theory and Social Work Practice*. New Brunswick, NJ: Aldine Transaction.

Social workers need to understand the multiple dimensions of clients' social networks to have a comprehensive understanding of natural supports for assessment and intervention (Hill, 2002). Practitioners often examine the characteristics of a client's social network, which include size, frequency of contact, density (i.e., the extent to which people in one's network know and have contact with one another), reciprocity, durability (i.e., the length of time one has known those in one's network), intimacy, and proximity (i.e., the geographic distribution of those in one's network; Berkman, 1983; Ezell & Gibson, 1989; Hirsch, 1979; Kaufman, 1990; Wellman, 1981).

Social support can be defined as the emotional, instrumental, or financial aid that can be obtained from members of an individual's *social network*, or the web of social relationships that surround that person. Social networks are referred to as "natural" when they are formed spontaneously without the involvement of professionals (Li, Edwards, & Morrow-Howell, 2004). Natural helpers are found at many levels of the community and in many social roles. In addition to friends, neighbors, and relatives, others in a community, such as clergy, shopkeepers, or even postal delivery persons, may hold roles that are beneficial, offer assistance, or have personalities that indicate a willingness to help others (Bisman, 2003; Farris, 2007; Kelley & Kelley, 1985). Natural helpers can provide numerous types of support, including enhancing resilience (see Chapter 7), providing information and referrals, providing tangible sources of support, and helping with environmental problems that are encountered within the community (Pyles & Lewis, 2007; Waller & Patterson, 2002).

In an era of scarce resources and erosion of public support for many human services, there is a debate among policy makers about the relative importance of natural social networks versus formal services (Greene, 2005; Muramatsu & Campbell, 2002; Tennstedt, 1999). However, evidence currently suggests that natural social networks seem to work best when undergirded by the support of basic formal services (Greene, 2005). Nonetheless, the nature of the relationship between formal providers and natural helpers is a delicate one that requires social workers to exercise great care so that they do not usurp the position of the natural helper.

Culture and Natural Support Systems

An ecological view of human behavior assumes the importance of cultural context as it shapes behavior and is shaped by people (Devore & Schlesinger, 1998; Germain, 1991). For example, Lucas, Goldschmidt, and Day (2003) described the importance of viewing drug abuse among women as related to relational problems or situational stress. In their research on alcohol use by pregnant African American women, these authors reported that intervention approaches must "emphasize the health and developmental consequences of alcohol use [and] must also explore psychological and socioenvironmental influences that increase a woman's vulnerability for continued alcohol use during pregnancy" (p. 281).

To be sensitive to the client's cultural background, social workers should direct intervention efforts to multivariable systems and make use of natural systems and life experiences of ethnic minority clients.

Extended family structure is another factor that needs to be considered in social work interventions with ethnic minorities. Reiss (1981) pointed out that Asian/Pacific-American families usually expect to resolve their life problems within a tightly organized social support network. For example, the well-organized Vietnamese community in New Orleans mobilized quickly after 2005's Hurricane Katrina (Pyles & Lewis, 2007). They advocated for the return of families and the preservation of resources needed to rebuild. Other researchers have analyzed caregiving relationships in diverse families. Korean families, for example, have a different caregiving hierarchy than North American families (Cohen & Lee, 2007). In Korean families the most common care provider is the daughter-in-law, as the older son's family typically provides care. However, it is the husband's wife who is the primary care provider (Lee, Yoon & Kropf, 2007). If the social worker does not give ample attention to this common feature of the culture, he or she may not be fully accepted.

When working with natural social networks in contexts different from those familiar to the social worker, a host of other issues must also be considered. The perception that a person needs help or support, and from what source, can be influenced by one's cultural background or social class. In Vietnamese and Indian cultures, for example, a family member's emotional or social problem is thought to be the family's responsibility; in such cultures it is inappropriate to seek help from outsiders, particularly formal service providers (Land, Nishimoto, & Chau, 1988; R. G. Lewis & Ho, 1975).

The literature suggests further questions relevant for work with natural social networks among diverse populations (Devore & Schlesinger, 1998; Whittaker & Garbarino, 1983). They include the following:

- How is the need for help defined by client groups, and to whom do people turn for help?
- How are the relative merits of formal versus informal help viewed by different client groups?
- What role does discrimination and the use of power play in clients' decisions about the need for help and help seeking, and in client–social worker determinations about options for intervention?
- What are the various sources of informal help used by different segments of the population?
- How does the use of formal or informal help affect the sense of autonomy and competence among diverse groups of clients?

Natural Social Networks as Buffers against Oppression

The ecological perspective is concerned with societal power relationships and redressing inequities, including those associated with age, gender, sexual orientation, physical or mental disability, and race and ethnicity (Brotman, Ryan, & Cornier, 2003; Germain & Gitterman, 1995; Greene, 2007). Ecological theorists suggest that environments need to be more nutritive or supportive and offer a better goodness of fit for minority individuals. These theorists are also concerned with how minority Americans are devalued and the effect this devalued status—and the accompanying social injustice and discrimination—has on development (Ho, 1992; Pinderhughes, 1983, 1989).

Theorists have long questioned whether social support systems have the potential to be buffers against societal oppression (Greene, Taylor, Evans, & Smith, 2002; Logan, Freeman, & McRoy, 1990). Martin and Martin (1985) traced the historical roots of the helping tradition among black families, concluding that the formerly strong tradition of natural helping among African Americans had been devastated by overwhelming social and political change, including the Great Depression, northern migration, and the gradual adoption of a patriarchal and capitalistic value system. The revival of a strong helping tradition would require the institutionalization of race consciousness, a goal that in the authors' opinion had yet to be realized (Martin & Martin, 1985, p. 96).

Despite Martin and Martin's rather discouraging conclusion, there is evidence that the church and extended family networks still provide important sources of support for African Americans (Devore & Schlesinger, 1998; Lucas et al., 2003; Martin & Martin, 1985; McAdoo, 1978; Robinson-Dooley, 2005; Stack, 1975). Although the realities of institutional racism and discrimination within formal service systems have necessitated the creative use of helping networks among African American families, overburdened natural networks have their limits (Garbarino, 1983; Solomon, 1976). For example, there is ample evidence that the 2005 Gulf Coast hurricanes Katrina and Rita devastated strong extended family and neighborhood networks within the African American communities (Pyles & Lewis, 2007).

Social networks among African Americans are different in nature and scope from those in the pre-Depression years (Martin & Martin, 1985), yet clearly the long tradition of self-help is still alive (Bagley & Carroll, 1998). For example, Pyles and Lewis (2007) discussed how the council members of African American residents in New Orleans public housing developments contributed to post-Hurricane Katrina recovery by forming mutual aid groups. However, questions remain: Without changes that address the most basic inequalities faced by African Americans, how effective can natural social networks be? Can social workers use an ecological approach with natural networks among African American clients without acknowledging a responsibility for involvement in broad societal change as well?

Another area in which social support has been studied is in the identity formation of adolescent lesbian women. Swann and Anastas (2003) collected data from 205 lesbian or "questioning" young women aged 16 to 24 to determine various dimensions of their sexual identity development. Their findings indicated that it is impossible to separate the process of identification of the "individual" from the "group." This supports the notion that "identity development during adolescence happens through the identification with a peer group. Therefore, as lesbian adolescents search to understand themselves, like their heterosexual peers, they need a peer group that can mirror and affirm their sexual orientation" (p. 121).

Natural Networks and Mutual Helping

For decades, research on the response to natural disasters such as floods or hurricanes has suggested that there is a high level of mutual helping. *Mutual helping* involves assistance to and from people, sharing stories and building a sense of camaraderie (Blundo & Greene, 2007; Cox, 2005). Understanding community altruism may lessen a perceived threat and be less psychologically injurious (Janoff-Bulman, 1992). For example, in a study of a flooded Mormon community, Bolin (1989) observed that mutual helping was already in place before the actual crisis. In a similar vein, Greene (2008-b) recorded the stories of older adults who survived Hurricane Katrina. She found that survivors strived to reestablish routines and important network connections. When disconnected from their networks, they befriended others, thus establishing new, temporary communities to provide mutual aid.

Social Supports and Economic Well-Being

Ecological theorists argue that goodness of fit can be strongly, if not primarily, influenced by abuses of power by dominant groups that prevent equal access to housing, health care, education, and economic distribution. Germain and Gitterman (1995) suggested that the negative person–environment fit resulting from the misuse of power impairs human growth and development. They argued that, although interpersonal counseling may be helpful, many life stresses are created by society and must therefore be solved at the societal level.

Although the social work literature related to social class and ecologically oriented practice with natural social networks is limited, it does contain intriguing findings that have important implications for practice. With some consistency, the literature challenges the romantic notion that members of the lower socioeconomic strata take care of one another through strong social networks (Auslander & Litwin, 1988; Camasso & Camasso, 1986; Fischer, 1982).

Camasso and Camasso (1986), in their study of social support as a mediator of psychological distress among medical assistance recipients, found that when there is an imbalance of needs and resources, people become less willing to help. For example, when people feel threatened by the neediness of others or vulnerable to exploitation by others, their efforts to enhance neighborhood support might fail (Garbarino, 1992, 1995). In addition, enhancing natural social networks is insufficient: "Efforts also must be made to modify established social structures and processes that generate stress (e.g., unstable employment, poverty, residential mobility, crime)" (Camasso & Camasso, 1986, p. 388).

For children growing up in underserved communities, the challenges in the environment may overwhelm their coping strategies. Hilarski (2005) found that substance abuse by African American and Hispanic youth was related to their level of anxiety and depression and to the level of violence in their neighborhoods. She concluded that it is not enough to suggest that parents need to improve their caregiving (e.g., monitoring behaviors). Instead, the addition of community-level protective factors (e.g., responsive and nurturing community associations) is necessary to combat substance-abusing behaviors. Marsiglia, Miles, Dustman, and Sills (2002) found family and school ties to be the strongest protective factors in determining drug use among urban Latino youth. They decried the absence of after-school and community center supports in this process. They also called for a careful assessment of the existence and use of after-school opportunities in communities and for advocacy to fund more programs.

Others have described the importance of using an ecological perspective to understand dropout rates of high school students. At-risk youth need to be understood from an ecological perspective, as underlying causes of dropping out of school are often complex and interwoven (Franklin, Garner, & Berg, 2007). For example, students who are not doing well in school are at particular risk for teen pregnancy and substance abuse (Aloise-Young & Chavez, 2002; Franklin, Corcoran, & Harris, 2004). In addition, engaging in risky behavior such as substance abuse increases teens' risk of failing or dropping out of school. Protective factors, such as family involvement and alternative schools that have specific outreach to at-risk youth, are crucial (Miller & MacIntosh, 1999).

Promoting Self-Sufficiency through Social Networks

The ecological perspective suggests that individuals may develop life problems when there is "a lack of good fit between the coping capacities of the person and the qualities of the impinging environment" (Swenson, 1979, p. 233). Moreover, social support networks as informal helpers can function parallel to formal social welfare services on behalf of the client (Pancoast & Collins, 1987). Whittaker (1983) captured this idea well in his statement that

> a good deal of what ails the human services at present will be greatly improved by an infusion of ordinary lay people—friends, neighbors, kinfolk, and volunteers—doing what they do best: providing support, criticism, encouragement, and hope to people in distress. (p. 43)

Some such innovative programs incorporate volunteer sponsors, cultural mentors, or consultants to aid families in working toward their goals and ensuring their integration into the larger community (see Aidetti, 2005; Almeida, Woods, Messineo, & Font, 1998; Parker, 2003).

Whittaker suggested that social workers use a blend of formal and informal services to enhance person–environment fit and promote self-sufficiency. Older adults are an example of an underserved population in the traditional mental health system for whom formal and informal services have been used (Kimmel, 1990). Elderly persons, particularly women, are often at risk for social isolation and in need of various supports to maintain independent living (J. S. Lewis, 1993; J. Lewis & Harrell, 2002).

During the past several years, the social work literature on gerontology has examined or evaluated specific practice interventions involving older adults and their social networks (Feingold & Werby, 1990; Kaufman, 1990; McDermott, 1989; Seltzer, Ivry, & Litchfield, 1987; Seltzer, Litchfield, Lowy, & Levin, 1989). One example is the faith-based service initiative, which is a source of social involvement for many older adults (Gallup & Lindsay, 1999; Levin & Taylor, 1997). A study of religious congregations in Philadelphia ($N = 1,393$) had the goal of identifying the magnitude and benefits of providing services through such communities (Cnaan, Boddie, & Kang, 2005). This research found that about half of the congregations had some type of formal service provision mostly targeted toward the older population. The researchers argued that the clergy in these congregations are an important source of outreach and connection for older adults in their congregations and should be viewed as potential partners in service provision to older adults.

In an interesting case study of a housing complex for the elderly, Feingold and Werby (1990) described an otherwise well-designed component of a program (a dinner plan) that neglected to ensure choice and control by the residents. Such a seemingly minor issue as assigned seating ignored residents' desire to choose their own dinner companions and thus to benefit from their own natural networks. Clearly, natural social networks are important among older adults, even in sheltered settings where residence itself implies some loss of autonomy.

Kaufman (1990) presented a model that case managers who are developing long-term-care service plans for functionally impaired elderly persons can use to assess social networks. In addition to expressing the need for understanding the various structural and interactional characteristics of these social networks, he presented guidelines to case managers for evaluating the relevant values and attitudes of their clients. He emphasized the importance of understanding feelings about dependence or independence, familial obligations and expectations, and the role of government and formal organizations in meeting people's needs in influencing help-seeking and service-use behaviors (Kaufman, 1990).

Although the research cited has contributed to further specification in the thinking about ecological practice with natural social networks among the older persons, there still is a great need for expansion of this knowledge, particularly as it relates to diverse groups of elders such as members of racial and ethnic minority groups (Gibson, 1987; Sokolovsky & Vesperi, 1990; Taylor & Chatters,

1991), the very old (Kropf & Pugh, 1995), and persons who are homosexual (Grossman, D'Augelli, & O'Connell, 2001).

Empowerment through Social Networks

The ecological perspective suggests that client empowerment is a critical approach to social work practice (E. O. Cox, 2001; Glicken, 2004). Social networking among women as a means of empowerment has been a constant theme in the feminist literature of the past two decades, as evidenced by the emergence of *Affilia: Journal of Women and Social Work* and the Association for Women in Social Work. The social work literature on social networks as a component of help for women includes models of practice with battered women (Wood & Middleman, 1992), rural women (Olson, 1988), homeless women (Hagen & Ivanoff, 1988), lesbian alcoholics (Schilit, Clark, & Shallenberger, 1988), and women as advocates in post-hurricane recovery and rebuilding (Pyles & Lewis, 2007). Although none of these studies focused primarily on natural social network interventions, they all addressed the importance of these interventions as part of the empowerment process essential to women's growth and development.

Men's social networks have recently been given greater attention. Some evidence suggests that men are at risk for insufficient peer and social support, especially in times of crisis or during stressful life experiences such as raising a child or caring for a spouse with a disability (Kramer & Thompson, 2002; Nicholas, McNeill, Montgomery, Stapleford, & McClure, 2003). Paying attention to the support networks and the needs of men is necessary and involves a different way of conceptualizing help-seeking behaviors and intervention approaches (Kosberg, 2005).

What conclusions can be drawn from this summary of the social work literature on ecological practice applications using natural social networks and diverse client populations? Is there sufficient evidence that the ecological perspective provides a way to use natural social networks in helping diverse groups? What have social workers learned from these applications to date? What other questions about this approach remain? What are the challenges ahead for the profession if application of this approach with diverse populations is to progress and benefit clients?

Practice Applications with Diverse Cultural Groups

It is conceptually useful to think of interventions in two main areas: those which engage existing networks and seek to enhance their functioning, and those that create new networks, or "attach" a formerly isolated person to a network. (Swenson, 1979, p. 225)

The ecological perspective on human behavior offers a positive view of people's capabilities. It strongly emphasizes the importance of client empowerment as a vehicle for strengthening competence in affecting the goodness of fit between self and the environment at all systems levels. In the ecological practice approach, the social worker and client are viewed as partners in the process of assessing transactions with environmental systems to seek solutions that positively affect the client's life situation. Social workers must be prepared to honor clients' perceptions of the meaning of their life situations and environmental demands, and they must be open to a creative search for a broader range of interventions (Schriver, 2003; see Table 10.2).

The ecological perspective has provided the foundation for well-known practice models such as the life model (Germain & Gitterman, 1980; Gitterman & Germain, 2008) and the competence-based approach to practice (Maluccio, 1979). From the life model perspective, the social worker's purpose is to strengthen adaptive capacities of individuals and influence environments so that transactions are growth promoting (Germain & Gitterman, 1995). The competence-based model also defines problems in transactional terms (i.e., person-environment fit) and focuses on the purposive use of life experiences as interventions (Greene, 2008b). When attention is given to environmental transactions and clients' cultural context, "issues of race, gender, class, and sexual orientation in culturally diverse groups [are] at the core of therapeutic intervention" (Almeida et al., 1998, p. 414).

More recently, risk and resilience ecological frameworks have been put forth for assessment and intervention (Corcoran & Nichols-Casebolt, 2004; Greene, 2008c). These frameworks articulate risk and protective factors across the microsystem (individual and family level), mesosystem (neighborhood, school, church/synagogue), and macrosystem (poverty, discrimination, segregation) levels (Queiro-Tajalli & Campbell, 2002). Greene (2008c) articulated the resilience-enhancing model of social work practice, which is heavily influenced by

Table 10.2
Guidelines for the Ecological Approach to Social Work Intervention

- View the person and environment as inseparable.
- Be an equal partner in the helping process.
- Examine transactions between the person and environment by assessing all levels of systems affecting a client's adaptiveness.
- Assess life situations and transitions that induce high stress levels.
- Attempt to enhance a client's personal competence through positive relationships and life experiences.
- Seek interventions that affect the goodness of fit among a client and his or her environment at all systems levels.
- Focus on mutually sought solutions and client empowerment.

Source. Greene, R. R. (2008a). The ecological perspective: An eclectic theoretical framework. In R. R. Greene (Ed.), Human Behavior Theory and Social Work Practice. New Brunswick, NJ: Aldine Transaction.

the ecological perspective. The foundation of the resilience-enhancing model is to assess particular risk situations of the client using a multisystem framework, the degree of person-environment fit, and the particular coping strategies and competencies that the client possesses. This model has been applied in various client populations and social work contexts (Greene, 2008c).

Critique

There is some controversy surrounding the ecological perspective; specifically, a criticism that it is too diffuse to guide practice (Wakefield, 1996a, 1996b). This contention has been refuted by some scholars who have provided examples that the ecological system can offer a useful framework to guide practice at multiple system levels (Corcoran & Nichols-Casebolt, 2004; Greene & Watkins, 1998; Jakes & Brookins, 2004; Rothery, 2001). In particular, the ecological perspective recognizes that transactions between individuals and their environments can enhance or interfere with life situations, and thereby be a source of support or stress. This is an important principle in social work with diverse populations. It is a particularly useful premise because it suggests that the social worker needs to explore the opportunities available to clients in the structures and institutions of society that may appear to be closed to them by virtue of race, class, gender, or age (Germain, 1991).

Despite efforts to develop theoretical frameworks and practice models that allow for a more comprehensive and inclusive view of human behavior, much work remains to be done to develop effective use of these frameworks across culture, gender, age, social class, and so on (Ephross-Saltman & Greene, 1993). As Greene (2007) stated, "It is critical that practitioners make an extra effort to recognize the risk and protective factors that may be unique to a particular population or individual" (p. 56). Furthermore, social work practitioners must also be aware of their own cultural issues in their relationships with clients, and their beliefs or views about their clients' situations and experiences. One such innovation is the use of the cultural context model, which incorporates this value into practice by using multicultural teams of therapists who work in tandem observing one another and giving feedback on practitioner cultural competence and bias (Parker, 2003).

In an early critique of the life model, a practice model based upon the ecological perspective, Gould (1987) proposed a conflict model from a feminist perspective. Gould's model allows for conflict as a necessary ingredient in institutional reorganization without negating the person-in-environment paradigm. Especially in the case of disenfranchised groups, she believed it is unduly optimistic to assume that the "needs of individuals and the needs of society can be met simultaneously" (Gould, 1987, p. 348). Gould is one of many social workers who has stressed the primary importance of making sociostructural change before a goodness of fit can be reached between clients and their environments (Queiro-Tajalli & Campbell, 2002; Queiro-Tajalli & Smith, 1998).

Social workers using an ecological perspective are aware of the need to respect the client's own experience and act in an advisory rather than a directive role with natural social networks. For example, Waller and Patterson (2002) studied natural helpers in the Navajo Nation of Arizona. Natural helpers were found to provide a range of social supports to their communities that extended over extensive time periods. The need for social workers and other traditional formal helpers to understand the informal social support structure in operation in this community is critical. Additionally, Estes and Blundo (2007) described a resilience perspective in helping to develop the parenting skills of African American mothers and grandmothers. In this situation, the social worker had a good working relationship with the natural support networks.

The social work literature on the ecological approach to working with natural social networks among diverse client populations has prompted a number of observations and provocative questions for the profession. Although the ecological perspective and the models that have evolved from it are relatively recent, and proven practice models take time to develop, it seems reasonable to expect theorists to have made more progress in this regard. It is not clear what may have contributed to their slow progress. Some social workers had hoped that the use of informal helping networks would be able to meet the needs formerly addressed by formal services that were being downsized. But even during the mid-1980s, it became apparent that "informal helping networks [offered] no easy solution to the crisis in public support for basic human services" (Pancoast & Collins, 1987, p. 181).

Another disappointment with the application of the ecological approach, particularly among disadvantaged client groups, has been the fact that the profession did not become more actively involved in broad sociostructural change efforts (Specht & Courtney, 1995). In addition, social workers did not escape the national climate of the 1980s, during which there was a "disappearance of community" (Carter & McGoldrick, 2005, p. 379). Nevertheless, despite these reservations, a new model of ecological social work practice is emerging that rests on a nonhierarchical philosophy of human well-being (Ungar, 2002). Theorists who believe in this approach, known as *deep ecology*, propose that people attend to how they live in their world environment with an ethical commitment to solving human and environmental concerns. Maximizing human welfare becomes a moral obligation. Social workers have a great deal of knowledge about natural social networks gleaned from their work on the front line. Undoubtedly, systematic documentation of that knowledge can advance practice models that guide practitioners in an ecological approach to practice with diverse client populations.

References

Almeida, R., Woods, R., Messineo, T., & Font, R. (1998). The cultural context model: An overview. In M. McGoldrick (Ed.), *Revisioning Family Therapy: Race, Culture, and Gender in Clinical Practice* (pp. 414–431). New York: Guilford Press.

Aloise-Young, P. A., & Chavez, E. L. (2002). Not all school dropouts are the same: Ethnic differences in the relation between reason for leaving school and adolescent substance use. *Psychology in the Schools*, 39, 539–547.

Arditti, J. A. (2005). Families and incarceration: An ecological approach. *Families in Society*, 86, 251–261.

Auslander, C. K., & Litwin, H. (1988). Social networks and the poor: Toward effective policy and practice. *Social Work*, 33, 234–238.

Bagley, C. A., & Carroll, J. (1998). Healing forces in African-American families. In H. I. McCubbin, E. A. Thompson, A. I. Thompson, & J.A. Futrell (Eds.), *Resiliency in African American families* (pp. 117–142). Thousand Oaks, CA: Sage.

Beck, E., Britto, S., & Andrews, A. (2007). *In the Shadow of Death*. New York: Oxford Press.

Berkman, L. F. (1983). The assessment of social networks and social support in the elderly. *Journal of the American Geriatrics Society*, 37, 743–749.

Berkman, L. F., & Syme, S. L. (1979). Social networks, host resistance, and mortality: A nine year follow-up study of Alameda County residents. *American Journal of Epidemiology*, 109, 186–204.

Bisman, C. D. (2003). Rural aging: Social work practice models and intervention dynamics. *Journal of Gerontological Social Work*, 41(1/2), 37–58.

Blundo, R., & Greene, R. R. (2007). Survivorship in the face of traumatic events and disasters: Implications for social work. In R. R. Greene (Ed.), *Social Work Practice: A Risk and Resilience Perspective* (pp. 160–176). Belmont, CA: Brooks/Cole.

Bolin, R. (1989). Natural disasters. In R. Gist & B. Lubin (Eds.), *Psychosocial Aspects of Disaster* (pp. 61–85). New York: Wiley.

Bronfenbrenner, U. (1979). *The Ecology of Human Development*. Cambridge, MA: Harvard University Press.

Brotman, S., Ryan, B., & Cornier, R. (2003). The health and social service needs of gay and lesbian elders and their families in Canada. *The Gerontologist*, 43, 192–202.

Camasso, M. J., & Camasso, A. E. (1986). Social supports, undesirable life events, and psychological distress in a disadvantaged population. *Social Service Review*, 60, 378–394.

Carter, B., & McGoldrick, M. (Eds.). (2005). *The Expanded Family Life Cycle: Individual, Family, and Social Perspectives* (3rd ed.). Boston: Allyn & Bacon.

Cnaan, R. A., Boddie, S. C., & Kang, J. J. (2005). Religious congregations as social service providers for older adults. *Journal of Gerontological Social Work*, 45(1/2), 105–130.

Cohen, H., & Lee, Y. (2007). Dementia caregivers: Rewards in multicultural perspectives. In R. R. Greene (Ed.), *Contemporary Issues of Care* (pp. 299–324). New York: Haworth Press.

Corcoran, J., & Nichols-Casebolt, A. (2004). Risk and resilience ecological framework for assessment and goal formulation. *Child and Adolescent Social Work Journal*, 21, 211–235.

Cox, E. O. (2001). Community practice issues in the 21st century: Questions and challenges for empowerment-oriented practitioners. *Journal of Community Practice*, 9, 37–55.

Cox, G., & Powers, G. T. (1998). An ecological approach to developing resilience in elementary school children. In R. R. Greene & M. Watkins (Eds.), *Serving Diverse Constituencies: Applying the Ecological Perspective* (pp. 135–166). New York: Aldine de Gruyter.

Cox, K. (2005). Examining the role of social network intervention as an integral component of community-based, family-focused practice. *Journal of Child and Family Studies*, 14, 443–454.

Estes, T., & Blundo, R. (2007). Parenting skills among African American mothers and grandmothers: A resiliency perspective. In R. R. Greene (Ed.), *Social Work Practice: A Risk and Resilience Perspective* (pp. 138–159). Belmont, CA: Brooks/Cole.

Ezell, M., & Gibson, J. W. (1989). The impact of informal social network on the elderly's need for services. *Journal of Gerontological Social Work*, 14(3/4), 3–18.

Farris, K. D. (2007). The role of African-American pastors in mental health care. In R. R. Greene (Ed.), *Contemporary Issues of Care* (pp. 159–182). New York: Haworth Press.

Feingold, E., & Werby, E. (1990). Supporting the independence of elderly residents through control over their environment. *Journal of Housing for the Elderly*, 6(1/2), 25–32.

Fischer, C. (1982). *To Dwell among Friends: Personal Networks in Town and City*. Chicago: University of Chicago Press.

Franklin, C., Corcoran, J., & Harris, M. B. (2004). Risk, protective factors, and effective interventions for adolescent pregnancy. In M. W. Fraser (Ed.), *Risk and Resiliency in Childhood and Adolescents* (2nd ed., pp. 195–219). Washington, DC: NASW Press.

Franklin, C., Garner, J., & Berg, I. K. (2007). At-risk youth: Preventing and retrieving high school dropouts. In R. R. Greene (Ed.), *Social Work Practice: A Risk and Resilience Perspective* (pp. 115–137). Belmont, CA: Brooks/Cole.

Gallup, G. J., & Lindsay, D. M. (1999). *Surveying the Religious Landscape: Trends in U.S. Beliefs*. Harrisburg, PA: Morehouse.

Garbarino, J. (1983). Social support networks: Rx for the helping professionals. In J. K. Whittaker & J. Garbarino (Eds.), *Social Support Networks: Informal Helping in the Human Services* (pp. 3–28). Hawthorne, NY: Aldine de Gruyter.

Garbarino, J. (1992). The meaning of poverty in the world of children. *American Behavioral Scientist*, 35, 220–237.

Garbarino, J. (1995). *Raising Children in a Socially Toxic Environment*. San Francisco: Jossey-Bass.

Germain, C. B. (Ed.). (1991). *Social Work Practice: People and Environments*. New York: Columbia University Press.

Germain, C. B., & Gitterman, A. (1980). *The Life Model of Social Work Practice*. New York: Columbia University Press.

Germain, C. B., & Gitterman, A. (1995). Ecological perspective. In R. L. Edwards (Ed.-in-Chief), *Encyclopedia of Social Work* (19th ed., Vol. 1, pp. 816–824). Silver Spring, MD: NASW Press. Gibson, R. C. (1987). Reconceptualizing retirement for black Americans. *The Gerontologist*, 27, 691–698.

Gitterman, A. & Germain, C. (2008). *Life Model of Social Work Practice: Advances in Theory and Practice*. New York: Columbia University Press.

Gitterman, A., & Shulman, L. (2005). *Mutual Aid Groups, Vulnerable and Resilient Populations, and the Life Cycle*. New York: Columbia University Press.

Glicken, M. D. (2004). *Using a Strengths Perspective in Social Work Practice: A Positive Approach for Helping Professions*. Boston: Pearson Education.

Greene, R. R. (2005). The changing family of later years and social work practice. In L. Kaye (Ed.), *Productive Aging* (pp.107–122). Washington, DC: NASW Press.

Greene, R. R. (Ed.). (2007). *Social Work Practice: A Risk and Resilience Perspective*. Monterey, CA: Brooks/Cole.

Greene, R. R. (2008-a). The ecological perspective: An eclectic theoretical framework. In R. R. Greene (Ed.), *Human Behavior Theory and Social Work Practice* (pp. 199-

236). New Brunswick, NJ: Aldine Transaction.

Greene, R. R. (2008-b). Reflections on Hurricane Katrina by older adults: Three case studies in resiliency and survivorship. *Journal of Human Behavior and the Social Environment*,16(4), 57-74.

Greene, R. R. (2008-c). Resilience. In T. Mizrahi & L. Davis (Eds.), *Encyclopedia of Social Work* (20th ed., Vol. 3., pp. 527-531). Silver Spring, MD: NASW Press.

Greene, R. R., Taylor, N. J., Evans, M. L., & Smith, L. A. (2002). Raising children in an oppressive environment. In R. R. Greene (Ed.), *Resiliency: An Integrated Approach to Practice, Policy and Research* (pp. 241–276). Washington, DC: NASW Press.

Greene, R. R., & Watkins, M. (Eds.). (1998). *Serving Diverse Constituencies: Applying the Ecological Perspective.* New York: Aldine de Gruyter.

Greenglass, E., Fiksenbaum, L., & Eaton, J. (2006). The relationship between coping, social support, functional disability and depression in the elderly. *Anxiety, Stress, and Coping*, 19(1), 15–31.

Grossman, A. H., D'Augelli, A. R., & O'Connell, T. S. (2001). Being lesbian, gay, bisexual and 60 or older in North America. *Journal of Gay & Lesbian Social Services*, 13(4), 23–40.

Hagen, J. L., & Ivanoff, A. M. (1988). Homeless women: A high risk population. *Affilia*, 3(1), 19–33.

Haynie, D. L., Silver, E., & Teasdale, B. (2006). Neighborhood characteristics, peer networks, and adolescent violence. *Journal of Quarterly Criminology*, 22, 147–169.

Hilarski, C. (2005). Exploring predictive factors for substance use in African American and Hispanic youth using an ecological approach. *Journal of Social Service Research*, 32(1), 65–86.

Hill, M. (2002). Network assessments and diagrams: A flexible friend for social work practice and education. *Journal of Social Work*, 2, 233–254.

Hirsch, B. J. (1979). Psychological dimensions of social networks: A multimethod analysis. *American Journal of Community Psychology*, 7, 263–277.

Ho, M. K. (1992). *Minority Children and Adolescents in Therapy.* Newbury Park, CA: Sage.

Jakes, S. S., & Brookins, C. C. (2004). Introduction: Understanding ecological programming: Merging theory, research and practice. *Journal of Prevention & Intervention in the Community*, 27(2), 1–11.

Janoff-Bulman, R. (1992). *Shattered Assumptions: Toward a New Psychology of Trauma.* New York: Free Press.

Kaufman, A. V. (1990). Social network assessment: A critical component in case management for functionally impaired older persons. *International Journal of Aging and Human Development*, 30, 63–75.

Kelley, P., & Kelley, V. R. (1985). Supporting natural helpers: A cross-cultural study. *Social Casework*, 66, 358–366.

Kimmel, D. C. (1990). *Adulthood and Aging* (3rd ed.). New York: Wiley.

Kosberg, J. E. (2005). Meeting the needs of older men: Challenges for those in helping professions. *Journal of Sociology and Social Welfare*, 32(1), 9–31.

Kramer, B. J., & Thompson, E. H., Jr. (Eds.). (2002). *Men as Caregivers: Theory, Research and Service Implications.* New York: Springer.

Kropf, N. P., & Pugh, K. (1995). Beyond life expectancy: Social work with centenarians. *Journal of Gerontological Social Work, 23*(3/4), 121–137.

Land, H., Nishimoto, R., & Chau, K. (1988). Interventive and preventive services for Vietnamese Chinese refugees. *Social Service Review*, 62, 468–483.

Lee, M. H., Yoon, E., & Kropf, N. P. (2007). Factors affecting burden of South Koreans providing care to disabled older adults. *International Journal of Aging and Human*

Development, 64(3), 245-262.

Levin, J. S., & Taylor, R. J. (1997). Age differences in patterns and correlates of the frequency of prayer. *The Gerontologist*, 37, 75–88.

Lewis, J., & Harrell, E. (2002). Older adults. In R. R. Greene (Ed.), *Resiliency: An Integrated Approach to Practice, Policy, and Research* (pp. 277–292). Washington, DC: NASW Press.

Lewis, J. S. (1993). *Independent Living among Community Based Elderly: The Impact of Social Support and Sense of Coherence.* Unpublished dissertation, University of Maryland, Baltimore.

Lewis, R. G., & Ho, M. K. (1975). Social work with Native Americans. *Social Work*, 20, 379–382.

Li, H., Edwards, D., & Morrow-Howell, N. (2004). Informal caregiver networks and use of formal services by inner-city African American elderly with dementia. *Families in Society*, 85, 55–62.

Lin, N., Simeone, R. S., Ensel, W. M., & Kuo, W. (1979). Social support, stressful life events, and illness: A model and an empirical test. *Journal of Health and Social Behavior*, 20, 108–119.

Logan, S. M. L., Freeman, E. M., & McRoy, R. G. (Eds.). (1990). *Social Work Practice with Black Families: A Culturally Specific Perspective.* New York: Longman.

Lucas, E., Goldschmidt, L., & Day, N. L. (2003). Alcohol use among pregnant African American women: Ecological considerations. *Health & Social Work*, 28, 273–283.

Maluccio, A. (1979). Competence and life experience. In C. B. Germain (Ed.), *Social Work Practice: People and Environments* (pp. 282–302). New York: Columbia University Press.

Marsiglia, F. F., Miles, B. W., Dustman, P., & Sills, S. (2002). Ties that protect: An ecological perspective on Latino/urban preadolescent drug use. *Social Work With Multicultural Youth*, 11, 191–220.

Martin, J. M., & Martin, E. P. (1985). *The Helping Tradition in the Black Family and Community.* Silver Spring, MD: NASW Press.

McAdoo, H. P. (1978). The impact of upward mobility on kin-help patterns and reciprocal obligations in black families. *Journal of Marriage and Family*, 40, 761–778.

McDermott, C. J. (1989). Empowering the elderly nursing home resident: The resident rights campaign. *Social Work*, 34, 155–157.

McGoldrick, M., & Carter, B. (2005). Remarried families. In B. Carter & M. McGoldrick (Eds.), *The Expanded Family Life Cycle: Individual, Family, and Social Perspectives* (pp. 417–435). Boston: Allyn & Bacon.

Miller, D. B., & MacIntosh, R. (1999). Promoting resilience in urban African American adolescents: Racial socialization and identity as protective factors. *Social Work Research*, 23, 159–170.

Muramatsu, N., & Campbell, R. T. (2002). State expenditures on home and community based services and use of formal and informal personal assistance. *Journal of Health and Social Behavior*, 43, 107–124.

Nicholas, D. B., McNeill, T., Montgomery, G., Stapleford, C., & McClure, M. (2003). Communication features in an online group for fathers of children with spina bifida: Considerations for group development among men. *Social Work With Groups*, 26(2), 65–80.

Nuckolls, K. B., Cassel, J., & Kaplan, B. H. (1972). Psychosocial assets, life crisis and the prognosis of pregnancy. *American Journal of Epidemiology*, 95, 431–441.

Olson, C. S. (1988). Blue Ridge blues: The problems and strengths of rural women. *Affilia*, 3(1), 5–17.

Pancoast, D. L., & Collins, A. (1987). Natural helping networks. In A. Minahan (Ed.-

in-Chief), *Encyclopedia of Social Work* (18th ed., pp. 177–182). Silver Spring, MD: NASW Press.

Parker, L. (2003). A social work justice model for clinical social work practice. *Affilia*, 18, 272–288.

Pinderhughes, E. B. (1983). Empowerment for our clients and for ourselves. *Social Casework*, 64, 331–338.

Pinderhughes, E. B. (1989). *Understanding Race, Ethnicity, and Power: The Key to Efficacy in Clinical Practice*. New York: Free Press.

Pyles, L., & Lewis, J. S. (2007). Women of the storm: Advocacy and organizing in post-Katrina New Orleans. *Affilia*, 22(4), 385-390.

Queiro-Tajalli, I., & Campbell, C. (2002). Resilience and violence at the macro level. In R. R. Greene (Ed.), *Resiliency: An Integrated Approach to Practice, Policy, and Research* (pp. 217–240). Washington, DC: NASW Press.

Queiro-Tajalli, I., & Smith, L. (1998). Provision of services to older adults within an ecological perspective. In R. R. Greene & M. Watkins (Eds.), *Serving Diverse Constituencies: Applying the Ecological Perspective* (pp. 199–220). Hawthorne, NY: Aldine de Gruyter.

Reiss, D. (1981). *The Family Construction of Reality*. Cambridge, MA: Harvard University Press.

Robinson-Dooley, V. (2005). *The Subjective Appraisal of Well-Being of Aging African American Men*. Unpublished doctoral dissertation, University of Georgia, Athens.

Rothery, M. (2001). Ecological systems theory. In P. Lehmann & N. Coady (Eds.), *Theoretical Perspectives for Direct Social Work Practice* (pp. 65–82). New York: Springer.

Schilit, R., Clark, W. M., & Shallenberger, E. A. (1988). Social supports and lesbian alcoholics. *Affilia*, 3(2), 27–40.

Schriver, J. M. (2003). *Human Behavior and the Social Environment: Shifting Paradigms in Essential Knowledge for Social Work Practice* (4th ed.). Boston: Allyn & Bacon.

Scott, D. (2000). Embracing what works: Building communities that strengthen families. *Children Australia*, 25(2), 4–9.

Seltzer, M. M., Ivry, J., & Litchfield, L. C. (1987). Family members as case managers: Partnership between the formal and informal support networks. *The Gerontologist*, 26, 722–728.

Seltzer, M. M., Litchfield, L. C., Lowy, L., & Levin, R. J. (1989). Families as case managers: A longitudinal study. *Family Relations*, 38, 332–336.

Solomon, B. B. (1976). *Black Empowerment: Social Work in Oppressed Communities*. New York: Columbia University Press.

Specht, H., & Courtney, M. E. (1995). *Unfaithful Angels: How Social Work Has Abandoned Its Mission*. New York: Free Press.

Stack, C. (1975). *All Our Kin: Strategies for Survival in a Black Community*. New York: Harper & Row.

Stevens, J. L., Martina, C. M. S., & Westerof, G. J. (2006). Meeting the need to belong: Predicting effects of a friendship enrichment program for older women. *The Gerontologist*, 46, 495–502.

Swann, S. K., & Anastas, J. W. (2003). Dimensions of lesbian identity during adolescence and young adulthood. *Journal of Gay & Lesbian Social Services*, 15(1/2), 109–125.

Swenson, C. (1979). Social networks, mutual aid and the life model of practice. In C. B. Germain (Ed.), *Social Work Practice: People and Environments* (pp. 215–266). New York: Columbia University Press.

Taylor, R. J., & Chatters, L. M. (1991). Religious life of black Americans. In J. S. Jackson (Ed.), *Life in Black America* (pp. 105–123). Newbury Park, CA: Sage.

Tennstedt, S. (1999, March). *Family Caregiving in an Aging Society.* Paper presented at the U.S. Administration on Aging Symposium "Longevity in the New American Century," Baltimore, MD.

Ungar, M. (2002). *A Deeper, More Social Ecological Social Work Practice.* Chicago: University of Chicago Press.

Wakefield, J. C. (1996a). Does social work need the eco-systems perspective? Part 1. Is the perspective clinically useful? *Social Service Review*, 70, 2–32.

Wakefield, J. C. (1996b). Does social work need the eco-systems perspective? Part 2. Does the perspective save social work from incoherence? *Social Service Review*, 70, 184–213.

Waller, J. A., & Patterson, S. (2002). Natural helping and resilience in a Dine' (Navajo) community. *Families in Society*, 83, 73–84.

Wellman, B. (1981). Applying network analysis to the study of support. In B. H. Gottlieb (Ed.), *Social Networks and Social Support* (pp. 171–200). Beverly Hills, CA: Sage.

Whittaker, J. K. (1983). Mutual helping in human service practice. In J. K. Whittaker & J. Garbarino (Eds.), *Social Support Networks: Informal Helping in the Human Services* (pp. 29–70). Hawthorne, NY: Aldine de Gruyter.

Whittaker, J. K., & Garbarino, J. (Eds.). (1983). *Social Support Networks: Informal Helping in the Human Services.* Hawthorne, NY: Aldine de Gruyter.

Wood, G. G., & Middleman, R. R. (1992). Groups to empower battered women. *Affilia*, 7(4), 82–95.

11

Power Factors in Social Work Practice

Roberta R. Greene

[Social workers cannot ignore] the consequences of negative valuations directed toward members of stigmatized groups ... and the relationship between power, powerlessness, and the processes of human growth and development. (Solomon, 1976, pp. 13-17)

Social workers' interest in and concern for social equity and quality of life has been a continuing and unifying theme in the historical development of the profession. The social work profession has also been committed to meeting the needs of and providing opportunities for at-risk and oppressed populations through social reform. In addition to their interest in the well-being of individuals, families, and groups, social workers have long held the belief that it is important to help people exert their influence to obtain basic resources, such as housing, food, clothing, and health care. Although activities have not always been consistent, social workers have also been involved in bringing about change in social, structural, and institutional factors that contribute to unemployment, poverty, and discrimination (Garcia & Van Soest, 2006).

Social workers who are concerned about power relationships in the therapeutic relationship recognize that difficulties with individual clients sometimes reflect the power "organization of larger political, economic, or social structures" (Burghardt & Fabricant, 1987, p. 456). Although social workers tend to view themselves as egalitarian change agents, they are also susceptible to the sociohistorical issues of power, racism, and other forms of privilege of the general society. As members of society and an institutionalized professional group, as well as representatives of agencies, social workers are inevitably caught up in the dynamics of power issues (Burghardt & Fabricant, 1987; Pinderhughes, 1983, 1989; Scott, 1971; Solomon, 1976, 1982, 1991).

Therefore, it is not surprising that there has been an attempt to find (a) human behavior theories that address the concept of power and (b) practice strategies that emphasize client empowerment. Lowenstein (1976) was among the earlier proponents urging social workers to address the consequences of unequal power relations in human behavior theories. She contended that the Freudian concepts of the conflict between a person's emotions and societal control be reinterpreted as a power struggle and that the concept of power be introduced into all courses on human behavior. Similarly, Max (1971) argued that because power "is located or latent in every level of society," social workers need to understand power theory and strategies of institutional change (p. 275). More recently, Garcia and Van Soest (2006) proposed that social workers understand how oppression bestows power and advantage on some people while denying it to others. They suggested that promoting social justice and redressing social inequities is the foundation for culturally competent social work practice.

This chapter examines theoretical assumptions related to the concept of power derived from general systems, ecological, and feminist theories. It discusses human behavior concepts that present the client–social worker relationship as a microcosm of societal power issues. It describes ways in which social workers can become more effective in recognizing and dealing with their own biases rooted in their power status and offers strategies for bringing parity to the helping relationship.

The Concept of Power

Power as a concept has been applied universally to all forms of human behavior— not only to explain intergroup behavior but also to explain dyadic relationships and individualistic behavior. (Wilson, 1973, p. 15)

Common Features of Power

Power may be considered the "more or less unilateral ability (real or perceived) or potential to bring about significant change, usually in people's lives, through the actions of oneself or of others" (Weber, 2007). Differential power is a marked feature in all complex societies (Anderson, Carter, & Lowe, 1999). Power differentials may occur at the *personal level*, relating to a person's sense of control and effecting one's sense of empowerment; the *interpersonal level*, referring to one's influence over others; the *institutional level*, relating to the extent discrimination is embedded in an organization; and the *structural level*, locating oppression in societal institutions (Cohen & Greene, 2005). According to Foucalt (1980), "Power is everywhere ... because it comes from everywhere." (p. 93)

Inequality in power has seven common characteristics:

1. inequality in social resources, social position, and political and cultural influences;
2. inequality in opportunities to make use of existing resources;
3. inequality in the division of rights and duties;
4. inequality in implicit or explicit standards of judgment, often leading to differential treatment (in laws, the labor market, educational practices, etc.);

5. inequality in cultural representations: devaluation of the powerless group, stereotyping, references to the "nature" or (biological) "essence" of the less powerful;

6. inequality in psychological consequences: a "psychology of inferiority" (insecurity, "double-bind" experiences, and sometimes identification with the dominant group) versus a "psychology of superiority" (arrogance, inability to abandon the dominant perspective);

7. social and cultural tendency to minimize or deny power inequality: (potential) conflict often represented as consensus, power inequality as "normal" (K. Davis, Leijenaar, & Oldersma, 1991, p. 52).

In addition, there are differences in power relations based on knowledge, ability, expertise, gender, ethnicity, class, and so forth.

Power Abuse

Power is a complex phenomenon central to a person's sense of mastery, competence, or psychological well-being. It is related to the capacity to produce desired effects on others, and to the status and roles assigned within a group and within the larger society. Power differentials account for aggrandizement of some individuals and marginalization of others. They also have an effect on human developmental processes. That is, when "specific groups, types, or classes of people are treated as if they are expendable and replaceable," their hope can be undermined and their development subverted (Goldenberg, 1978, p. 9). The abuse of power can make people experience themselves as hoping to be a true member of society while being psychologically separated by oppression. This idea was captured by Wicker (1986), who argued that "racism is more than prejudice. It is power plus prejudice" (p. 30).

Webb (2000) cautioned that social work as a profession is not immune to the politics of power. He contended that social work is about change in human behavior and in the environment. He argued:

> The capacity to effect changes, bar nature's capacity, e.g. earthquakes, is at the root a human capacity and a form of power. In so far [*sic*] as social work is about making changes to the condition of human life, social work is fundamentally about the use of various kinds of power (p. 2).

Preferential Treatment or Privilege

Access to unearned privilege maintains inequality and contributes to an abuse of power (hooks, 1990; Swigonski, 1996). *Privilege* bestows economic, social, judicial, and political advantages on people who most fit the norms of mainstream society (Garcia & Van Soest, 2006). Privilege is associated with preferential treatment, access to a disproportionate share of resources, and the subordination of women and certain racial and ethnic groups (Danziger, 1987).

For example, McIntosh (1988, 1995) discussed the consequences of the U.S. system of advantages that favor white men while devaluing women and people of color (see Table 11.1). McIntosh suggested that people act as if male privilege were a secret, making it even more powerful and oppressive.

Table 11.1
Types of Privilege Reflected in Statements

Type of Privilege	Sample Statement
The freedom to associate exclusively or primarily with members of your own group	I can, if I wish, arrange to be in the company of people of my race most of the time. (p. 5)
The level of social acceptance you can presume across varying contexts	If I should need to move, I can be pretty sure of renting or purchasing housing in an area in which I want to live. (p. 5)
	Whether I use checks, credit cards, or cash, I can count on my skin color not to work against the appearance of financial reliability. (p. 6)
	I do not have to educate my children to be aware of systemic racism for their own daily protection. (p. 6)
The ability to see members of your group in a positive light in history records, in texts, in media, and as role models	When I am told about our national heritage or about civilization, I am shown that people of my color made it what it is. (p. 6)
	I can be pretty sure that if I ask to speak to the person in charge, I will be facing a person of my own race. (p. 7)
Freedom from stereotyping	I can swear, or dress in second-hand clothes, or not answer letters, without having people attribute these choices to the bad morale, poverty, or illiteracy of my race. (p. 7)
	I can do well in a challenging situation without being called a credit to my race. (p. 7)
	I can be late to a meeting without having the lateness reflect on my race. (p. 8)
The ability to be oblivious to other groups in your culture	I can remain oblivious to the language and customs of people of color who constitute the world's majority without feeling any penalty for such obliviousness. (p. 7)

Source: McIntosh, P. (1988). *White Privilege and Male Privilege: A Personal Account of Coming to See Correspondences through Work in Women's Studies* (Working Paper No. 189, pp. 5–8). Wellesley, MA: Wellesley College Center for Research on Women.

Power as Demeaning

Power may also be associated with the capacity to demean others and the ability to force an individual to do something against his or her will. Power may be considered particularly oppressive when people are forced to do something against their will, as in the case of slavery and the oppression of indigenous peoples during the European settlement of America. Despite many forms of oppression and deliberate attempts to destroy Native cultures, Indians have struggled to retain their cultural identification. For example, most indigenous families have been negatively influenced by the legacy of the Indian boarding school system in which many children reported experiencing racism from teachers and staff (Weaver, 2000).

Indian students often continue to face negative experiences when attending colleges that expect them to meet mainstream institutional expectations. For example, Weaver's (2000) study of the experience of American Indian social workers in social work programs found that they felt oppressed by the hierarchical, bureaucratic educational system. Students also felt that they had to compromise their cultural identity to succeed in school. Particularly troublesome for them was the expectation to be verbal in small groups and to maintain constant eye contact. Weaver urged that educators learn the *orthogonal model of cultural identification*, in which people identify simultaneously with more than one culture; this identification has positive implications for health and social issues (Weaver, 1996).

Various contextual factors can also impact an individual's capacity for domination over others. One example is the atrocities that were committed at Abu Ghraib prison during the War on Terrorism. As Mohanty (2006) argued, defining the war as an assault on terrorism and as a crusade of the civilized against the uncivilized led to distortions of power by U.S. soldiers that were the foundation for the acts of torture and humiliation of the prisoners. When viewing the photographs of the prisoners—naked, posed in vulnerable and demeaning positions, and frightened—it is striking the look of power and dominance.

Power and the General Systems Perspective: Basic Assumptions

The concept of ethnosystems ... emphasizes the interdependent, interrelatedness of ethnic collectivities ... and makes it possible to study the variations in cultural patterns and social organization, language and communication, the degree of power over material resources, and political power. (Greene, 2008, p. 184)

Power as Natural

General systems theorists suggest that social systems exist in relatively continuous harmony because of their well-coordinated functions. Power is considered an inherent, fixed property of these systems (Longres, 2000; Parsons, 1951, 1964; see Table 11.2). From this perspective, each system naturally develops a

Table 11.2
Power Issues in Social Work Practice

General Systems Theory

- All social systems have an organizational structure and therefore have a status or power hierarchy.

- Personal and positional resource differentials are associated with differences in power. Resources are an interpersonal factor influenced by gender or ethnicity/race.

- As a social system, the client–social worker relationship has inherent power issues that may mirror those found in the general society. Societal beliefs and practices tend to view professionals as authorities or experts over the lay public.

Ecological Theory

- Power is related to the reciprocal process of goodness of fit between the person and the environment.

- A goodness-of-fit metaphor suggests that nutritive environments offer the necessary resources, security, and support at the appropriate times and in the appropriate ways. Such environments enhance the cognitive, social, and emotional development of community members.

- When environments are not nutritive, the match tends to be poor. Hostile environments, in which there is a lack or a distortion of environment supports, inhibit development and the ability to cope.

- The client–social worker relationship goal is empowerment, or a process of increasing personal, interpersonal, or political power to improve client's life situation, knowledge, skills, or material resources.

Feminist Theory

- Power is unlimited and can be widely distributed through empowerment strategies. Empowerment is a political act in which people take control over their own lives and make their own decisions.

- Power is a process in which people personally and collectively transform themselves. Power is derived from a person's internal energy and strength and requires openness and a connection with others.

- Whenever possible, the personal power between the therapist and the client approaches equality.

system of power and control that is associated with how it is organized. In this manner, conflict and change are avoided, and the system remains well integrated. This view of power as being natural and necessary to group functioning has been applied in role theory, general systems theory, and many schools of family treatment. Power, then, is related to a community's or family's underlying structure and general capacity to meet collective obligations and goals.

Social Stratification

Because power is a natural feature of systems, it results in *social stratification*, a societal ranking of individuals based on such indices as income, occupation, and education. In addition, social stratification and social class groups center around race or skin color; ethnicity; religion; gender; health and physical abilities; age; and, more recently in U.S. society, sexual orientation. These power and prestige hierarchies are then associated with societal inequities (Pincus, 2000).

The notion of social class usually suggests that there is a group consciousness on the part of members, both of their own group status and that of others. When social classes are clear and closed, there is little movement between and among status groups (Anderson et al., 1999). In addition, when status is assigned by some characteristic beyond a person's control (e.g., skin color, gender, national origin, or age), a caste or caste-like society exists (DuBois, 1969).

The Dual Perspective

Chestang (1972) and Miller (1980) used a systems analysis to discuss the *dual perspective*, which portrays the impact for clients who simultaneously live in two cultures with unequal power: (a) the dominant or sustaining system, that is, the source of power and economic resources; and (b) the nurturing system, or the immediate social environment of the family and community. Miller suggested that the social worker's assessment of stress produced by institutional and dominant environment factors can lead to an understanding about "whether the target of change [intervention] should become the client, the larger system, or both, or whether it is appropriate to intervene at all" (p. 60).

Ethnosystems

Solomon (1976) developed the concept of an ethnosystem to understand how minority families, specifically African American families, fit within the larger power context of other ethnosystems and societal institutions. An *ethnosystem* is defined as a "collective of interdependent ethnic groups with each group sharing unique historical and/or cultural ties and bound together by a single, political system" (p. 45). Social workers can understand their client's resource base by using this schema to map the relative power position of ethnic groups, including those who are new Americans.

Family and Goodness of Fit

A family's sense of capacity or power to function effectively depends on its fit with the environment (Auerswald, 1971; Bronfenbrenner, 1986; Sotomayor, 1971; see Chapter 8 for a discussion of the family). However, many families face the burden of insurmountable environmental pressures and limited access to resources. They may be seen as ineligible for work, struggling with unresponsive educational systems, and blocked from entering the social and economic mainstream. Hence, a "cycle of poverty and exclusion is perpetuated" (Hartman & Laird, 1983, p. 189).

Minority individuals and families in particular face this ecological challenge (Harrison, Wilson, Pine, Chan, & Buriel, 1990). Ecological theorists believe that the ecological challenges facing ethnic minorities are not sudden, temporary economic calamities but derive from a long history of oppression and discrimination. The process of discrimination often leading to poverty is seen as a

> cycle of powerlessness in which the failure of the larger social system to provide needed resources operates in a circular manner.... The more powerless a community the more the families within it are hindered from meeting the needs of their members and from organizing the community so that it can provide them with more support. (Pinderhughes, 1983, p. 332)

According to the ecological perspective, then, power evolves through social structures when the majority or dominant group maintains control or power over subordinate groups. This process of social stratification also involves denying subordinates access to resources and controlling the expectations for lifestyles, life chances, and quality of life. In addition, a group's relative power affects how individuals and families perceive themselves and their life opportunities.

Power and the Feminist Perspective: Basic Assumptions

> *Feminism is a transformational politics, a political perspective concerned with changing extant economic, social, and political structures. (Van Den Bergh & Cooper, 1986, p. 1)*

Gender and Power

According to a book on the gender of power by K. Davis et al. (1991), a theory of power relevant to women must define how women are valued as a social category. From another point of view, Sands and Nuccio (1992) questioned the social work profession's very use of categories such as gender, race, ethnicity, and class, when addressing its mission to overcome oppression. They suggested that there is a danger that the "very categories promulgated to stem oppression are themselves oppressive in their superficiality" (Sands & Nuccio, 1992, p. 493). Indeed, they asserted, the very construction of categories returns people, full circle, to oppressive hierarchical relationships. Instead, they proposed that practitioners be cognizant of clients' multiple voices. For example, feminist theorists contend that it is not possible to describe the essential woman or man. This essentialism tends to treat historical and social constructions as fixed, natural, and absolute (Tice, 1990, p. 135).

Feminist scholars have called for theories that "are nonuniversal, [but open to the] multiplicity and diversity of experiences" (Frazer & Nicholson, 1990, p. 21). Because feminist scholars are suspicious of any universal norms that fit all women or men, they would "replace unitary notions of 'woman' with plural and complex descriptions of feminine gender identity" (Tice, 1990, p. 135; see Chapter 5 on role theory). Feminist theory has also addressed social work activities that are centered around social reform and the existing relationships of patriarchal power and authority (Hooyman, Summers, & Leighninger, 1988). For example, feminism posits that social roles should not be assigned solely on the basis of gender and strives for the equality of men and women (Valentich, 1986).

Conceptualizing Power

How power is conceptualized has been a central concern of feminist theorists. Although different branches of feminists share many ideas, they also speak in multiple voices on different philosophical and political concerns. *Liberal feminists* work to attain political rights and opportunities for all and to change the inequality that exists between men and women within the political system. *Socialist feminists* strive to eliminate oppression and the resulting sexism, racism, and classism that they say stems from patriarchal capitalism. *Radical feminists* work toward a society in which patriarchy no longer predominates and women's caring and loving qualities predominate (Nes & Iadicola, 1989).

Generally speaking, feminists reject the notion that power is limited and that people need to be placed into the dichotomous conditions of haves and have-nots (Van Den Bergh & Cooper, 1986). They do not accept that there is a limited supply of property or money, with the controllers of the supply dominating or censuring personal and societal behaviors (Hooyman, 1980). Feminist theorists also reject the traditional definition of power in terms of who can maintain domination or control (Bricker-Jenkins & Hooyman, 1986), or an "imposition-from-without model" (Albrecht & Brewer, 1990, p. 4).

Feminists view the meaning of power as multiple, unfixed, and open to interpretation (Van Voorhis, 2008). The multiple meanings of power are related to a particular social, political, and historical context (Sands & Nuccio, 1992). Power is also expressed at a more personal level or in the microprocesses of everyday life (Foucault, 1983). This philosophy of *local power* shifts the focus to "routine, habitual and practical features of human conduct in the constitution of social life" (K. Davis et al., 1991, p. 10; see Chapter 6 on social construction).

Because power "hovers everywhere and underlies everything," it is a primary concept in the analysis of social life (Giddens, 1984, p. 226). Giddens argued that the structural properties of social systems do not exist outside day-to-day, face-to-face interactions. Rather, power has the following five dimensions:

1. Power is integral to social interaction, which includes, but is not limited to, social institutions or political collectives.
2. Power is intrinsic to human agency, which encompasses people's desires and intentions.
3. Power is relational, involving relations of dependence and autonomy.
4. Power is enabling as well as constraining and includes restrictions and opportunities.
5. Power is processual, which involves how people routinely construct, maintain, change, and transform their relations of power.

Empowerment

According to feminist theorists, power is unlimited and can be widely distributed through empowerment strategies rather than through domination. *Empowerment*, then, is viewed as a political act in which people take control over their own lives and make their own decisions (Simon, 1994). Hence, "the personal is political" is a major assumption of feminist theory (Van Den Bergh & Cooper, 1986, p. 612). Power is expressed as a process by which people personally and collectively transform themselves. It is derived from a person's internal energy and strength and requires openness and a connection with others (Albrecht & Brewer, 1990).

Power Differentials and Intervention Strategies

If our institutional response and problem-solving endeavors are directed to the elimination of powerlessness, then we are truly "starting where the client is." (Pinderhughes, 1978, p. 14)

Power is "an often unspoken but central dynamic in cross cultural encounters" and therefore needs to be addressed in the clinical social work relationship (Pinderhughes, 1989, p. 109). Political, economic, and social aspects of professional social work authority—the established right granted by society to make decisions on certain issues—also must be taken into consideration (Briar & Miller, 1971; Dworkin, 1990).

This section reviews and explores the power differential and control issues that may exist in the social worker–client relationship. It notes the potential difficulties in providing a service that maximizes client competence and feelings of self-worth (see Table 11.3).

General Systems Perspective: Authority

From a structuralist systems perspective, power that is viewed as legitimate, such as that associated with professional power, is called *authority*. The authority

Table 11.3
Guidelines for Power Parity in the Client-Social Worker Relationship

- Recognize that the social worker has the potential to be an agent of social control and/or social change. Bring awareness of sociohistorical issues of power, racism, and privilege of the general U.S. society to the client–social worker relationship.

- Examine power issues related to practical features of everyday social life within social, cultural, political, and historical contexts.

- Recognize and deal with practitioner biases rooted in power statuses and offer strategies for bringing parity to the helping relationship.

- Identify a client's psychological issues related to oppression.

- Identify social, structural, and institutional factors that produce client stress and inequalities.

- Determine whether the target of change should become the client, the larger system, or both, or whether it is appropriate to intervene at all.

- Employ empowerment and advocacy strategies that enhance client strengths.

of the expert, such as a social worker, is said to stem from education, knowledge, credentials, expertise, status, and agency position. Martin and O'Connor (1989) asserted that the client–social worker relationship is an example of an authority relationship with the social worker in the advantaged position. From this perspective, the client–social worker relationship is "structured by the organization prior to the arrival of worker or client" (Martin & O'Connor, 1989, p. 104).

Perceived differences in socioeconomic status are of importance to social workers, and socioeconomic differences have profound influences on how individuals interact, communicate, and perceive the world. "Social work technology has developed from essentially middle-class conceptions of the universe" (L. V. Davis & Proctor, 1989, p. 260). Because cross-class helping relationships may be affected by the client-therapist status differential, practitioners working with economically different clients must ask, *Does my economic status impact on the extent to which I can be helpful?*

From this perspective, the interviewer (social worker)–interviewee (client) interaction is one of reciprocal, mutual efforts of the participants to influence each other. However, because the interviewer has more power, the influence potential of that person is greater (Kadushin & Kadushin, 1997). The interviewer/social worker has reward power, or the power to control access to special services and to the therapy he or she provides. He or she also has expert power or specialized knowledge and skills and, in some cases, may have coercive power or the ability to control. For these reasons, social workers need to be aware of their own power biases as well as of techniques that will help them avoid power abuses.

A social worker who uses a practice theory that calls for him or her to be an expert who diagnoses, teaches, and treats must be cautioned, particularly in cross-cultural social work, not to use the helping role to satisfy his or her own needs for power (Pinderhughes, 1983). To avoid this difficulty, interventions should be based on an understanding of power dynamics, and the social worker should use strategies that enable clients to turn a sense of powerlessness into a sense of power. Such interventions focus on client strengths and reinforce coping mechanisms that exercise choice and self-assertion. They may also incorporate strategies that increase client information about and knowledge of resource options.

Ecological Perspective

The ecological perspective suggests that people may live in a specific neighborhood or environmental niche that carries negative valuations (Greene, 2008a). An understanding of the interaction between oppressed people and an oppressing society must involve an appreciation of and respect for the special coping capacities and resources necessary to survive and function in such hostile environments. As noted earlier, residents may feel powerless to change their situation. Social workers may focus on "individual pathology," rather than on how to provide vital resources, services, and opportunities (Fong & Furuto, 2001).

Victim Versus Survivor

Others have argued against the perspective of client as victim (Goldstein, 1983, 1990, 1992; Greene, 2002; Weick, 1992). For example, Weick suggested that a strengths perspective toward human development assumes a form of individual power. In addition, Goldstein (1992) argued that neither the concept of pathology nor the concept of strength is based on objective fact. Rather, each concept is socially constructed and reflects public and professional attitudes and beliefs (see Chapter 6 on social construction). The reflection of attitudes and beliefs is expressed in the situation of people who are positive for HIV and who prefer to be called "persons with AIDS" (or "PWAs") rather than "AIDS victims."

Another example involves the various portrayals in the social work professional literature of how to view people who have experienced domestic violence (L. V. Davis, 1987). Initially, wife abuse was linked to societal forces outside the individual, such as norms permitting men to physically abuse women. Some theorists asserted that "victims" played a role in their own difficulty. Today, women are viewed as survivors who need services to gain control over their lives, and men who batter are encouraged to seek treatment.

Empowerment

Empowerment is "a process of increasing personal, interpersonal, or political power so that individuals can take action to improve their life situation" (Gutierrez, 1990, p. 149). *Empowerment* is gaining the capacity to manage emotions, knowledge, skills, or material resources in a way that makes possible more effective performance of valued social roles and receipt of individual satisfaction. Empowerment strategies are guided by the philosophy that interventions "should enhance mental, spiritual, and physical wellness, as well as social justice" (Cox & Joseph, 1998, p. 169). The goal of empowerment is to avoid replicating within the social worker-client relationship the relative powerlessness that a client experiences in society (Gutierrez, Parsons, & Cox, 1998). The social worker who works using an empowerment model aims to reduce "institutionally derived powerlessness caused by social injustice and societal inconsistency" (Bush et al., 1983, p. 103). Persons who have belonged to stigmatized categories all their lives can be assisted in developing interpersonal skills and performing valued social roles (Amaro & Raj, 2004; Gutierrez, Joo Oh, & Gillmore, 2004; Solomon, 1976). Therefore, empowerment encompasses problem-solving strategies and the building of support networks.

A systemic process of empowerment involves influencing the external social system to be less destructive and requires working with extrafamilial systems, such as houses of worship, businesses, or schools. Making surrounding systems more responsive to people's vulnerabilities and needs; addressing the power differential; and assisting clients to exert their personal, political, and economic power are the ultimate goals of empowerment (Simon, 1994; Zippay, 1995). The need to make surrounding social systems more responsive is particularly keen for clients who experience "interacting oppressions" such as the multiple interacting effects of gender and race among women of color (Morris, 1993, p. 99).

To the extent that powerlessness may be an issue with every client who seeks help, empowerment may be viewed as a necessary component of all human services methods and techniques (Greene, 2008a). Empowerment as a goal of social work practice assumes that the knowledge and skills the practitioner uses in working with the client (system) will maximize the client's own effectiveness and opportunities. The client participates in a helping process that "redefines his [or her] self-worth, competence and ability to affect his [or her] social and physical worlds" (Solomon, 1976, p. 342). Finally, rather than view empowerment as an ideal to which to aspire, social workers need to implement empowerment strategies within a client's cultural context, adapting techniques accordingly (Yip, 2004).

Barriers to Empowerment

It must be remembered that many agencies designed to assist the poor and those less powerful hold power over those individuals. Agency personnel and policies determine which services are available to whom and under what circumstances; for example, seemingly simple matters such as the times when services are available and how physical space is designed are controlled. Problem solving through empowerment may be impeded by several factors. Empirical studies have demonstrated that there is often little consensus between social workers and clients on such important matters as the definition of the problem, the interventions needed, and the goals and outcome of treatment. These issues can remain areas of contention throughout the relationship or can bring about early termination of services.

In addition, many current approaches to intervention and to problem solving tend to ignore the organizational or sociopolitical environments in which they take place (Greene, 1989). These forces often make clinical problem solving a "political act by which the participants seek to accomplish a more satisfactory redistribution of power and control" (Murdock, 1982, p. 418). By recognizing the omnipresence of conflict in social relationships (including the helping relationship), the practitioner can consciously adopt strategies to "maintain mutual respect in the client-social worker relationship and to avoid the effects of power discrepancies" (p. 420).

Advocacy

Advocacy, an approach closely aligned with empowerment, is another means of redressing power differentials between the client and social worker. Advocacy involves "acting as a partisan" in a social conflict and using one's professional expertise in the interest of the client (Harbert & Ginsberg, 1979, p. 234). Social workers operating as partisans attempt to influence another individual or group to make a decision that the person or group would not otherwise make in the welfare and interests of the client, who by definition is in a less powerful position than the decision-maker (Sosin & Caulum, 1983).

Advocacy can occur at three levels: (a) the *individual level*, focusing on the manner in which a certain client or group is assisted in a specific situation, such as the acceptance of a client for service; (b) the *administrative level*, centering on convincing decision-makers to alter agency regulations, such as the verification procedures used in public welfare; and (c) the *policy level*, influencing legislative or regulatory provisions, such as changes in health policy. Within professional practice, social workers are often in roles and situations in which they need to advocate for a particular position, client system, or social change. Schneider and Lester (2001) provided a conceptual framework for advocacy skills in social work practice. They discussed the following:

- recognizing the complexity of the number of factors and variables that are a part of advocating for change on any level,
- acknowledging the knowledge base that provides the foundation for advocacy skills, and

- evaluating effectiveness by identifying desired outcomes of advocacy-related efforts (p. 90).

These three principles help social workers determine the particular nature of the situation that requires advocacy efforts, the particular knowledge or skills that are needed to bring about change, and the effectiveness of their advocacy efforts.

Advocates, therefore, organize their social work activities around obtaining goods, services, other resources, and power for clients (Biegel, Shore, & Gordon, 1984). Advocacy as an intervention strategy is concerned with the balance of power between the client as a member of a minority or other disenfranchised group and the larger society (Greene, 1988). The advocate generally takes action to rectify unfair or unjust practices and the inequitable distribution of resources (Green, 2008a). From the advocate's point of view, the client's problems are not personal or psychological deficits but rather stem or arise from discrimination in social and economic opportunities (Dodson, 1988; Prunty, 1980). Techniques of intervention challenge the system's inequities that seem to contribute to or cause difficulties, rather than focus solely on the relief of the individual client.

"To negate advocacy on any level is to dismiss a basic tenet of social work practice" (Sosin & Caulum, 1983, p. 15). Advocacy on behalf of one or more clients implies that the condition facing the client has broader ramifications or exists at the macrosystem level. That is, rather than attempt to improve a difficulty on a case-by-case basis, the social worker takes measures such as testifying before boards of directors or legislative bodies about the overall need. Advocacy as an approach to intervention recognizes that many clients "have serious social systems' problems and have spent a great deal of time, effort, energy and resources in trying to cope with them.... [Therefore, the social work advocate focuses on the] reality oriented problem" that the clients bring (Prunty, 1980, p. 183).

Feminist Perspective

Although there is no single definition of feminist therapy, many theorists view it as a collaborative process between the client and practitioner that attempts to alleviate or remediate the social, cultural, and psychological barriers to women's optimal functioning. The goal of feminist counseling is remediation on both the psychological and social levels. This view emphasizes a clarification of individual autonomy as well as an attempt to change structural properties in the family and in the economy (Russell, 1986; Valentich, 1986).

Practitioners may identify their own biases and better assist women to act on their own behalf through a number of therapeutic goals. According to Van Den Bergh and Cooper (1987), there are seven general feminist helping principles:

1. A client's problems are interpreted within a sociopolitical framework. This underscores the notion of "the personal as political."

2. Automatic submission to traditional sex (gender) roles is questioned, yet supported for pursuing a free choice of lifestyles.
3. Treatment is focused on articulating and augmenting clients' strengths rather than centered on pathologies. Therapy seeks to be an empowering process, whereby clients increase their ability to control their environments to get what they need.
4. Encouragement is given to the development of an independent identity that is not defined by one's relationships with others.
5. Reassessment of women's relationships with other women is encouraged so that bonding between women is valued as highly as developing relationships with men.
6. Emphasis is placed on developing a balance between work and interpersonal relationships.
7. Whenever possible, the personal power between therapist and client approaches equality. (p. 613)

Feminist practitioners believe that it is important for the helping relationship to involve two equals. Theorists tend to see the social worker as expert as being detrimental to growth because of the dependency this view may generate (Bricker-Jenkins & Hooyman, 1984). As in all social work practice, the practitioner strives to treat the client with dignity and respect, but social worker expertise is shared. Skills tend to be externally and empowerment-oriented; these include (a) problem solving, interpersonal, and life management skills; and (b) participation in collective action, such as networking and joining support and self-help groups (Bricker-Jenkins & Hooyman, 1984).

There is continuing concern about how sexist attitudes may affect practice and the profession. *Renaming*, or the right to describe and name one's own experiences, has increasingly become the therapeutic and political goal shared by the Civil Rights and women's movements. It involves using new words for people, altering meanings through language, remembering old definitions, and expanding existing definitions (Van Den Bergh, 1982). The development of feminist therapies has also involved the reconceptualization of diagnostic categories (Brown, 1992). This reconceptualization is based on the idea that client assessment and treatment may reflect societal inequities and, therefore, may be racist, sexist, or heterosexist in nature. Hamilton and Jensvold (1992) argued that an example of the misuse of diagnostic categories is the widespread, often misplaced diagnosis and treatment of women for depression, rather than the addressing of issues of status, poverty, employment, and family roles.

The skepticism about universal truths and concern for individualizing the client is also reflected in family treatment approaches (Hoffman, 1990; also see Chapter 8). For example, Hoffman contended that the family therapy literature has long been dominated by a masculine vocabulary based on strategies that portray family members as either "one-up" or "one-down." She suggested that family therapists need to replace the notion of the feedback loop, which assumes a static communication and balance within families, with the idea of "intersubjective loops of dialogue," which express multiple stories (p. 8). She went on to state that this intervention approach leads to empowerment of women and ethnic minorities within the treatment milieu.

Community responses to violence can promote a rebalancing of power within communities as well. Rituals have been used to promote healing within groups and communities in both Eastern and Western religions. Galambos (2001) described a community-level therapeutic ritual for survivors of rape. A candlelight vigil promotes healing for both the community and the individuals who experienced the assault. Through this event, healing is initiated at both the individual and collective levels.

Respect for client strengths and an awareness of and attention to societal factors in problem definition are common features contained in the three power perspectives presented (see Table 11.2). Acknowledgement of power as a critical factor in shaping human behavior creates a therapeutic atmosphere in which clients can "achieve self-actualization without inhibiting that of others" (Bricker-Jenkins, 1991, p. 272).

References

Albrecht, L., & Brewer, R. M. (1990). *Bridges of Power: Women's Multicultural Alliances.* Philadelphia: New Society.

Anderson, R. E., Carter, L., & Lowe, G. (1999). *Human Behavior in the Social Environment: A Social Systems Approach* (5th ed.). Hawthorne, NY: Aldine de Gruyter.

Amaro, H., & Raj, A. (2004). On the margin: Power and women's HIV risk reduction strategies. *Sex Roles*, 42, 723–749.

Auerswald, E. H. (1971). Families, change and the ecological perspective. *Family Process*, 10, 263–280.

Biegel, D. E., Shore, B. K., & Gordon, E. (1984). *Building Support and Networks for the Elderly.* Beverly Hills, CA: Sage.

Briar, S., & Miller, H. (1971). *Problems and Issues in Social Casework.* New York: Columbia University Press.

Bricker-Jenkins, M. (1991). The propositions and assumptions of feminist social work practice. In M. Bricker-Jenkins, N. R. Hooyman, & N. Gottlieb (Eds.), *Feminist Social Work Practice in Clinical Settings* (pp. 271–303). Newbury Park, CA: Sage.

Bricker-Jenkins, M., & Hooyman, N. (1984, March). *Feminist Ideology.* Discussion paper presented at the 30th Annual Program Meeting of the Council on Social Work Education, Silver Spring, MD.

Bricker-Jenkins, M., & Hooyman, N. (1986). *Not for Women Only: Social Work Practice for a Feminist Future.* Silver Spring, MD: NASW Press.

Bronfenbrenner, U. (1986). Ecology of the family as a context for human development: Research perspectives. *Developmental Psychology*, 32, 723–742.

Brown, L. S. (1992). A feminist critique of the personality disorders. In L. S. Brown & M. Allow (Eds.), *Personality and Psychopathology: Feminist Reappraisals* (pp. 206–228). New York: Guilford Press.

Burghardt, S., & Fabricant, M. (1987). Radical social work. In A. Minahan (Ed.-in-Chief), *Encyclopedia of Social Work* (18th ed., pp. 455–462). Silver Spring, MD: NASW Press.

Bush, J. A., Norton, D. G., Sanders, C. L., & Solomon, B. B. (1983). An integrative approach for the inclusion of content on blacks in social work education. In J. C. Chunn, P. J. Dunston, & F. Ross-Sheriff (Eds.), *Mental Health and People of Color* (pp. 97–125). Washington, DC: Howard University Press.

Chestang, L. (1972). *Character Development in a Hostile Environment* (Occasional Paper No. 3). Chicago: University of Chicago, School of Social Service Administration.

Clark, K. (1965). *Dark Ghetto: Dilemmas of Social Power*. New York: Harper & Row.

Cohen, H., & Greene, R. R. (2005). Older adults who overcame oppression. *Families in Society*, 87, 1–8.

Cox, E. O., & Joseph, B. H. R. (1998). Social service delivery and empowerment. In L. Gutierrez, R. J. Parsons, & E. O. Cox (Eds.), *Empowerment in Social Work Practice: A Sourcebook* (pp. 167–186). Pacific Grove, CA: Brooks/Cole.

Danziger, S. (1987). Poverty. In A. Minahan (Ed.-in-Chief), *Encyclopedia of Social Work* (18th ed., pp. 294–302). Silver Spring, MD: NASW Press.

Davis, K., Leijenaar, M., & Oldersma, J. (Eds.). (1991). *The Gender of Power*. Newbury Park, CA: Sage.

Davis, L. V. (1987). Battered women: The transformation of a social problem. *Social Work*, 32, 306–311.

Davis, L. V., & Proctor, E. (1989). *Race, Gender, and Class: Guidelines for Practice with Individuals, Families and Groups*. Englewood Cliffs, NJ: Prentice Hall.

DePoy, E., & Gilson, S. F. (2004). *Rethinking Disability: Principles for Professional and Social Change*. Belmont, CA: Brooks/Cole.

Dodson, J. (1988). Conceptualizations of black families. In H. P. McAdoo (Ed.), *Black Families* (2nd ed., pp. 77–90). Newbury Park, CA: Sage.

Draper, B. (1979). Black language as an adaptive response to a hostile environment. In C. B. Germain (Ed.), *Social Work Practice: People and Environments* (pp. 267–281). New York: Columbia University Press.

DuBois, W. E. B. (1969). *Darkwater Voices from within the Veil*. New York: Shocken Books.

Dworkin, J. (1990). Political economic and social aspects of professional authority. *Families in Society*, 71, 534–541.

Fong, R., & Furuto, S. (Eds.). (2001). *Culturally Competent Practice: Skills, Interventions, and Evaluations*. Boston: Allyn & Bacon.

Foucault, M. (1980). *Power/Knowledge: Selected Interviews and Other Writings, 1972–1977*. New York: Pantheon Books.

Foucault, M. (1983). *Beyond Structuralism and Hermeneutics*. Chicago: University of Chicago Press.

Frazer, N., & Nicholson, L. J. (1990). Social criticism without philosophy: An encounter between feminism and postmodernism. In L. J. Nicholson (Ed.), *Feminism/Postmodernism* (pp. 19–38). New York: Routledge.

Galambos, C. (2001). Community healing rituals for survivors of rape. *Smith College Studies in Social Work*, 71, 441–457.

Garcia, B., & Van Soest, D. (2006). *Social Work Practice for Social Justice: Cultural Competence in Action*. Alexandria, VA: Council on Social Work Education.

Germain, C. B. (1987). Human development in contemporary environments. *Social Service Review*, 61, 565–578.

Germain, C. B., & Gitterman, A. (1995). Ecological perspective. In R. L. Edwards (Ed.-in-Chief), *Encyclopedia of Social Work* (19th ed., Vol. 1, pp. 816–824). Silver Spring, MD: NASW Press.

Giddens, A. (1984). *The Constitution of Society*. Cambridge, England: Polity Press.

Goldenberg, I. I. (1978). *Oppression and Social Intervention*. Chicago: Nelson Hall.

Goldstein, H. (1983). Starting where the client is. *Social Casework*, 64, 267–275.

Goldstein, H. (1990). The knowledge base of social work practice: Theory, wisdom, analogue, or art? *Families in Society*, 71, 32–43.

Goldstein, H. (1992). Victors or victims: Contrasting views of clients in social work practice. In D. Saleeby (Ed.), *The Strengths Perspective in Social Work Practice* (pp. 27–38). New York: Longman.

Greene, R. R. (1988). *Continuing Education for Gerontological Careers*. Washington, DC: Council on Social Work Education.

Greene, R. R. (1989). The growing need for social work services for the aged in 2020. In B. S. Vourlekis & C. G. Leukefeld (Eds.), *Making Our Case: A Resource Book of Selected Materials for Social Workers in Health Care* (pp. 11–17). Silver Spring, MD: NASW Press.

Greene, R. R. (2002). *Resiliency: An Integrated Approach to Practice, Policy, and Research*. Washington, DC: NASW Press.

Greene, R. R. (2008a). The ecological perspective: An eclectic theoretical framework. In R. R. Greene (Ed.), *Human Behavior Theory and Social Work Practice*. New Brunswick, NJ: Aldine Transaction.

Greene, R. R. (Ed.) (2008b). *Human Behavior Theory and Social Work Practice*. New Brunswick, NJ: Aldine Transaction.

Gutierrez, L. (1990). Working with women of color: An empowerment perspective. *Social Work*, 35, 149–153.

Gutierrez, L., Joo Oh, H., & Gillmore, M. R. (2004). Toward an understanding of (em)power(ment) for HIV? AIDS prevention with adolescent women. *Sex Roles*, 42, 581–611.

Gutierrez, L. M., Parsons, R. J., & Cox, E. O. (1998). Creating opportunities for empowerment-oriented programs. In L. Gutierrez, R. J. Parsons, & E. O. Cox, (Eds.), *Empowerment in Social Work Practice: A Sourcebook* (pp. 220–223). Pacific Grove, CA: Brooks/Cole.

Hamilton, J. A., & Jensvold, M. (1992). Personality, psychopathology, and depressions in women. In L. S. Brown & M. Ballou (Eds.), *Personality and Psychopathology: Feminist Reappraisals* (pp. 116–143). New York: Guilford Press.

Harbert, A., & Ginsberg, L. (1979). *Human Services for Older Adults: Concepts and Skills*. Belmont, CA: Wadsworth.

Harrison, A. O., Wilson, M. N., Pine, C. J., Chan, S. Q., & Buriel, R. (1990). Family ecologies of ethnic minority children. *Child Development*, 61, 347–362.

Hartman, A., & Laird, J. (1983). *Family-Centered Social Work Practice*. New York: Free Press.

Hoffman, L. (1990). Constructing realities: An art of lenses. *Family Process*, 29, 1–12.

hooks, b. (1990). *Yearning: Race, Gender, and Cultural Politics*. Boston: South End Press.

Hooyman, N. R. (1980, September). *Toward a Feminist Administrative Style*. Paper presented at Social Work Practice in Sexist Society: First NASW Conference on Social Work Practice With Women, Washington, DC.

Hooyman, N. R., Summers, A., & Leighninger, L. (Eds.). (1988). *Women Working Together: A Collection of Course Syllabi about Women*. New York: Commission on the Role and Status of Women in Social Work Education, Council on Social Work Education.

Jargowsky, P. A., & Sawhill, I. V. (2006). *The Decline of the Underclass* (Social Policy Center on Children and Families Brief No. 36). Washington, DC: Brookings Institution.

Kadushin, A., & Kadushin, G. (1997). *The Social Work Interview: A Guide for Human*

Service Professionals (4th ed.). New York: Columbia University Press.

Kaniasty, K., & Norris, F. (1999). The experience of disaster: Individuals and communities sharing trauma. In R. Gist & B. Lubin (Eds.), *Response to Disaster: Psychosocial, Community, and Ecological Approaches* (pp. 25–61). Philadelphia: Brunner/Mazel.

Lemann, N. (1986a, June). The origins of the underclass, Part 1. *Atlantic Monthly*, 257, 31–35.

Lemann, N. (1986b, July). The origins of the underclass, Part 2. *Atlantic Monthly*, 258, 54–55.

Longres, J. F. (2000). *Human Behavior in the Social Environment* (3rd ed.). Belmont, CA: Wadsworth.

Lowenstein, S. F. (1976). Integrating content on feminism and racism into the social work curriculum. *Journal of Education for Social Work*, 12(1), 91–96.

Martin, P. Y., & O'Connor, G. G. (1989). *The Social Environment: Open Systems Applications*. New York: Longman.

Max, J. (1971). Power theory and institutional change. *Social Service Review*, 45, 274–288.

McIntosh, P. (1988). *White Privilege and Male Privilege: A Personal Account of Coming to See Correspondences through Work in Women's Studies* (Working Paper No. 189). Wellesley, MA: Wellesley College Center for Research on Women.

McIntosh, P. (1995). White privilege and male privilege: A personal account of coming to see correspondence through work in women's studies. In M. L. Andersen & P. H. Collins, *Race, Class, and Gender: An Anthropology* (pp. 76–87). New York: Wadsworth.

Miller, S. (1980). Reflections on the dual perspective. In E. Mizio & J. Delany (Eds.), *Training for Service Delivery for Minority Clients* (pp. 53–61). New York: Family Service of America.

Mohanty, C. T. (2006). U.S. empire and the project of women's studies: Stories of citizenship, complicity and dissent. *Gender, Place and Culture*, 13(1), 7–20.

Morris, J. K. (1993). Interacting oppressions: Teaching social work content on women in color. *Journal of Social Work Education*, 29, 99–111.

Moynihan, D. P (1965). *The Negro Family*. Washington, DC: U.S. Department of Labor.

Murdock, A. (1982). A political perspective on problem solving. *Social Work*, 27, 417–421.

Nes, J. A., & Iadicola, P. (1989). Toward a definition of feminist social work: A comparison of liberal, radical and socialist models. *Social Work*, 34, 12–21.

Parsons, T. (1951). *The Social System*. New York: Free Press.

Parsons, T. (1964). Age and sex in the social structure. In R. L. Coser (Ed.), *The Family: Its Structure and Functions* (pp. 251–266). New York: St. Martin's Press.

Pincus, F. L. (2000). Discrimination comes in many forms: Individual, institutional and structural. In M. Adams, W. J. Blumenfeld, R. Castenada, H. W. Hackman, M. L. Peters, & X. Zuniga (Eds.), *Readings for Diversity and Social Justice* (pp. 31–35). New York: Routledge.

Pinderhughes, E. B. (1978). Power, powerlessness, and empowerment in community mental health. *Black Caucus Journal*, 10–15.

Pinderhughes, E. B. (1983). Empowerment for our clients and for ourselves. *Social Casework*, 64, 331–338.

Pinderhughes, E. B. (1989). *Understanding Race, Ethnicity, and Power: The Key to Efficacy in Clinical Practice*. New York: Free Press.

Prunty, H. (1980). The "how-tos" of advocacy for the caseworker. In E. Mizio & J. Delaney (Eds.), *Training for Service Delivery to Minority Clients* (pp. 181–188). New

York: Family Service of America.

Report of the National Advisory Commission on Civil Disorders. (1968). New York: Bantam Books.

Russell, M. (1986). Teaching feminist counseling skills: An evaluation. *Counselor Education and Supervision*, 25, 320–331.

Sands, R. G., & Nuccio, K. (1992). Post-modernization feminist theory and social work. *Social Work*, 37, 489–502.

Schneider, R. L., & Lester, L. (2001). *Social Work Advocacy: A New Framework for Action.* Belmont, CA: Brooks/Cole.

Scott, C. A. (1971). Ethnic minorities in social work education. In A. M. Pins (Ed.), *The Current Scene in Social Work Education* (pp. 24–25). New York: Council on Social Work Education.

Simon, B. L. (1994). *The Empowerment Tradition in American Social Work.* New York: Columbia University Press.

Solomon, B. B. (1976). *Black Empowerment: Social Work in Oppressed Communities.* New York: Columbia University Press.

Solomon, B. B. (1982, July). *Power, the Troublesome Factor in Cross-Cultural Supervision.* Paper presented at the Smith College School of Social Work, Amherst, MA.

Solomon, B. B. (1991). Social work values and skills to empower women. In A. Weick & S. T. Vandiver (Eds.), *Women, Power and Change* (pp. 206–214). Washington, DC: NASW Press.

Sosin, M., & Caulum, S. (1983). Advocacy: A conceptualization for social work practice. *Social Work*, 28, 12–18.

Sotomayor, M. (1971). Mexican-American interaction with social systems. *Social Casework*, 51, 316–322.

Swigonski, M. E. (1996). Challenging privilege through Africentric social work practice. *Social Work*, 41, 153–161.

Thomas, A., & Sillen, S. (1972). The mark of oppression. In A. Thomas & S. Sillen, *Racism and Psychiatry* (pp. 45–56). New York: Brunner/Mazel.

Tice, K. (1990). Gender and social work education: Directions for the 1990s. *Journal of Social Work Education*, 26, 134–144.

U.S. Census Bureau. (2005). *Income, Poverty and Health Insurance Coverage in the United States, 2005* (Publication No. P60-231). Washington, DC: Housing and Household Economics Statistics Division.

Valentich, M. (1986). Feminism and social work practice. In F. J. Turner (Ed.), *Social Work Treatment* (pp. 564–580). New York: Free Press.

Van Den Bergh, N. (1982). Renaming: Vehicle for empowerment. In J. Penfield (Ed.), *Women and Language in Transition* (pp. 130–136). Albany: State University of New York Press.

Van Den Bergh, N., & Cooper, L. B. (Eds.). (1986). *Feminist Visions for Social Work.* Silver Spring, MD: NASW Press.

Van Den Bergh, N., & Cooper, L. B. (1987). Feminist social work. In A. Minahan (Ed.-in-Chief), *Encyclopedia of Social Work* (18th ed., pp. 610–618). Silver Spring, MD: NASW Press.

Van Voorhis, R. M. (in press). Feminist theories and social work practice. In R. R. Greene (Ed.), *Human Behavior Theory and Social Work Practice.* New Brunswick, NJ: Aldine Transaction.

Weaver, H. N. (1996). Social work with American Indian youth using the orthogonal model of cultural identification. *Families in Society*, 77, 98–107.

Weaver, H. N. (2000). Culture and professional education: The experience of Native American social workers. *Journal of Social Work Education*, 36, 415–428.

Webb, S. A. (2000). The politics of political social work: Power and subjectivity. *Critical Social Work*, 1(2).

Weber, M. (2007). *Basic Concepts in Sociology*. Retrieved August 27, 2007, from *http:// en.wikipedia.org/wiki/Power_(sociology)*

Weick, A. (1992). Building a strengths perspective for social work. In D. Saleeby (Ed.), *The Strengths Perspective in Social Work Practice* (pp. 18–26). New York: Longman.

Wicker, D. G. (1986). Combating racism in practice and in the classroom. In N. Van Den Bergh & L. B. Cooper (Eds.), *Feminist Visions for Social Work* (pp. 29–44). Silver Spring, MD: NASW Press.

Wilson, W. J. (1973). *Power, Racism, and Privilege*. New York: Free Press.

Wilson, W. J. (1985). Cycles of deprivation and the underclass debate. *Social Service Review*, 59, 541–559.

Yip, K. (2004). The empowerment model: A critical reflection of empowerment in Chinese culture. *Social Work*, 49, 479–487.

Zippay, A. (1995). The politics of empowerment. *Social Work*, 40, 263–267.

Index